JAMES STEWART,

Earl of Moray

JAMES STEWART,

EARL of MORAY

A POLITICAL STUDY *of the* REFORMATION *in* SCOTLAND

by *MAURICE LEE, Jr.*

GREENWOOD PRESS, PUBLISHERS
WESTPORT, CONNECTICUT

TO MY PARENTS

PREFACE

MARY QUEEN OF SCOTS *is one of the best-known figures in history. Her fame has spread far beyond the specialized world of the professional historian, and all sorts of books have been written about her by all kinds of people. Hence it might seem, on first glance, that nothing could be less necessary than another book on the Marian period in Scotland.*

This was, in fact, my opinion until I started to examine thoroughly the source materials and the secondary works dealing with this era. Then it became clear that no one had treated Mary's reign from the point of view of the most powerful group in Scotland, the nobility. Previous writers had studied the period either as a part of Mary's personal biography or as the first few chapters in the story of Scottish Protestantism —this latter treatment being equivalent, very often, to a biography of Knox. In either case the nobility was generally slighted. While their importance was recognized, the Scottish lords were dismissed as a group of

greedy, unprincipled ruffians: unprincipled and wicked
in the eyes of Mary's defenders; unprincipled but useful (if Protestant) to her detractors. It need hardly be
added that the majority of these authors were biased; indeed, their controversies occasionally descended to the
level of personal abuse.[1]

In these circumstances it seemed necessary to reconsider the political and religious strife of this period from
the point of view of this powerful and important class.
This has been done, in the following pages, by a detailed
study of the career of one of the most important of
them, James Stewart, Earl of Moray, bastard brother of
the Queen and, in his later years, Regent of Scotland for
the infant James VI. Moray has been chosen not because he was a typical Scottish lord but because he was
the leader of the Protestant party in Scotland during the
critical years which followed the establishment of the
Reformed Religion there. That Mary's career was tragi-
cally romantic was her own doing; that it was a political and religious failure as well was due to Moray as
much as to any other person, not even excepting Knox
or Cecil or Elizabeth herself.

In view of the excitement and controversy this period has caused, it is surprising that so few of the figures
in the Marian drama have received biographical treat-

---

[1] See, for instance, the unedifying dispute over the Casket Letters between
Andrew Lang and T. F. Henderson in the *Scottish Historical Review*, V
(1907–8), 1–12, 161–74.

ment. Only Mary, Knox, and Maitland seem to have stirred the imagination of historians. Moray has had no previous full-scale biography. This holds true also of Mary' father, James V, of Cardinal Beaton, Châtelherault, Morton, and Lennox, and of virtually all the other Scots discussed in these pages. This work is, in some sense, an attempt to repair this deficiency in respect to Moray.

I should like to take this opportunity to express my thanks to Professor E. Harris Harbison of Princeton University, who contributed most generously of his time and counsel while this work was being written, and whose advice has been valuable throughout.

MAURICE LEE, JR.

Princeton, N.J.
June 1951

Contents

JAMES STEWART,

Earl of Moray

CHAPTER I

The Coming of Protestantism

To the theatrically minded observer, the story of the sixteenth century reads like a colossal drama, the protagonist of which is a movement—Protestantism. The play has a long prologue, the Captivity, the Schism, Lollardy, the Hussites, mysticism, Conciliarism, the Renaissance, and the humanist Papacy being the leading elements. The drama itself begins with Martin Luther and his Ninety-five Theses; complications appear in the 1530s, with the entrance onto the stage of John Calvin and Henry VIII. The crisis years of Protestantism, very appropriately from the dramatist's point of view, come in mid-century, from the signing of the Peace of Cateau-Cambrésis in 1559 to approximately 1573, when it became apparent that massacre and armed repression, in France and in the Low Countries, would not succeed in making the new movement a mere memory. From this point the drama moves rapidly to its conclusion. Ten years after the explosive events of 1588 the curtain falls: Philip II, the champion of militant Catholicism, dies in disillusionment, leaving his country shattered, and the King of France, once a Protestant himself, signs the Edict of Nantes.

Contemporaneous with the rise of Protestantism were the almost continuous wars between the two great Catholic dynasties, the Hapsburgs and the Valois. To this struggle was due, in very large part, the survival of Protestantism in its early years. The exigencies of war and politics caused the Most Christian King and His Most Catholic Majesty to overlook the behavior of a man like Henry VIII and to bid for his support as they had in the days when Henry was writing anti-Lutheran tracts. So Protestantism spread, since the natural defenders of the old Church had other business which they considered more pressing.

By the later 1550s, however, the Protestant position began to worsen. True, Charles V had been forced to acquiesce in the legal recognition of Lutheranism in the Empire, but on the other hand, the Hapsburg-Valois wars ended in 1559, at Cateau-Cambrésis. Worse still, Catholicism was showing signs of revival. The Council of Trent, and the Popes themselves, had set about the long-overdue task of reform, and the new Jesuit order was beginning its campaign to reconquer men's minds. It seemed quite possible that France and her Imperial-Spanish rivals would unite under the moral leadership of a purified Papacy to crush heresy and reaffirm triumphantly the unity of Christendom.

Under these circumstances the survival of Protestantism depended on two factors: England, Catholic under Mary Tudor, must once again become a Protestant state; and the two great Catholic powers, France and Spain, must be so occupied by the suppression of heresy at home and so suspicious of each other in foreign affairs as to make effective political and military cooperation for religious purposes impossible. If either of these conditions had not held, Protestantism would have been destroyed: for if England had remained Catholic, the French and Dutch Protestants would have been defeated eventually; and if France and Spain had had their hands free and had been able to cooperate, England must have been crushed. Hence the crucial importance of the years 1559–73, for in those years it was made clear that England would definitely join the Protestant camp, that the Protestants of France and the Netherlands could not be crushed by their Catholic rulers, and that those rulers were at odds with each other more often than not.[1]

What has all this to do with the career of a Calvinist lord in a European backwater such as Scotland? The answer is, that owing to a series of historical accidents the maintenance of England in

[1] The year 1573 was marked by the recall of Alva from the Netherlands and by the Edict of Boulogne, which ended the fourth "War of Religion" in France on terms not unfavorable to the Huguenots, in spite of the massacre of St. Bartholomew's Day in the previous year.

the Protestant camp depended to a very great extent on the course of events in the land of her northern neighbor.

The childlessness of Mary Tudor, and her death in November 1558, brought to the English throne her half-sister Elizabeth. The new Queen owed her throne to Henry VIII's break with Rome; and however she might try to befool the representatives of the old faith on the Continent by occasional leanings toward Catholicism when the diplomatic situation seemed to require it, she was committed to the Protestant side. But what if Elizabeth should die? By hereditary right, the English crown would pass to the heir of her father's sister Margaret, and that heir was Scotland's Queen, a girl just turning sixteen when Elizabeth mounted the throne, Mary Stewart, wife to the heir to the crown of France, and, needless to add, no Protestant.

There were two ways out of this dilemma that presented themselves to Elizabeth's chief adviser, Sir William Cecil—aside from the most satisfactory solution of all, which would have been a suitable marriage for the Queen and the birth of an heir to the throne. The first course was to deny or somehow to pass over Mary's right to the crown; the second was to render her possible succession harmless by binding her permanently to the Protestant cause. The success of either of these policies, however, depended upon the domination of Scotland by a party which was both Protestant and Anglophile. If Scotland were Catholic, it would naturally remain faithful to its "auld alliance" with France, and would serve as a base for the forcible assertion of Mary's claim to the throne of England—in Catholic eyes a better claim than that of Elizabeth, who was a bastard by Catholic standards. Even a Protestant Scotland was not enough: for Scotland had arrived at a sense of nationhood under the repeated hammering of English armies since the days of Edward I. The "auld enemy" was England, and Protestantism and hatred of England could go hand in hand. Only a Protestant, pro-English Scotland would serve, for only then could England force her political and religious views on Mary as a necessary prerequisite for her recognition as Elizabeth's successor. Only then, if it became necessary to set Mary aside, would it be possible to work out a *modus vivendi* with the northern kingdom which would have some chance of success and which would enable England to deal with the Catholic Powers on the Continent untroubled by the fear of a possible attack from the north.

In the light of these considerations, the importance of James Stewart, Earl of Moray, becomes clear. To Moray more than to any other one man, not even excepting Knox, was due the triumph of the Protestant, Anglophile party in Scotland; for Scotland became Protestant, and stayed that way, on account of a political party headed by the nobility, above all by Moray, rather than on account of a reforming clergy.[2] The founding of this party was not Moray's work. But he became one of its leaders during its struggle with the Catholic, pro-French party, the so-called Wars of the Congregation, and after that struggle he soon became its most important political leader, along with Maitland of Lethington. He remained its head through the vicissitudes of Mary's personal rule in Scotland; after her fall it was he, in the name of his party, who governed Scotland. By the time of his death he had so wrought that the victory of his political and religious principles was assured, as the history of his country from his death in 1570 to the accession of James VI to the English throne in 1603 amply demonstrates. It is primarily from this point of view that the career of Moray will be considered in the following pages.

ii

Before we take up the story of Moray in detail, however, it would be well to set the stage, as it were. What sort of country was Scotland in the sixteenth century—what were the conditions with which Moray had to deal in the course of his political career?

The most obvious fact about sixteenth-century Scotland is that Scotland, unlike her southern neighbor, was still a medieval country, both politically and economically. The power of the nobility, collectively (and even, on occasion, individually, though this was rare), was far greater than that of the King. To this situation the chronic wars with England and the dynastic misfortunes of the

---

[2] On this question see P. Hume Brown, "The Scottish Nobility and their Part in the National History," *Scottish Historical Review*, III (1905–6), 157–70.

successors of the Bruce were the major contributors. Scotland did enjoy some periods of comparatively stable government, but the King was never able to assert his power above that of any possible feudal combination—a situation which lasted until well after the death of Moray.

Even in the best of times the royal authority did not extend over all of Scotland. Scotland, like all Gaul, was divided into three parts—the Highlands, the Lowlands, and the Border. In the Highland and Border districts the power of the King was seldom more than nominal, because of the Crown's lack of a standing army and of money. In both areas great numbers of people lived by brigandage. The Highlander, whose loyalty was to his clan chief, not to the King, robbed Lowlanders and other Highlanders. The Borderer robbed in England, an occupation frequently encouraged by the government. In order to prevent complete anarchy, the Crown generally had to rely on certain Highland and Border nobles, who were given power and privilege in return for keeping order. In this way there arose certain great families, the heads of which became very powerful: the Gordons (earls of Huntly) and the Campbells (earls of Argyle) in the Highlands; the Hepburns (earls of Bothwell), the Humes, and others on the Border. This, of course, was no solution to the problem; in exchange for a certain amount of security from disorder, the Crown raised up a series of petty kings who could and often did defy the government with impunity.[3] Even in the Lowlands the power of the nobility was very great. Here lay the domains of various branches of the House of Stewart, of the Hamiltons, next heirs to the throne, and of the Douglases—now no longer as great as they had once been, but a power to be reckoned with nonetheless.

The financial resources of the Crown were hopelessly inadequate; they were, in fact, those of a medieval monarch. Taxation on a national scale, such as the English kings had been levying for centuries, was still reserved for great emergencies or special occa-

[3] See Andrew Lang, *A History of Scotland from the Roman Occupation*, I, 370–72, for a discussion of the political aspects of the Highland problem. I. F. Grant, *The Social and Economic Development of Scotland before 1603*, pp. 472–550, is a thorough treatment of the social and economic situation in the Highlands.

sions. For example, in the seven years of Mary's personal rule, at a time when the deficit was steadily mounting, the only instance of national taxation was a levy of £12,000 in October, 1566, for the baptism of Prince James.[4] The revenue that did exist was collected in a manner which Rait compares unfavorably with that existing in England under Henry II. Taxes were "farmed out" for collection to the sheriffs, whose offices had become hereditary by the sixteenth century.[5] Thus there would have been no money to pay a standing army even if the kings had been able to create one; but they were unable to do this, owing to the steadfast opposition of the nobility.[6]

Under these conditions it is easy to see why the nobility did not object to the theoretically extensive powers of the Crown. The Privy Council, the Parliament, and the Convention of Estates [7] had no legal authority independent of the Crown. But the Crown was never independent of one faction, at least, of the great nobles. Each noble hoped to be a member of the ruling faction, in which case the legal machinery of Parliament and Privy Council would be very useful in attacking his opponents. Conversely, if a great noble disliked an enactment of Parliament or Council, he generally ignored it, and a major expedition would be required to force him into line. Such an expedition was also required to stop a feud. Feuds were frequent and bloody in Scotland, partly because of the great strength of family feeling and partly because the nobility had never had occasion to sink their differences in order

[4] Grant, *Social and Economic Development*, p. 236. *The Register of the Privy Council of Scotland*, I, 485–87.

[5] R. S. Rait, *The Scottish Parliament before the Union of the Crowns*, p. 12, n. 1. J. MacKinnon, *The Constitutional History of Scotland from Early Times to the Reformation*, pp. 265–66.

[6] See the account in G. Buchanan, *The History of Scotland*, II, 387–90, of the violent reaction of the nobility when, in 1556, Mary of Guise, then Regent, proposed to create a standing army supported by taxation.

[7] The Convention of Estates is described in R. S. Rait, *The Parliaments of Scotland*, pp. 145–46, as an informal, limited reproduction of Parliament. After 1567, when burgesses were formally admitted, its personnel was about the same as that of Parliament. The chief difference between the two was that the Convention had no judicial function. On these points see *ibid.*, pp. 5, 127–64. This book, and those referred to in note 5, are excellent on constitutional and parliamentary problems. See especially MacKinnon, *Constitutional History*, pp. 212–41, 267–88, for discussions of the constitutional position of King and Parliament respectively.

to present a united front to the Crown. It is mainly because of
these feuds that Scottish history appears on the surface to be a
mere chronicle of ambushes, assassinations, treasons, stratagems,
and spoils.

The power of the nobility was based on possession of the land,
by far the most important source of wealth in sixteenth-century
Scotland. That power was increased by a legal system and a system of land tenure which gave the Crown practically no right
to intervene between the tenant-in-chief and his inferiors.[8] The
consequence was that the average tenant was loyal to his immediate superior, not to the King.[9] This, however, does not mean
that the nobility was wealthy. By and large they were chronically
short of cash, which explains the ease with which outsiders—
Henry VIII, for instance—were able to bribe them. But in respect
to funds they were no worse off than the Crown.[10]

The ordinary tenant had very little protection against his lord.
Most land was held on short-term lease, and evictions were frequent.[11] This was the peasant's chief complaint; other important
grievances were the tithes demanded by the Church and the
monopoly held by the towns over trade, markets, and crafts.[12]
The peasant's standard of living was precariously close to the subsistence level at all times, and occasionally, in times of dearth, below it. Famine was his greatest fear; that he did not suffer from it
more than he did was due, surprisingly enough, to the policy of
the government. The nobility was aware that a prolonged famine
would cause political difficulties; it would also do more direct
harm, since rents were largely paid in kind.[13] While a bad harvest

[8] On this point see Grant, *Social and Economic Development*, pp. 64–65, 174–78,
205–18, 244–47, and MacKinnon, *Constitutional History*, pp. 258–60.
[9] P. Hume Brown, *Scotland in the Time of Queen Mary*, pp. 181–84. Rait, *Scottish Parliament*, p. 8.
[10] For a discussion of the question of the power of the nobility, see Grant, *Social
and Economic Development*, pp. 171–218.
[11] On this point see November 12, 1549, Mary of Guise to the Cardinal of Guise
and the Duc d'Aumâle, in A. Teulet, ed., *Relations politiques de la France et de
l'Espagne avec l'Ecosse au XVIe siècle*, I, 197–206. For the problem of land
tenure, including the so-called "kindly" tenancies, see Grant, *Social and Economic Development*, pp. 244–64.
[12] E. Percy, *John Knox*, pp. 221–22.
[13] Grant, *Social and Economic Development*, p. 298.

could not be prevented, its effects were mitigated by forbidding exports in favor of keeping the home market well supplied. This policy applied not only to agricultural produce, but also to articles of common consumption such as tallow, salt, coal, and herring.[14] And, unlike many laws, these were for the most part strictly enforced. That this policy was dictated by largely selfish motives there can be no doubt; but it redounded to the advantage of peasant as well as noble, and was wise, if unprogressive, given the predominantly rural nature of the Scottish economy.

The Scottish towns, or burghs, were small and relatively unimportant. The largest of them, Edinburgh, had a population of only about 9,000 in 1560.[15] Most burghs were poor, and a great many of their inhabitants, especially in the lesser burghs, supported themselves partly or wholly on the arable lands of the burgh.[16] This is a striking indication of the unimportance of commerce and industry by comparison with agriculture.

In the middle of the sixteenth century about thirty-five towns were "royal burghs"; these towns "possessed the sole right of carrying on crafts, selling and buying commodities, and in . . . [them] fairs and markets alone could be held." [17] Other towns, "burghs of regality and barony," served as local markets only; the inhabitants of these burghs could trade only within the burgh itself.[18] This monopoly was irksome to the peasantry, but the all-powerful nobility found ways of turning it to account, and so they let it continue.[19]

The volume of business carried on by the towns was small. The principal exports were raw materials and foodstuffs—wool, hides and skins, and fish—and some few manufactured items. The chief imports were manufactured goods, especially luxury and semi-luxury products, iron, timber, wine, preserving salt, and, in times of famine, food.[20] At the beginning of the sixteenth century it was

---

[14] *Ibid.*, pp. 355–56. *Register of Privy Council*, I, 114, 127, 137, 334, 402, 559–60, 571–72.   [15] Grant, *Social and Economic Development*, p. 351.
[16] *Ibid.*, pp. 111–12, 305–6.   [17] *Ibid.*, pp. 367, 374–75.   [18] *Ibid.*, pp. 372–73.
[19] *Ibid.*, pp. 356–57, 372–73, 380. See also *Register of Privy Council*, I, 191–92, 285.
[20] Grant, *Social and Economic Development*, pp. 321–24. Brown, *Scotland in the Time of Queen Mary*, pp. 135–37.

estimated by a foreign observer that the government obtained from the duties on this trade about one third as much money as it got from its strictly feudal sources of revenue.[21] At the same time, on a much larger volume of business, over half the revenue of the English Crown, apart from extraordinary subsidies, benevolences, and loans, came from customs receipts and fines for the violation of customs regulations.[22] This clearly demonstrates the economic backwardness of Scotland, in relation to the more advanced nations of Western Europe.

The comparative weakness of the burghs within Scotland is also striking. Politically, the burghs were dominated by the merchant guilds. Craft guilds did not develop in Scotland until the late fifteenth century; throughout the sixteenth century a great issue in most burghs was the attempt of these new organizations to break the stranglehold of the merchant guilds on municipal governments.[23] When this merchant control is placed side by side with the economic policy of the government, dominated as the latter was by noncommercial motives, the political insignificance of the burgher class is quite obvious. The burghs wanted one thing above all from the government—a continuance of their monopoly —and this they got. They would have appreciated peace and order, and they were able to provide these desirable commodities, to some extent at least, by means of their own courts, provided no nobleman took it into his head to cause a disturbance. If this happened, the town government was generally helpless.[24]

The burghs, the burgher class, and economic problems as a whole were not very important in Scottish politics in the sixteenth century. The support of the small, not very wealthy, but growing middle class could be useful to an aristocratic politician; Moray certainly found it so on more than one occasion. But Moray and

[21] Grant, *Social and Economic Development*, p. 207.
[22] F. C. Dietz, *English Government Finance 1485–1558*, p. 80.
[23] On these points see Grant, *Social and Economic Development*, pp. 376, 414–15, 424–25, 428–34.
[24] See, for instance, the account in John Knox, *History of the Reformation in Scotland*, II, 315–21, of the Bothwell-Arran fracas in Edinburgh in December 1561.

his fellow nobles were concerned with other matters. The towns-men played a role in the drama of Moray's life, but merely as extras, and not very vocal ones at that.[25]

In sharp contrast to the burgher class and to the powerful but chronically impecunious nobility stood the Catholic Church—very wealthy, politically and socially powerful, and hopelessly corrupt. No branch of the Church in Europe was more riddled with vice; this helps to explain why it succumbed so easily to the Protestants. The testimony of all contemporaries, Catholic and Protestant alike, agrees on this point.[26] There were all the usual vices: sexual immorality, clerical ignorance and rapacity, plural-ism, and the like. By the sixteenth century, too, appointments to the higher offices had fallen into the hands of the King, which meant the virtual monopolization of these offices by the nobility. This led to poor appointments, nepotism, and the distribution of abbeys and priories *in commendam*, frequently to children. King James V (1513–42), for example, took care of five of his bastard sons in this way, among them Moray, then known as Lord James, who became Prior of St. Andrews at the age of seven.

Owing to royal control of appointments, a member of the rul-ing faction could lay his hands temporarily on a share of the Church's wealth. But a bishop or an abbot might die, and, given the sudden reversals of fortune common in Scottish politics, it might not be possible to control the nomination of his successor. In order to obtain permanently the revenue of the benefice, re-course was had to a comparatively new type of land tenure, the feu farm. This had been devised to meet the most common griev-ance of the Scottish tenant—insecurity of tenure; it was both permanent and hereditary. In the case of secular lands, it did not benefit the tenant very much, since landlords generally raised

[25] The above paragraphs on the towns have been drawn mainly from Grant, *Social and Economic Development*, Section II, Chapters 7 and 8. This book is excellent on all aspects of social and economic history in this period. See also MacKinnon, *Constitutional History*, pp. 289–307, and Brown, *Scotland in the Time of Queen Mary*, pp. 112–76.

[26] See, for instance, Cardinal Sermoneta's letter to Paul IV in 1556, in J. H. Pol-len, ed., *Papal Negotiations with Mary Queen of Scots*, pp. 528–30. For a typical Protestant view, see Buchanan, *History*, II, 350–51.

rents enormously before granting this type of lease.[27] For Church lands, however, the device suited the nobility perfectly. It became common in the 1530s, when James V permitted the feuing of Church lands on a large scale in order to help the clergy meet certain obligations to him. In consequence, a bishop or abbot, scion of a noble family as he was, feued his lands to his relatives so that after his death the family would continue to profit. This process reached its height in the late 1550s, when the higher clergy began to fear the triumph of Protestantism and the possible confiscation of Church lands.[28] The Papacy objected to this excessive feuing but was unable to put a stop to it.[29]

Finally, this corrupt and secularized Church proved utterly unable to reform itself. In the last decade of Catholic supremacy in Scotland, from 1549 to 1559, three Church Councils were held. All of them passed excellent statutes against the prevailing vices in the Church, which statutes had absolutely no effect whatever.[30] As one authority has put it, "The best proof that a religious revolution was needed is the fact that the Church was fully conscious of its own shortcomings, yet was powerless to set itself in order." [31]

Given the condition of the Scottish Church, it is not surprising that Protestantism became a serious problem. In general, the first groups to be affected by the new dispensation were the lesser lords, the junior branches of the great families, some clergy, and the wealthier burgesses.[32] During the reign of James V, however, Protestantism did not receive any encouragement from the government. James had been able to milk his clergy very satisfactorily;

---

[27] For feu farming, see Grant, *Social and Economic Development*, pp. 265–86.
[28] On the question of Church lands, see *ibid.*, pp. 219–27; R. K. Hannay, "On the Church Lands at the Reformation," *Scottish Historical Review*, XVI (1918–19), 52–72, and "A Study in Reformation History," *Scottish Historical Review*, XXIII (1925–26), 18–33.   [29] *Ibid.*, p. 32.
[30] For the text of these statutes, see D. Patrick, ed., *Statutes of the Scottish Church*, pp. 84–191. On the question of the effectiveness of the reforms, see Mary of Guise's letter to the Council of 1559, *ibid.*, pp. 156–60.
[31] P. Hume Brown, *John Knox*, I, 42–43. For good general surveys of the condition of the Church at this time, see W. L. Mathieson, *Politics and Religion: a Study of Scottish History from the Reformation to the Revolution*, I, 19–33, and Lang, *History of Scotland*, I, 421–33. The Church's constitutional position is discussed in MacKinnon, *Constitutional History*, pp. 308–34.
[32] Lang, *History of Scotland*, I, 422.

like the French kings, he had no pressing motive to change his religion. On the contrary, he had the strongest reasons for not going over to Protestantism. In the first place, he was a sincere Catholic himself. Second, his foreign policy, the traditional anti-English policy of Scotland, meant, after England's break with Rome, a pro-Catholic policy, to which he steadily adhered, despite the hectoring of Henry VIII. Finally, James depended on the higher clergy for his administrative officials, since the vicissitudes of his youth had conditioned him to grave suspicion and dislike of most of his great nobles. For example, Cardinal Beaton was his chief adviser during the last years of his life and was almost certainly the author of the policy which led to the disaster of Solway.

At the time of James's death in 1542, there was a sort of spiritual vacuum in Scotland. Protestantism was as yet a state of mind, and, truly, a protesting one, exemplified best by Sir David Lindsay, a royal official, a close friend of James V, and a very fine poet and satirist.[33] Something had to happen, and the scales were weighted in favor of Protestantism, not only because of the moribund condition of the Church but also because of the stake of the nobility in Church property, a stake which might well be lost in the event of a successful Catholic reform. Since the vacuum existed, however, just how it would be filled hinged on the solution given to political problems. It is to the political scene, then, that we must now turn.

iii

King James V died on December 14, 1542, apparently of melancholia induced by the shameful rout of his army at Solway Moss in November. This disaster was attributable to James's following the traditional Scottish policy of alliance with France and hostility to England, a policy which had been complicated and envenomed in recent years by the religious differences between James and his uncle Henry.

The Scottish crown now passed to James's week-old daughter Mary. A regency was, of course, necessary. After a struggle with

[33] There is a good study of Lindsay's attitude toward the Church: W. Murison, *Sir David Lyndsay*.

the late King's chief adviser, Cardinal Beaton, James Hamilton, Earl of Arran, heir apparent to the Scottish throne, won this coveted office. Arran was an ineffectual man, dominated by desire for pelf and for advancement for himself and his family. At the moment he was reputed to be a Protestant.

Arran's victory in the struggle for the regency pleased Henry VIII, who now decided to try to use Arran and the Scottish Protestants to work a revolution in Scottish foreign policy, and, in fact, to bring Scotland under his domination. His weapon was money rather than force. Henry sent home the Scottish nobles captured at Solway with full pockets and with instructions to further Henry's policy. Henry proposed that Mary be wed to his son, Prince Edward. This was reasonable enough, but the conditions attached to the marriage scheme made it clear that Henry's object was domination rather than a friendly alliance between equals.[34] This the Scots simply would not stomach. "There is not so little a boy but he will hurl stones against it," one of Henry's "assured lords" told Sir Ralph Sadler, the official English envoy to Scotland.[35] The result was that late in 1543 Arran reconciled himself with Beaton, turned his back on Protestantism, and renewed the ancient alliance with France.[36]

Thus failed a premature attempt to create a Protestant, pro-English party in Scotland. The reasons for the failure are numerous. First, the convinced Protestants in Scotland were few in numbers and had no organization. Protestantism was still a state of mind or a political rallying ground rather than a creed; there was an immense dissatisfaction with the existing Church, but nothing yet to take its place. It was not until Knox arrived on the scene that Scottish Protestantism became an organized fighting force.

Second, Protestantism suffered from its political connections.[37]

[34] On this point see Lang, *History of Scotland*, I, 461–63; Mathieson, *Politics and Religion*, I, 9–11; D. H. Fleming, *Mary Queen of Scots*, p. 181.
[35] *Ibid.*, pp. 183–84.
[36] The best account of the confusing maneuvers of 1543 is to be found in Lang, *History of Scotland*, I, 458–75.
[37] As an indication of the political uses to which religious opinions were put at this time, it is interesting to note that the Parliament which authorized negotiations with England in March 1543 permitted the circulation of the Bible in the vernacular; that which renewed the French alliance in December 1543 passed

Of the great nobles who called themselves Protestants in 1543, it is safe to say that not more than one or two were sincere. They professed Protestantism because they were bribed by Henry VIII, or for some equally worldly consideration. This fact was perfectly evident to the Scots, who flocked to the standard of Beaton: the latter, whatever his motives, was at least determined to preserve the independence of his country.

Finally, no small share of the blame for failure rests with Henry himself. Had he moved cautiously, had he been willing to sacrifice his ambition for immediate domination in Scotland to his professed policy of an Anglo-Scottish marriage which was to be contracted between equals, he might have been able to bring about the triumph of the pro-English party in Scotland. The French alliance was by no means popular; twice within thirty years it had led to a national military disaster. Sentiment in Scotland for an alliance with England was growing.[38] But no patriot could accept English friendship on Henry's terms, for that meant loss of independence. So it was that the Catholic Church and the French alliance got a new lease of life.

Henry reacted violently to the miscarriage of his schemes,[39] and the result was further war between the two countries, throughout which, as in the past, every Scottish defeat merely intensified the determination of the smaller nation to resist and to maintain its independence. In the course of the struggle Beaton was assassinated by some personal enemies who also were paid agents of Henry VIII, but this did not help Henry particularly. Arran besieged the murderers in St. Andrews, which they had seized in order to do away with the Cardinal, and captured them with the aid of a French fleet.[40]

The death early in 1547 of both Henry VIII and Francis I marks the turning point in the struggle, even though the great English

---

an act for the repression of heresy. *The Acts of the Parliament of Scotland*, II, 425, 443.

[38] Brown, *John Knox*, I, 40.

[39] See his instructions to Hertford in April 1544, quoted in Fleming, *Mary Queen of Scots*, pp. 189–90.

[40] For a good account of the siege of St. Andrews Castle, see Lang, *History of Scotland*, II, 1–8.

victory at Pinkie was won later in that year. The new English government soon had its hands full with domestic problems, while Henry II of France was far more interested in Scotland than his father had been. The result was that by 1548 very substantial French aid began to arrive. At the same time pressure was applied to Arran by the French and by Mary of Guise, the widow of James V, to permit the marriage of Mary to the Dauphin. Arran, who had been actively promoting the marriage of his own son to Mary, looked askance at this project, but French pressure and the bribe of a French dukedom won him over. In July 1548 the Scottish Parliament consented to the French proposals, which included a stipulation that Mary was to be sent to France to be brought up. In August 1548 the little girl sailed for France, accompanied by a numerous train, a member of which was her half-brother, Lord James Stewart.[41]

It is high time that the reader was introduced to the subject of this work. Lord James was born in 1531,[42] an illegitimate son of James V and of Margaret Erskine Douglas, wife of Robert Douglas of Lochleven.[43] We know very little of his childhood, except that he was well provided for by his father.[44] In 1538 he was made Commendator of the Priory of St. Andrews, one of the wealthiest monastic foundations in Scotland; Strachan, the Rector of the University of St. Andrews, was sent to Rome in that year to get the necessary papal dispensation.[45] Lord James evidently lived in St. Andrews after 1538; in the 1540s he attended the University

[41] On these points see Fleming, *Mary Queen of Scots*, pp. 13–14, 193–98; T. F. Henderson, *Mary Queen of Scots*, I, 57–68.

[42] The date is established beyond dispute by a papal document dated August 30, 1534, which gave Lord James a dispensation from bastardy as a handicap to ecclesiastical preferment. *Historical Manuscripts Commission, 6th Report*, Appendix, p. 670.

[43] She married him in 1527; *The Scots Peerage*, VI, 369. In April 1536 James V, then engaged in negotiations for his French marriage, broke them off temporarily and consulted the Pope on the possibility of getting a divorce for her so that he could marry her—a move which, if successful, would probably have meant that Lord James would have been King. King James's effort was unsuccessful, however. Lang, *History of Scotland*, I, 438–40.

[44] For the amounts spent on clothing, etc., for Lord James during James V's reign, see *Accounts of the Lord High Treasurer of Scotland* (henceforth abbreviated *Treasurer's Accounts*), VI, 181 ff.

[45] J. M. Anderson, ed., *Early Records of the University of St. Andrews*, p. xix.

there.[46] He was in close contact with his mother at Lochleven; [47] after his father's death, when Lord James was eleven, the revenues of the priory, nominally his but actually in the King's hands till then, evidently passed to his mother, for we find the Laird of Lochleven paying the priory's share of a tax in February 1547.[48] Just when they passed into his own hands is uncertain, but undoubtedly shortly thereafter. In 1548, the year of his voyage to France, he made his mark in the military sphere for the first time, helping to repulse English raids in Fife, at East Ferry in January and at St. Monans in June.[49] He did not linger in France; he was back in Scotland by November 1548.[50]

The war with England dragged on for a year and a half after Mary's voyage to France and went in favor of the Scots and their French allies. Peace was finally made in April 1550, on terms favorable to France and Scotland. This was a great victory for the policy of Beaton, now being carried on by Mary of Guise. The latter was a very able woman, naturally enough devoted to the Franco-Catholic cause in Scotland. She was well aware of the incapacity of Arran, who, she knew, cherished family ambitions that might lead him, now that French military aid was no longer an absolute necessity, to try to upset the French marriage. So she resolved on nothing less than the ouster of Arran as Regent and his replacement by herself.[51] In this she was ultimately successful,

[46] *Treasurer's Accounts*, VII, 163–64. Lord James is listed as having matriculated in 1545, but owing to the methods of enrollment used at St. Andrews at this time, this may mean that he was nearer ending his studies than beginning them. Anderson, *University of St. Andrews*, pp. xxvi, 148, 251–52.
[47] Some of the priory's valuables were stored at Lochleven during the war with England in the 1540s. C. Innes, ed., *Registrum Honoris de Morton*, I, 6.
[48] *Treasurer's Accounts*, IX, 59.
[49] This dating is taken from R. Lindsay of Pitscottie, *The Chronicles of Scotland*, II, 104, 108–9. This is the only chronology which will fit with the fact of Lord James's presence on the voyage to France. Fleming, *Mary Queen of Scots*, p. 197, has expressed his doubts as to whether Lord James did go, but cites only one piece of contemporary evidence in favor of his view, and that of the flimsiest, since the reason given for Lord James's remaining at home does not make sense, and the weight of contemporary evidence definitely favors the contrary opinion. Fleming's case really rests on the chronology of the fighting in Fife, which Lindsay of Pitscottie clears up. It is true that the excellent Mackay edition of Lindsay was not available when Fleming wrote, and previous editions lent support to his view.   [50] *Treasurer's Accounts*, IX, 256.
[51] This was not a new idea; it had occurred to Jacques de la Brosse in 1543, when

chiefly because of the fact that she had the support of France and of virtually every important Scottish faction except that of Arran's own family. Even the Protestants supported her, since she had been conciliatory toward them and since Arran's brother, now Archbishop of St. Andrews, was disliked by them as the visible symbol of Popery. So in April 1554, Arran, now Duke of Châtelherault in the French nobility, laid down his power, much to the disgust of the Archbishop, and Mary of Guise was proclaimed Regent.[52]

With the elevation of its leader to the regency, the triumph of the pro-French, Catholic party seemed complete. Yet in six short years Scotland was ruled by a Protestant, pro-English faction. How is this dramatic reversal to be explained?

The fact is that ever since the debacle of 1543, in spite of the seeming triumph of its foes, Protestantism had been steadily making headway in Scotland. There were numerous reasons for this. The Catholic Church was corrupt and unable to reform itself, as has been pointed out. Moreover, Protestantism profited by the preaching and martyrdom of George Wishart, the first important Calvinist leader in Scotland, who was executed for heresy by Beaton in March 1546.[53] It was the Cardinal's last successful act of persecution, and it backfired, for it made a martyr of Wishart and unquestionably stimulated the ardor of those who assassinated the Cardinal two months later.[54]

More important were the changes in the political situation. It was during these years that Protestantism lost its invidious connection with England and ceased to be identified in the popular mind with loss of independence and the dominion of the "auld

---

he was sent to Scotland in the successful French attempt to retain the Scottish alliance. G. Dickinson, ed., *Two Missions of Jacques de la Brosse*, Introduction, pp. 12–13.

[52] Fleming, *Mary Queen of Scots*, pp. 16–17, 19–20, 199–202, 207–8. Brown, *John Knox*, I, 284–85. Henderson, *Mary Queen of Scots*, I, 81–83, 89–93. Lord James, who supported Mary of Guise, was rewarded in 1555 by the commendatorship of the Priory of Pittenweem, and of Mâcon in France. J. Robertson, ed., *Inventaires de la Royne Descosse Douairière de France*, p. xxxix.

[53] Foxe's account of Wishart's trial, quoted by Knox, *History*, I, 149–68, shows that Wishart's beliefs were essentially Calvinistic.

[54] Mathieson, *Politics and Religion*, I, 14.

enemy." Two events were primarily responsible for this. The capture of Beaton's murderers in St. Andrews in 1547, seemingly a disaster of the first magnitude for Protestantism, since it lost at one stroke its important religious and political leaders, among them Knox, was really an advantage, for these men were looked on as little better than English agents—which, indeed, many of them were. When they made their way back to Scotland after a term in the French galleys, as eventually almost all of them did, they had learned wisdom. Furthermore, Protestantism could now be diffused by those that were left in Scotland free from the stigma of Englishry.[55] More important was the accession of Mary Tudor in England and the beginning of Catholic persecution there. Many English and Scottish Protestants fled to Scotland, among them some very able preachers. England being Catholic, Protestantism was now definitely free of any taint of association with English political ends.

Among the reasons that led Protestants south of the Tweed to flee north was a cessation of persecution in Scotland. Archbishop Hamilton, Beaton's successor, though a thorough rascal in many respects, did not persecute, partly because of the fate of his predecessor, partly because on family grounds, he opposed the thoroughgoing pro-French policy of Mary of Guise, as did his brother the Regent. When Mary of Guise became Regent, she, too, did not persecute, for Protestant support had smoothed her path to power, and she was forced to depend upon that support to remain in power. Indeed, the Archbishop did not reconcile himself to the loss of the regency by his brother, whom he had been able to dominate. In this situation the new Regent judged it wise to conciliate her Protestant subjects, since she believed that they would not be politically dangerous.[56]

Not only did the new Regent refrain from persecution, but her positive actions gave a further fillip to Protestantism, although this was far from her intention. As has been said before, the French alliance was becoming more and more unpopular.[57] It is true that

[55] *Ibid.*, pp. 37-38. See also Lang, *History of Scotland*, II, 22-23, 31-34.
[56] *Ibid.*, 28-29. Pollen, *Papal Negotiations*, p. xxiii. Mathieson, *Politics and Religion*, I, 42-44.
[57] Even under James V the French alliance was unpopular in some quarters. MacKinnon, *Constitutional History*, p. 223.

during the 1540s anti-French feeling was submerged in the wave of anger aroused by the perfidy of Henry VIII; but even during the war there were outbreaks in Edinburgh against the French.[58] Mary of Guise herself realized that the behavior of the French soldiery was losing friends for France, and she got rid of the majority of them as quickly as she could after the war was over.[59] But Mary of Guise neglected to learn the primary political lesson of the 1540s, which was this: that the Scots had rallied to the Catholic, pro-French party not merely out of hatred of England, still less out of enthusiasm for France or the Catholic Church, but out of a desire to maintain their independence. This independence they were prepared to defend, from whatever quarter the attack upon it should come. In the 1550s England was no longer threatening it. On the other hand, there was good reason to think that France was.

All the world was painfully aware of the fate of a country in the sixteenth century when its crown fell to a woman. Burgundy, Spain, Bohemia, Hungary, and now, it seemed, England had fallen into the Hapsburg net for just this reason. It now seemed likely that Scotland would be swallowed up by France in the same way. The Scots had done their best to stipulate for their independence when they agreed to the French marriage for Mary; now that the pressing danger which had caused them to make that agreement had passed, they became far more sensitive to the possibility of French encroachments on that independence. Mary of Guise, far from attempting to allay this suspicion, or even understanding it, conferred most of the real administrative power on French officials, thereby alienating the all-powerful nobility, and especially those members of it—such as the Earl of Huntly, the greatest Catholic lord—who felt that they had special claims on her gratitude.[60] The Regent's tax scheme of 1556, mentioned above,[61] increased Scottish fears. It was not simply the desire to maintain

---

[58] John Leslie, *The History of Scotland*, II, 315.
[59] November 12, 1549, Mary of Guise to the Cardinal of Guise and the Duc d'Aumâle, in Teulet, *Relations politiques*, I, 197–206. Brown, *John Knox*, I, 278.
[60] Henderson, *Mary Queen of Scots*, I, 92. P. F. Tytler, *History of Scotland*, VI, 60. Huntly was nominally Chancellor under Mary of Guise, but the real power was exercised by the Vice-Chancellor, De Rubay, a Frenchman.
[61] See above, p. 8, note 6.

their traditional power but suspicion of France as well that led the nobility to oppose this plan.

Thus the elements of political and religious revolution all existed in Scotland in the 1550s, and it was at this moment—in 1555, to be exact—that John Knox returned home to take advantage of them. A great deal has been written about this extraordinary man; only a few biographical details need be given here.[62] Knox had been rescued from the puddle of papistry, to use his own phrase, by Wishart in the early 1540s. Though not one of the murderers of Beaton, he joined them in St. Andrews in April 1547 and preached for the first time there. Like the others, he was sent to the galleys; on his release he went to England, where his work during the reign of Edward VI is well-known. Upon Mary's accession he fled to the Continent, winding up at Geneva, where he became an earnest disciple of Calvin. As his religious views became more radical, Knox became more uncompromising in holding to them. It was at once his strength and his weakness that he became less and less able to understand, or to sympathize with, any viewpoint other than his own.

It was as a thoroughgoing Calvinist that Knox returned to his native land, where he made two vitally important contributions to the Protestant cause. Those who first welcomed him to Scotland were mostly burgesses: Protestantism still drew most of its support from this group and the lesser gentry.[63] Knox knew, however, that the nobility was the class he must reach if Protestantism was to succeed. So, with the assistance of the Protestant gentry, principally John Erskine of Dun and James Sandilands of Calder, Knox arranged to meet and to convert, or to strengthen in their "political" faith, many important people, among them Lord James, whom Knox saw in the house of Sandilands in the course of the winter.[64] Now this is not to argue that the nobility turned Protestant solely on account of Knox or other preachers. The question of Church lands was in the back of many minds,

[62] The best modern biography is that by P. Hume Brown, which supplanted the older but still useful work of T. McCrie. For a critical view see Andrew Lang, *John Knox and the Reformation.*
[63] Brown, *John Knox,* I, 294. Lang, *History of Scotland,* I, 422–23, II, 31–34.
[64] Brown, *John Knox,* I, 303.

especially those of the great earls such as Argyle and Morton. But some of the men who turned from Rome were sincere, and Lord James was certainly one of these, as even his critics admit.[65] So Knox gave to Protestantism what it had not had before: a group of aristocratic leaders whose motives were in some cases laudable, in some selfish, but in no case unpatriotic.

Knox's second contribution was equally important: he turned the various elements of Protestant belief and feeling in Scotland into a distinctive, fighting creed with a distinctive, Calvinistic stamp. The key question, which illustrates Knox's work best, was that of the Mass. Knox, of course, regarded the Mass as idolatry. Many men who considered themselves Protestants had been attending Mass, simply in order to conform to the law. Knox argued against this practice and won his point, even convincing Maitland of Lethington, no mean feat, since Maitland was not in the habit of thinking in theological terms.[66] Thus the Protestant party, as formed by Knox in this short visit—he left Scotland in July 1556—became for the first time a unified, cohesive group with influential leaders and well-defined principles, a group which was likely to clash with the old religion in a very short time. This was by far the most important contribution Knox made to the Reformation in Scotland, though some of his later actions, during the struggle with Mary, were more spectacular. As one authority has put it, "had Scotland never seen him again [after 1556], the eventual direction both of politics and religion could not have been widely different from what it has actually been." [67]

That a clash did not come immediately between the adherents of the old faith and the new was due to Mary of Guise. Although her use of Frenchmen in high office was unpopular, nothing in the first three years of her administration, if we except the tax scheme of 1556, gave any ground for complaint. She was a good executive; she interested herself personally in the administration

[65] Consider the testimony of two of Lord James's bitterest critics on this point: J. Skelton, *Maitland of Lethington and the Scotland of Mary Stuart*, II, 264–65; J. Hosack, *Mary Queen of Scots and Her Accusers*, p. 504.
[66] Knox, *History*, I, 247–49.
[67] Brown, *John Knox*, I, 317. Knox's own account of his work during this visit is in his *History*, I, 245–54. See also Brown's account, *John Knox*, I, 293–316.

of justice and did what she could for the peasantry, who were feeling the adverse effects of feuing and of rising prices.[68] Her temporizing religious policy kept the two factions from flying at each other's throats. In fact, so favorable to the Protestants did she show herself that some of Knox's noble supporters sent him an optimistic letter on March 10, 1557, inviting him to return to Scotland. This letter, signed by Lord James among others, has been characterized as a revolutionary document, since the signers announced that they were ready to hazard lives and goods in behalf of the new dispensation. That this is a misinterpretation is indicated by a significant phrase in the letter: the writers believe that the "friars, enemies to Christ's Evangel, [are] in less estimation, both with the Queen's Grace, and the rest of the nobility of our realm." [69] It is evident that the lords expected to accomplish the desired religious change without resorting to revolution and that they desired Knox's presence in order to put further pressure on the Regent.

Knox accepted the invitation and left Geneva, but his reply evidently gave the lords pause, for on his arrival in Dieppe he found two letters awaiting him which indicated that he, too, had misinterpreted the lords' intentions; their advice now was to wait a while before coming. Knox's letter to the lords from Dieppe indicates that they did well to head him off, for the Reformer now urged them, in their capacity as nobles as well as Protestants, to rebel against French tyranny and Popery.[70]

The events of the last months of 1557 mark a definite turning point in the regency of Mary of Guise and in the history of Scottish Protestantism as well. The crisis was precipitated by the last installment of the Hapsburg-Valois wars, into which England had been dragged by this time as the reluctant ally of Spain. France was naturally anxious that Scotland should fall on England's rear, as she so often had in the past. There was absolutely no Scottish interest to be served by such a war. Relations with

[68] Leslie, *History of Scotland*, II, 359, 365, 483–84. A. I. Cameron, ed., *The Scottish Correspondence of Mary of Lorraine*, pp. xiv–xv.
[69] The letter is given in Knox, *History*, I, 267–68.
[70] *Ibid.*, pp. 269–72.

England were peaceful enough, and the government of Mary Tudor was straining hard to be conciliatory, in the hope of preventing an attack. After receiving the French request for aid, however, Mary of Guise summoned the Scottish nobility to war on the "auld enemy." [71]

The Regent received a rude shock. Unquestionably she expected that she had but to command, in the case of a war against England, and obedience would automatically follow.[72] She did succeed in getting the nobility to agree to a declaration of war, by provoking an English raid,[73] but beyond this they would not go. They professed their readiness to defend their country against an invasion, but, after a retaliatory raid led by Huntly, they absolutely refused to enter England in force.[74] Anti-French feeling was largely responsible for this attitude: it was felt that Scotland had acted as a French catspaw often enough. Flodden and Solway had not been forgotten.[75] Since the English did not launch an invasion, fighting was at a minimum; it consisted largely of border raids by D'Oysel's Frenchmen and by supporters of the Regent such as the Earl of Bothwell.

These events brought about a decisive reaction in two directions. In the first place, they produced in Mary of Guise an overwhelming distrust of the Scottish nobility, Catholic and Protestant alike, for even the Catholic Huntly sided with her enemies. They also served as a danger signal, which Mary of Guise had perforce to ignore. As a Frenchwoman, a Guise, and a mother, she was committed to the policy of French domination in Scotland.[76] Peaceable domination if possible; but if not, then domination by force. She now became aware that the latter method was the only possible one, since the nobility could not be led to acquiesce in

[71] Leslie, *History of Scotland*, II, 368–70.
[72] See March 29, 1557, D'Oysel to François de Noailles, in Teulet, *Relations politiques*, I, 291–95. D'Oysel was the commander of the French forces in Scotland. [73] Buchanan, *History*, II, 391.
[74] Leslie, *History of Scotland*, II, 371–74.
[75] Lang, *History of Scotland*, II, 35–36.
[76] For example: D'Oysel, in a letter of March 30, 1555, to the Duke of Guise, said that the Regent would follow his, Guise's, advice in regard to the war with England, which was obviously about to break out soon. A. Teulet, ed., *Papiers d'état relatifs à l'histoire de l'Ecosse au XVIe siècle*, I, 720–23.

French control of their country. For the moment it was necessary to continue the temporizing policy she had hitherto followed, but she was now ready to discard it as soon as possible.

The war policy of Mary of Guise, contrary to the national interest as it was, provoked in the Protestant camp a reaction which was certainly intensified by the incendiary letters pouring from Knox's pen.[77] On December 3, 1557, the earls of Argyle, Glencairn, and Morton,[78] Argyle's son, Lord Lorne, and Erskine of Dun signed a document which was to become known as the First Band of the Lords of the Congregation.[79] This document was clearly revolutionary: the signers agreed to hazard lives and goods for the setting forth of the true religion, without any reference to pious hopes that the necessary change might come peaceably. Just how or when they were to go about instituting the change they did not say, nor did they act at once. The band was not so much a clarion call to arms as an indication that the signatories would act in the future, when the action they contemplated became feasible or necessary. The significance of the band was that, for the first time, the Protestant party which Knox had supplied with cohesiveness and leadership was prepared to act. Worldly motives were not lacking: the anti-French motive was there, and both Morton and Lorne (who became Earl of Argyle in 1558) were greedy for Church land. But "Christ's Evangel" was the rallying cry, and Glencairn, a single-minded zealot, and Erskine of Dun, a transparently honest man respected even by the Catholic party, were quite sincere.

Clearly a struggle was impending. And it was at this point that Lord James became an important figure in Scottish politics.

[77] Knox by this time was preaching sedition. In a letter of December 17, 1557, he advised his friends that they might disobey the authorities if the latter, upon being asked, refused to further the word of God. D. Calderwood, *The History of the Kirk of Scotland*, I, 323–26. See also Brown, *John Knox*, I, 348–58.

[78] Morton was now head of the House of Douglas, since the Earl of Angus had died earlier in the year, leaving a minor heir and a disputed succession to his earldom.   [79] It is given by Knox, *History*, I, 273–74.

CHAPTER II

The Wars of the Congregation

IN AUGUST 1557 an unsuccessful raid into Northumberland was made by a party of Scots led by Lord James and by Lord Robert, Commendator of Holyrood—another bastard of James V—and Lord Hume, the great Border chieftain.[1] This event marked the initial venture of Lord James into high politics, and in view of his later career it seems somewhat surprising that he should have started as an adherent of Mary of Guise.

It was to be expected that Lord James, before his conversion to Protestantism, would be an ally of the Regent out of family interest. He was a Stewart, and he knew that with the Hamiltons in power no political career would be open to him. So he supported Mary of Guise in her bid for office and was rewarded, as we have seen, by the grant of additional benefices, both in Scotland and in France. He saw no reason to change his position immediately after his conversion, since Mary of Guise was tolerant of Protestants and since she was on bad terms with Archbishop Hamilton.

With the solidification of the Protestant party as a result of Knox's visit, however, the problem arose as to what policy should be followed. All members of the Protestant group agreed that, ideally, the government should itself be Protestant and enforce the new religious views; all agreed that the first step was to try to induce the Regent to see religious matters as they did. Knox's efforts at persuasion were laughed at by the Regent, however.[2]

[1] P. Ridpath, *The Border History of England and Scotland*, pp. 585–86.
[2] John Knox, *History of the Reformation in Scotland*, I, 252. From this point on, Knox's hostility to Mary of Guise was marked.

If Mary of Guise could not be won to Geneva, what then? Should the Protestants continue to go along with her tolerant policy or should they forcibly insist that she accept the truth of Protestant teaching and turn on the "pestilent Papists"? One group, headed by Knox and the preachers, was for action.[3] The first overt act of this group was the signing of the band of December 1557. Action did not follow at once, however; the political leaders of this faction were aware that they simply did not have the strength to force their views on the Regent as long as she continued to tolerate them, since on the question of action the Protestant party was by no means united.

The other wing of the Protestant party, including Lord James, felt that action now would be very unwise. The problem as they saw it was twofold: how to effect the religious change, and how to prevent Scotland from sinking to the status of a French province. From the Catholic, pro-French point of view there was one grave weakness in the existing system: that France was committed to a policy of absentee government for Scotland. The Queen, as prospective wife of the Dauphin and future Queen of France, would perforce reside in France. This meant that Scotland must be ruled by a series of regents. As long as Mary of Guise lived, this weakness would not be important, but on her death it would be impossible for France to commit the government to another French regent without provoking a rebellion. So there would in all probability be another Scottish regent, and the logical choice was Châtelherault. Once the government was in Scottish hands again, the Protestant party could make its bid for power, win the vacillating Châtelherault, who was not on particularly good terms with France at the moment, and make the dominance of Protestantism in Scotland the necessary condition for continued loyalty to Scotland's absentee ruler and to the French alliance. So thought Lord James and his friends.

The objection to the policy of the activist wing of the Protestants from this point of view was that it would lead to a clash with

[3] The evolution of Knox's views on this question, particularly with reference to political theory, is traced by J. W. Allen, *A History of Political Thought in the Sixteenth Century*, pp. 109-12.

the Catholic party before the death of Mary of Guise. In this case France would undoubtedly act to put down any rebellion. There would be a religious and a political struggle at the same time, and this Lord James and those who thought like him wished to avoid. Under only one condition would the policy of the activists be justified: England must be willing to support it. As long as Mary Tudor reigned in England such an idea was preposterous.

The weaknesses in the position of the Fabian wing of the Protestant party were two. First, their enthusiastic coreligionists might make some move which would stir the government into action. In fact, Lord James himself had unwittingly almost done as much by signing the invitation to Knox in March 1557; it had been only just possible then to head off the Reformer, whose return would certainly have precipitated matters. Second, Mary of Guise might change her policy and begin to persecute. If this happened, of course, the Protestants would have to fight, come what may, or surrender.

Mary of Guise was quite ready to change her policy, but the time was not yet ripe. Her daughter was not yet married to the Dauphin; not until the marriage had taken place and the marriage treaties been ratified could she afford to turn against the Protestant party.

Parliament was summoned for December 1557, and there a letter from Henry II was read, which requested that commissioners be sent to France to negotiate the marriage treaty.[4] Parliament assented and named nine commissioners, among them Lord James.[5] Three of these men were Protestants. The support given by the Protestants to the marriage indicates the triumph in Protestant councils of the Fabian view, for the moment at least. Their policy was to support the marriage, which was inevitable, and at the same time to see to it that the rights of Châtelherault were carefully safeguarded.[6]

[4] The letter is printed in R. Keith, *The History of the Affairs of Church and State in Scotland*, I, 348–49.
[5] D. H. Fleming, *Mary Queen of Scots*, p. 210. Lord James's mother arranged his finances for the trip, borrowing sufficient money to support him. A. I. Cameron, ed., *The Scottish Correspondence of Mary of Lorraine*, pp. 411–13.
[6] E. Percy, *John Knox*, pp. 252–54.

The commissioners sailed in February 1558. On their arrival they received full powers from Mary to negotiate for her.[7] They found the French very compliant. The integrity of Scotland, its ancient laws and liberties, and the rights of Châtelherault were fully protected.[8] The Scots commissioners were satisfied, and the marriage was celebrated on April 24.[9]

The reason for the French compliance with the Scottish demands was simple. On April 4 Mary had set her hand to three rather shocking documents. In the first two she agreed that if she died without issue, Scotland and her rights to the English succession were to be granted to the King of France as a free gift; or, if it were not feasible for him to govern Scotland permanently, he was to hold Scotland till he was repaid the costs of its defense and of her education. In the third document, Mary announced that all promises made in her name, or by her, past or future, which contravened the terms of the first two documents, were void.[10] Conduct such as this speaks for itself.

The commissioners consented to swear fealty to the Dauphin as titular King of Scotland,[11] but when they were asked by the French to agree to bring the Scottish crown to France to crown him, they flatly refused, on the ground that this would be a violation of their instructions.[12] When four of the commissioners died before returning to Scotland, in the space of four months, the deaths were, quite naturally, attributed to poison.[13] This did not endear France to the Scots. Lord James was taken ill at the same time but survived; however, according to Buchanan, he suffered from a stomach ailment for the rest of his life.[14]

---

[7] *Ibid.*, p. 259. P. F. Tytler, *History of Scotland*, VI, 68. A. Labanoff, ed., *Recueil des lettres de Marie Stuart*, I, 46–50.

[8] The marriage contract is in *The Acts of the Parliament of Scotland*, II, 511–14.

[9] For a contemporary description of the marriage, see A. Teulet, ed., *Relations politiques de la France et de l'Espagne avec l'Ecosse au XVIe siècle*, I, 302–11.

[10] The three documents are in Labanoff, *Recueil*, I, 50–56.

[11] The oath is in Keith, *History*, I, 363–64.

[12] G. Buchanan, *The History of Scotland*, II, 395.

[13] W. L. Mathieson, *Politics and Religion: a Study of Scottish History from the Reformation to the Revolution*, I, 48.

[14] Buchanan, *History*, II, 395. R. Lindsay of Pitscottie, *The Chronicles of Scotland*, II, 127, says that Lord James was "hanged by the heels" to get the poison to drop out of his mouth. The atomic age does have its advantages.

The commissioners who did come home arrived in October, and Parliament was summoned for November 29. It approved the actions of the commissioners, including the marriage treaty, and it also agreed, at the instance of Mary of Guise, that the Dauphin should be vested with the crown matrimonial for the duration of the marriage only—in other words, he was to be King while his wife lived. True to his cautious policy, Lord James supported the Regent's request. He also backed the formal declaration made in this Parliament by Châtelherault that the granting of the crown matrimonial should not prejudice his rights in the succession.[15] Lord James and his friend, the new Earl of Argyle,[16] were deputed to take the crown to France. But they never went.

The reason for their failure to depart was the threatening aspect of the religious situation, which was now coming to a head. The activists in the Protestant party were becoming stronger, and events were playing into their hands. Just after the signing of the band in December 1557 the Protestants decided on a religious policy which was decidedly moderate.[17] A petition was drawn up, which was presented to Mary of Guise by a group headed by Sandilands of Calder. The Protestants requested the use of a vernacular Bible, interpretation of the Scriptures by "qualified persons," the use of the vernacular in the administration of baptism and the Eucharist—the latter to be administered in both kinds—and, finally, a reform of the wicked lives of the clergy.[18] Mary of Guise returned a temporizing answer to the petition, as she was still in need of Protestant support in the matter of the marriage treaty. Provided there were no public assemblies in Edinburgh and Leith, Protestants might worship as they wished till Parliament acted on the religious question.[19]

All this was in line with Fabian policy; but a piece of Catholic stupidity followed [20] which gave strength to the views of the

[15] *Acts of Parliament*, II, 504–8.
[16] Argyle, the former Lord Lorne, was also a relative of Lord James; his wife was another of the bastards of James V.
[17] T. McCrie, *The Life of John Knox*, I, 437–41. Knox, *History*, I, 275–76.
[18] *Ibid.*, pp. 302–6.   [19] *Ibid.*, p. 307.
[20] I have followed Knox's dating here in placing the Sandilands petition before the death of Miln. Other accounts, that of Buchanan for instance, place it after; but the changed tone of Protestant requests after Miln's death lend weight to

activists. In April 1558 an old man, Walter Miln, a parish priest who had turned Protestant, was executed for heresy. This exasperated the Protestants; their preachers now taught openly throughout the country, in Edinburgh and Leith, too,[21] and when several of them were summoned for trial, the western gentry appeared in arms before Mary of Guise on July 19 to present a remonstrance.[22]

The Regent was not yet prepared to act: the marriage treaty was still unratified. She denied any foreknowledge of the Miln affair, and was believed; [23] upon the hierarchy fell the odium of having done the old man to death. The summons to the preachers was withdrawn.[24] She did not even act when, on September 1, 1558, the celebration of St. Giles' Day was broken up by a Protestant mob in the streets of Edinburgh.[25] This riot was a significant indication of the popular temper. The preachers, almost to a man proponents of action, were doing their work well.

The Regent had promised to take action on the religious question in Parliament; so when that body was summoned in November to approve the French marriage treaty, a new Protestant petition was presented to Mary of Guise. The tone of this document was bitterly anti-Catholic.[26] The Regent would do nothing. Lord James and the Fabians were not sorry, but the activists issued a formal Protestation, announcing that they would adhere to their religious views; that they did not propose to obey any laws which might restrict them, such as the heresy laws; that if any violence ensued, it was not their fault, since their attempt at orderly change had failed; and, finally, that all they wanted was a religious change —they had no ulterior political motives.[27]

With the dissolution of the Parliament in December 1558 it is possible to see how greatly the situation had changed in the course of the year. The marriage of Mary had taken place and had been

Knox's dating. The relevant passages are in Knox, *History*, I, 307-8, and in Buchanan, *History*, II, 396-400.
[21] As Calderwood put it, "The Gospel flourished wonderfully" (*The History of the Kirk of Scotland*, I, 343).
[22] *Ibid.*, pp. 344-45. Mathieson, *Politics and Religion*, I, 51-52.
[23] Knox, *History*, I, 308-9.   [24] *Ibid.*, p. 258.
[25] Knox's description of this affair is amusing. See *ibid.*, pp. 258-61.
[26] *Ibid.*, pp. 309-12.   [27] *Ibid.*, pp. 312-14.

approved; therefore the support of the Protestants was no longer necessary to the Regent. She could now play the Catholic, pro-French game to the hilt, and the situation abroad looked favorable, since it was evident that France and Spain would soon make peace. Furthermore, it would be necessary to act soon, for the Protestant attitude was becoming more and more rigid. Throughout the year 1558 the Protestants had moved steadily toward a policy of action, nicely illustrated by the difference in tone between the Sandilands petition and that presented to the Regent in November. And for the first time it could be claimed for the activists that their policy made political sense. For in November 1558 Mary Tudor died and was succeeded by Elizabeth. The daughter of Anne Boleyn was a potential ally against the Regent. The accession of Elizabeth certainly contributed heavily to the increasing desire for action in Protestant ranks.

With the new year the Regent decided to change her tactics. In March 1559 a Provincial Council, the last held in Scotland by the medieval Catholic Church, met in Edinburgh. It proved un-compromising in its support of the ancient faith. Mary of Guise cordially supported its stand and had several of its statutes pro-claimed publicly on March 23.[28] The Protestants disregarded them, and "in this meantime did the town of Perth . . . embrace the truth," which further annoyed the Regent. She ordered Lord Ruthven, the Provost of Perth, to put an end to Protestantism there; he replied that he could not coerce men's consciences.[29] The result was that in April, after some hesitation on the part of the Regent owing to the mingled threats and pleas of the Protes-tant leaders, four of the leading Protestant ministers were sum-moned to Stirling on May 10 to answer for their violation of the recent proclamations.[30] This summons, as it turned out, led di-rectly to civil war.

In these circumstances it is easy to see why Lord James and Argyle did not go to France with the crown matrimonial. Lord James, as his conduct in May 1559 was to make clear, still clung

[28] "Historie of the Estate of Scotland," in D. Laing, ed., *Miscellany of the Wodrow Society*, I, 56. Mathieson, *Politics and Religion*, I, 57.
[29] Knox, *History*, I, 316.
[30] *Ibid.*, pp. 316–17. Mathieson, *Politics and Religion*, I, 58.

to his Fabian policy, and with him stood a number of Protestant lords, Argyle being the most important. The situation was very confused, mainly because many great nobles were motivated not by religious considerations but by greed. Huntly, for instance, was a Catholic; but no one trusted Huntly, who was a shifty, unscrupulous intriguer. Morton, a hard-headed and devious politician, was a Protestant, but he disliked the favor which the Protestants had shown to Châtelherault: it might lead the Regent to recall the Duke's enemy, the exiled Earl of Lennox, with whom Morton was at odds over the earldom of Angus. Many other nobles were equally cautious, and for similar reasons.

All signs pointed to an armed struggle between the two camps, however, and Lord James, who was by no means foolish, must have read those signs aright. He should have realized that the policy of Fabianism was bankrupt, broken with the Regent, and thrown his very considerable influence on the side of his coreligionists. With him he could have carried Argyle and the great majority of the Fife gentry, who were Protestants already and who were awaiting his signal. For by April 1559 it was quite clear that the two necessary conditions of the Fabian policy no longer held: the zealots in the party had slipped their collars, and the Regent had turned her back on the policy of toleration.

Why, then, did Lord James hold back? In the first place, he was naturally cautious, averse to getting himself into a position from which there would be no retreat. Second, it was by no means certain that the English government would come to the aid of the Protestants, whereas it was certain that France would help Mary of Guise. Elizabeth had just signed the Peace of Cateau-Cambrésis. The war had not been a success for England, and it seemed likely that Elizabeth would eschew any foreign adventures for a time, especially in view of the uncertain domestic situation. Third, there was the problem of Châtelherault, who was trying to keep a foot in both camps.[31] Without Châtelherault the Protestant position would be impossible; with him, it would be possible to

---

[31] For Châtelherault's position at this time, see January 22, 1559, Sir Henry Percy to Sir Thomas Parry, *Calendar of State Papers, Foreign Series, Elizabeth* (henceforth abbreviated *C.S.P., For., Eliz.*), I, 97–99.

add to the religious appeal the political one of defense of the Duke's dynastic rights against French usurpations. These considerations undoubtedly led Lord James to cling to the Fabian policy, to keep things as they were until Mary of Guise should disappear from the scene, when it would be possible to accomplish the religious revolution without violence.

The writer is aware that there is virtually no direct evidence for the preceding analysis. This, however, seems to be the only theory which satisfactorily explains the actions of the various elements in the Protestant party in the eighteen months or so which preceded the outbreak of the civil war, and especially those of Lord James. The conventional explanation, that there were only two types of Protestant—zealots such as Knox and Glencairn, and worldlings such as Maitland and Morton—is far too simple since it does not take account of what we have called the Fabian faction, which started out with fair prospects of success but which, by force of circumstances, was to be overwhelmed.[32]

ii

The date set by the Regent for the appearance of the preachers at Stirling was May 10, 1559. They determined to obey the summons, and at the same time not to go forward alone. Consequently, in the first days of May, there swarmed into Perth, which had been set as the meeting place, a multitude of Protestants. Knox says they were unarmed.[33] Erskine of Dun was sent to the Regent to explain that the purpose of the assembly was not to overawe justice but simply to indicate the popular support which the Protestants had. On the subject of Mary of Guise's reply to Erskine of Dun a debate has long raged among the learned. Unquestionably she re-

---

[32] John Leslie, *The History of Scotland*, II, 383–84, attributes Lord James's behavior to disappointed ambition. While in France in 1558, Lord James asked his sister for the earldom of Moray; on the advice of her mother, Mary refused the request but held out hopes of ecclesiastical preferment if he were loyal. So Lord James hated the Regent. Thus Leslie. Not only is there no evidence for this story besides Leslie's word—that of a bitter opponent—but the story also fails to explain why Lord James did not align himself at once with the opponents of the Regent's policy and use his influence against the granting of the crown matrimonial. The story simply does not fit the facts of Lord James's behavior.
[33] Knox, *History*, I, 317.

quested him to prevent the mob from coming to Stirling. Whether she then promised unconditionally to postpone the summons to the preachers, or to postpone it if the mob dispersed, or made no promise at all, is the question. What actually happened is quite clear, however. Erskine understood the Regent to have promised to postpone the summons, and he so reported to his coreligionists at Perth. Consequently no one appeared at Stirling on May 10, and Mary of Guise promptly ordered the preachers to be "put to the horn"—outlawed—for nonappearance.

This was the spark which touched off the powder keg, which was much more likely to explode now, owing to the return of John Knox. On the day after the horning of the preachers Knox preached a violent sermon against idolatry. This touched off the first of those iconoclastic demonstrations which disfigured the Reformation in Scotland. First the church in which Knox preached, and then the neighboring monasteries, were entered and "purged," not without looting. Knox in his *History* [34] says that he attempted to prevent the destruction; this is contradicted by his later actions, however, and by his letter of June 23, 1559, to Mrs. Locke, his mother-in-law.[35]

Unquestionably the wanton destruction caused by the reformers in the course of the civil war is one of the least attractive features of the movement. Almost all the Protestant leaders, laymen such as Glencairn and Lord James as well as preachers such as Knox, were responsible for the devastation at one place or another and at one time or another. It must be said in behalf of the Protestants, however, that they have been blamed for a great deal which was not their doing. The troops of Henry VIII in the war of the 1540s, and the avarice and neglect of many of the Catholic clergy played their part, as a prince of the Church stated in a letter to the Pope in 1556.[36] The Protestants tended to confine their real wrecking to monasteries. Ordinary churches were stripped of images but were left standing and usable, in most cases. The dam-

[34] *Ibid.*, p. 319.
[35] On this point see Andrew Lang, *John Knox and the Reformation*, pp. 112–14. The letter is in *C.S.P., For., Eliz.*, I, 331–35.
[36] Cardinal Sermoneta to Pope Paul IV, in J. H. Pollen, ed., *Papal Negotiations with Mary Queen of Scots*, pp. 528–30.

age attributed to the reformers has been greatly exaggerated.[37]

The Regent, when she heard of the riots at Perth, was not pleased. She summoned the nobility to meet with her to reduce the town to obedience. Knox and his friends, when they heard of this, were not idle. The multitude—armed, this time—began to reassemble in Perth. The Regent arrived at the town with a force of some eight thousand men about May 24 and encamped at Auchterarder, a few miles away.[38] Knox meanwhile had issued appeals for support which were not without effect; the Earl of Glencairn made a rapid march with 2,500 men from his seat of power in the west, and further reinforcements poured into Perth from Fife and Angus and from the town of Dundee.[39]

Lord James, still clinging to his hope of peace but becoming ever less certain of it, had joined the Regent's forces on the assurance of the latter that she desired peace.[40] Just what was in the Regent's mind is uncertain. If she had been in possession of an overwhelming superiority of strength at Perth, she would probably have tried to eliminate the Protestants at one stroke. But the large numbers and unyielding attitude of the Protestants evidently convinced her that to provoke a battle would be unwise, since even if she won, there would be a rebellion, and a defeat would be disastrous. So she decided to negotiate, and those she selected to send to the Perth Protestants were Lord James, Argyle, and Lord Sempill.

On May 25 the three men met the representatives of the embattled Protestants, Erskine of Dun and Wishart of Pitarrow. Lord James and his colleagues put the key question right away: Did the Protestants plan "to hold that town against the authority, and against the Queen Regent?" For they had been told that the Protestants "meant no religion, but a plain rebellion." "No," came the answer. "If the Queen's Grace would suffer the religion there begun to proceed, and not trouble their brethren . . . that had professed Christ Jesus with them, that the town, they them-

---

[37] On this point see McCrie, *John Knox*, I, 450–56.
[38] P. Hume Brown, *John Knox*, II, 9–11.
[39] Knox, *History*, I, 335–36. Buchanan, *History*, II, 405–6.
[40] Knox, *History*, I, 343.

selves and whatsoever to them pertained, should be at the Queen's commandment." [41]

The Regent was by no means pleased with this reply, which, if accepted, would mean a virtual condoning of the behavior she had set out to punish. But the opportune arrival of Glencairn and his West Country levies tipped the scale. So Lord James and Argyle were sent back again to arrange an agreement on the terms laid down by the Protestants, with the further concession that no French troops were to be quartered in Perth. In return, the Protestants agreed to disband and allow the Regent to enter Perth, which she did on May 29.[42]

During these negotiations increasing pressure had been put on Lord James and Argyle to declare for the Congregation, as the Protestants were called. Knox accused them of infidelity to their religion. They replied that they had promised the Regent that they would labor for peace and would assist her if the Protestants were unwilling to accept reasonable terms of agreement. But now they consented in writing on May 31 to join the Congregation; they further promised that if the Regent infringed the Perth agreement in any way, they would join forces with their brethren to resist her.[43] The policy of delay was dead, and its proponents had joined the activists.

Lord James had undoubtedly seen the handwriting on the wall for some time. Nevertheless he had worked, and worked hard, for his temporizing policy. It is likely that the thing which gave the *coup de grâce* to his Fabianism, in his own mind at least, was the very settlement at Perth which he had just negotiated. The terms were very favorable to the Protestants—far too favorable, in fact, for the Regent to accept them permanently, as the zealots themselves well knew. Knox announced publicly the day after the agreement was made that "I am assured, that no part of this promise made shall be longer kept . . . [when] the Queen and her Frenchmen have the upper hand." [44] If this were true, and Lord James obviously believed it was true, it followed that the Regent was determined to crush the Protestants and was simply

41 *Ibid.*, pp. 337–39.   42 *Ibid.*, pp. 340–42.   43 *Ibid.*, pp. 343–45.
44 *Ibid.*, pp. 343–44.

biding her time till a favorable opportunity presented itself. There was no choice but to surrender or fight. Lord James chose to fight. It was unfortunate for his reputation that he had to change sides in the way he did, however, for it left him open to a charge of treachery to the Regent which his enemies then and since have not been slow to make.

Mary of Guise soon gave him a pretext for shifting sides openly. She evaded the spirit of the compact by garrisoning Perth with Scots in French pay. She ousted Lord Ruthven from the provostship of the town, an act which was construed as punishing Ruthven for his Protestant leanings.[45] Consequently, on June 1, Lord James and Argyle announced that the Regent had violated the terms of the agreement and that they would keep their word and join the Congregation.

It is worth pausing here for a moment to ask what the objectives of the Protestants were at the moment of Lord James's break with the Regent. Obviously they wished complete freedom of worship for themselves. From Knox's manifestos during the Perth affair it may be further inferred that they did not intend to tolerate the public exercise of the Catholic religion or permit any religious or political power to the Catholic hierarchy.[46] But did they intend a "plain rebellion"? The answer to this question is neither a simple *yes* or *no*. It was clear to Lord James that a religious uprising while Mary of Guise was still Regent would lead to a political upheaval as well, a fact which zealots such as Knox did not see; the latter were doubtless sincere in their disclaimers of any political ends. Lord James's whole policy had been directed to timing the religious revolt so as to have no political revolt involved in it, and he had failed. But now that the revolt had come, the Protestant party did not face the consequences of their behavior squarely, because they could not. They did not have English aid, and they did not have Châtelherault. Rumor was already busy with the story that Lord James was aiming at the crown; James Melville, a Scot in the service of Montmorency, was sent on a mission from France in June to find out whether he had any such ambition.[47] But Lord

[45] Lindsay of Pitscottie, *Chronicles*, II, 150–51. [46] Knox, *History*, I, 326–36.
[47] Lord James had been legitimated in 1551. *Registrum Magni Sigilli Regum*

James well knew that such a design would be the surest possible means of ruining both himself and the Protestant cause. Châtelherault, the next heir to the throne, was the man they needed. His continuance in the Regent's camp, and the political confusion engendered in Protestant ranks as a consequence, was a major cause of the early failures of the Congregation.

Lord James and Argyle headed for St. Andrews, the seat of Archbishop Hamilton, announcing their decision to "reform" that town and calling on their friends to meet them there on June 4. Knox followed, preaching at some small towns en route; they were promptly "reformed." He proclaimed his intention of doing the same at St. Andrews itself; a threat against his life by the Primate did not deter him. His sermon was preached on June 11, and the usual destruction followed. The buildings of Lord James's abbey seem to have been spared, however.[48]

This repetition of the happenings at Perth aroused the Regent. She sent forth what troops she had with her at Falkland immediately on this occasion, hoping to crush the Protestants before they could collect their forces. She did not reckon with the fact that Fife was one of the most Protestant sections in Scotland. Lord James determined to bar the approach to St. Andrews at the town of Cupar; by the time the two armies met face to face, on June 13, his little troop of horse had been swollen to a force of three thousand men. "It appeared as [if] men had rained from the clouds," wrote Knox.[49] So it must have seemed to D'Oysel and Châtelherault, who commanded the Regent's army. There was nothing for it but to negotiate, and Lord James was willing enough. Since the Protestants were still claiming that all they wanted was a religious settlement and that they had no political designs, it was incumbent on them to negotiate whenever their opponents wished to do so. A truce was arranged, to last for eight days, during which time representatives of both sides would confer to try to arrive

Scotorum, IV, 128. Melville accepted Lord James's assurance that he had no ulterior motives and that he was loyal to Mary of Guise, who, he said, was being misled by bad advice from France. Sir James Melville, *Memoirs of his own Life*, pp. 81–82.
[48] Knox, *History*, I, 346–50. Brown, *John Knox*, II, 18, n. 1.
[49] Knox, *History*, I, 351.

at a settlement. Meanwhile the French troops were to withdraw from Fife, except those regularly garrisoned there.[50]

While awaiting the representatives of the Regent—who never came, incidentally—Lord James and Argyle wrote to Mary of Guise demanding that she remove the garrison from Perth.[51] Having received no satisfaction, and nothing having happened during the truce, they determined to oust the Regent's men by force. They arrived at Perth on June 24 and forced the garrison to capitulate on the twenty-fifth.[52] They left Perth the following day, having heard that the Regent was preparing to seize Stirling in force. This would cut off the Protestants in Fife from their fellows in the Lothians, and make communication with the west very difficult indeed: Stirling was in many respects the military key to Scotland. By means of a night march Lord James and Argyle arrived before the Regent's army. After pausing for a few days, during which time the usual "reforming" took place, the Congregation moved on to Edinburgh, on learning that the Regent had retreated to Dunbar. The Protestant forces entered the capital on June 29.[53]

Although the seizure of the chief city in the kingdom appeared on the surface to be a great victory for the Protestants, it soon became evident that their zeal had outrun their resources. From the military point of view they were not well off. Edinburgh Castle was not in their hands but in those of Lord Erskine, who had been appointed its governor in 1554; he was neutral in the struggle, but tended to favor the Regent. Furthermore, the character of the forces of the Congregation worked against them. They were feudal levies which could not be held together more than a few weeks, and there was no money to pay mercenaries. Mary of Guise's forces, though far smaller at this point than those of the Congregation, were mainly French, well-trained veterans, and

[50] The terms are given by Knox, *ibid.*, pp. 353–54.
[51] On June 15, 1559. *C.S.P., For., Eliz.*, I, 317. This letter shows that the ostensible reason for the shift of the two men was the question of the Perth garrison.
[52] For the events at Perth, see Knox, *History*, I, 358–61.
[53] This is the date given by Knox, *ibid.*, p. 362. T. Thomson, ed., *A Diurnal of Remarkable Occurrents that Have Passed within the Country of Scotland*, p. 53, gives June 28.

of course they would not desert her. The Regent also had a marked advantage in artillery.[54] Finally, the vast majority of the Scottish nobility was still noncommittal or nominally on the Regent's side. Those who were zealous Protestants had already shown their colors; there would be no new accessions to the Congregation until the situation clarified.[55]

Far worse were the political difficulties in which the Protestants now found themselves. They had been steadily claiming that they had no political aims: all they wanted was a satisfactory religious settlement. But the seizure of Edinburgh made these claims seem to smack of hypocrisy. The Regent was quick to take advantage of the opening afforded her, and her proclamations pointed out the inconsistencies in her opponents' behavior. Obviously, she claimed, they were merely using religion as a means of disguising their true aim, the overthrow of her authority.[56] Privately she began to circulate rumors that the real key to the Congregation's actions was the political ambition of Lord James—he wanted the crown.[57] The purpose of this story, for which there was no evidence, then or now, was to keep Châtelherault on her side, and she succeeded.[58]

The Regent's charges had a devastating effect. The Protestants could not meet the political challenge squarely; so, in respectful fashion, as befitted law-abiding subjects, they offered obedience to the Regent if they might have religious liberty, the cancellation of the outlawing of the preachers, and the return to France of the Regent's French troops.[59] Mary of Guise conceded the second point, but had no intention of granting the other two. She played for time, however, with great skill.[60] While these negotiations were going on, the army of the Congregation was slowly melting

[54] Buchanan, *History*, II, 415.
[55] Kirkcaldy of Grange, writing to Sir Henry Percy on July 1, gives an optimistic picture of Protestant strength; when the list of lords he gives as being favorers of the cause is checked with other sources, it develops that only sixteen of these men were with the Congregation at this time. Some of these sixteen were very influential people, to be sure, but the number is small. *C.S.P., For., Eliz.,* I, 349–51.
[56] See, for instance, the proclamation of July 1, *ibid.,* 348–49.
[57] Knox, *History*, I, 368.
[58] July 8, 1559, Sir James Croft to Cecil, *C.S.P., For., Eliz.,* I, 365–66.
[59] Knox, *History*, I, 366–67.   [60] For the negotiations see *ibid.,* pp. 368–70.

away; the Regent's unanswered charges against the Congregation were taking their toll. "Some of our own number began to murmur," Knox lugubriously admits.[61] At last, on July 22, Mary of Guise decided that she was strong enough to move. On the twenty-third Leith, which the Protestants had counted on to support them, surrendered to the Regent without a struggle. The last hope of the Congregation was Edinburgh Castle: if Lord Erskine could be persuaded to shift sides, all would yet be well. Lord James, his nephew,[62] was deputed to deal with him. Erskine not only would not join the Protestants, but he also threatened to fire on them if they attempted to defend Edinburgh against the Regent.[63]

So there was nothing for it but to make the best possible terms with Mary of Guise. On July 24 a settlement was arranged at Leith. The Congregation was to get out of Edinburgh in twenty-four hours. Edinburgh was to have the religion it chose. Neither side was to molest the other on religious questions, and that meant that Protestants were not to seize clerical rents or indulge in iconoclasm. The truce was to run till January 10, by which time, presumably, Parliament would be called to effect a permanent settlement.[64]

This was regarded by both sides as a mere truce, made to be broken when convenient, as their behavior during subsequent months showed. About the middle of August some thousand Frenchmen arrived with their wives and families, with more to follow; this implied a permanent occupation and caused such feeling that the Regent was forced to issue a proclamation on August 28 to justify it.[65] At about the same time, in order to assure a secure port of entry for further French reinforcements, Mary of Guise began to fortify Leith.

[61] *Ibid.*, p. 368.   [62] Erskine was the brother of Lord James's mother.
[63] *Ibid.*, pp. 374–76.
[64] The terms are in Teulet, *Relations politiques*, I, 334–35. In passing, it is interesting to note that on July 29 the Protestants on the Edinburgh town council refused to allow a vote to be taken on the question whether Edinburgh should be Catholic or Protestant. There were evidently many Catholics in the town still, but, as was later the case in France, the Protestants were active and influential out of all proportion to their number. Keith, *History*, I, 487–89.
[65] Knox, *History*, I, 396–99. Brown, *John Knox*, II, 44.

The problems of the Congregation were far more serious: it was essential to remedy the military and political weaknesses revealed during June and July. Furthermore, on July 10 Mary and Francis had ascended the French throne; the entire resources of that kingdom would now be at the Regent's command. The immediate problem was to hold the present members of the Congregation together; this was done in the traditional Scottish fashion by a band signed at Stirling on August 1, in which it was agreed that no one of them would enter into negotiations of any kind with the Regent without notifying the others.[66] Thus they hoped to prevent the piecemeal detaching of their members by Mary of Guise. This done, the lords separated, agreeing to meet at Stirling again on September 10.

This, however, was but a palliative; the cure consisted in getting the support of England and winning Châtelherault. To these problems the Congregation seriously addressed itself. As early as May 24 Kirkcaldy of Grange, a Protestant Fife laird and a fine soldier, who possessed the qualities and defects of the typical military man, wrote a letter to Sir Henry Percy describing the events at Perth and wanting to know what Percy thought the English attitude would be in the event of a serious upheaval. This letter was sent on to Sir William Cecil, Elizabeth's principal Secretary of State, by Percy with a request for instructions on how to handle it.[67]

The possibility of a rebellion in Scotland gave Cecil much to think about. There was a very complex diplomatic problem involved here which would require very careful handling. If it had simply been a question of intervention in Scotland, there probably would have been no hesitation on England's part. The difficulty was France. Cecil knew well enough that France planned to make of Scotland a dependency of the French crown. In fact, it seemed certain that French ambition did not stop there, for shortly after Elizabeth's accession, Henry II had taken the momentous step of quartering the English arms on the escutcheon of the Dauphin and his wife, thereby implying that they were the rightful rulers

[66] Knox, *History*, I, 382.
[67] *C.S.P., For., Eliz.*, I, 278. May 31, 1559, Percy to Cecil, *ibid.*, p. 295.

of England. All this was an incentive to action: if the vital Scottish link could be snapped, the grandiose French schemes could be brought to nothing. Cecil was convinced that the link must be snapped. But how? If England intervened openly, France would declare war. This might not be so bad, in spite of England's weakness, if Cecil could rely on the support of Spain. This was most uncertain, however. English intervention would probably produce tremendous Spanish pressure to mediate, which could not be evaded for long. And if the question once got to the conference table, England would be beaten, since the French legal case was unassailable.

The alternative to open intervention was to see to it, by one means or another, that the Congregation was strong enough to overturn the Regent and the French power without an English army. Money could be sent—*sub rosa*, of course. But more important was a good legal case, and in this respect Cecil, like Lord James, grasped the importance of Châtelherault. Further, Cecil saw the means of bringing about Châtelherault's adhesion to the Congregation. He knew that the Duke was a man without a mind of his own, subject to the strongest influence near him. The Duke's eldest son, the Earl of Arran, an energetic if somewhat unstable young man, currently in France, was just the man to win over his father, for he was a strong Protestant, already in difficulties with the French government on that account. On June 13 Cecil wrote to the English ambassador in France, Sir Nicholas Throckmorton, instructing him to smuggle Arran out of the country and into England.[68] At the same moment, it is interesting to note, Lord James and his friends had come to the same conclusion: Arran must be got home.[69] Beyond this, however, Cecil would not go until he could gauge the relative strength of the parties better, except to give the Congregation unofficial encouragement by way of his Border officials.[70]

The Protestant leaders, heartened by these evident signs of friendship, on July 19 addressed to Cecil and his mistress a formal

[68] *Ibid.*, pp. 312–13.   [69] June 14, 1559, Croft to Sir Thomas Parry, *ibid.*, p. 316.
[70] E.g., July 8, 1559, Cecil to Croft, *ibid.*, p. 365; July 11, 1559, Cecil to Percy, *ibid.*, pp. 371–72.

appeal for aid. Their aims, they said, were to promote Protestantism and friendship with England; they had no idea of a political
rebellion unless they were driven to it by Catholic tyranny.[71]
Cecil did not relish this request. He knew very well that English
intervention would create a political issue, even if none already
existed; and intervention on the pretext offered by the Congregation would seriously antagonize Spain. The Secretary therefore
wrote a noncommittal reply, on July 28, telling the Congregation
that he approved of its religious and political objectives as it had
outlined them, and giving it military and financial advice. But he
refused to promise help of any kind.[72]

This letter was far from revealing Cecil's true feelings toward
the Protestant cause in Scotland, of course. It simply reflected the
political uncertainties of the moment. On the same date, July 28,
the Secretary wrote a private letter to Knox which made it clear
that the ambiguity of the official answer was due to necessity, not
conviction; Knox was encouraged to persevere.[73] Practical considerations also dictated the letter to Knox, for if the Congregation really believed that England would not help it, it might come
to terms with the Regent. Cecil urged Croft to give the Congregation further encouragement in order to prevent any such occurrence.[74]

The truce of July 24, however, forced Cecil to come to some
decision. It revealed two facts to his trained eye: first, that the
Congregation would not be strong enough to do the job unaided;
and second, that if the Congregation were left to itself much
longer, it might reach an agreement with the Regent. Cecil was
deceived on this last point, since the information he got concerning the terms of the truce was inaccurate. Knox had deliberately
spread false accounts of these terms, so that it would be possible
later to claim that the Regent had broken the agreement and thus
to justify further action by the Congregation in the eyes of the
world.[75] The terms as received by Cecil were so favorable to the
Protestants as to justify his fear that Mary of Guise might return

[71] Ibid., pp. 389–90, 396–97.   [72] Ibid., pp. 423–25.   [73] Ibid., pp. 425–26.
[74] July 29, 1559, Cecil to Croft, ibid., pp. 429–30.
[75] Lang, Knox and the Reformation, pp. 142–48.

to her former policy of appeasement. Consequently, on August 8, Cecil made his first move: Sir Ralph Sadler, a "career diplomat" with an intimate knowledge of Scottish affairs, was sent north, ostensibly to help negotiate with the Regent's government on the various matters left undecided by the recent peace treaty. His real job was quite different: it was to sow dissension between Mary of Guise and the Congregation. He was also given £3,000 to dole out to the Protestants as he saw fit.[76]

A section of Sadler's instructions throws light on the position of Lord James in the complex situation as it existed in early August. Sir Ralph was to find out if Lord James really did have designs on the crown; if he did, and if Châtelherault continued "cold," it would be well to encourage Lord James. This is by no means the only piece of evidence we have with respect to the importance of Lord James. Whatever small measure of success the Congregation had achieved up to this point was due to his having joined it. This was recognized even in France: on July 4 Throckmorton wrote to Cecil that the Guises believed that he, Argyle, and Erskine of Dun, were the key figures on the Protestant side, and must be killed if Protestantism was to be rooted out.[77] Cecil and his agents knew it too: in a memorandum written on July 18 the Secretary stressed the necessity of keeping Lord James and Argyle from swinging back to the Regent.[78]

As it turned out, it was unnecessary for Sadler to bring up the question of Lord James's regal ambitions. At last the policy of the Congregation was bearing fruit with Châtelherault. On August 9 he wrote to Cecil, asking him to see that Arran got home safely.[79] The leaders of the Congregation were delighted; a tone of increased confidence pervades their letters from August 9 on. Lord James had received letters from Francis and Mary bitterly reproaching him for his behavior. On August 12 he replied, declaring that he had done "no thing against God nor the debtful obedience toward your Highness and the Queen's Grace my Sover-

---

[76] Sadler's instructions are in *C.S.P., For., Eliz.*, I, 460–61. It is evident from them that Cecil was still misled as to the terms of the July truce.   [77] *Ibid.*, pp. 356–57.
[78] *Ibid.*, p. 386. See also, July 11, 1559, Croft to Cecil, *ibid.*, p. 372.
[79] *Ibid.*, p. 465.

eign," as Francis would realize if he were "truly informed." [80]
It was the letter of a man profoundly convinced that his cause
was just and that it would prevail. A day later he and Argyle wrote
an equally confident letter to Cecil, urging him to send aid, since
they could not finance themselves by seizing Church property as
Henry VIII had, and as Cecil had advised: they were not the
government. [81]

Everything now hinged on the arrival of Arran, who finally
got to England toward the end of August. [82] At this time Cecil
wrote a highly significant memorandum outlining his policy toward Scotland. Cecil's goals were to drive the French out of Scotland, establish the Protestant religion there, and make of Scotland
an English ally. The kingdom was to be governed by Scots, not
French; a committee appointed by the Estates, since the Queen
was absent, was the method suggested. If the Queen proved irreconcilably hostile to all this, it might even be necessary to turn
over the kingdom to the next heir; hence the importance of
Châtelherault. [83] The significance of this document lies in the fact
that nowhere in it is there any idea that England should rule in
Scotland. All that Cecil wanted was a friendly, Protestant neighbor. Had Henry VIII been willing to settle for this, he might well
have got it. English political intelligence had improved considerably since the days of Bluff Hal and Cardinal Beaton.

The appearance of Arran in the north of England coincided
with a very important meeting between Sadler and Henry Balnaves, representing the Congregation, in which it was agreed that
England would aid the Congregation, but only with money, and
secretly for the nonce. Sadler gave Balnaves £2,000 on the assurance that the Congregation would take the field again soon. [84] On
these lines, Cecil hoped, England would be able to continue: a
relatively small expenditure of money might turn the scale in favor
of the Congregation, and England's objective might be attained
without the open intervention that would produce such unpleasant international complications.

[80] Knox, *History*, I, pp. 386–87.   [81] C.S.P., *For.*, *Eliz.*, I, 469–70.
[82] August 31, 1559, Cecil to Sadler, *The State Papers and Letters of Sir Ralph Sadler*, I, 417–18.   [83] C.S.P., *For.*, *Eliz.*, I, 518–19.
[84] September 8, 1559, Sadler and Croft to Cecil, *Sadler Papers*, I, 430–36.

iii

The Earl of Arran, accompanied by an English agent, Thomas Randolph, entered Scotland on September 8 and was met by Lord James and Argyle. Within two weeks Châtelherault joined the Congregation.[85] Plans were now made to act as soon as possible. On September 19 a letter was sent to Mary of Guise, requesting her to desist from fortifying Leith, on the ground that this was a breach of the agreement of July 24.[86] The Protestants knew well that the Regent would never accede to such a request, as was made quite clear by their fresh endeavors to win over the neutral lords. If they had any doubts as to the possibility of the Regent's making concessions, they must have vanished when the news came of the arrival of more French troops. October 15 was the date set for the Congregation to gather in full strength.[87]

The Regent was in a tight corner. Few important Scotsmen were on her side. The nominally Catholic nobles were mostly mere intriguers; by this time her only active supporters were the Primate, the Earl of Bothwell, and Lords Borthwick and Seton.[88] She complained of the negotiations which the Congregation had been conducting with England, to no avail.[89] She appealed for French aid, which she got, and continued to fortify Leith. She attempted, with no particular success, to split the Congregation; the lords remained faithful to their mutual promise not to negotiate individually with her. Her effort to detach Lord James is interesting. On September 30 she sent John Spens of Condie, a lawyer, to him with an equivocal promise to "set forward" Protestantism, but basing her main appeal on the ground that she knew that the motive of the forthcoming rebellion was not religion, but the overthrow of Mary and the crowning of a Hamilton. It was not likely that such a letter would appeal to Lord James: after all, a month or two earlier the Regent had been broadcasting the

---

[85] September 21, 1559, Arran to Cecil, in J. Stevenson, ed., *Selections . . . Illustrating the Reign of Mary Queen of Scotland*, pp. 73–75. September 21, 1559, Knox to Croft, *Sadler Papers*, I, 455–57.   [86] Knox, *History*, I, 413–14.
[87] September 23, 1559, Balnaves to Sadler and Croft, *Sadler Papers*, I, 461–63.
[88] Mathieson, *Politics and Religion*, I, 64.
[89] Teulet, *Relations politiques*, I, 340–44, 346–52.

very same tale about him. Lord James's reply was polite but un-obliging.[90] The Regent had somewhat more success, by Knox's own admission, in the propaganda war which broke out as both sides attempted to win the support of the waverers of all classes.[91]

Cecil was pleased by the Congregation's activity, of which he was kept fully informed by his agents. On October 5 he sent Sadler £3,000 more and urged the Protestants to hurry up and attack Leith, for reports out of France indicated that the Guises were preparing a really formidable relief expedition.[92] But owing to the late harvest, the Congregation could not come together before October 15. On that day, however, its members joined forces, and on the sixteenth, headed by Châtelherault, they entered Edinburgh once more.

Now the Protestants took a step for which Cecil had long been waiting. They wrote again to the Regent, demanding that she cease fortifying Leith; on receiving the expected refusal, on October 21, they formally deposed Mary of Guise from the regency, in the name of Francis and Mary, and set up a committee to govern the kingdom, in which Châtelherault, Arran, and Lord James had the key positions.[93] This was a transaction of the first importance. It was now plain to all that the Congregation's aims were political as well as religious; as soon as it had Châtelherault on its side to give the color of legality to its action, it took the plunge. In the document of October 21 deposing the Regent, the reasons the Congregation gave for this step were almost entirely political—principally, of course, the defense of Châtelherault's rights against French usurpation. As has been pointed out, Lord James had seen from the beginning that it was impossible to separate religion from politics, and he had worked ceaselessly for this result, once he had been convinced by the course of events

[90] Knox, *History*, I, 418–21.
[91] *Ibid.*, pp. 421–33, 437. The behavior of both sides at this time is a nice illustration of the common sixteenth-century belief that revolutions are due to individuals, not to religious, political, economic, or social forces.
[92] October 6, 1559, Cecil to Sadler, *Sadler Papers*, I, 485. October 8, 1559, Sadler and Croft to Randolph, *ibid.*, pp. 487–88.
[93] For instance, any authorization of expenditure of funds had to have the signature of one of these three. *Ibid.*, pp. 539–40. The record of all these transactions is in *C.S.P., For., Eliz.*, II, 46–51.

that it would be impossible to delay the religious upheaval till after the departure, by death or otherwise, of Mary of Guise. The two necessary conditions for success now obtained: the Congregation had Châtelherault, and it had England. Cecil was now much more apt to give it support, for he had feared that, owing to some turn of fortune, Catholic and Protestant might come together against the "auld enemy." But the deposition of Mary of Guise made the breach between the two parties irreparable.

At this point the Congregation obtained an addition to its ranks of the greatest importance in the person of William Maitland of Lethington, who had been Mary of Guise's Secretary of State. Maitland was a man of a rather different stripe from those we have hitherto met with. Although a Protestant, he did not think in religious terms: his political behavior, unlike that of Lord James, was not motivated by the desire to establish the new religion and eliminate the old. Neither was he motivated primarily by personal ambition for money or power, as was the case with Châtelherault. Maitland was first and foremost a diplomatist: he invariably planned in terms of Scotland's relations with foreign powers. And here his guiding principle was a desire for the union of Scotland and England—by alliance and, eventually, by personal union. Maitland never swerved from the pursuit of this goal, and, being a realistic, secular-minded politician—Machiavellian, if you like— he was prepared to adopt whatever means might offer the best chances of success. Hence his reputation for unreliability and changeableness, for he, almost alone in Scotland in his time, thought in terms which were neither religious nor personal.

The importance of Maitland in the life of Lord James can hardly be overestimated. From this point—October 1559—their careers were intertwined. More important, Maitland won Lord James over to his view that the political goal of Scotland should be a permanent alliance with England. Hitherto the Congregation had sought for friendship with the "auld enemy" out of dire necessity; it had to have English aid in order to win. As has been pointed out, Lord James would have been perfectly content to remain loyal to Mary and to the French alliance, before May

1559, if Protestantism had been established. Since that time his policy, and that of the Congregation, had involved political disloyalty to France without the obvious counterbalance of permanent friendship with England. The coming of Maitland supplied that counterbalance—and made a permanent convert of Lord James. To the day of his death Lord James's two fixed principles were the dominance of Protestantism at home and friendship with England abroad.

This digression on Maitland has been made because of the broader implications of his impact on the Congregation. It has been pointed out that the survival of European Protestantism depended on England's remaining Protestant; this in turn hinged on the domination of Scotland by a Protestant, Anglophile party, because of the succession question. The party was now created; shortly it was to dominate. The remainder of the career of Lord James is the story of how that party, after many vicissitudes, successfully met the one great challenge to its supremacy, in a struggle which cost Lord James his life in the heyday of his success.

iv

The Congregation, having seized Edinburgh and "deposed" Mary of Guise, was now faced with the problem of enforcing its will on the Regent. For this task it was, if anything, in a worse military position than it had been in July. True, it had received some English money. It also had Châtelherault. But £3,000 was very little, and the gaining of the Duke was of no immediate advantage. First of all, Châtelherault was timid and inept; secondly, the behavior of the Congregation had made a true prophet of Mary of Guise. She had been saying all along that the Protestants intended a political coup, and so it had turned out. The armies of the Congregation were still feudal levies for the most part, no better than before. Lord Erskine was still neutral; other lords were still bystanders. There even was treachery in the ranks of the Congregation.[94] And the Regent had twice as many Frenchmen as she had had before.

[94] Knox, *History*, I, 452.

Recourse was had to England. The English were willing to supply their friends with more money; on October 31 they gave Cockburn of Ormiston £1,000. Unfortunately for the Congregation, Ormiston was waylaid on his way home by the Earl of Bothwell, one of the few noble supporters of the Regent, and relieved of his burden.[95]

This was the beginning of a black week for the Congregation. On hearing of the disaster, Lord James and Arran set out in pursuit of Bothwell, who escaped from his Border fortress in the nick of time.[96] During their absence the French issued from Leith and inflicted a sharp defeat on part of the remaining forces of the Congregation. Five days later, on November 6, another French sally resulted in a serious defeat for Lord James himself, who was almost captured before being able to make good his retreat. This reduced the Congregation to despair. Lord James and Arran vainly endeavored to prevent the evacuation of Edinburgh. Once again the Congregation departed in confusion from the capital, leaving behind most of its artillery.[97]

Lord James and his fellows retired to Stirling, where two important decisions were taken. The leaders determined to split their forces: Châtelherault and the western earls were to base themselves on Glasgow, while Arran and Lord James were to hold on in Fife. More important, it was decided to send Maitland to England to plead for open intervention.[98]

On the decision of England the fate of the Congregation hung. It was quite clear that even with English financial aid the Congregation could not beat the Regent: it did not have the resources to do so, and far too many of the Scottish nobles were neutral. Open English support would turn the trick, for besides bolstering the Congregation militarily it would bring in the lords who still hung off—not only Protestants such as Morton, but in all probability Catholics such as Huntly, who were more interested in power than in religion. So Sadler and Croft implied in a letter

[95] October 25, 1559, Knox to Croft, *C.S.P., For., Eliz.*, II, 59–60. October 27, 1559, Croft to Knox, *Sadler Papers*, I, 523–24. Knox, *History*, I, 455.
[96] November 3, 1559, Randolph to Sadler and Croft, *Sadler Papers*, I, 536–38.
[97] November 11, 1559, Randolph to Sadler and Croft, *ibid.*, pp. 563–66. Knox, *History*, I, 465.   [98] *Ibid.*, I, 473; II, 5.

to Cecil.[99] The latter, after the discomfiture of the Congregation on November 6, came to the same conclusion.[100] The most pressing need of the Congregation, from a military point of view, was a fleet, which would protect Fife from invasion and at the same time prevent French reinforcements from arriving. Ably seconded by Maitland, Cecil persuaded his mistress to authorize the sending of one on December 16, with instructions to seize French ships and to prevent any new French landing.[101]

A fleet might stave off disaster for the Congregation, but only an army could win for it, and here Elizabeth was likely to stick. Nevertheless Cecil persuaded her; Elizabeth was doubtless aided to make up her mind by his threat of resignation and by Throckmorton's account of the domestic situation in France, which indicated that a Protestant revolt against the Guises would break out very shortly.[102] On December 25 instructions were issued to the Duke of Norfolk, who had been appointed Lieutenant General in the north, to prepare an army.[103]

The news of these transactions was more than welcome to the Scottish Protestants, who were being pressed hard by the Regent. The latter had not been idle. She had entered Edinburgh after the Congregation's departure in November and had done her best to win Lord Erskine and the castle, unsuccessfully.[104] She was now planning to take the offensive. Lord James meanwhile was in Fife, preparing for the coming attack. The Regent on November 25 had issued an order to seize his property because of his treason, as she termed it. She apparently was quite astonished at Lord James's "stiffness"; his reply to this order was to seize one of the Regent's supply ships in the Forth, on November 30.[105] On

[99] On November 8. *Sadler Papers*, I, 550–55.
[100] See his letter of November 12, 1559, to Sadler and Croft, *ibid.*, pp. 566–75.
[101] *C.S.P., For., Eliz.*, II, 199–202.
[102] J. E. Neale, *Queen Elizabeth*, pp. 91–92. See also the report of the Council to Elizabeth on December 24, 1559, *C.S.P., For., Eliz.*, II, 220–24.
[103] *Ibid.*, pp. 233–37. Even after this Elizabeth was hopeful of not having to send the army, but Norfolk finally convinced her of the military necessity of doing so. S. Haynes, ed., *The Burghley Papers (1542–1570)*, pp. 217–18, 220–22.
[104] Brown, *John Knox*, II, 64.
[105] November 30, 1559, John Wood (Lord James's secretary) to Randolph, *C.S.P., For., Eliz.*, II, 152–53. Knox supplies us with some evidence on Lord James's character and motives at this time. In a letter to Mrs. Locke on December

the same date Lord James and Arran wrote to Sadler and Croft asking for money, which they got, partly to pay their men and partly to bribe Lord Erskine to remain neutral.[106] On December 20 they wrote again, begging the English to hurry and send the fleet, since the Regent was planning to invade Fife. Open English intervention, they added, would bring in the neutral lords on their side.[107]

The invasion of Fife began in January, 1560. Lord James and Arran were far inferior in numbers, and could only fight a delaying action against the French. The evident objective of the French was St. Andrews, which would be a port of entry for the expected reinforcements far safer from the now-dreaded English attack than was Leith. Lord James and Arran fought a skillful and harassing campaign, enormously aided by the severe winter and by the fact that the French had to march along the coast to keep in contact with their seaborne supplies. For twenty-one days, says Knox, the two Scottish commanders never changed their clothes or even took their boots off.[108] The progress of the campaign, from day to day almost, may be traced in the dispatches passing to and from Sir Ralph Sadler at Berwick.[109] Lord James's letters became steadily more pessimistic. Then, suddenly, everything changed. On January 23 Admiral Winter and the English fleet arrived in the Forth, after having been delayed by a storm. The French were cut off from their supplies and had to retreat.

The arrival of Winter marks the turning point of the struggle from the military point of view. The Regent, although she still held Stirling, was virtually confined to the general area between Edinburgh and Dunbar, with her main stronghold at Leith. The Congregation was jubilant. Its next step was to formalize the agreement with England in order to pave the way for the entry of the English army. This consumed most of the month of February; meanwhile, Lord James busied himself with mopping up

31, he reported that Lord James had spent 3,000 crowns since May and was at the end of his financial resources. Calderwood, *History of the Kirk*, I, 561. Lord James obviously was not profiting from the war.
[106] *Sadler Papers*, I, 620, 623-26   [107] *Ibid.*, pp. 647-49.
[108] Knox, *History*, II, 9.   [109] See *Sadler Papers*, I, 667 ff.

in Fife.[110] All signs now pointed to success, especially since news had arrived of the destruction of the French relieving force by the storm which had also delayed Winter.[111] This was, perhaps, the first "Protestant wind" in history. Late in February Lord James sailed from Pittenweem in an English ship and arrived at Berwick on the twenty-fourth to help negotiate the formal agreement with England.

The Treaty of Berwick, as the agreement came to be known, was signed on February 27, 1560, and was, essentially, a mutual defense pact against France. There was no mention of religion. The English agreed to intervene in Scotland to defend the realm against the French and to protect the rights of Châtelherault, in whose name the Scots at Berwick were acting. Any conquests made were to be handed over to the Congregation. No peace was to be made which did not guarantee Scottish freedom. In return the Scots were to aid England if France should invade the latter country, and were to give six hostages for the duration of the treaty. The Scots further stated that the treaty, and their behavior in general, was in no way intended to cast doubt on their loyalty to Francis and Mary, their legitimate sovereigns. The treaty was to last for the duration of the marriage of Francis and Mary, plus one year.[112]

From the signing of the Treaty of Berwick till the end of the struggle some four months later, the events in Scotland were the focus of European attention. The crucial decisions were made not on the battlefield around Leith, which became the center of military activity, but in the diplomatic dovecotes. In both respects the Congregation remained in the background. England now virtually took over the military and political direction of the alliance. The struggle took on the aspect of a conflict between England and France, with influence in Scotland the prize. It will not

[110] January 31, 1560, Winter to Norfolk, *C.S.P., For., Eliz.*, II, 346–47. February 4, 1560, Randolph to Sadler and Croft, *Sadler Papers*, I, 699–703.
[111] January 11, 1560, Elizabeth to Norfolk, in Haynes, *Burghley Papers*, p. 223.
[112] Knox, *History*, II, 46–52. The treaty was negotiated by the Duke of Norfolk for England, and by Lord James, Maitland, and four others for the Congregation, in the name of Châtelherault.

be described in detail here, since it more properly belongs to English than to Scottish history.

It became apparent in March that the English gamble was going to succeed: the Guises, faced with a difficult domestic crisis, were unable to make a large-scale military effort on behalf of the Regent. Therefore France began to negotiate almost as soon as the ink on the Berwick agreement was dry. Proposals for a settlement were made to Elizabeth on March 2; on March 19 the Regent attempted to get in touch with Lord James through Lord Erskine, in an effort to forestall the English invasion.[113] No agreement was reached, but the entry of the English army into Scotland was delayed for a month. Elizabeth was hopeful of making a settlement without the expense of a war, but at last she became convinced that the French were simply playing for time, and Norfolk was ordered to go forward.[114] In the first days of April the English army, approximately eight thousand strong, commanded by Lord Grey, joined forces with the Congregation at Prestonpans.[115] Three days earlier the Regent had been received into Edinburgh Castle, still neutral, by Lord Erskine. The allies had the better of a skirmish outside Leith on April 6 and settled down to a siege.[116]

The most important contribution of the Congregation during these weeks was its final success in winning over the neutral lords, chiefly Huntly and Morton. Lord James took a prominent part in these negotiations.[117] The task was not easy, however. As

[113] *C.S.P., For., Eliz.*, II, 423–24, 459.
[114] March 22, 1560, the Council to Norfolk, in Haynes, *Burghley Papers*, pp. 267–68. On the French attitude see, February 19, 1560, the Duke of Guise and the Cardinal of Lorraine to Mary of Guise, *C.S.P., For., Eliz.*, II, 384–87; April 26, 1560, Tiepolo to the Doge and Senate of Venice, *Calendar of State Papers, Venetian* (henceforth abbreviated *C.S.P., Ven.*), VII, 196.
[115] Brown, *John Knox*, II, 72. On the question of the size of the English army, see G. Dickinson, ed., *Two Missions of Jacques de la Brosse*, pp. 88–89, n. 2.
[116] April 6, 1560, Grey, etc., to Norfolk, *C.S.P., For., Eliz.*, II, 509–10.
[117] For details, see Lindsay of Pitscottie, *Chronicles*, II, 167; March 8, 1560, Lord James to Norfolk, *C.S.P., For., Eliz.*, II, 439–40; March 27, 1560, Maitland to Cecil, *ibid.*, p. 483; *ibid.*, III, 24–25; June 7–8, 1560, Randolph to Norfolk, *ibid.*, 107–9; May 24, 1560, Morton to Cecil, in Haynes, *Burghley Papers*, pp. 315–16; Knox, *History*, II, 61–64. Lord James also did his best, throughout April and May, to win over his uncle Erskine, without success. De la Brosse's "Journal of the Siege of Leith," in Dickinson, *Two Missions of Jacques de la Brosse*, pp. 93 ff.

Maitland complained to Cecil on April 17,[118] one reason why men such as Huntly and Morton delayed so long in joining the Congregation was the continuing negotiation between France and England, which was now going on at the site of the military operations. These discussions, which hampered the prosecution of the siege, were very embarrassing to the Congregation. As has been pointed out, Maitland and Lord James were convinced of the value of a permanent Anglo-Scottish alliance, but they were by no means certain that England had any such view. They were aware of the difficult diplomatic situation in which England found herself, partly owing to Spanish pressure,[119] and they feared that the English might well reverse their policy and, in return for concessions on questions not directly affecting the interests of the Congregation, make an agreement with France which would expose the Scots to the vengeance of the Regent. They did not wish any negotiations to take place till after Leith had been captured, yet they could not force the English to break them off. Consequently they followed a policy of rigidly insisting on their demands and of pointing to the Treaty of Berwick at every mention of concessions. The Scottish demands were simple. The French must go—troops and officials and Regent. The fortifications of Leith must be dismantled. The French must recognize the Treaty of Berwick.[120] Once again, there was no mention of religion, partly to spare the susceptibilities of Elizabeth, partly because the Congregation now felt confident that, once the French were removed, it would have everything its own way. The French were willing to make some concessions on the first two points, but they could not swallow the Treaty of Berwick. It was illegal, they held, and absolutely must be abandoned. The Scots would not budge. Maitland, who handled the negotiations for the Congregation, had doubtless foreseen this result. It was a shrewd maneuver on his part, for the English could justify their own behavior to the world in general and to Spain in particular only by upholding the

[118] *Calendar of State Papers Relating to Scotland and Mary Queen of Scots* (henceforth abbreviated *C.S.P., Scot.*), I, 364.
[119] For the Spanish effort to mediate, see Teulet, *Relations politiques*, II, 52 ff.; *C.S.P., Ven.*, VII, 149 ff.
[120] April 9, 1560, Grey, etc., to Norfolk, *C.S.P., For., Eliz.*, II, 519-20.

validity of the Treaty of Berwick, once the Scots had brought it into the discussion. So, on April 25, the negotiations broke down.[121]

An attempt was now made to end the impasse by force, but the full-scale assault on Leith on May 7 was hopelessly mismanaged, and the French had little difficulty in repelling it. This undoubtedly made the Congregation more amenable to negotiation, the threads of which were once more taken up by the Regent. She invited the Protestants to send a deputation to Edinburgh Castle to confer with her. This was done on May 12. The negotiations collapsed on the question of the Treaty of Berwick, as they had before,[122] but now the Congregation became aware of a new factor, which might well mean an end to the deadlock. The Regent was dying. Once she was gone, there would be no French authority left in Scotland, and the French would be forced to make the necessary concessions. So, indeed, it turned out.

Elizabeth now determined to make a serious effort to end the struggle, which was proving expensive, by sending Cecil himself to negotiate with the French.[123] The latter and his colleague Wotton went north early in June, met the French envoys at Newcastle, and resolved to push on to Edinburgh, where a truce was arranged, to begin on June 17.[124] Negotiations then began. They were considerably simplified by the death of the Regent on June 10. Mary of Guise was both a good and an intelligent woman and in ordinary circumstances would have made an excellent ruler, as the early years of her regency amply demonstrated. It was her misfortune to rule at the time of the religious upheaval, and because of that very fact she did her beloved France and her own kin far more harm than good by being in the seat of power. For a French, Catholic regent meant that the religious

[121] For a running account of the negotiations from the allied side, see *ibid.*, pp. 519 ff., especially Maitland's letter to Cecil on April 26, 1560, pp. 588–90. The report of the French negotiator, the Bishop of Valence, is in A. Teulet, ed., *Papiers d'état relatifs à l'histoire de l'Ecosse au XVIe siècle*, I, 571–96.

[122] May 11, 1560, Grey, etc., to Norfolk, *C.S.P., For., Eliz.*, III, 45–46. May 14, 1560, Maitland to Cecil, *ibid.*, pp. 56–57. See also the account in de la Brosse's "Journal," in Dickinson, *Two Missions of Jacques de la Brosse*, pp. 151–57.

[123] Cecil's instructions are dated May 26, 1560. *C.S.P., For., Eliz.*, III, 85–87.

[124] *Ibid.*, pp. 115–16.

question was entangled with the issue of French domination. Had Châtelherault still been Regent, in all probability the policy which Lord James had intended to put into effect on Mary of Guise's departure would have been put into operation at once, and France, at the price of religious concession—no great feat for the ally of the Grand Turk—would have been able to retain her Scottish ally. But it was not to be.

Cecil now set to work in earnest. At every turn he was aided by Maitland and Lord James, whose chief function was to hold the leaders of the Congregation in line. This task they performed successfully, with the aid of a clause in the final agreement guaranteeing the restoration of their French income and property to all members of the Congregation. The clause pleased Châtelherault, needless to say; Lord James, however, even though he profited by it, was afraid that it might pave the way for a revival of French influence in Scotland, and thus become a danger to the "amity" with England.[125] "Surely the Lord James is a gentleman of great worthiness!" Cecil exclaimed in a letter to Petre.[126]

The two crucial points in the negotiation were those of the armorial bearings of Francis and Mary and the Treaty of Berwick. By threats Cecil got the French to agree that Francis and Mary would stop using the English title and arms. On the second point, the negotiations almost collapsed. On July 1 Cecil, having done his best, was prepared to go home.[127] Next day, however, the French finally gave in, although they had been instructed to admit nothing into the treaty which remotely resembled a sanctioning of the Treaty of Berwick.[128] They agreed to a clause which stated that Francis and Mary were making an agreement with their subjects because of the intercession of Elizabeth and therefore would fulfill the promises now made. This was vague enough, but it certainly implied that Elizabeth was justified in dealing with the Congregation.

Once these matters were settled, the other points at issue be-

---

[125] July 8, 1560, Cecil and Wotton to Elizabeth, in Haynes, *Burghley Papers*, pp. 354–57.   [126] On June 23. *Ibid.*, pp. 332–33.
[127] July 1–2, 1560, Cecil and Wotton to Elizabeth, *ibid.*, pp. 335–41.
[128] Andrew Lang, *A History of Scotland from the Roman Occupation*, II, 68.

tween France and England were easily disposed of. The separate Franco-Scottish agreement, which was cast in the form of a royal grant, contained virtually everything the Congregation wanted, except that the religious question was not settled.[129] No foreign troops were to be brought into Scotland, or war or peace made, without the consent of the Estates. The Leith fortifications were to be demolished. No foreigners were to hold important offices, and no financial office was to be entrusted to a cleric. Parliament, which the Congregation had summoned for July 10, was to be prorogued till August 1 in order to obtain the consent of the Sovereign to hold it; it was then to be held in the customary manner and be a legal Parliament. The Estates were to select twenty-four men, of whom Mary could chose seven and the Estates five,[130] to make up a council to govern the country. A general amnesty was proclaimed, except to those whom the Estates decided to exclude as unfit. Representatives were to be sent to Francis and Mary to negotiate on religious matters, but clerical property was not to be disturbed, and the Estates must do justice to those churchmen who had suffered during the war. The nobles were to agree to observe this treaty and punish violators of it.[131]

These treaties, known collectively as the Treaty of Edinburgh, though they were two separate agreements, were proclaimed on July 6, 1560. They represented a complete victory for Protestantism, for England, for the Congregation. The French had been driven from Scotland, and in place of Mary of Guise there now ruled a group of nobles, the leaders of which were Protestants—either from conviction, like Lord James, or from hope of gain, like Morton—and which included Catholic members such as Huntly who were simply intriguers. Their power was legally assured by the treaty, for though Mary could name the majority of the council that was to rule, the Estates, which would be dominated by the Congregation, could pick the men from whom she was to choose. The only means of enforcement of the treaty was

---

[129] Some of the lords wanted this in the treaty; Cecil and Maitland dissuaded them. June 25, 1560, Cecil to Norfolk, in Haynes, *Burghley Papers*, p. 333. June 26, 1560, Cecil to the Council, *C.S.P., Scot.*, I, 433–35.

[130] Or, if either party saw fit, the numbers could be eight and six.

[131] The texts of the treaties are given by Keith, *History*, I, 291–306.

the old and often ineffectual Scottish method of the band. Thus Scotland was once more turned over to its nobles, and to Protestant nobles at that. The desires of an absent, Catholic ruler were not likely to be respected. Worse still, from that ruler's point of view, the triumphant nobility had won because of the aid rendered them by a foreign state, heretical and anti-French, whose obvious policy it would be to maintain its Scottish Protestant friends in power by all means at its command.

The Protestant party in Scotland had won by dint of becoming an Anglophile party as well. Lord James and his coreligionists were now in power. It remained to be seen how they and their English friends would use their victory.

CHAPTER III

The Problems of Victory

THE VICTORIOUS Protestants were not long in capitalizing on their victory. Peace was made on July 6; less than two weeks later, just after the French and English troops had left,[1] they made their first move. On July 19 the Congregation appointed five men—including one layman, Erskine of Dun—as "superintendents" of the Kirk.[2] Their duties were to keep an eye on the ministers in a specified area, and to travel around that territory performing the functions of a minister in those places where no regularly appointed clergyman was located. They were looked on as temporary officials only: the office would be abolished as soon as the Kirk had an adequate supply of ministers. The significance of the superintendents was this: that without any legal sanction, while Catholicism was still the law of the land, even before the meeting of Parliament—at which, by implication at least, religious matters were not to be discussed [3]—the Protestants made it quite clear that there was to be but one Church in Scotland, theirs, and that they intended to use the forthcoming meeting of Parliament to legalize their newly won supremacy.

The Parliament which met in August 1560 was by all odds the most important ever held in Scotland. Its deeds have been dwelt

---

[1] Both armies left on July 15. *C.S.P., For., Eliz.,* III, 192. Lord James accompanied the English army to Berwick. John Knox, *History of the Reformation in Scotland,* II, 84.

[2] *Ibid.,* pp. 84–87. It is interesting to note that in the 1560s some Catholic bishops who turned Protestant became superintendents.

[3] The Treaty of Edinburgh, on which the legality of the Parliament rested, provided that religious problems were to be dealt with by the sovereigns, in consultation with representatives of the Estates. See Andrew Lang, *A History of Scotland from the Roman Occupation,* II, 73.

on at length by Scottish historians and so will not be discussed in any great detail here. A few aspects of this momentous, and unquestionably illegal, meeting must be mentioned, however.[4] The great question was, of course, the religious one. Under the influence of Knox, a violently anti-Catholic petition was handed in. It demanded in unmeasured language the abolition of Popery and the establishment of the true religion.[5] Not everyone was happy about this, especially those nobles who had profited from the feuing of Church lands. They wanted no discussion of this question, which they feared the preachers might raise, and their point of view prevailed. Consequently the petitioners were instructed by Parliament to draw up a declaration confined to doctrine. This was promptly done; on August 17 the Confession of Faith was presented to Parliament and approved with but few dissenting votes.[6]

It is not necessary here to discuss the theology of the Scottish Protestants as outlined in the Confession, since this feature of Scottish history has received a great deal of attention. It will suffice to borrow the words of Knox's biographer, who says that the Confession was a "compendium of Calvinistic theology in the fully developed form it had assumed in Calvin's later days." [7] There was one section of it, however, which is worth a passing glance: that on the obedience due the civil magistrate. As given by Knox, the section states that the magistrates are to be obeyed, since God has given them authority, not only in civil affairs "but also for the maintenance of the true Religion, and for suppressing of idolatry and superstition." [8] The obvious implication is that if the magistrate himself is an idolater, he should no longer be obeyed. Randolph says that Maitland and Wynram, the Subprior of St. Andrews, to whom the Confession was submitted before

[4] For a discussion of the constitutional and legal questions involved here, see R. S. Rait, *The Parliaments of Scotland*, pp. 195–205, and W. L. Mathieson, *Politics and Religion: a Study in Scottish History from the Reformation to the Revolution*, I, 80–82.   [5] Knox, *History*, II, 88–92.
[6] The Confession is given in Knox, *ibid.*, pp. 93–120. On the question of the dissenters, see July 29, August 19, 1560, Randolph to Cecil, *C.S.P., Scot.*, I, 452, 466–67; Knox, *History*, II, 121; R. Keith, *The History of the Affairs of Church and State in Scotland*, III, 4.   [7] P. Hume Brown, *John Knox*, II, 122.
[8] Knox, *History*, II, 118–19.

its presentation to Parliament, deleted this section.[9] This may be; or it is possible, as Lang opines, that they merely toned it down.[10]

Parliament also authorized a committee of divines to draw up a treatise on Church governance and related matters.[11] This was the famous Book of Discipline.[12] It was not presented to the August assembly but to the meeting of the Estates on the following January. Once again, there is no need to discuss this work in detail.[13] It is worth noting, however, that here the problem of Church property was squarely dealt with. Knox and his colleagues insisted that the property of the Catholic Church—except that of the monastic foundations, most of which had already been expropriated in one way or another, and hence was virtually irrecoverable—be turned over to the new Church, in order to support its ministers and to carry out Knox's highly laudable and ambitious social and educational projects. Many lords, thinking of their own pocketbooks, wanted no part of this. Knox singled out Lord Erskine for special abuse, "for besides that he has a very Jezebel to his wife, if the poor, the schools, and the ministry of the Kirk had their own, his kitchen would lack two parts and more, of that which he unjustly now possesses." Maitland, too, was assailed, for he termed Knox's plan a "devout imagination." [14] These two were not alone. Even those who did approve, including Lord James, did so with the proviso that those holders of benefices who had turned Protestant should keep their revenues as long as they provided for the ministers in their districts.[15] The Book of Discipline itself did not become the law of the land, but its program was that followed by Knox and his colleagues throughout this period, and they continued to press for a solution of the property question on terms favorable to themselves.

The August Parliament took one more vitally important step

[9] September 7, 1560, Randolph to Cecil, *C.S.P., Scot.*, I, 477–79. Randolph was soon to be appointed resident ambassador in Scotland, to remain in that capacity until early in 1566.

[10] Lang, *History of Scotland*, II, 76–77. Lang devotes some twenty pages, pp. 72–92, to a closely written critique of Knox's theology, which is interesting but, it seems to me, not entirely fair.   [11] Brown, *John Knox*, II, 125.

[12] It is given by Knox, *History*, II, 183–258.

[13] Brown, *John Knox*, II, 122–51, gives a full analysis of it.

[14] Knox, *History*, II, 128.   [15] *Ibid.*, pp. 129–30.

in religious affairs. On August 24 three acts were passed which abolished papal jurisdiction in Scotland, repealed all laws favorable to the Catholic Church, such as heresy laws, and forbade the saying or hearing of Mass on pain of death for the third offense.[16] It also refused, in defiance of the Treaty of Edinburgh, to deal with the complaints of those Catholic clerics who had suffered in the civil war, and it further declared all feus lately made by Catholic prelates to be void.[17] The purpose of this last measure was not to restore the feued Church property to the prelates, but to absolve the recipients of the feus, who were too strong to be dispossessed by force, from paying rent. No Catholic would be able to get a favorable decision on such a question from a court of law.[18]

All this was not calculated to smooth the ruffled feelings of Scotland's legal sovereigns; nor were some of Parliament's other actions. Besides giving its approval to the Treaty of Edinburgh, it also voted to confirm the Treaty of Berwick, despite Maitland's qualms.[19] To add insult to injury, James Sandilands of Calder, a man of no great political importance, and a convinced Protestant, was sent to France to obtain the assent of Francis and Mary to the doings of Parliament and to the Treaty of Edinburgh. It could hardly have come as a surprise to the Protestant leaders that Sandilands's mission was a total failure.[20] Francis and Mary regarded the Parliament as illegal, and they refused to assent to any of its acts. Nor would they ratify the Scottish part of the Treaty of Edinburgh.[21] Worse still, it began to be rumored in Scotland that

[16] *The Acts of the Parliament of Scotland*, II, 534–35.
[17] On these two points see the letter of Thomas Archibald, a servant of the Archbishop of Glasgow, to his master in France, August 28, 1560, in Keith, *History*, III, 7–10.
[18] This was true even after Mary's return, according to the Jesuit Gouda, who visited Scotland in 1562. "Whenever anyone comes into a court of law, the magistrates always inquire first if they are 'Papists.' . . . Should they be Papists, they can get very little, if any, attention paid to their cause." September 30, 1562, Gouda to Laynez, in W. Forbes-Leith, ed., *Narratives of Scottish Catholics under Mary Stuart and James VI*, p. 74.
[19] July 29, 1560, Maitland to Cecil, *C.S.P., Scot.*, I, 451–52.
[20] G. Buchanan, *The History of Scotland*, II, 434, says that the Sandilands mission was authorized by the Congregation more to sound out Francis and Mary than with any expectation that they would consent to the Acts of Parliament.
[21] September 17, November 17, 1560, Throckmorton to Elizabeth, *C.S.P., For., Eliz.*, III, 298–303, 391–96. A. Teulet, ed., *Papiers d'état relatifs à l'histoire de*

the French planned to make a new effort to reconquer the country in the spring of 1561, a story which gave encouragement to those elements in Scotland, largely Catholic, which disliked the August settlement.[22]

The leaders of the Congregation were well aware that Francis and Mary, and many people in Scotland as well, would dislike the decisions taken in July and August. Some important people had not voted for the Confession of Faith. Others disliked the confirmation of the Treaty of Berwick.[23] The powerful and shifty Huntly was already causing trouble; on September 1, Lord James met with Argyle and Athol at Perth, where the three agreed to stand together against Huntly if he changed sides.[24] The Catholic Athol's membership in this coalition was short-lived. Briefly, a Catholic reaction was to be expected, the likelihood of which was increased by the uncertain legal position of the Protestants and by the fact that a victorious coalition, political or military, almost always falls apart after victory has been won.

To the Protestants there was but one solution to the problem. If England were on their side, they would be safe. How could they be sure of retaining English support? The answer leaped at them, the obvious answer in a dynastic age. Marry their leader— or, rather, the son of their leader—to Elizabeth.

The idea of the Arran marriage was not a new one. Alexander Whitelaw, one of the Congregation's agents, had suggested it to Cecil, through Throckmorton, in June 1559.[25] But it became a serious proposition for the first time in August 1560. At the Parliament it was decided that an embassy should be sent to Elizabeth to ask formally for her hand. The Parliament even had the gall to

---

l'Ecosse au XVIe siècle, I, 623–28. October 5, 1560, Francis II to the Bishop of Limoges, ibid., pp. 636–37. November 16, 1560, Francis II to the Scottish Estates, ibid., pp. 638–39.
[22] Knox, History, II, 131. The Venetian Ambassador in France also felt that France was simply playing for time, would never ratify the Treaty, and would attack in Scotland soon. November 25, 1560, Surian to the Doge and Senate of Venice, C.S.P., Ven., VII, 273–74.
[23] August 15, 1560, Randolph to Cecil, C.S.P., Scot., I, 460–62. Marischal and Athol are specially mentioned as opposing its confirmation, because they disliked England.   [24] September 7, 1560, Randolph to Cecil, ibid., pp. 477–79.
[25] June 28, 1559, Throckmorton to Cecil, C.S.P., For., Eliz., I, 340–41.

request Francis and Mary to support this marriage.[26] The ambassadors selected, Glencairn, Morton, and Maitland, left for England, after some delay, in mid-October.[27]

It was obvious that if Elizabeth married Arran, the Congregation's problems would be over. England would then be permanently committed to the support of the Protestant party against France and against dissident elements within Scotland. England in turn would reap the benefit of a friendly neighbor, and the considerably greater potential one that the children of this marriage, or even its principals, would some day rule over the whole island, if Mary died without issue.

Here we come to the crux of the question: did the Protestants plan, if Elizabeth married Arran, to depose Mary and put Arran on the throne at once? Some writers on Scottish history have assumed that the Protestants could have had no other object in such a proposal, simply because they could not have made it palatable to England on any other basis. There are good reasons for doubting this, however. In the first place, the Hamiltons were by no means popular. Most of the Catholic nobles would certainly oppose any attempt at deposition, and there were many Protestants, such as Marischal, who out of dislike of the Duke and his family would also refuse to go along.[28] Any premature attempt to make Arran King would almost certainly have caused a revolt.

Yet the Protestants certainly believed that Arran would some day be elevated to the throne, or they would not have made the proposal to Elizabeth. They believed thus, however, not because they planned to depose Mary, but because they thought that Mary would soon die, before her husband, and would die childless. The evidence all points in this direction. All the foreign ambassadors in France during Mary's marriage to Francis noted her bad health; it was rumored that she would soon be dead, that she suffered from

[26] August 31, 1560, the Scottish Estates to Francis II, in A. Teulet, ed., *Relations politiques de la France et de l'Espagne avec l'Ecosse au XVIe siècle*, II, 150–52.
[27] *C.S.P., For., Eliz.*, III, 358–59.
[28] See Randolph's letter to Cecil on August 25, 1560, on the question of the opposition to the Arran marriage, *C.S.P., Scot.*, I, 469–73.

an incurable disease.[29] Mary's early death was the bait that the Protestants held out to Elizabeth, whose character they could not have so misread as to believe that she would approve the deposition of a fellow monarch in such circumstances, and for whose benefit they had insisted on their loyalty to Francis and Mary throughout the civil war.

Only thus, too, can we explain the attitude taken toward the marriage by Maitland and Lord James. Maitland adopted a *faute de mieux* position. He disliked the haste with which it was pressed on Elizabeth.[30] He knew enough of Arran to realize that he was a poor instrument for strengthening the Anglo-Scottish friendship. His letters to Cecil on the subject, before the departure of the embassy to England, were distinctly lacking in fervor.[31] Being an accomplished politician, he well knew that the deposition of Mary would produce a revolt. Yet he gave his support to the marriage. On what other basis but that he believed that Arran would be King soon in any case, and that that occurrence might as well be put to use?

Lord James is a still clearer case in point. He was far more enthusiastic than was Maitland—he was "marvelous earnest" on the subject, said Randolph.[32] He certainly recognized the advantages of the Arran marriage to Protestantism. Yet to assume that he would favor the deposition of his sister in favor of the enemies of his house—he was a Stewart, after all—before that sister's attitude to the Treaty of Edinburgh and the August Parliament was definitely known, is to place a great strain on one's credulity, especially when it is considered that a Hamilton king might well mean his own political extinction. Lord James may have reasoned that, given the incapacity of the Hamiltons and his own great power and influence in Protestant ranks, his power in Scotland might remain unimpaired, but this was by no means certain, considering the nepotism of the Hamiltons. The explanation that best fits the

[29] D. H. Fleming has collected these medical rumors in *Mary Queen of Scots*, pp. 27–29, 213–16.
[30] On this point see August 19, 1560, Randolph to Cecil, *C.S.P., Scot.*, I, 466–67.
[31] For instance, that of September 13, 1560, *ibid.*, pp. 479–80.
[32] August 19, August 25, 1560, Randolph to Cecil, *ibid.*, pp. 466–67, 469–73.

facts of Lord James's behavior is the one given: that he expected the early demise of his sister and was playing his cards accordingly.

All this is but speculation on what might have been, however, for the decision lay in the hands of Elizabeth. To Cecil's great annoyance,[33] the Queen would not follow up her successes in Scotland, in spite of Throckmorton's alarmist letters from France.[34] She had no intention whatever of marrying Arran. Her flirtation with Lord Robert Dudley was at its height in the latter half of 1560; it was in September that Lord Robert's wife died in mysterious circumstances. On December 8 Elizabeth informed Maitland and his colleagues that she was not presently disposed to marry and that Arran should look elsewhere for a bride.[35]

It was during this same month of December that there came from France the astonishing and unexpected news of the death of Francis II.[36] His death and the simultaneous rejection of Arran by Elizabeth mark a turning point in Scottish history. The two events produced a decisive shift in the policy of the Congregation and made a breach between the Hamiltons and Lord James which was never fully healed.

There was one great advantage for the Congregation in the death of Francis: the threat of a French invasion was virtually eliminated, along with the influence of the Guises in French councils. In these circumstances, the rejection of Arran by Elizabeth became far less serious. Not that Maitland and Lord James were any less anxious for an English alliance, but the overmastering, immediate necessity for it was gone; other, slower methods could be used. Scottish bargaining power was now greater, and there was no further need for the Arran proposal, which would have brought with it the unpleasant prospect of dominance by the Hamiltons. For it was now apparent to Maitland and Lord James that they had made a serious miscalculation. Whatever the state of Mary's health, she had outlived Francis, and she would probably come home. This being the case, the acceptance of Arran by

[33] August 27, 1560, Cecil to Throckmorton, *C.S.P., For., Eliz.*, III, 262–63.
[34] See, for instance, that of October 10, 1560, *ibid.*, p. 347.
[35] *Ibid.*, p. 436.   [36] Knox, *History*, II, 137–38.

Elizabeth would have put them, and Elizabeth too, in an impossible position. The sighs of relief on all sides, excepting the Hamiltons, must have been enormous.

But there was still the problem of Mary to be dealt with. A meeting of the Estates was called in January to determine the Protestants' position, and it was decided to send Lord James on an unofficial mission to Mary. He was selected for two reasons: because he was a sincere Protestant who could not be swayed by blandishments to forsake the cause, as Mary of Guise had learned to her sorrow, and because the Protestants felt that Mary would be friendlier to him than to any other important leader.[37]

Lord James's purpose in this mission was to determine Mary's attitude toward Scottish affairs in general and some points in particular—to "fully grope her mind." He was to assure her of the Protestants' loyalty to her and to find out how she felt about them. He was to intimate as plainly as possible that there were limits to that loyalty, however: the Protestants would resist any attempt to suppress Protestantism or to bring foreign troops with her on her return. Knox also wanted him to inform her that public or private exercise of the Catholic religion was forbidden. Lord James would not go so far as this. Public Masses, no; but "to have it secretly in her chamber, who could stop her?" The implication being that he, for one, would not try.[38]

The fact was that the death of Francis and the rejection of Arran had split the ranks of the Congregation. Even before December many of the intriguing Catholics and dubious Protestants who had joined the Congregation for gain were shying off. The death of Francis, while it ended the possibility of a French invasion, encouraged them to persevere in the hope that Mary, when

[37] On this point see December 31, 1560, Throckmorton to the Council, *C.S.P., For., Eliz.*, III, 471–74. Mary's confidence in her brother doubtless stemmed in part from the fact that Lord James had already requested her to restore the revenues from his French benefices to him. Mary evidently saw in this a means of securing his support. November 29, 1560, Throckmorton to Elizabeth, *ibid.*, p. 412.

[38] Knox, *History*, II, 142–43. The above two paragraphs are drawn mainly from Maitland's letter to Cecil of February 6, 1561, *C.S.P., Scot.*, I, 509–11. The only other important action of the January meeting was to ratify the Book of Discipline in qualified form, as mentioned above. Maitland in his letter termed this an "earnest embracing of religion."

she returned, would favor them. Early in 1561 the Catholic members of this group met and determined to send their own representative, John Leslie, the historian and future Bishop of Ross, to Mary in an attempt to commit her to their policy, which, it developed, was one of force.[39]

The Hamiltons were in agonies. The Duke and Arran had been upset by Elizabeth's rejection of the latter, and they dreaded the arrival of Mary. The only thing they could think of was to avoid the anticipated blow by getting Mary to marry Elizabeth's baffled suitor, a plan which Knox viewed with favor. Early in January Arran, having heard the bad news from London, was in communication with his Queen.[40] The reaction of Lord James and Maitland to this maneuver is illuminating. They were very angry.[41] So long as they were threatened by a French invasion and so long as the accession of a Hamilton to the throne seemed inevitable, they had been willing enough to have Arran marry Elizabeth; but in the changed circumstances they wanted no part of Hamilton rule.

The policy of Lord James and Maitland was essentially that laid down in Lord James's unofficial instructions. They knew that Mary was bound to come back and that it was necessary to come to terms with her. They were prepared to make the best of it, provided that her return was not incompatible with the continued dominance of Protestantism and the friendship with England. But why should their Francophile, Catholic Queen even consider such a policy? Because of the gigantic bait of the English succession. On this thread their whole policy toward Mary hung. It was up to Elizabeth to name her successor, if she wished. While Elizabeth had no particular interest in union with Scotland, or in religion for religion's sake, there were those around her, notably Cecil, who did; and Elizabeth was interested in the welfare of her realm, and that welfare was intimately tied up with a friendly, Protestant Scotland. If Elizabeth was to be persuaded to recognize Mary as her heir presumptive, it would only be on the ironclad assurance

[39] John Leslie, *The History of Scotland*, II, 451.
[40] Knox, *History*, II, 137. January 3, 1561, Randolph to Cecil, *C.S.P., Scot.*, I, 504–5.
[41] February 26, 1561, Randolph to Cecil, *ibid.*, pp. 518–21. April 9, 1561, Throckmorton to Cecil, *C.S.P., For., Eliz.*, IV, 55–56.

that the policy of Maitland and Lord James would be the permanent policy of Mary. In other words, only Maitland and Lord James could deliver the English throne to Mary without war. This was their unspoken offer to their Queen: adopt our program, and we shall get England for you.[42]

There was one other group that should be mentioned. Knox and his extremist followers regarded the coming of Mary with unconcealed aversion. They dreaded its effect on religion, and they looked on all who attempted to make any sort of arrangement with "our Jezebel" as corrupt timeservers. Knox, being utterly unable to understand Maitland, had never trusted him, of course. But that Lord James, who was rightly regarded as a zealous Protestant, should be ensnared by Mary was more than Knox could bear. "My Lord, my Master, may not thus be used: he has that honor to be the Queen's brother; and therefore we will that all men shall understand that he must tender her as his sister; and whosoever will counsel him to displease her . . . shall not find him their friend; yea, they are worthy to be hanged that would so counsel him." [43] From this point on, Lord James was to find himself hampered at every turn by the zealousness of his old associates, and especially of Knox, who could not understand the complexities of Lord James's policy.

Thus was Scotland divided on the matter of the return of Mary. On the one side were those who welcomed the Queen's return and hoped to profit from it [44]—the Catholics, both sincere and timeserving, as well as the great majority of the Protestant lords, including Lord James. On the other side stood the Hamiltons and the Protestant extremists, both of whom dreaded her return, though for widely divergent reasons.

[42] There were those who suspected that Lord James, in undertaking the mission to France, was simply trying to worm himself into his sister's confidence, get the earldom of Moray from her, and then rule with the aid of his relatives and friends. April 28, 1561, Randolph to Throckmorton, in D. M. Rose, "Mary Queen of Scots and Her Brother," *Scottish Historical Review*, II (1905), 152–53. Lord James was certainly not devoid of personal ambition, but it never operated to the exclusion of considerations of policy, and did not in this case.
[43] Knox, *History*, II, 266.
[44] As early as January 10 Maitland reported to Cecil that he had noticed a tendency among the nobles to pay court to Mary. *C.S.P., For., Eliz.*, III, 494.

ii

Now that Mary's husband was dead, the Scottish Queen was in a position to formulate a policy of her own for the first time.[45] A great deal hinged on what that policy should be. Mary herself quickly recognized the basic facts of her position. Her real importance, in the eyes of Europe and in her own, lay in the fact, not that she was Queen of Scotland, but that she was the legitimate heiress of England if Elizabeth should die without issue. All of Mary's subsequent policy turned on this point: she wanted the English throne. This was her end. The problem lay in the choice of means.

Broadly speaking, there were two methods of reaching the seat of Elizabeth. The first was by peaceful means, by Elizabeth's sanction. This involved returning to Scotland as the friend of the Protestant leaders there, allowing them to be her chief advisers, seeking Elizabeth's friendship at every turn, particularly on the point of her possible remarriage, keeping her Catholicism in the background and her French relatives at arm's length. In other words, she must identify herself completely with the policy of Maitland and Lord James, at least until she arrived on the English throne, and probably thereafter as well, for by then the restoration of Catholicism would in all likelihood be out of the question.

This was one possibility. The other way of accomplishing her end was by force. This had the advantage, to Mary, of the restoration of Catholicism throughout the island. It also had the disadvantage of requiring, in all probability, foreign troops for its accomplishment, and involved a Catholic marriage as a necessary preliminary. There were any number of matches which would make the scheme feasible. Charles IX might do, but unfortunately that did not look very practicable at the moment, owing to the antagonism between Mary and her Guise relatives on the one hand and Catherine de Medici, who now controlled French policy, on the other. Or, just possibly, a native Catholic might do—Mary was

---

[45] The literature on Mary is enormous. The best biography is that of T. F. Henderson. The work of D. H. Fleming also deserves to be mentioned, on account of its voluminous and critical notes.

unaware as yet of the actual strength of the English and Scottish
Catholics. Already rumor was busy with the name of Lord Darnley, the son of the Earl of Lennox.[46] But the really desirable match
was with Don Carlos, son of the mighty Philip of Spain. Once
such a marriage was accomplished, Mary could proceed, with her
foreign and local Catholic levies, to crush the Scottish Protestants
and then turn her attention to Elizabeth.

These were the alternatives that faced Mary after the death of
Francis. The second was the more attractive, Mary being a good
Catholic, but also looked to be far more difficult of accomplishment. Nevertheless the young Queen and her Guise relatives decided, early in 1561, to try it, without closing the door to the alternative plan. As early as January 10 Throckmorton reported to
his sovereign that the Guises wanted a Spanish husband for
Mary.[47] This did not suit Elizabeth at all, needless to say, nor did
it please Catherine de Medici, who dreaded such an increase in
Guisan power. Catherine's opposition eventually proved effective;
she threatened Philip with an alliance with England if Mary married any Hapsburg prince, and Philip, who was aware that Elizabeth, in those circumstances, would certainly side with France,
decided that discretion was the better part of valor, for the time
being at least. The negotiations were shelved for the moment.[48]

While these transactions were still pending, the two messengers
from Scotland arrived in Lorraine, whither Mary had gone after
her period of strict mourning, probably in order to help her relatives negotiate with Spain in a place as far removed from Catherine
de Medici as possible. The Catholic representative, Leslie, arrived
first, the day before Lord James. The burden of his message was
that Lord James was not to be trusted and should be shown the
inside of a French prison. Mary should come home and land at
Aberdeen, where Huntly's levies would be awaiting her; she could
then march south and crush the Protestants in their Lowland
strongholds.[49] Mary was not convinced. Even if Huntly, whom

[46] On December 23, 1560, Randolph passed on to Cecil Châtelherault's advice to
keep an eye on Lennox and his family. C.S.P., Scot., I, 498–500.
[47] C.S.P., For., Eliz., III, 489–91.
[48] On these negotiations see T. F. Henderson, Mary Queen of Scots, I, 121–24.
[49] Leslie, History of Scotland, II, 451–55.

she did not trust, had the strength to perform what he had promised, which was very unlikely indeed, she would lose her freedom of action and become a mere puppet. She decided to listen to what Lord James had to say.

Lord James did not see his sister till April 15, nearly three months after he had been authorized to do so by the Estates. His delay was due primarily to Mary's action in sending four commissioners to Scotland as part of her policy of keeping two irons in the fire. On January 12 she wrote to the Scottish Estates, notifying them that the commissioners were coming, with powers to summon the Estates legally; that Gilles de Noailles would follow, to propose the renewal of the French alliance; and that she would be coming home soon herself and was ready to forgive and forget.[50] Mary's messengers arrived on February 18;[51] Noailles appeared on March 11 and was informed that he must await the forthcoming meeting of the Estates, set for May 20, for an answer to his proposals.[52]

At this point Lord James, who had waited to see what Mary's envoys had to say, decided that he could leave; he started his journey on March 18, evidently accompanied by a large train.[53] He traveled south through England and conferred with Cecil and Elizabeth. The probable subject of these talks was the attitude to be adopted in case Mary attempted to bring French soldiers with her on her return—whether or not this would constitute an "invasion" under the terms of the Treaty of Berwick.[54] Elizabeth also pressed him to procure Mary's ratification of the Treaty of Edinburgh. Lord James sidestepped this demand, saying that he was traveling in an unofficial capacity.[55] For reasons that will be pointed out below, Lord James was now by no means as en-

[50] A. Labanoff, ed., *Recueil des lettres de Marie Stuart*, I, 80–84.
[51] T. Thomson, ed., *A Diurnal of Remarkable Occurrents that Have Passed within the Country of Scotland*, p. 64. February 26, 1561, Randolph to Cecil, *C.S.P., Scot.*, I, 518–21. Mary's instructions to her messengers are in Labanoff, *Recueil*, I, 85–88.
[52] *C.S.P., For., Eliz.*, IV, 16–17. Knox, *History*, II, 142. March 14, March 20, 1561, Randolph to Cecil, *C.S.P., Scot.*, I, 525–27, 532–33.
[53] *Ibid.*, pp. 509, 525–27.
[54] February 6, 1561, Maitland to Cecil, *ibid.*, pp. 509–11.
[55] March 29, 1561, Elizabeth to Throckmorton, *C.S.P., For., Eliz.*, IV, 38–39.

thusiastic in regard to the Treaty of Edinburgh as he and his fellows had once been.

Early in April Lord James arrived in France. Having passed through Paris, where he saw the worried Throckmorton, he set out for Lorraine before April 9.[56] On the fifteenth he met Mary at St.-Dizier.[57] He was with her for some five days, and was back in Paris on the twenty-third.[58]

On the subject of this interview a great controversy has raged. Lord James has been charged with treacherously revealing to Throckmorton the secret plans of his sister. The charge is based on the ambassador's letter to Elizabeth on April 29, in which he says that Lord James, on his return to Paris, "came to my lodging secretly unto me and declared unto me at good length all that had passed between the Queen, his sister, and him." [59] Lord James himself made no secret of his interview with Throckmorton, however; [60] furthermore, Mary herself must have been perfectly aware that Lord James would pass on the information he obtained from her to his English friends. This is clear from the contents of Lord James's revelations, and also from his—and consequently Throckmorton's—opinion that Mary would not entrust a temporary commission of regency to him because of his refusal to change his views on religious matters or to renounce his friendship with England.[61]

What then was discussed by Mary and her brother? Though Throckmorton does not mention it—this was Lord James's side of the conversation, not Mary's—Lord James doubtless gave Mary the message entrusted to him by the Estates. According to Leslie, Lord James also asked for the earldom of Moray.[62] The question

[56] April 9, 1561, Throckmorton to Cecil, *ibid.*, pp. 55–56. The ambassador disliked the coming of Lord James; he feared that the Guises, who, he said, were all-powerful with Mary, would attempt to win Lord James over by offering him a Cardinal's hat, or failing that, would use force against him. He urged Elizabeth to forbid the trip, in vain. March 31, 1561, Throckmorton to Elizabeth, *ibid.*, pp. 41–45. [57] Leslie, *History of Scotland*, II, 454.
[58] April 23, 1561, Throckmorton to Cecil, *C.S.P., For., Eliz.*, IV, 75–76.
[59] *Ibid.*, p. 84.
[60] See his letter to Mary on June 10, 1561, in D. M. Rose, "Mary Queen of Scots and Her Brother," *Scottish Historical Review*, II (1905), 157–62.
[61] May 1, 1561, Throckmorton to Elizabeth, *C.S.P., For., Eliz.*, IV, 90–92.
[62] Leslie, *History of Scotland*, II, 454.

of the Treaty of Edinburgh likewise came up. Throckmorton had written Lord James and Mary on April 13, asking for ratification.[63] Mary told her brother that she would not ratify it till she returned to Scotland. Lord James informed Throckmorton of this. Treachery! But on May 1 the ambassador wrote Elizabeth that Mary had given him exactly the same answer.[64]

Mary also told Lord James, according to Throckmorton, that she wanted to dissolve the league between England and the Scots —no great revelation in view of Noailles's mission. She would try to get the Estates' consent for her marriage to a foreign prince. This was required of her by the Treaty of Haddington of 1548, the first French marriage agreement, signed in her name, and the commissioners she sent to Scotland after Francis's death had already promised in her name that she would not marry without seeking the advice of the Estates.[65] She did not think highly of the King of Denmark as a prospective suitor—but everyone knew that it was not the King of Denmark that Mary wanted to marry.

Now we come to three pieces of evidence which indicate very clearly that Mary did not reveal her secret intentions to her brother. She would not permit him to go to Nancy with her. Lord James opined, accurately enough, that this had something to do with the Spanish negotiations then going on. If Mary had taken her brother fully into her confidence, she would have permitted him to go with her.[66] Secondly, she said that she meant to return to Scotland by sea. She did, of course, but only after she had been refused a safe-conduct through England by Elizabeth. It seems likely that Mary was attempting, by this remark, to reduce English pressure for ratification of the Treaty of Edinburgh before she got home, by making it clear that she was not dependent on Eliza-

---

[63] C.S.P., For., Eliz., IV, 58.   [64] Ibid., pp. 90–92.
[65] February 26, 1561, Randolph to Cecil, C.S.P., Scot., I, 518–21.
[66] Some writers, notably Lang (History of Scotland, II, 102–3), have stated that Lord James did go to Nancy with Mary, basing their evidence on a letter written from that town by Mary on April 22, 1561 (in Labanoff, Recueil, I, 94). Henderson (Mary Queen of Scots, I, 157–59), demolishes this theory completely. Aside from the inherent improbability of Lord James's having told a lie which could be so easily exposed, if he were at Nancy on the twenty-second and at Paris on the twenty-third, given the usual condition of sixteenth-century roads, he must have made the journey on a broomstick.

beth's goodwill to get home. Finally, and most conclusively of all, she told Lord James that she cared as little for the friendship of France as for that of England. This statement speaks for itself.[67]

It seems quite clear, then, that Lord James had no secrets to betray. Nevertheless he was well satisfied with the result of the interview. Mary had been most agreeable, and it seemed almost certain that on her return home she would adopt his and Maitland's policy and be content to be governed by them; they would then all work together on the problem of the English succession. There was the danger of a Spanish marriage, to be sure, but Mary would require, and had promised to seek, the consent of the Estates in such a contingency; that bridge could be crossed when the time came.[68] Lord James stayed in Paris about ten days, evidently awaiting the commission of regency he thought Mary might confer on him. He was disappointed in this expectation, and on May 4 began his journey home.[69]

Lord James returned to Edinburgh via London, contrary to his sister's wishes, and saw Elizabeth and Cecil once more. Here, according to Camden, he advised Elizabeth to intercept Mary on her return home.[70] There is, however, no other evidence for such a maneuver on Lord James's part; even Bishop Leslie says that Lord James was planning for his sister's return.[71] Furthermore, such a move was completely inconsistent with his whole policy, the policy of Protestant domination and of union with England, for the latter aspect of which first Arran, now Mary, was to be the instrument.[72] After his conferences with his English allies, Lord James arrived in Edinburgh on May 29. His return, and his apparent success with his sister, ended the possibility of

---

[67] The preceding paragraphs are based on Throckmorton's letter of April 29, 1561, to Elizabeth, *C.S.P., For., Eliz.*, IV, 82–88.

[68] Lord James is said to have told the King of Navarre that he was opposed to the Spanish marriage. This is what one might well expect; such a marriage would have wrecked his policy. May 4, 1561, Throckmorton to Elizabeth, *ibid.*, pp. 96–97.

[69] April 23, May 4, 1561, Throckmorton to Cecil, *ibid.*, pp. 75–76, 97–98. The ambassador was delighted with Lord James's firmness in not having fallen victim to the blandishments of the Guises, and he urged his sovereign in the famous letter of April 29, 1561, to reward him liberally.

[70] Lang, *History of Scotland*, II, 98.   [71] Leslie, *History of Scotland*, II, 455.

[72] On this whole question see Fleming, *Mary Queen of Scots*, pp. 235–36.

a religious clash at this time.[73] So, too, did the moderation of the
political leaders of the Congregation. Bishop Leslie admits that,
despite the vehemence of Knox, the Protestant nobles exiled
few Catholics, jailed fewer, and executed none.[74]

The Convention of Estates which met in late May and early
June was dominated by the Congregation. It absolutely refused
to renew the ancient league with France.[75] It further undertook
to deal with a violently anti-Catholic petition presented by the
General Assembly of the Kirk, the tenor of which was that the
laws passed by Parliament on August 24 should be enforced, and
that "all places and monuments of idolatry should be destroyed." [76] The petition was approved—by some Catholics even,
according to Lord James, who on June 5 informed Cecil of all that
had gone on since his return.[77] Arran, Argyle, and Glencairn were
commissioned by the Estates to see to the west, and "Lord James
was appointed to the North, where he made such reformation as
nothing contented the Earl of Huntly," [78] a task which occupied
him from about the middle of June till the end of July.

Before he set out on this reforming expedition, Lord James
wrote a very important letter to Mary on June 10, a letter which,
taken together with his letter of August 6 to Elizabeth,[79] is completely inconsistent with the charge that he wished England to
prevent her return. It is a friendly letter, full of sound, if Protestant, advice, and is clearly an attempt to drive home once more

---

[73] Thomson, *Diurnal of Occurrents*, p. 64. Knox, *History*, II, 156–61. There was a
severe "Robin Hood" riot in Edinburgh in the summer, however, of which there
is an interesting account in Thomson, *Diurnal of Occurrents*, pp. 65–66. These
"Robin Hood" festivities had been forbidden by the government of Mary of
Guise in 1555 in the interests of order, but they were still popular among the
lower classes and were frequently begun by disaffected elements in the population—in this case, by the Edinburgh craftsmen. There is a good account of a
similar Festival of the "Abbot of Unreason" in Sir Walter Scott's novel, *The
Abbot*.   [74] Leslie, *History of Scotland*, II, 463.
[75] Knox, *History*, II, 166–67.
[76] The petition is in Knox, *ibid.*, pp. 161–64. The General Assembly was a meeting, held twice a year in this period, of all important Protestants, lay and clerical,
the purpose of which was to decide on all matters pertaining to the Kirk. The
meetings were frequently timed to coincide with those of the Estates or Parliament. Almost always, in matters which required action by the civil power, the
Assembly's desires were summarized in a petition addressed to that power, as in
this case.   [77] *C.S.P., For., Eliz.*, IV, 129–30.
[78] Knox, *History*, II, 167–68.   [79] See below, pp. 83–84.

the points he had made during his visit to France. "There seemeth to me, Madame, no thing so necessary for quieting of your realm and weal of your whole affairs as your majesty's own presence." She will, of course, take the advice of those that "have the fear of God in their heart," that is, the Protestant party. But if she found it necessary to remain away from home longer than she expected, she should send a commission of regency to some person or persons she could trust. This was really very necessary, it should be added, since owing to the inoperativeness of the Treaty of Edinburgh there was no legally constituted government in Scotland. The kingdom was being governed by the leaders of the Congregation, sitting as a council, on a day-to-day basis. "Some there be that unfeignedly desire your Grace's advancement, and will employ themselves faithfully thereto only for their conscience [sic] sake, . . . others for this cause and for natural affection: some for both these causes and farther because that their particular weal hinges wholly hereupon. . . . Others there be, I confess, of the flat contrary conditions in all points," i.e., conscienceless, intriguing Catholics. Above all, "for the love of God, press no matters of religion, not for any man's advice on the earth," for tumults will be the inevitable result. There are those, Lord James continues, who want her to attempt a drastic alteration in the religious *status quo:* those who hate Protestantism, those who have suffered financial loss—Lord James was firm in opposing any restitution to Catholic clerics for losses suffered—and those who found it profitable to fish in troubled waters, from shifty, troublemaking nobles down to rascally informers.[80]

This letter was a piece of special pleading, to be sure, but it also revealed Lord James's conception of how the situation in Scotland should be handled by Mary. It was written in the confident tone of a man who is fairly certain that his advice will be taken. As a matter of fact, he was justified in that confidence, for by June the possibility of a Spanish marriage for Mary had vanished for the time being. Mary therefore decided that she would definitely

[80] The letter is printed in full in the *Scottish Historical Review*, II (1905), 157–62.

adopt the alternative policy, that of conciliation of her own Protestant subjects and, through them, of Elizabeth.[81]

Mary returned to Paris from Lorraine in June and was met by
Throckmorton with yet another demand that she ratify the
Treaty of Edinburgh. Mary once more refused, saying that she
would do nothing till she got back to Scotland and consulted with
the Estates.[82] The problem of the Treaty of Edinburgh was becoming more and more acute, since the attitude toward it of one
of the three parties involved had materially changed. The English
position remained one of unyielding insistence on ratification;
Mary's, one of continued dislike. But the Scottish Protestants were
beginning to regard the treaty far less favorably than before. As
long as Francis II lived they had been as eager as Elizabeth that
Mary ratify it, for obvious reasons. But the death of Francis, which
upset their calculations on the Arran marriage, also caused them
to change their minds on the treaty. The difficulty lay in the clause
which required Francis and Mary to cease using the English
armorial bearings, for that clause contained the word *deinceps*—
"hereafter." This seemed unimportant at the time, when, it will
be remembered, the Congregation expected that Mary would
die soon and that Elizabeth would wed the next heir, Arran. But
all that was changed now, for Mary was a widow, and *deinceps*
assumed tremendous importance, for it implied that Mary was
excluded from the English succession even if Elizabeth should die
without issue. This was a question of the utmost seriousness for
Maitland and Lord James, since, as has been pointed out, their
only hope of a *modus vivendi* with Mary lay in their being able
to deliver on the question of the English succession.

The rigid English attitude on ratification of the treaty was serious, because it meant that many of Maitland's and Lord James's
followers, less convinced than they of the value of permanent
friendship with England, would turn once more to France. Maitland vainly urged that England counter this tendency by scatter-
ing a little largess.[83] His task was made no easier by a minatory

[81] Sir James Melville, *Memoirs of his own Life*, pp. 88–89.
[82] June 23, 1561, Throckmorton to Elizabeth, *C.S.P., For., Eliz.*, IV, 150–52.
[83] June 10, 1561, Maitland to Throckmorton, *ibid.*, p. 136.

letter from Elizabeth to the Scottish council—which returned a
soft answer—telling them to hurry up and get Mary to ratify the
treaty, or serious trouble might result.[84] Elizabeth hoped, by this
show of firmness, to compel the Congregation, for its own sake,
to force the Scottish Queen to ratify. Elizabeth and Cecil still
wanted a friendly, Protestant Scotland, however, as Randolph's
instructions of March 17 show.[85] Maitland and Lord James, on the
other hand, were hopeful of bringing the English to reason on the
deinceps clause by pointing out to them the fact that if Mary had
no hope of peacefully succeeding Elizabeth, she would certainly
follow a pro-French, pro-Catholic policy.[86] In August Maitland
and Lord James made their move, in the form of a letter by the
latter to Elizabeth on the sixth.

Lord James began this famous letter in characteristically Calvinistic fashion by expatiating on the goodness of God, who had
miraculously transmuted the age-old enmity of England and Scotland into friendship. There was nothing to impede its continuance,
"if the heads could so heartily be joined in love as be the members." There was "but one root from which any variance can
grow": the succession question. Lord James went on, "I wish to
God the Queen my sovereign lady had never by any advice taken
in head to pretend interest or acclaim any title to that your Majesty's realm . . . but now since on her part some thing has been
thought of it, and first mentioned when the two realms were in
war together . . . I fear that unless that root may be removed,
it shall ever breed unkindness betwixt you"—a true prophecy.
Elizabeth could not yield on this question and allow Mary to use
the English arms, of course; yet Mary would think it hard if her
claims were passed over altogether and forever. Then, with protests as to his lack of qualification to discuss such a great matter,
Lord James came to the point: "What if your Majesty's title did
remain untouched, as well for yourself as the issue of your body?
Inconvenient were it to provide that to the Queen my sovereign

---

[84] Knox, *History*, II, 175–79.
[85] S. Haynes, ed., *The Burghley Papers (1542–1570)*, pp. 366–68.
[86] This is definitely implied in Randolph's letter to Cecil of August 9, 1561, *C.S.P.*,
Scot., I, 542–43, and in Maitland's of August 10, 1561, Keith, *History*, III, 211–16.

her own place were reserved in the succession of the crown of England? Which your Majesty will pardon me if I take to be next by the law of all nations . . . and in the meantime this isle to be united in perpetual friendship." [87]

Here, then, was the solution proposed by Lord James and Maitland. Elizabeth should recognize Mary as her successor if she died without issue; in return, Mary would surrender all her claims to the English throne until such time, and presumably, would ratify a revised Treaty of Edinburgh. This would have solved all of Lord James's and Maitland's problems, for Mary would be constrained to follow their advice lest Elizabeth change her mind, and Elizabeth, too, must remain friendly to them in order to keep Mary in line.

Lord James enclosed his letter to Elizabeth in a letter to Cecil of the same date, asking him to deliver it to the Queen if he saw fit.[88] Cecil probably did not see fit. This proposal was not a new thing by any means; it had perhaps been broached as early as December 1560.[89] Lord James had certainly discussed it with Lord Robert Dudley on his return from France in May.[90] Cecil, writing to Throckmorton in July, indicated his dislike of the plan.[91] He did not say why, but his objections can easily be surmised. Such a move would encourage the discontented in England, who would look for better times under a new ruler; it would also make the Scots far more difficult to handle. The Secretary reasoned that Maitland and Lord James could not do without English friendship anyway. There was no need to give up such a valuable card as the succession just yet in return for the ratification, which the Congregation was committed to deliver in any case.

No answer was returned to Lord James's letter, or to any of the earlier moves on the succession question, and meanwhile the time for Mary's return was approaching. By this time Elizabeth and Cecil did not want Mary to come home without having ratified the Treaty of Edinburgh, as was made clear by Elizabeth's letter

[87] C.S.P., Scot., I, 540–41.   [88] Ibid., p. 541.
[89] See Maitland's letter to Cecil on February 26, 1561, ibid., pp. 516–18. Also Fleming, Mary Queen of Scots, p. 288.
[90] October 7, 1561, Lord James to Lord Robert Dudley, C.S.P., Scot., I, 557–58.
[91] C.S.P., For., Eliz., IV, 187.

to Randolph on July 1.[92] When Mary asked for a safe-conduct through England on her way home, Elizabeth angrily refused. Not until it became evident that Mary was going anyway was the safe-conduct sent, and then it was too late: Mary had already left.[93] Of the Scottish leaders, Maitland was frankly worried. He feared that if Mary came home before a definite agreement between her and Elizabeth was reached, "wonderful tragedies" would ensue: Mary would do her best to ruin Protestantism.[94] Maitland's letters in August also indicate a very strong feeling of fear for himself if Mary returned before an agreement with England was reached. This feeling was intensified by a letter Mary wrote him on June 29, reproaching him for his dealings with England; he must prove loyal to her, she said, if he was to be trusted by her.[95] On August 9 Randolph reported to Cecil that Maitland wished Mary were "stayed" for a time, at least till an agreement could be reached.[96]

In the same letter Randolph also stated that Knox and the other Protestant zealots still regarded Mary's homecoming with aversion, which is by no means surprising. What is surprising is that Lord James was classed with Maitland as wishing that Mary were "stayed" for a while, for this was almost certainly not Lord James's view. He certainly felt, as did Maitland, that it would be necessary to have an agreement between Mary and Elizabeth soon, and before Mary's return if possible: hence his letter of August 6. Randolph evidently interpreted this attitude to mean that Lord James wanted Mary "stayed" until an agreement was reached. But Lord James saw—as Maitland, perhaps misled by his personal fears, did not—that negotiations for an agreement, and Anglo-Scottish amity, would not automatically end as soon as Mary set foot on Scottish soil. He had doubtless surmised the failure of the Spanish marriage negotiations he had perceived to be going on in April, when he was in France, and he knew that, at the moment, Mary had no choice, were she to come home, but to rely

92 *Ibid.*, pp. 166–67.   93 *C.S.P., Scot.*, I, 545.
94 Fleming, *Mary Queen of Scots*, pp. 250–52. See also August 10, 1561, Maitland to Cecil, in Keith, *History*, III, 211–16.
95 *C.S.P., For., Eliz.*, IV, 161.   96 *C.S.P., Scot.*, I, 542–43.

on Maitland and himself. His conviction was strengthened by the fact that on July 13 Mary had written to him, entrusting him with a matter of justice—a small affair, but a sign of confidence.[97] It must be conceded that Maitland's pessimistic prediction that Mary would attempt to subvert Protestantism and wreck the English alliance turned out to be accurate, but she tried this only after he and Lord James had failed to deliver the English succession to her, as we shall see.

The theory that Lord James wanted his sister delayed rests on Randolph's letter of August 9, on the highly suspect story of Camden in regard to Lord James's dealings in London in May, and on some statements by Cecil concerning the attitude of the Scottish Protestants in general. While accurate enough in regard to Maitland, Cecil's statements did not apply to Lord James. Throckmorton, at least, did not think so: on July 26 he wrote Cecil that Lord James, while in France, had done his best to persuade his sister to come home. "If he be now of another mind, I know not what he meaneth." [98] Against this theory stands also the evidence of Lord James's own letters to Mary and Elizabeth and of the results of his visit to France, which he obviously considered to be highly successful. It is clear that Lord James was not worried about Mary's return.

The object of all this concern was meanwhile preparing to leave her beloved France—forever as it turned out. Since the beginning of the year she had had much opportunity to use her very considerable diplomatic skill, fending off the repeated English requests for ratification of the Treaty of Edinburgh—first on one ground, then on another, and finally on the basis that she must return home first and consult with her Estates—yet never allowing the English a real opening through which to attack her.[99] On August 14 Mary bade farewell to France and set sail, accompanied by her four Marys (her ladies in waiting, all named Mary, who had been with her throughout her stay in France), three of her Guise uncles, and various and sundry other Frenchmen, including

[97] *C.S.P., For., Eliz.*, IV, 177.   [98] *Ibid.*, pp. 204–6.
[99] See, for instance, Throckmorton's letters of June 23 and July 26, 1561, *ibid.*, pp. 150–52, 198–204.

the author Brantôme. On the nineteenth, a gloomy day, her ships dropped anchor at Leith. "The very face of heaven . . . did manifestly speak what comfort was brought to this country with her, to wit, sorrow, dolor, darkness, and all impiety." Thus Knox.[100] A new phase in Scottish history was about to begin.

[100] Knox, *History*, II, 268–69.

CHAPTER IV

The First Year of Mary's Rule

IT BECAME APPARENT very shortly after Mary's arrival in Scotland that Lord James had correctly foreseen her course of action. On September 6, some eighteen days after she landed, the Queen selected her council. Of its seventeen members, four were Catholics, Huntly being the most powerful. The others were Protestants, and virtually all the important leaders of the Congregation were included.[1] The make-up of this council, which Maitland and Lord James dominated, showed very clearly that Mary planned to be advised by them. Randolph wrote to Throckmorton on August 26 that these two stood "in highest credit" with the Queen.[2]

The immediate problem was the religious one, of course, and it flared up on the first Sunday after Mary's return, on August 24. Mary held a private Mass that day in the chapel of her palace at Holyrood. The Protestant zealots were very angry; they attempted to rush the chapel and seize the "idolator priest." They were met by a solitary figure who barred the door—Lord James. It had been part of his bargain with his sister that she should be able to hear Mass privately, and he meant to keep his word, although the excuse he gave to his coreligionists at this moment was that he was there to prevent any Scot from attending Mass. And so "the godly departed with great grief of heart," since they dared not gainsay "the man whom all the godly did most reverence."[3]

[1] *The Register of the Privy Council of Scotland*, I, 158–61.
[2] *C.S.P., For., Eliz.*, IV, 277–79.
[3] This account is taken from John Knox, *History of the Reformation in Scotland*, II, 270–71.

This episode convinced Mary and her brother that something would have to be done very quickly about the religious question; so a proclamation was hastily drafted and made public on the following day. The gist of this document was that it would be unwise to attempt to solve the religious problem prematurely; therefore, no one was to "make alteration or innovation of the state of religion, or attempt any thing against the form which her Majesty found publicly and universally standing at her Majesty's arrival in this her Realm (i.e., Protestantism), under the pain of death," until the Estates settled the question.[4] This proclamation, while seemingly an important victory for Protestantism, was really a double-edged weapon. Protestantism, to be sure, was recognized, and given some official status, but at the same time the proclamation indicated very plainly that Mary thought the August Parliament to have been illegal, and hence Protestantism officially existed on royal sufferance only. This was to have repercussions eventually, as we shall see.

The attitude of Lord James and Maitland to Mary was most displeasing to Knox and the zealots, who wanted no compromise with iniquity. The split between the two branches of the Protestant party, which was already serious before Mary's return, now began to come into the open. On August 31 Knox preached a violent sermon in which he stated "that one Mass was more fearful to him than if ten thousand armed enemies were landed in any part of the Realm of purpose to suppress the whole religion."[5] Two days later, on Mary's official entry into Edinburgh, only the intervention of Huntly prevented the burning in effigy of a priest elevating the Host; the festivities had a sufficiently Protestant flavor as it was.[6] Lord James and Maitland were badly worried; in an attempt to restrain their overzealous ally, who might, if he continued, stir up another civil war or exasperate Mary into a pro-Catholic policy,[7] they arranged an interview between him and Mary: perhaps she could talk Knox around.

---

[4] Ibid., pp. 272–73.   [5] Ibid., p. 276.
[6] D. H. Fleming, Mary Queen of Scots, pp. 255–56.
[7] On this point see Randolph's letters of August 26, September 7, September 24, and October 12, 1561, C.S.P., For., Eliz., IV, 277–79, 295–96; C.S.P., Scot., I, 551–52, 555–57.

It must have been quite a meeting. Knox has left us a description of it, in which he is represented as having done most of the talking, which is probably true enough.[8] The discussion has become so famous that it would be superfluous to summarize it here. It did absolutely no good, as Lord James, who was the only other person present, must have realized. If anything, it did harm, since it left the two principals farther apart and more suspicious of each other than ever, and since it strengthened Knox's belief that Lord James and his fellows were betraying the cause out of a desire for worldly advancement. Randolph's attempts to convince Knox and his associates that Lord James was really acting in the best interests of Protestantism had no success.[9]

Knox was not the only problem Lord James had on his hands in the religious field. During September he had an altercation with Huntly, who boasted that, if the Queen so wished, he could raise the Mass "in three shires." Lord James somewhat acidly doubted his ability to do so.[10] Further trouble came from the Edinburgh town council, which on October 2 ordered all "monks, friars, priests, nuns, adulterers, fornicators, and all such filthy persons" to get out of town in twenty-four hours.[11] Mary was incensed, deposed the town officials, and ordered new ones chosen in their places. Knox laid the whole blame for this municipal *coup d'état*, of which he thoroughly disapproved, on the shoulders of Maitland and Lord James.[12] Mary's High Mass on All Saints' Day, November 1, touched off another acrimonious dispute between the preachers and the Protestant lords, which resulted in an agreement to write to Calvin on the question of the propriety of preventing monarchical idolatry by force. Nothing ever came of this, however.[13]

[8] Knox, *History*, II, 277–86.
[9] November 11, 1561, Randolph to Cecil, *C.S.P., Scot.*, I, 568–70.
[10] September 24, 1561, Randolph to Cecil, *ibid.*, pp. 555–57.
[11] Fleming, *Mary Queen of Scots*, pp. 52–53.
[12] October 7, 1561, Knox to Cecil, *C.S.P., For., Eliz.*, IV, 352–53. Knox had not entirely lost faith in Lord James, who was described by him in a letter to Calvin on October 24 as the only man at court who still opposed impiety; but even he, Knox lamented, would not take any active steps against the prevalent evils. A. Teulet, ed., *Relations politiques de la France et de l'Espagne avec l'Ecosse au XVIe siècle*, II, 172–73.
[13] Knox, *History*, II, 291–92. There is considerable mystery surrounding the

Enough has been said to indicate how serious the rift between the court party and the preachers was becoming. The situation was made worse by the action taken on the question of Church property. It will be recalled that Knox, in the Book of Discipline, had demanded that most of the property of the Catholic Church should be turned over to the Kirk. At the General Assembly of December, 1561, this demand was renewed. Maitland took the lead in opposing it, but the court party was willing to sponsor a request to the Queen that she make some provision for the Protestant ministers, many of whom had no visible means of subsistence.[14] During the winter the council came to a series of decisions. One third of the incomes of the Catholic clergy was allotted to the royal treasury; the clerics were to keep the remainder. Part of this revenue would be spent on the ministers, part on the ordinary expenses of government. The government appointed collectors, who were responsible to the Comptroller, Wishart of Pitarrow; these men collected all the revenues of the benefices, and then handed back two thirds to the holder. The dividing of the third between government and Kirk was entrusted to a solidly Protestant six-man committee including Lord James. This settlement of the property question survived, with few changes, till 1587.[15]

From the fiscal point of view this arrangement did not work very well. The amount received by the government almost tripled in the years 1562–1565—it decreased thereafter—but the deficit continued to mount. The share of the clergy seems never to have been more than half the value of the amount available for distribution, and was generally much less. Much of the remainder went

---

question of the letter to Calvin; it is discussed by T. F. Henderson (*Mary Queen of Scots*, I, 188–90).

[14] D. Calderwood, *The History of the Kirk of Scotland*, II, 159–61. The split between the lords and the preachers was sharply pointed up at this meeting when some of the former unsuccessfully raised the question of the legality of holding a General Assembly without the sovereign's consent.

[15] I. F. Grant, *The Social and Economic Development of Scotland before 1603*, p. 236. For details of the settlement, see *Register of Privy Council*, I, 192–94, 196–97, 199–206; Knox, *History*, II, 310. On this whole question see G. Donaldson, ed., *Accounts of the Collectors of Thirds of Benefices 1561–1572*, especially the introduction.

in pensions and in remission of payment of the thirds to various favored benefice holders, including Lord James.[16] Knox tells us that the ministers did not get enough to live on; nevertheless the money thus obtained was vital to them, as is shown by the fact that in 1565, when the Kirk received no funds from the thirds, the General Assembly had to threaten those ministers who were leaving their posts for more remunerative employment.[17] Knox, of course, detested the settlement, which so blasted his hopes. "I am assured," he said, "that the Spirit of God is not the author of it, for first I see two parts freely given to the Devil, and the third must be divided betwixt God and the Devil: well, bear witness to me . . . ere it be long the Devil shall have three parts of the third; and judge you then, what God's portion shall be." [18] Nevertheless, the settlement was not politically unfair, and the Protestants had made one very substantial gain: they had extracted from Mary a semi-official recognition of the new religion, since the state was now paying the stipends of the ministers.

Closely allied to this question was that of the feuing of Church lands. Lord James and his friends realized that they must settle this problem in a manner favorable to the nobility, as a reward for past support and to keep their party together. So, on September 10, 1561, it was forbidden to all to apply to Rome for confirmation of feu charters of Church lands acquired since March 6, 1559, on the ground that it was a waste of money to do so.[19] On December 22 it was declared that all feus made since March 1559 were to be valid until Whitsuntide of 1563—later extended to 1564—and that in the meantime Parliament would act.[20] In the Parliament of December 1564 Mary was given the power to confirm feu charters; the royal assent was declared to be as valid as that of the Pope had been. All feus made since March 1559 required this assent.[21] It was given only for a fee, of course; between 1564 and 1566 the Scottish treasury profited to the extent of

---

[16] R. Keith, *The History of the Affairs of Church and State in Scotland*, III, 370-85. Andrew Lang, *John Knox and the Reformation*, p. 210. Donaldson, *Accounts of Collectors*, Introduction, pp. xxiv-xxvi.
[17] Knox, *History*, II, 311, 515. Calderwood, *History of the Kirk*, II, 294-310.
[18] Knox, *History*, II, 310.   [19] *Register of Privy Council*, I, 162-63.
[20] *Ibid.*, pp. 192, 234-35.   [21] *The Acts of the Parliament of Scotland*, II, 545.

£9,104.[22] Thus did Lord James pay his debts to his party and secure the continued loyalty of many of its members to Protestantism. His action, much as one regrets to say it, probably had far more to do with the final success of the new religion than the preaching of Knox.[23]

Other than the religious question, Lord James's most serious concern in the latter months of 1561 was the problem of the Borders. For generations this area had been the home of outlaws, hardy souls who lived by raiding in England. Some members of practically every Border family lived in this way, a situation which made the establishment of law and order next to impossible.[24] This did not matter so much while England was regarded as the national enemy, but now it mattered a great deal, since the policy of the government was one of friendship with England. Lord James decided that the time had come to act.

On November 14, 1561, Lord James set out for Jedburgh, armed with a commission from the council which gave him *carte blanche* to do whatever he wished.[25] What he wished was to use force, which he did; a large number of thieves were caught and hanged out of hand.[26] He also compelled a number of the leading Borderers to sign an agreement which pledged them to stand surety for the production of criminals at future Border courts. If a signer had a criminal within his grasp and failed to capture him, he was liable for him.[27] This, Lord James judged, would mean either that criminals would henceforth be produced, or that the government could collect a fine from the men responsible for them. Furthermore, some of the Borderers were haled before the Privy Council on December 4 and forced to admit their negligence in pursuing thieves.[28] Lord James also inaugurated a policy of

[22] Grant, *Social and Economic Development*, p. 282. Many nobles chose to risk the lack of royal confirmation rather than pay up. *Ibid.*, pp. 283–84.
[23] On the whole problem of feu farming and Church lands see the works cited above, Chapter I, notes 27 and 28.
[24] The Scots were not the only culprits. For conditions in the English Border area, see September 12, 1559, Sadler to Cecil, *The State Papers and Letters of Sir Ralph Sadler*, I, 441–44.
[25] November 11, 1561, Randolph to Cecil, *C.S.P., Scot.*, I, 568–70. *Register of Privy Council*, I, 184–87. [26] Knox, *History*, II, 292–93.
[27] A. I. Cameron and R. S. Rait, eds., *The Warrender Papers*, I, 32–35.
[28] *Register of Privy Council*, I, 188.

cooperation with the English Border Wardens which led in 1563 to a comprehensive agreement on methods of law enforcement in this area.[29]

Thus was begun the cleaning up of the Borders, and to Lord James belongs the credit for being the first seriously to tackle a problem which had long cried for settlement and which required long years of weary effort before completion. Lord James did not live to see the day; right up to his death, Border lawlessness plagued him. It was no accident that on the day after his assassination his Border enemies raided England two thousand strong, a deed they would not have dared to do had he still been alive.[30]

More important than Border problems in Anglo-Scottish relations at this time, however, was the succession question. On September 1 Maitland, now in charge of Scottish foreign relations, was sent to England, ostensibly to notify Elizabeth of Mary's safe arrival and of her desire to live in amity with her cousin, but really to discuss this issue. The Scottish position was that laid down by Lord James in his letter of August 6; Maitland carried with him a letter to Cecil from his colleague which urged that this proposal be followed.[31] During this period, however, Lord James was not seriously involved in foreign affairs. He was content to trust the English negotiations to Maitland, and limited himself to writing occasional letters to Cecil and others in England, assuring them that Maitland spoke for him and urging them to adopt Maitland's suggestions.

Shortly after Maitland started for England, an envoy from Elizabeth, Sir Peter Mewtas, was making his way north to demand ratification of the Treaty of Edinburgh. Neither had much success. Mary treated Mewtas with courtesy, having been somewhat mollified by Elizabeth's belated *volte-face* on the safe-conduct,[32] but she refused to ratify the treaty and declared that it was neces-

---

[29] December 7, 1561, Randolph to Cecil, *C.S.P., Scot.*, I, 573–78. For the agreement, see P. Ridpath, *The Border History of England and Scotland*, pp. 609–14.
[30] Andrew Lang, *A History of Scotland from the Roman Occupation*, II, 226–27.
[31] It is dated September 1, 1561. *C.S.P., Scot.*, I, 548.
[32] August 26, 1561, Randolph to Throckmorton, *ibid.*, pp. 547–48.

sary to revise it before she would consider ratification.[33] Maitland fared no better. He pleaded lack of instructions when Elizabeth pressed him on the matter of ratification, but he could get nowhere on the succession question. Curiously enough, Elizabeth did not question Mary's legal right to succeed her. She based her whole case on political expediency and personal motives. If she declared Mary her successor, all the discontented in England would turn to Mary, probably raise a rebellion, as had happened in Mary Tudor's day, or even attempt to assassinate her. "This desire is without an example, to require me in my own life to set my winding-sheet before my eye . . . so long as I live I shall be Queen of England; when I am dead, they shall succeed that has most right. If the Queen your sovereign be that person, I shall never hurt her. . . ." [34] This remained Elizabeth's attitude to the succession question to the day of her death. As related to Maitland, it was largely a matter of personal motives, but, as pointed out in a previous chapter, there were also good political reasons for not recognizing Mary. Elizabeth did make one concession to Maitland: she agreed to consider a revision by commissioners of the *deinceps* clause of the Treaty of Edinburgh, but she changed her mind about this shortly afterward.

Matters having reached something of an impasse, Maitland, after returning home, began to press an idea which he had toyed with and mentioned somewhat tentatively while in England. This was the proposal that the two queens should meet face to face; at such a conference it would be possible to iron out all difficulties. Maitland spent the next few months jockeying for position. He wanted the proposal for the interview to come from England or, at the very least, to commit Cecil to the scheme before any formal proposal was made.[35] But Cecil and Elizabeth were not to

[33] October, 1561, Mary's reply to Elizabeth, A. Labanoff, ed., *Recueil des lettres de Marie Stuart*, I, 115–16.
[34] Maitland's account of this conversation, from which this quotation is drawn, is printed in J. H. Pollen, ed., *A Letter from Mary Queen of Scots to the Duke of Guise*, pp. 37–45.
[35] See October 7, 1561, Maitland to Cecil, *C.S.P., For., Eliz.*, IV, 351–52; October 24, 1561, Randolph to Cecil, *C.S.P., Scot.*, I, 561–64.

be caught. On November 23 Elizabeth wrote to Mary indicating that she was willing to discuss a revision of the treaty only through the normal diplomatic channels.[36] This forced Maitland into the open. During December he bombarded Cecil with letters asking for the latter's cooperation in framing a reply to this letter of Elizabeth's, indicating that Mary would put forward an official request on the succession question, and would also ask for an interview with Elizabeth. How would Elizabeth react? The question of the interview was delicate. Mary must not be snubbed, or the amity would vanish.[37]

Among the arguments used by Maitland in behalf of the interview was the possibility that Elizabeth might convert Mary to Protestantism. This, of course, would strengthen the Scottish hand enormously in the negotiations on the succession question. On December 7 Randolph wrote that Maitland and Lord James both felt that Elizabeth could turn the trick, if only the two queens could meet.[38] Maitland had prepared the ground for this move very carefully, having mentioned Mary's convertibility as early as October 25.[39] He may well have been sincere in this belief. Mary had been following a Protestant policy since her return to Scotland. Might she not become an Anglican, if some agreement on the momentous succession question could be reached? Lord James thought so, too; he gave Mary a pamphlet on the Colloquy at Poissy which Randolph had given him, evidently hoping she would see the light.[40] This hope of Maitland and Lord James helps to explain their irritation with Knox, whose constant railing at the Queen's idolatry was not calculated to speed Mary's conversion, and who was infuriated by the rumor that Mary might become an Anglican. Knox considered Anglicans little better than Papists, and preached a violent sermon against them.[41] Good relations with England could not be promoted thus.

Cecil was too wary to commit himself on the question of the

[36] *C.S.P., For., Eliz.*, IV, 410–11.
[37] *C.S.P., Scot.*, I, 572–73, 581. S. Haynes, ed., *The Burghley Papers* (1542–1570), pp. 375–76.   [38] *C.S.P., Scot.*, I, 573–78.   [39] *C.S.P., For., Eliz.*, IV, 379.
[40] October 24, 1561, Randolph to Cecil, *C.S.P., Scot.*, I, 561–64. As early as October 7 Lord James was writing hopefully to Cecil of Mary's possible Protestant leanings. *Ibid.*, p. 558.   [41] February 12, 1562, Randolph to Cecil, *ibid.*, pp. 602–3.

interview; Maitland's letters went unanswered. So the Secretary reluctantly decided that he would have to go ahead without a previous commitment by England. On January 5, 1562, Mary wrote a letter to Elizabeth which Maitland undoubtedly drafted. It was a skillful piece of work. Elizabeth's refusal to handle the problem of the Treaty of Edinburgh by commissioners, Mary wrote, was an infallible sign that she preferred a face-to-face discussion. The treaty was obnoxious to Mary on account of the question of her rights in the succession; it was unjust that "a matter of so great consequence is wrapped up in obscure terms." She would do anything reasonable required by the treaty, provided it was revised on this point. The easiest way to handle all this was clearly by means of a personal interview, at which Elizabeth could see more plainly than ever how much Mary loved her.[42]

Mary and Maitland had to wait three months for an answer, and in the meantime interesting things were going on in Scotland. The Queen decided to reward Lord James for his services, and on January 30, 1562, granted her brother the coveted earldom of Moray.[43] This gift remained a secret, however, for the moment, probably so as not to provoke Huntly, who had held the earldom off and on since the death of the previous earl, likewise a royal bastard, in 1544. On February 7 Lord James received instead the title of Earl of Mar and some of the lands of that earldom.[44] This title had been vacant for some time and was claimed by Lord Erskine—to whom it rightfully belonged—as head of the Erskine family. Lord James was Erskine's nephew. Eventually, after Lord James had become Earl of Moray, Erskine received the earldom of Mar, but Lord James seems to have retained some of its lands.[45]

The grant of the earldom of Mar was a wedding present. On February 8 Lord James married Agnes Keith, daughter of the Earl Marischal; he had been courting her for some time.[46] The ceremony was performed by Knox in St. Giles' Church, Edinburgh,

[42] Labanoff, *Recueil*, I, 123–27.
[43] J. Robertson, ed., *Antiquities of the Shires of Aberdeen and Banff*, IV, 742.
[44] *Ibid.*, pp. 743–44.   [45] See the charter of December 22, 1564, *ibid.*, II, 87–93.
[46] Randolph, who was something of a gossip, described the various love affairs going on at court, including this one, in his letter to Cecil on October 24, 1561, *C.S.P., Scot.*, I, 561–64.

and an enormous banquet followed at the Abbey of Holyrood, of which Lord Robert Stewart, half-brother of Lord James, was Commendator. The magnificence of the festivities displeased Knox, who publicly admonished Lord James to continue zealous for Protestantism, for "if hereafter ye shall be found fainter than . . . ye were before, it will be said that your wife hath changed your nature." [47]

Agnes, Countess of Moray, is a rather shady figure. She took little part in the politics of her day as long as Lord James was alive, although after his death she and her second husband, the Earl of Argyle, were prominent for a while owing to their fierce efforts to retain some of Mary's jewels, which Lord James had given her when he was Regent.[48] She was a forceful and shrewd lady and made Lord James an excellent wife; the marriage was a happy one. Lord James was one of the few men in Scottish public life in his day—Maitland was another—who was not given to wenching and about whose head no domestic scandal ever broke. Countess Agnes bore him three children; only two survived. The elder, Elizabeth, married James Stewart of Doun in 1580; he acquired his father-in-law's title and became famous in popular legend as the "bonny Earl o' Moray." The younger daughter, Margaret, married Francis, Earl of Errol.[49]

A month or so after Lord James's wedding the court was half alarmed, half amused over the Arran-Bothwell affair. As this business had considerable political significance and is interesting

---

[47] Knox, *History*, II, 313-15. February 12, 1562, Randolph to Cecil, *C.S.P., Scot.*, I, 602-3. There is an unpleasant side to this transaction. In his youth Lord James had been betrothed to the heiress of the Earl of Buchan and on the strength of this had managed to get most of the lands of that earldom into his own hands. G. Chalmers, *The Life of Mary Queen of Scots*, II, 421-23. Later in the year 1562 the lady married his half-brother, Robert Douglas, son of the Laird of Lochleven. This was the occasion of an angry letter from Lord James to his mother, in which he claimed to be dishonored by this marriage, although he admitted that obviously he could not marry the girl himself. He also refused to give up the Buchan lands he held. C. Innes, ed., *Registrum Honoris de Morton*, I, 9-10. Robert Douglas eventually became Earl of Buchan and a loyal supporter of Lord James; possibly the latter made some property adjustment with him. It is a pity that our knowledge of Lord James's transactions in real estate is so fragmentary, since he was obviously a gifted, and sometimes unscrupulous, operator in this field.　　　　　[48] Lang, *History of Scotland*, II, 250-51.
[49] Chalmers, *Mary Queen of Scots*, II, 426.

in portraying—in somewhat extreme form—the state of mind and the behavior of the Scottish nobility, it deserves to be recounted in some detail.

The Hamiltons had not been happy since the Queen's return. Mary trusted neither father nor son, and Lord James and Maitland, who had no use for them politically now, encouraged Mary's suspicions. Arran joined the Protestant extremists as a result, and put himself under the political tutelage of Knox.[50] The Hamiltons were touched in their most sensitive spot, the pocketbook, by the solution to the question of clerical property.[51] Rumors began to spread that they might revolt, and Mary decided to provide herself with a bodyguard.[52] In February 1562 Randolph wrote that Arran was behaving peculiarly.[53] In retrospect this looks like a typical English understatement.

The other character in the strange tragicomedy about to take place is widely known to readers of romance, for in five short years James Hepburn, Earl of Bothwell, was to drag his Queen into the mire and to be the key figure in a great historical romance and riddle. But by 1562 nothing in Bothwell's career foreshadowed what was to come. This Earl was simply a Border ruffian, a type only too common in Scotland, with the courage, cleverness, and complete lack of political intelligence of his class. He was constantly in debt, and a roisterer and wencher of the worst sort. His chief political principle was the typical Borderer's loathing of England, which was probably the consideration that kept him unflinchingly loyal to Mary of Guise during the civil war. As a result of his ambushing of Cockburn of Ormiston [54] he had become involved in a deadly feud with Arran. Their mutual fondness was not increased by an incident in December 1561, when Bothwell and Mary's uncle, the Marquis d'Elbœuf, a kindred spirit, paid a public and somewhat drunken visit to the house of an Edinburgh burgess whose daughter was reputed to be Arran's mistress. A

---

[50] Knox, *History*, II, 273–75.
[51] January 15, 1562, Randolph to Cecil, *C.S.P., Scot.*, I, 590–93.
[52] Knox, *History*, II, 293–94. December 7, 1561, Randolph to Cecil, *C.S.P., Scot.*, I, 573–78.
[53] *Ibid.*, pp. 604–7.   [54] See above, p. 53.

street fight almost ensued and was prevented only by the intervention of Lord James and Huntly.[55]

The last thing that anyone in Scotland expected was that Bothwell should reconcile himself with Arran. Yet this was exactly what happened. In March, 1562, Bothwell went to Knox, who, he knew, was close to Arran and to whose friendship he had a claim owing to the feudal relationship of the forebears of the two men. Bothwell told Knox that he could not afford to keep the feud going any longer; he was short of funds, and Arran's hostility made it necessary for him to keep a large body of retainers with him at all times. Knox, out of feudal loyalty to the Hepburns, promised to see what he could do. There was a political motive too: Bothwell, who was a Protestant, might follow Knox's lead in future, as Arran was doing. Arran was persuaded, not without difficulty, to agree. From bitter enemies the ill-assorted pair suddenly became fast friends.[56]

This was passing strange, but it was as nothing compared to what was to come. On March 27, four days after the reconciliation, Arran burst into Knox's study in great agitation. Bothwell, he said, had treasonably betrayed him. He had proposed that he and Arran should imprison the Queen in Dumbarton Castle, which was then in Hamilton hands, murder Lord James and Maitland, and rule the kingdom themselves. He, Arran, was determined to notify Mary, so that he could not be accused of treason. Given Bothwell's character, such a story was not in itself impossible. But it was apparent to Knox that Arran was definitely deranged, and he did his best to persuade Arran to forget about the whole business. The miserable Earl would not take this advice, wrote a letter to Mary, and fled to his father's house at Kinneil, whence he wrote to Lord James. Shortly thereafter both Arran and Bothwell were taken into custody while Mary decided what to do.[57]

It was perfectly obvious that Arran was mad. He spoke of being bewitched and asserted that he was Mary's husband.[58] Under the

[55] Knox, *History*, II, 315, 316–21.   [56] *Ibid.*, pp. 322–26.
[57] G. Buchanan, *The History of Scotland*, II, 455. Knox, *History*, II, 326–29. April 7, 1562, Randolph to Cecil, *C.S.P., For., Eliz.*, IV, 583–85.
[58] Knox, *History*, II, 329.

circumstances it was only just to dismiss the charge against Bothwell. But Lord James did not think in these terms. Although he
had formerly patched up his quarrels with Bothwell at Mary's request,[59] Lord James did not like him and regarded him as a political danger. Bothwell's hatred of England might lead him to
attempt to wreck Lord James's Border policy. Here was an opportunity to keep him out of mischief for a while. Mary was persuaded, and so Bothwell was clapped into Edinburgh Castle,
whence he escaped in August 1562. He was outlawed in November for failure to surrender himself; eventually he made his way
to France, whence he reappeared in Scotland during the crisis of
1565, as we shall see.[60]

Now, too, was the time to break the power of the Hamiltons:
so thought Mary and her brother. Arran was confined in Edinburgh Castle. The unhappy Earl never recovered his wits; he long
outlived all the other characters in this story and died in 1609. On
the father was visited the sin of the son: Châtelherault was forgiven for whatever part he might have played in the "conspiracy,"
but he was forced to surrender Dumbarton Castle to the Queen.[61]
The affair was a political blessing to Mary and Lord James, for
the Hamiltons' influence and usefulness in intrigue was based on
their proximity to the throne; now their candidate was a hopeless
lunatic. Lord James had got two birds with one stone, and his
position was stronger than ever.

At the height of the excitement over Arran's escapade the long-
expected English answer on the interview arrived in Edinburgh:
Elizabeth was willing, in principle, to meet Mary. The latter was
delighted, Randolph reported.[62] In connection with the interview

---

[59] October 12, 1561, Randolph to Cecil, *C.S.P., For., Eliz.*, IV, 295–96. *Register
of Privy Council*, I, 183–84. R. Gore-Browne, *Lord Bothwell and Mary Queen of
Scots*, pp. 123–25.
[60] Calderwood, *History of the Kirk*, II, 200–201. Buchanan, *History*, II, 465. It is
possible that Lord James's "raid" on Hawick in July 1562, when he seized about
fifty malefactors, was undertaken partly in order to capture some of Bothwell's
lawless Border followers, or at least to frighten them into inactivity. Randolph's letter of July 8, 1562, to Cecil hints as much. *C.S.P., Scot.*, I, 637–38.
[61] T. Thomson, ed., *A Diurnal of Remarkable Occurrents that Have Passed
within the Country of Scotland*, p. 72.
[62] March 31, 1562, Randolph to Cecil, *C.S.P., For., Eliz.*, IV, 574–77.

the Arran affair must have come as a great relief to Maitland and Lord James. Elizabeth might well have demanded that Mary marry Arran in return for a satisfactory settlement of the succession question, and the Scots would have found such a request very embarrassing. Nobody—the Hamiltons excepted—wanted Mary to wed Arran, but since the Protestant party had pressed him on Elizabeth as a suitable husband, they could not have refused to urge him on Mary now without offering a mortal insult to Elizabeth. The Earl's madness, however, struck this card from Cecil's hand.

On May 19, after some delay, probably caused by the aftermath of the Arran business, the Scottish Council gave its official consent to the proposed interview.[63] Maitland was sent to London to arrange the details of the meeting. The Scottish Protestants, Randolph reported, were delighted and were hopeful that Elizabeth would be able to convert Mary to Protestantism. Lord James, the ambassador went on, was especially favorable to the interview, although he was concerned about the state of affairs in France, and although he regretted that as yet he could detect no change in his sister's religious views. He—Lord James—hoped that Elizabeth would put religion above all other considerations during the meeting.[64]

Maitland did not have an easy time in London. English opinion was divided; many of the council opposed the interview on account of the situation in France, where religious strife had actually broken out.[65] If Elizabeth met the niece of the Duke of Guise while that gentleman was engaged in the extermination of the Huguenots, the latter would obviously think that Elizabeth had abandoned them, and this would have a serious bearing on the future of Continental Protestantism, and, consequently, on that of Elizabeth herself. The Queen was impressed by these arguments,

[63] *Register of Privy Council*, I, 206.
[64] June 17, 1562, Randolph to Cecil, *C.S.P., For., Eliz.*, V, 100–102.
[65] April 17, 1562, Throckmorton to Cecil, *ibid.*, IV, 608–10. June 10, 1562, Maitland to Mary, in M. Philippson, *Histoire du règne de Marie Stuart*, III, 455–58. June 14, Sir H. Sidney to Throckmorton, *C.S.P., For., Eliz.*, V, 93. The English Council's opinion that a meeting would be unwise was given on June 20. Keith, *History*, III, 328–29.

but in late June and early July it looked as though the French factions might compose their differences. So, on July 11, Maitland set out for home in high spirits. He had not succeeded in getting the English to make any concessions on the succession question beforehand, as he had wished, but at least the meeting would take place, and the English were no longer insisting on immediate ratification of the Treaty of Edinburgh. The bold diplomatic démarche of January had succeeded.[66]

Then news came to London of a rupture of negotiations in France; once again the factions were at each other's throats. This brought a quick reversal of the English position: on July 15 Elizabeth decided that the interview must be postponed.[67] In an endeavor to lighten the blow, she informed Mary that she had every intention of meeting her next year, and Mary could pick the date, between May 20 and the end of August. Mary was bitterly disappointed, and so were her advisers; nevertheless she accepted Elizabeth's proposal.[68] Maitland somewhat wearily wrote *finis* to this episode in his letter to Cecil of July 29, in which he expressed the hope that Anglo-Scottish friendship would not suffer from what had passed and from the current behavior of the Guises.[69]

Meanwhile, on June 18, there had arrived in Scotland a papal agent, Nicholas Gouda, whose principal aim was to get Mary to send representatives to the Council of Trent. Lord James disliked this, because he feared that if Mary saw Gouda, and Elizabeth learned of it, Anglo-Scottish friendship would suffer, and all chance of the interview vanish.[70] His representations to this effect had some influence on Mary, who did not see Gouda until after the interview had been postponed. Even then Gouda received but cold comfort from the Queen. She assured him of her constancy in the Catholic faith, but she refused to act on Gouda's suggestions.

[66] *C.S.P., For., Eliz.*, V, 157–58. See also January 15, February 27, 1562, Maitland to Cecil, *C.S.P., Scot.*, I, 588–90, Haynes, *Burghley Papers*, pp. 379–81.
[67] *C.S.P., For., Eliz.*, V, 162–64.
[68] July 25, 1562, Sidney to Cecil, *C.S.P., Scot.*, I, 641. Labanoff, *Recueil*, I, 150–56. August 16, 1562, Randolph to Cecil, *C.S.P., For., Eliz.*, V, 246–47.
[69] *C.S.P., Scot.*, I, 641–42.
[70] June 26, 1562, Randolph to Cecil, *ibid.*, pp. 634–35. July 11, 1562, De Foix's memoir to the French government, in Teulet, *Relations politiques*, II, 188.

He had no better luck with the Scottish clergy. Scotland was in a bad way, Gouda felt. The chief difficulty, in his opinion, lay in the fact that Mary had no Catholic advisers around her. Protestants ruled the country, he moaned, and threatened the Queen with an English invasion if she displayed any Catholic leanings in matters of policy.[71]

Throughout Mary's reign Catholic observers in Europe, as well as those who visited Scotland, were almost unanimous in holding Lord James chiefly responsible for conditions in Scotland. He was their special *bête noire*: get rid of him, and the old religion might be able to win out. Edmund Hay, a Scottish Jesuit, wrote to Laynez in January 1564 as follows: "All that may be suggested . . . will be premature, not to say absolutely useless, as long as . . . Lord James is alive, or at any rate as long as he continues to govern the kingdom, which he has done ever since the Queen's return. He holds all the heretics, except the Earl of Hamilton [sic], so completely under control by interest, and all the Catholics, who are fewer in number, by fear and by the use of the royal authority, which is scarcely even nominally in possession of the Queen, that no one ventures to oppose his will." [72] No one else, not even Knox, was mentioned with such dislike as was Lord James. Such a feeling was a highly significant, albeit unintentional, tribute to the importance of Lord James in making and keeping Scotland Protestant.

Since the interview with Elizabeth had been postponed, Mary decided to make a progress in the north, a project she had had in mind for some time.[73] Her councillors, Randolph reported, were not overly enthusiastic about the trip, but they acquiesced in the Queen's wishes.[74] Mary began her journey in mid-August, and before the end of the month she had arrived in Aberdeen.

She had not been there long when it became evident to all that she was displeased with her greatest northern subject, the Earl

---

[71] This paragraph has been drawn mainly from Gouda's long letter to Laynez on September 30, 1562, in J. H. Pollen, ed., *Papal Negotiations with Mary Queen of Scots*, pp. 129–39.
[72] W. Forbes-Leith, ed., *Narratives of Scottish Catholics under Mary Stuart and James VI*, pp. 80–81.   [73] Fleming, *Mary Queen of Scots*, pp. 74, 300–301.
[74] August 10, 1562, Randolph to Cecil, *C.S.P., Scot.*, I, 645–47.

of Huntly. The latter had clattered into Aberdeen at the head of 1,500 men to pay his respects, though he had been forbidden to bring more than one hundred.[75] Consequently Mary refused to visit him at his home at Strathbogie, in spite of the wishes of her council.[76] A more serious cause of quarrel was the behavior of Huntly's son, Sir John Gordon. This sharp-witted and venture-some young man was at feud with Ogilvie of Findlater over some property. In June he almost killed Ogilvie of Airlie in a brawl in Edinburgh. The Edinburgh officials seized Sir John, but he escaped and fled north to his father.[77] Huntly was too cautious to sanction such behavior, and Sir John once more made his submission to Mary, once more repented of it, and once more escaped. On September 10 the council proclaimed that in view of this state of affairs, Sir John was not to be helped by anyone and that the property in dispute with Ogilvie was to be surrendered to the Crown.[78]

This decision was taken at Tarnaway, the principal seat of the earldom of Moray, for Mary was on the way to Inverness. That day Lord James publicly assumed the title of Earl of Moray, by which he is best known to posterity.[79] On the following day Mary arrived at Inverness. There she received a rude shock. The captain of the castle refused to open its gates without a direct order from Huntly or his eldest son, Lord Gordon. But the castle was in no condition to stand a siege, and on the following day it was surrendered. An example was made of the captain, who was hanged on the spot.[80]

This was open defiance of royal authority, and Huntly could have been outlawed at once. That this was not done is clear proof

[75] *Acts of Parliament*, II, 572.
[76] August 31, 1562, Randolph to Cecil, *C.S.P., Scot.*, I, 649–50.
[77] Knox, *History*, II, 345–46.
[78] *Register of Privy Council*, I, 218–19. Philippson, *Histoire*, II, 83–86.
[79] The date of Lord James's assumption of the title is not certain. It is mentioned by Randolph on September 18, 1562 (*C.S.P., Scot.*, I, 650–52), and it may not have occurred until after the *contretemps* at Inverness. I have followed Henderson, *Mary Queen of Scots*, I, 238–39, in dating it on the tenth.
[80] September 18, 1562, Randolph to Cecil, *C.S.P., Scot.*, I, 650–52. There is a confusion of dates here: Randolph says Mary arrived at Inverness on the ninth, but in view of the date and place of the council's proclamation referred to in note 78, she must have arrived on the eleventh.

that Mary's object at this time was to reduce the Earl to obedience, not to wreck him utterly. To say, as some of Mary's extreme partisans have, that the whole northern progress was a deep-laid plot on the part of Moray in order to destroy his great Catholic rival is nonsense. Mary herself planned the trip, and she had no interest in destroying Huntly, despite his shiftiness and despite his opposition to the interview with Elizabeth and to the policy of Maitland and Moray.[81] She certainly wished to reduce his power, which was that of a petty king in the north. It was Huntly's own blunders that precipitated his downfall.

Mary remained in Inverness for about a week and then began to make her way back to Aberdeen. It was rumored that Sir John Gordon would ambush her on the way, but nothing happened. The Castle of Findlater was summoned by the Queen to surrender, and refused.[82] Consequently, on her return to Aberdeen, Mary decided that the time had come for strong measures. One hundred twenty hagbutters were levied, and messengers were sent south to summon, among others, Moray's military henchmen, Kirkcaldy of Grange and the Master of Lindsay. On September 25 Captain Hay was sent to Strathbogie to demand the surrender of Huntly's cannon, which Huntly had used to overawe his Highland foes. Huntly received him with protestations of loyalty, and his Countess, playing on Mary's religious sympathies, showed Hay her private chapel, full of Catholic vestments. Mary was not moved.[83]

Huntly was now in a painful dilemma. He had virtually no supporters outside his own family. Now, it seemed, he must either surrender and yield up his power and his son to Mary, or else defy her openly. He did neither, a policy which was to prove fatal, for each day of delay only strengthened Mary's belief in his guilt and increased her own military strength in proportion to his. On October 9 an attempt was made to surprise the Earl at Strathbogie; the latter barely managed to escape and fled to the wilds of Bade-

[81] July 15, 1562, Randolph to Cecil, *C.S.P., For., Eliz.*, V, 161–62.
[82] September 24, 1562, Randolph to Cecil, *C.S.P., Scot.*, I, 652–54.
[83] September 30, 1562, Randolph to Cecil, *ibid.*, pp. 654–56.

noch.[84] Finally, on October 15, it was determined to outlaw Huntly on the seventeenth if he did not submit by that time, a decision made all the more necessary by a direct military attack by Sir John on Mary's forces besieging Findlater. No submission was forthcoming, and on the seventeenth Huntly was put to the horn.[85]

The end now came with surprising speed. Huntly might have defied the government for a long time in Badenoch, especially with winter coming on, but he most unwisely decided to measure his strength with his foes, possibly on account of the rumor that there was treachery in the ranks of the Queen. The decisive battle was fought outside Aberdeen, at Corrichie, on October 28. Huntly was outnumbered, outgeneraled by Moray, who was in command of the Queen's forces, and quickly defeated. He was captured, but died—of apoplexy, probably—before he could be led off the battlefield. Two of his sons were taken also. Sir John was one, and he was speedily executed, but not before he had confessed to various treasonable designs against Mary, Maitland, and Moray. Similar confessions were extracted from some of Huntly's servants, in one case even before Corrichie, which lends some credence to them.[86] It is not likely that Huntly had such ideas before his outlawry, but after that time it is quite possible, and his advance on Aberdeen which ended at Corrichie may be reasonably interpreted as an attempt to seize Mary's person before she got back to the Lowlands.[87]

While all this was going on, wild rumors circulated in southern Scotland. Knox, who suspected that a reckoning with Huntly might be in the offing, exerted himself to keep the south quiet, and on September 4 persuaded many of the western gentry to sign

[84] October 12, 1562, Randolph to Cecil, *ibid.*, pp. 657–59.
[85] October 23, 1562, Randolph to Cecil, *ibid.*, pp. 660–61. *Register of Privy Council*, I, 219–20.
[86] On the question of the confessions, see Randolph's letters of October 23 and November 18, 1562, *C.S.P., Scot.*, I, 660–61, 668–70.
[87] A rather unconvincing defense of Huntly is offered by T. Duncan, "Mary Stuart and the House of Huntly," *Scottish Historical Review*, IV (1906–7), 365–73. Duncan regards Moray as a deep-dyed villain. The best sources for the whole Huntly affair are Randolph's letters, cited above.

a Protestant band. This was aimed at Châtelherault, who was the father-in-law of Huntly's heir, Lord Gordon. Châtelherault, in his present discontented state of mind, might be expected to welcome a plot against the regime. Knox's efforts were effective, however; the Duke remained quiet.[88]

Lord Gordon was tried and condemned for treason, early in 1563, but was not executed; Moray is said by Knox to have interceded for him with Mary.[89] Huntly himself, or rather his corpse, was adjudged guilty of treason in Parliament in 1563. So was the Earl of Sutherland, a relative of Huntly's, but he had escaped to the Continent.[90]

What did Mary think of the ruin of her greatest Catholic subject? After she had learned the full extent of Huntly's plans, she appeared to regard the Earl as a double-dyed traitor and to be thoroughly satisfied at all that had occurred. She knew that her Catholic friends in Europe would not be pleased; in January 1563 she wrote to her uncle the Cardinal of Lorraine and asked him to make her excuses for her "if I have failed in any part of my duty towards religion." Father Pollen regards this letter as indicating that Mary now repented of her behavior toward Huntly; it can be much more readily interpreted as an apologetic for something that had to be done.[91] It is significant that Mary, even after she had broken with her brother and the Protestants and was posing as a Catholic martyr, never accused him of misleading her on the question of Huntly.[92] When the latter's son and Sutherland were restored by the Parliament of April 1567, it was on the ground of a technical irregularity in their condemnations, not because they had not been guilty.[93]

As for Moray, he could look on the results of the northern progress with a good deal of satisfaction. He had obtained his coveted earldom, the revenues of which were estimated by Ran-

[88] Knox, *History*, II, 347–51. [89] *Ibid.*, p. 360.
[90] Fleming, *Mary Queen of Scots*, p. 80.
[91] Pollen, *Papal Negotiations*, pp. lviii, 162–63. The letter is printed in Labanoff, *Recueil*, I, 175–76.
[92] Moray was accused by his enemies of arranging the ruin of Huntly in a venomous proclamation in May 1568, but this was probably the work of Archbishop Hamilton rather than Mary. See Fleming, *Mary Queen of Scots*, pp. 486–89.   [93] *Acts of Parliament*, II, 577–81.

dolph to amount to 1,000 marks a year.[94] Furthermore, his grateful sister had rewarded him with no mean share of the spoils of Huntly's richly furnished house at Strathbogie, some additional northern property, and the sheriffdoms of Elgin and Forres and of Inverness.[95] More important, the ruin of Huntly climaxed a year of highly successful internal political consolidation. The greatest potential enemies of the policy of Maitland and Moray, the Gordons and the Hamiltons, had been reduced to helplessness. Secure in the Queen's confidence, the two statesmen seemed to be monarchs of all they surveyed.

Yet Moray's position was by no means as advantageous as it appeared to be. He had paid a price for his successes. He and Maitland had very seriously alienated Knox and the preachers. The General Assembly of June 1562 had revealed that the split was as deep, if not deeper, than before.[96] This did not matter so much as long as Moray retained the confidence of the Queen; but should he and his sister ever fall out, the defection of the zealots would have serious consequences. As far as Knox himself was concerned, this probably would not be disastrous, for Knox was no fool, and he knew that in the last analysis he and Moray must stand or fall together. But the rank and file of Protestants, whom Knox had been telling for some time now that Moray was becoming a worldly-minded politician, little better than Maitland, might well wash their hands of the Earl if he clashed with Mary. This was a fact of which Moray was not fully aware, and it almost ruined him.

The attitude of the zealots did not make a great deal of difference, of course, provided Moray could count on his sister. This, in turn, depended on something that he was unable to control— the attitude of England on the question of the succession. Mary had thus far put herself in the hands of Maitland and Moray in the expectation that they would be able to arrange a satisfactory solution of this question. England had been friendly, to be sure,

[94] September 30, 1562, Randolph to Cecil, *C.S.P., Scot.,* I, 654–56.
[95] J. Robertson, ed., *Inventaires de la Royne Descosse Douairière de France,* p. xxiv. Chalmers, *Mary Queen of Scots,* II, 433–35.
[96] See the account of this meeting in Knox, *History,* II, 337–45.

but no commitments had been made. Mary had never renounced her other policy, that of a Catholic marriage and of a reduction of the whole island by force. This policy could easily be revived; if this took place, the political consolidation of 1562 would probably work to Mary's advantage, for Hamilton and Gordon alike had been ruined, not in the name of the Congregation, but in that of the Queen. In spite of the seemingly dominant position of Moray, the initiative, by the end of the year 1562, had passed into Mary's hands. If she chose the Catholic policy, Moray, owing to the split in the Protestant ranks, would be in a very grave position. It remained to be seen what Mary's choice would be.

CHAPTER V

The Queen's Marriage

WHILE Mary was in the north, events in England were taking an unpleasant turn. Elizabeth had intervened openly in the civil war in France on the side of the Huguenots, against the Guises and the government. This placed Mary in a highly embarrassing position.[1] Far worse, however, was the situation which developed out of Elizabeth's illness. The Queen's attack of smallpox—for a while her life was despaired of —brought the realities of the succession question grimly home to English statesmen. There was much discussion, and from it emerged one glaring fact, which quickly reached Scotland: almost no one favored Mary.[2]

Mary decided that there was nothing to be gained by intervening in the French war, but she did not plan to remain entirely passive. She was preparing a major shift of policy. Since the middle of 1561 she had been playing the Protestant game, in the hope that the prize of the English succession would fall to her peacefully. She had gotten nowhere. It was time, Mary thought, to adopt an alternative course of action. This was the pro-Catholic policy, involving a Catholic marriage and, ultimately, the forcible overthrow of English and Scottish Protestantism and of Elizabeth herself. This had been tried early in 1561, when the Guises attempted to get Don Carlos as a husband for Mary, and it had failed then. Mary now decided to try again, encouraged by the fact that Catherine de Medici's power for harm was considerably reduced

[1] See November 14, 1562, Maitland to Cecil, *C.S.P., Scot.*, I, 666–68.
[2] J. E. Neale, *Queen Elizabeth*, pp. 117–18. November 18, 1562, Randolph to Cecil, *C.S.P., Scot.*, I, 668–70.

by her alliance with the Guises, into which she had been forced by the religious situation in France. This time, of course, the Guises could not handle the negotiations for Mary. They were to be entrusted to Maitland.

Maitland was perfectly willing. A worldly politician and diplomatist in a religious country and age, he had no religious scruples to restrain him. His goal was political: the union of England and Scotland, and religion was simply an element to be considered in the political game. A Protestant himself, he would have preferred the solution for which he had worked in 1561–62, but he was willing to try the Catholic solution. If Mary wed Don Carlos, the union of the island would follow, and soon: for nothing could stand against the might of Spain—so everyone believed, at least, until Elizabeth's navy proved otherwise many years later. As for his coreligionists, Maitland, one must regretfully conclude, was prepared to sacrifice them if necessary. During his negotiations with Quadra, the Spanish ambassador in London, he raised the question of safeguards for Protestantism but made no real effort to pin the Spaniard down.[3]

Moray, of course, was informed of the Spanish marriage plan —it could hardly be kept from him. Since with Moray religion was a paramount motive, we might expect to find him denouncing the plan from the housetops. Yet, strange to say, he offered no objection at all. In fact, Maitland even told Quadra that the marriage had Moray's sanction.[4] Here is a paradox which requires explanation.

It is obvious that Moray really was opposed heart and soul to the Spanish marriage. He was perfectly aware of its consequences, the union of the island under Catholic auspices and the ruin of Protestantism. He was anxious to set Mary on the English throne, to be sure, but only by means of an agreement with England which would insure the continued dominance of his religion. To suggest, as Henderson had done, that he was really won over to

---

[3] See Quadra's letter of March 18, 1563, to Philip II, in *Calendar of State Papers, Spanish (Elizabeth)* (henceforth abbreviated *C.S.P., Span.*), I, 305–12.
[4] *Ibid.*, pp. 305–12. See also, on this point, January 3, 1562, Quadra to the Duchess of Parma, *ibid.*, p. 222.

the Spanish match by assurances that Protestantism would be guaranteed, or by promises of power for himself, is nonsense.[5] Moray was well aware of the value placed by Catholics on their promises to heretics. In spite of all this, Moray was constrained to go along with Mary's plans because he found himself in a nasty political dilemma. On the surface, at least, his power and influence were still great. But the moment he crossed the Queen on a major issue and broke with her, his power would be gone, unless he could carry the Protestant moderates with him. His old allies, the Protestant zealots, were estranged from him and not very influential, in spite of the preaching of Knox—and this had been largely Moray's own doing. He and Maitland were the leaders of the moderates. He could only be absolutely certain of the moderates if Maitland were with him, and in this case Maitland was not.[6] Even if Maitland were in the opposite camp, Moray would be able to carry the moderates with him, he judged, if a serious threat to the religion—and consequently to the pocketbook, in many cases —could be brought home to them: that is to say, in the event that the marriage negotiations actually succeeded. If this happened, there is no doubt that Moray would have raised the banner of religion and national independence, Elizabeth would have been forced to support him, and the situation of 1559 would have repeated itself. But the mere fact that the negotiations were going on would not be enough to win the moderates. So he held his peace.

This was the pass to which Moray had been brought by his policy of the last two years. He had relied too heavily on being able to control Mary through his influence with England; the initiative had passed from his hands, and he was now faced with the possibility of having to raise a rebellion—truly the last resource of a politician in any era. Yet one should not criticize Moray too severely, for there was almost no other course open to him than the one he took. He had gambled on English cooperation, and thus far the gamble had not succeeded. But the situation was

[5] T. F. Henderson, *Mary Queen of Scots*, I, 261–63.
[6] For the relations of the two at this time, see June 3, June 26, 1563, Randolph to Cecil, *C.S.P.*, *Scot.*, II, 9–12, 16.

by no means desperate as yet. Possibly the Spanish negotiations
might fail—Moray must have prayed that they would. Possibly,
whether they failed or not, Elizabeth might be goaded into a
counteroffer so attractive that Mary would once more change
her course. If all else failed, a revolt could always be raised, with
good prospects of success. The outlook was not bright, but all
was far from lost.

Maitland set out for London in February 1563. His official instructions were largely in the nature of a pretext for getting him
into England.[7] His real purpose was to negotiate with Spain. These
negotiations were long and complicated, and need not detain us
unduly.[8] Maitland was marvelously adroit, and he almost succeeded. He shrewdly played on Philip's fear that Mary had a
French marriage offer in her pocket and would accept it unless
Philip offered Don Carlos. By mid-August that procrastinating
potentate was worked up to such a pitch that he was almost prepared to rise to Maitland's bait. But he reconsidered, as he always
did, and by the end of the year he had changed his mind, although
he did not definitely put an end to the possibility of the match
till August 1564.[9]

Circumstances which Maitland and his sovereign could not
control conspired to bring their grandiose scheme to naught.
Philip had agreed to discuss the Carlos marriage only because he
feared that Mary might wed Charles IX.[10] Thus, in the last analysis, the fate of the Carlos match was to be determined by the attitude of France, that is to say, of the Guises and of Catherine de
Medici. Early in 1563 the religious situation in France had brought
the Guises and Catherine into a close alliance. This, on the surface,
appeared to favor Mary's cause, for her Guise relatives could now
be expected to neutralize Catherine's unchanged hostility to a
Spanish marriage for Mary. Surprisingly enough, things worked

---

[7] They are given in A. Labanoff, ed., *Recueil des lettres de Marie Stuart*, I, 161–69.
[8] The best sources are the letters of Quadra to Philip II, *C.S.P., Span.*, I, 305 ff.
J. H. Pollen, ed., *Papal Negotiations with Mary Queen of Scots*, pp. lxv–lxviii,
177–78, is a good nutshell summary. There are good accounts in Henderson,
Mary Queen of Scots, I, 259–69, 279–81, and in M. Philippson, *Histoire du règne
de Marie Stuart*, II, 175–95, 209–17.
[9] Henderson, *Mary Queen of Scots*, I, 279, 288–89. *C.S.P., Span.*, I, 370–71.
[10] June 15, 1563, Philip II to Quadra, *ibid.*, pp. 331–34.

out just the other way: Catherine was able to convince the Guises that the Spanish match would be the ruin of France.[11] The result was that the Cardinal of Lorraine began to negotiate on behalf of Mary, but with no authorization from her, for the hand of an Austrian archduke. Maitland and Mary were furious when they discovered what the Cardinal was up to, but by then it was really too late. Philip paused. The death of Quadra at a crucial point in the negotiations further delayed matters. By this time Catherine had been able to penetrate Maitland's designs; she and the Cardinal informed Philip that she had not offered the hand of Charles IX to Mary, and had no intention of doing so.[12] This, and the serious illness of Don Carlos late in 1563, virtually ended the scheme. In November Philip indicated that Mary should wed the Archduke.[13]

It was impossible, naturally, in so faction-ridden a country as Scotland, to prevent some rumor of these negotiations from leaking out. The Scottish Catholics began to take heart. At Easter time in 1563 many of them, Archbishop Hamilton included, were bold enough to say Mass. This was a violation of the Proclamation of August 1561, and Knox protested vehemently. In so doing he had the support of Moray, who could not allow such a challenge to Protestantism to go unpunished. The consequence was that in April Knox had another interview with Mary, his third, and it was fairly amicable.

Among other things, there was discussed at this interview the recent appointment of Ruthven to the council, which Moray had opposed.[14] This appointment marks the temporary eclipse of Moray as the leader of Mary's domestic administration; until late in 1564 he was but one among many.[15] He was not entirely power-

---

[11] Philippson, *Histoire*, II, 179–81.   [12] *Ibid.*, pp. 215–16.

[13] *Ibid.*, pp. 226–29. Mary had no intention of marrying the Archduke, since a Catholic husband who could not increase her material power would have been worse than useless to her. Mary never ceased to hope for the Spanish match, even as late as 1565. January 23, 1565, Alava to Philip II, in A. Teulet, ed., *Relations politiques de la France et de l'Espagne avec l'Ecosse au XVIe siècle*, V, 5–9. April 26, 1565, De Silva to Philip II, *C.S.P., Span.*, I, 420–26.

[14] February 28, 1563, Randolph to Cecil, *C.S.P., For., Eliz.*, VI, 166–69. John Knox, *History of the Reformation in Scotland*, II, 370–76.

[15] On this point see, for example, the government's handling of the problem of

less, however. In fact, the reason for the friendly tone of the interview between the Queen and Knox was that Mary had decided to do as the preacher and Moray wished, and to punish Archbishop Hamilton and the others; they were jailed in May.[16] The Queen judged that it would be premature to provoke a rupture with the Protestants, with the Spanish match not yet concluded. Furthermore, Parliament was about to meet—the first Parliament since Mary's return. Mary knew very well that the Protestant zealots would press for a carrying out of the promise of 1561 that Parliament would act on the religious question. She was by no means anxious that such a demand be raised while the Spanish negotiations were in progress; so she had to keep Knox and the moderates divided. Hence her order to imprison the Archbishop; such an action might mollify the moderates. He was released, after some delay, after Parliament was dissolved.[17]

Moray, probably with considerable misgivings, finally decided to go along with his sister and not to raise the religious question at this Parliament. To back Knox would mean an immediate breach with his sister, which, for reasons pointed out above, he did not want at this time. If the Spanish match fell through, the delay could do no harm; if it did not, Moray wanted to raise the cry of "Religion in danger!" as a weapon against Mary, and he judged that Protestantism's lack of legal standing would add potency to his warning cry at such a time.

This was a major blunder. Mary had given her word to effect a religious settlement at her first Parliament. She must either have capitulated or else defied Moray and Knox, and the latter course would undoubtedly have alienated all the Protestant moderates. Probably no immediate rebellion would have ensued, but the Protestant lords, whose suspicions of their Catholic Queen had been lulled by such events as the ruin of Huntly, would have been on the alert. At Mary's first pro-Catholic gesture Scotland would have been in flames.

the rebellious Clan Gregor. *The Register of the Privy Council of Scotland*, I, 248–50, 255–58, 269–72.
[16] May 20, 1563, Randolph to Cecil, *C.S.P., For., Eliz.*, VI, 355.
[17] June 19, 1563, Randolph to Cecil, *C.S.P., Scot.*, II, 15–16. On this point see also D. H. Fleming, *Mary Queen of Scots*, pp. 374–76.

But Moray allowed his sister to escape from this very serious dilemma. Worse still, by his conduct he provoked an open breach with Knox. The preacher was infuriated by Moray's policy, and the latter's attempt to justify himself by saying that the time to press for a settlement of the religious question was on the occasion of Mary's marriage was contemptuously brushed aside. Moray, said Knox, was more interested in having his earldom confirmed than in furthering Protestantism. One remark led to another, and the two men parted in furious anger. "The matter fell so hot betwixt the Earl of Moray and some others of the Court, and John Knox, that familiarly after that time they spoke not together more than a year and [a] half." Knox, as usual, had the last word; he sent Moray a wounded letter which closed as follows: "I praise my God I this day leave you victor of your enemies, promoted to great honors, and in credit and authority with your Sovereign. If so ye long continue, none within the Realm shall be more glad than I shall be; but if that after this ye shall decay (as I fear that ye shall), then call to mind by what means God exalted you; which was neither by bearing with impiety, neither yet by maintaining of pestilent Papists." [18] The minor reforms pushed through the Parliament, which met in late May and early June, did not mollify the zealots.[19]

In August, while the Queen and the court were absent from Edinburgh, a disturbance broke out as a result of Mass being said in the Queen's chapel at Holyrood. The Protestants contended that this was illegal, since Mary was not there; nevertheless two of them were arrested for what would be called, today, disturbing the peace.[20] Knox, who was ever on the watch for the thin edge of the Popish wedge, took alarm, and on October 8 wrote a circular letter to all the Protestants of Scotland, urging them to come to Edinburgh on the day of the trial of their brethren in order to support them and the religion.[21] This was the usual procedure at Scottish trials; the side with the biggest number of retainers invariably had the better case.

[18] Knox, *History*, II, 381–83.
[19] The doings of this Parliament are in *The Acts of the Parliament of Scotland*, II, 535–45.   [20] Knox, *History*, II, 393–94.   [21] *Ibid.*, pp. 395–97.

Mary, when she heard of this letter, rejoiced. At last she had caught Knox in a false step: he had clearly committed treason by summoning the Queen's lieges without authority. So thought many Protestants, too. Moray temporarily forgot his anger and begged the Reformer to throw himself on Mary's mercy in order to get off lightly. He wanted no open clash that would force him to take sides and thus to antagonize either Mary or the zealots. Maitland joined in the plea, but Knox was adamant.[22] The Secretary decided it was high time that Knox was taught a lesson.

On December 21, 1563, the council met to hear the case.[23] Knox was accompanied to the trial by a great crowd of followers, who pushed up the stairs to the very door of the council chamber. Mary demanded if the Reformer acknowledged having written the letter. He had. Was he not sorry? Maitland asked. Why should he be? Because he had convened the Queen's lieges without her permission. Had this not been done, Knox wondered, in 1559, by many of the gentlemen sitting at the council board?

Checkmate! No Protestant could vote to condemn Knox now for the same action which the members of the Congregation had engaged in, and the council knew it. The Protestants there could not confess the illegality of their behavior then without bringing the whole structure they had so laboriously constructed down around their heads. Knox easily handled further attempts by Mary and Maitland to make capital out of other phrases in the letter. He was acquitted and, to Maitland's further chagrin, was given a vote of confidence by the General Assembly of December 1563, which ordered him to continue to warn the flock whenever he saw danger approaching.[24]

Moray was greatly relieved. It had been a difficult year for him, made no easier by a severe famine which tripled the price of food;[25] but with the acquittal of Knox, which he had voted for, to Mary's annoyance,[26] and with the evident fading of the Spanish danger, things were improving. Furthermore, a new possibility had developed, which bade fair to solve all his problems at once.

[22] *Ibid.*, pp. 399–403.
[23] December 21, 1563, Randolph to Cecil, *C.S.P., Scot.*, II, 29–30.
[24] Knox, *History*, II, 403–15.   [25] *Ibid.*, pp. 369–70.
[26] February 21, 1564, Randolph to Cecil, *C.S.P., Scot.*, II, 43–48.

ii

It was not to be expected that Mary's matrimonial negotiations with the Continental powers could long go unnoticed by Elizabeth and her ministers. In the course of an interview with Maitland—so the latter told Quadra—Elizabeth turned the conversation to the subject of Mary's marriage and suggested that Mary could do worse than to marry Lord Robert Dudley. Maitland was startled and puzzled. He scarcely knew whether to regard the overture seriously or not, and for the moment he turned it aside with a joke.[27] By June, when Maitland was passing through London on his return from a trip to France, the English were definitely aware that something detrimental to their interests was in the wind. Maitland was peremptorily informed by Elizabeth that if Mary married Don Carlos, or, indeed, any Hapsburg, Elizabeth would be forced to regard her as an enemy.[28]

The very idea of Mary's marriage with a powerful Catholic prince was enough to give Elizabeth and Cecil many a sleepless night, for obvious reasons. Such a marriage was the most serious threat imaginable to Elizabeth's throne. The solution which Elizabeth preferred, and for which she and Cecil steadily worked, was that Mary should never marry at all.[29] Just how this was to be accomplished in the long run was never clear—Elizabeth's tactics during the next two years were improvised from day to day, almost—but that was what she wanted. If it proved impossible to keep Mary from marrying again, as well it might, it was imperative that she marry someone who was no threat to Elizabeth and who could be controlled by her: in other words, an English noble. Randolph was instructed, on August 20, 1563, to repeat Elizabeth's warning of June to Mary and to indicate that she should wed an Englishman.[30]

Randolph delivered his message to the Scottish Queen early in September, but he got very cold comfort indeed.[31] Moray, with

[27] March 28, 1563, Quadra to Philip II, *C.S.P., Span.*, I, 312–15.
[28] June 26, 1563, Quadra to Philip II, *ibid.*, pp. 337–40.
[29] This was guessed as early as 1561 by Chantonnay, the Spanish ambassador in Paris. July 26, 1561, Chantonnay to Philip II, in Teulet, *Relations politiques*, II, 166–71.   [30] *C.S.P., Scot.*, II, 19–20.
[31] September 4, 1563, Randolph to Cecil, *ibid.*, pp. 21–22.

whom Randolph was instructed to consult, regarded the English tactics with mixed feelings. He dared not move while the Spanish match was still in the balance, and he was clearly disappointed that Cecil had made no definite counteroffer. On September 23 he wrote an interesting letter to his English colleague in which he explained himself as far as he dared. Mary would not be hasty in accepting any suitor, he trusted. He, Moray, would work for a solution which would further Anglo-Scottish amity, but he could not prevent Mary from weighing the offers of foreign princes.[32] He could not write more without betraying his sovereign; but between the lines of the letter he was pleading with Cecil to make a definite proposal, and one of sufficient attractiveness to enable him to work for it with Mary, as a reasonable alternative to a Catholic marriage. His behavior in this matter had the approval of Knox, with whom, be it remembered, he was not on speaking terms. Knox knew very well that Moray wanted no Catholic husband for Mary.[33]

As it happened, Moray's fear that the English tactics would prove ineffective was needless, owing to the failure of the negotiations for the Spanish match. Toward the end of 1563 Mary once more picked up the threads of her English policy and asked that Elizabeth indicate whom she would have her marry. In December Randolph delivered his mistress's answer to Mary: any English noble would do, but no one man was singled out officially.[34] These tactics irritated Moray and Maitland, who again were working together, now that the latter had abandoned hope of the Spanish match. Moray was especially anxious: here was a chance to lay the ghost of a foreign marriage once and for all, if Elizabeth would only be reasonable. Randolph's letter of February 21, 1564, which indicated that Moray and Maitland had just about reached the end of their patience, at last drove Elizabeth to act. In March Randolph was instructed to indicate to Mary that Elizabeth wished her to marry Lord Robert Dudley.[35]

[32] *Ibid.*, pp. 22–23.   [33] October 6, 1563, Knox to Cecil, *ibid.*, p. 24.
[34] Randolph's instructions are dated November 16, 1563. *Ibid.*, p. 27. See also Randolph's letter of December 31, 1563, *ibid.*, pp. 31–34.
[35] *Ibid.*, pp. 43–48, 54–55.

This was an offer worthy of a lending-library romance. Lord Robert was most unsuitable in every respect as a husband for a reigning queen of an ancient house, who had once sat on the proudest throne in Europe. The Dudley family history in the sixteenth century was stained with treason. Lord Robert himself was suspected of having murdered his wife and was more than suspected of sharing Elizabeth's bed. Mary's first reaction was to treat the offer as a joke.[36] Yet on second thought she decided not to do so. The Spanish match had gone a-glimmering, for the time being at least, and Elizabeth could hardly expect Mary to wed someone like Lord Robert without an ironclad guarantee on the succession question. Besides, there was another consideration involved here—it will be discussed presently—which made it imperative to be on good terms with Elizabeth at this time. So, contrary to her inclination, Mary did not laugh or explode in Randolph's face.

The advice of Maitland and Moray must have carried weight too. Neither of them had any illusions as to the character of Lord Robert, and both realized that Mary could and would not marry him without a definite settlement on the succession question. But if they could force the necessary concessions from Elizabeth, they were willing to risk everything to get Mary to marry him, as their subsequent conduct was to make abundantly clear.

Moray especially was zealous in the cause. Such a solution would safeguard the English alliance and Protestantism, place both on a permanent basis, and end the Catholic threat once for all. Those who believe that Moray's every move was dictated by greed and personal ambition are hard put to it to explain his conduct in this matter, for it is perfectly obvious that, had Mary married Dudley, Moray's political influence would have been very greatly reduced. His policy in this case was perfectly honest and selfless, for he himself recognized that his political eclipse would be the result of the Dudley marriage.[37]

All elements of the Protestant party would unite behind this

[36] March 30, 1564, Randolph to Cecil, *ibid.*, pp. 55–59.
[37] March 1–3, 1565, Randolph to Cecil, *ibid.*, pp. 129–34.

marriage, Moray felt, for Knox was an admirer of Lord Robert.[38] Such a union would be highly gratifying to Moray, for the Protestant moderates and the zealots were still poles apart; the chief sore point was still the Queen's Mass.[39] The situation was just about the same as it had been ever since Moray had taken his stand at the chapel door back in August of 1561, except that the events of 1563, described above, had widened the rift. At the General Assembly of June 1564 a long debate took place between Knox and Maitland, who was supported by the "court party," including Moray. The discussion was most revealing, for it clearly pointed up the differences between the two points of view. The key question, of course, was that of resistance to an idolatrous prince. To Knox's quotation of Biblical examples—Jezebel was his favorite, needless to say—Maitland replied, "They were singular motions of the Spirit of God, and appartain nothing to this our age." [40] It need hardly be added that neither side was able to convert the other. Moray regretted the split, hoped that the Dudley marriage would heal it, and still maintained his moderate position. "In all that time the Earl of Moray was so formed to John Knox, that neither by word nor write was there any communication betwixt them." [41]

Maitland had told Randolph, the day after the latter had mentioned Dudley's name to Mary, that the Scots favored a meeting of commissioners of both countries to discuss the conditions under which the marriage might take place.[42] This did not suit the English at all, since Elizabeth and Cecil did not wish the Scots to see how insincere they really were in offering Dudley to Mary. They still did not want her to marry at all; nevertheless, they would doubtless have sped Lord Robert to Edinburgh posthaste

[38] See his letter of October 6, 1563, to Dudley, *ibid.*, p. 25.
[39] There were other difficulties, too, chiefly connected with the stipends of the ministers and the teinds. Moray was unable to make good his promises to settle these matters satisfactorily to Knox. D. Calderwood, *The History of the Kirk of Scotland*, II, 223–28, 241–47. Knox, *History*, II, 417–18.
[40] The debate is given at length by Knox, *ibid.*, pp. 425–61.
[41] *Ibid.*, p. 461. This sentence closes Book IV of Knox's *History*, the last that was unquestionably written by Knox. Book V is generally regarded as the work of another, who compiled it from Knox's notes after his death. It will be referred to in these footnotes, for convenience's sake, as though it were written by Knox.
[42] March 30, 1564, Randolph to Cecil, *C.S.P., Scot.*, II, 55–59.

if Mary had agreed to marry him without conditions. But no one in Scotland, not even the most convinced believer in the Anglo-Scottish alliance, much less Mary herself, would have Dudley without a guarantee on the succession question. Even with such a guarantee, it is by no means certain that Mary would have married him, though it is the writer's opinion that in the end she would have. But this is pure conjecture. The spring and summer of 1564 were spent in fruitless negotiation, Maitland attempting to pin Cecil down, and the latter refusing to be pinned.[43] Moray took almost no part in the negotiations at this stage.

Mary was content to let the diplomatic maneuvering go on, though her faith in English sincerity of purpose was probably not very great. It was necessary to be on good terms with Elizabeth in order to pave the way for a counterstroke of her own, revolving around the person of Mary's second cousin, Henry, Lord Darnley, eldest son of Matthew Stewart, Earl of Lennox.

Lennox had been living in exile in England for twenty years, as a result of his treacheries during the struggle between Henry VIII and Cardinal Beaton. Bluff Hal had rewarded the Earl beyond his deserts by bestowing on him the hand of Lady Margaret Douglas, daughter of Margaret Tudor, Mary's grandmother, by her second husband, Archibald Douglas, Earl of Angus. Lord Darnley thus stood very close to the English throne—in fact, his claim was, after Mary's, the best, and was enhanced in the eyes of many by the fact that he was an Englishman born. The Lennox family had suffered its ups and downs in recent years; Elizabeth disliked them on account of their Catholic leanings. But early in 1563 they were received favorably at court and made much of by Elizabeth. On June 16, 1563, she went so far as to write to Mary, asking that they be permitted to return to Scotland.[44] The reason for this is not far to seek: Elizabeth was alarmed by Mary's marriage negotiations, and was building up Darnley, whose religious opinions were still unformed, despite his mother's Catholi-

---

[43] In this connection it is interesting to note that the proposal that Mary and Elizabeth should meet was revived, by the English this time, and rejected by the Scottish Council, on the ground that it would simply delay matters. June 5, 1564, Randolph to Cecil, *ibid.*, pp. 64–65.   [44] *C.S.P., For., Eliz.*, VI, 415.

cism, as a potential successor, to the exclusion of Mary, should the latter marry a Catholic prince from the Continent.[45]

Matters stood thus when, at the end of 1563, Mary's hopes of the Spanish match began to fade and when, shortly thereafter, the Dudley match was proposed to her. For the first time she began seriously to consider the possibility of marrying Darnley. This marriage had much to recommend it. It would strengthen her claim to the English throne. Since the Countess of Lennox was looked on as the leader of the English Catholics, Spain, France, and the Pope could be expected to approve. Knox did not like it, to be sure,[46] but his opposition might be discounted if Elizabeth and the Protestant moderates could be brought to consent. Even if they did not, the marriage might still be feasible if the Catholic powers would support Mary with sufficient vigor, in which case the same result would be forthcoming as in the case of the Spanish match.

The key to the situation would lie, of course, in the attitude of Elizabeth. In this respect Mary had a couple of useful cards to play, which Elizabeth had inadvertently put into her hand. The first was Elizabeth's repeated assurance that she would welcome Mary's marriage to any suitable English nobleman. Who could be more suitable than Lord Darnley? The second was Elizabeth's letter of June 1563 in behalf of Lennox. Shortly after Randolph's proposal of Dudley, Mary made it known that she was acceding to her good sister's request and was willing to welcome Lennox home.[47]

This rather annoyed Elizabeth and Cecil, who were by no means anxious to have Mary wed Darnley, given the serious religious and political implications of such a marriage. Elizabeth adopted a characteristic shift. Moray and Maitland were told that it was no longer desirable that Lennox be allowed to go to Scotland, and they were requested to get Mary to rescind the permission she had granted to Lennox to return.

[45] On this point see Philippson, *Histoire*, II, 59–63.
[46] May 3, 1564, Knox to Randolph, in John Knox, *Works*, VI, 541–42. Knox already suspected that Mary might be planning to marry Darnley.
[47] May 22, 1564, Randolph to Cecil, *C.S.P., Scot.*, II, 63–64.

This touched off an explosion. On July 13, 1564, both men wrote angry letters to Cecil, rejecting the suggestion as utterly dishonorable and indulging in some highly sarcastic language at Cecil's expense.[48] Moray and Maitland knew very well that there was a matrimonial angle involved in the return of Lennox, but neither of them was worried about it. As far as Moray was concerned, the Dudley marriage, with suitable guarantees on the succession, was what he wanted. If Elizabeth should not be accommodating in regard to the marriage of her chosen suitor with Mary, she certainly would never permit Mary to wed Darnley, who was, after all, an English subject. The idea that Mary might marry Darnley without Elizabeth's consent, if the Dudley business fell through, and revert to the Catholic policy involved in the Spanish match, had not crossed Moray's mind as yet. And in any case this was not a question of Darnley, but of Lennox.

Furthermore, Moray had no objection to the return of Lennox. The latter was a Stewart and, presumably, would work with him in his pro-English policy, since to oppose England would mean, for Lennox, the loss of his English estates. Besides, Lennox's return would further weaken the Hamiltons, for whom Moray had no use at all at this point.[49] As for religious matters, Moray in his letter of July 13 to Cecil brushed aside the latter's argument that Lennox's coming might weaken the Protestant position in Scotland. Moray's critics have fastened on this fact and loudly proclaimed him a hypocrite for saying, in the following year, that the Darnley marriage was a menace to Protestantism. They conveniently overlook the fact that by that time circumstances were vastly different and that, as we shall see, Moray had good grounds for his belief that his religion was in danger.

So Elizabeth was hoist with her own petard, and was forced to permit Lennox to return to Scotland, which he did, in September 1564. Thus was completed the first phase of Mary's plan to pave the way for the Darnley marriage and at the same time to retain her freedom of action. She still might choose Dudley, if Elizabeth

[48] *Ibid.*, pp. 67–69.
[49] There was a long-standing feud between the Hamiltons and Lennox, and the former had acquired a good deal of property from the forfeited estates of the Earl, which now, presumably, they would have to disgorge.

proved reasonable on the subject of the succession. Mary expected little from this, but was willing to give Elizabeth every chance, in order to force the English Queen to show to the world the patent insincerity and, indeed, shamefulness of the Dudley proposal. Meanwhile, it was necessary to remain on good terms with Elizabeth in order to get Darnley into Scotland, so that Mary could marry him, preferably with Elizabeth's consent, but if necessary against her wishes. There was no need to hurry; the Lennox family would never marry Darnley elsewhere so long as there was a chance for Mary's hand.

If Elizabeth consented to, or at least did not actively oppose, the Darnley match, there would be no problem for Mary. But if, as Mary evidently considered likely, Elizabeth should oppose the marriage, it could not be a useful match politically unless it were put on a pro-Catholic basis. It was necessary to prepare for such a step, but Mary could not show her hand until she had gotten Darnley into Scotland, and until the Dudley offer was definitely shown to be insincere. So Mary, in September 1564, restored her brother to full control of internal affairs, a position he had not held since shortly after Corrichie. It was rumored that he would be made Lieutenant-General of the kingdom.[50] Other favors were showered on the Protestant party: George Buchanan, for instance, was given the temporalities of the Abbey of Crossraguel.[51] Mary did all this in order to lull the Protestants on both sides of the Tweed into a false sense of security, so that they would not penetrate her real schemes in regard to Darnley. Moray and his friends allowed themselves to be lulled. They regarded these favors as an earnest of Mary's desire to arrive at a settlement with Elizabeth on the Dudley match—for which purpose, indeed, Mary could effectively use them, if Elizabeth proved reasonable. Mary's true frame of mind was revealed by her choice of advisers.

[50] September 19, 1564, Kirkcaldy to Randolph, *ibid.*, p. 75. October 13, 1564, Bedford to Cecil, *C.S.P., For., Eliz.*, VII, 223. One of Moray's first acts was to seize twenty-four pirates at Leith, on September 17. *C.S.P., Scot.*, II, 76–78. Further evidences of his renewed hold on power were the council's promulgation in December of a strictly Protestant decree against sexual misdemeanors, and a serious attempt on its part, early in 1565, to put an end to the lawlessness in the west. *Register of Privy Council*, I, 296 ff.
[51] October 24, 1564, Randolph to Cecil, *C.S.P., Scot.*, II, 84–88.

Moray had the same administrative power he possessed in 1562, but he did not now have his sister's ear. Nor did Maitland. For now "began Davie to grow great in court," writes Knox.[52] "Davie" was an Italian musician, David Riccio (or Rizzio), who had come to Scotland a few years previously in the train of an ambassador from Savoy. By the end of 1564 he had become Mary's confidential secretary in all matters pertaining to the Catholic powers of the Continent, and he seems to have served her both loyally and well. The rapidly increasing influence of this base-born foreigner was looked on with extreme distaste by the nobility, especially by the Protestants. Knox labeled him a "poltroon and vile knave";[53] he was generally suspected of being a papal agent.[54] Such was the man who now possessed the confidence of the Queen.

Mary's most elaborate attempt to throw dust in the eyes of Elizabeth was the dispatch, in September 1564, of Sir James Melville, an accomplished courtier, on a special mission to the English Queen. Mary had written an angry letter to Elizabeth on the occasion of the latter's curious proposal regarding Lennox. Melville was to explain away the sharp phrases in the letter, and to humor Elizabeth without making any real concessions.[55] Elizabeth was taken in by the smooth flattery and plausible explanations of the wily Sir James; on October 4 she consented to the holding of a conference between commissioners of both kingdoms to discuss the Dudley marriage, a move she and Cecil had been resolutely avoiding since March.[56]

The conference was held at Berwick from the nineteenth to the twenty-third of November. It appeared that in one sense Melville had done his work too well, for Elizabeth made absolutely no concessions whatever.[57] Mary must marry Dudley, now Earl of

[52] Knox, *History*, II, 422.   [53] *Ibid.*, I, 235.
[54] Sir James Melville, *Memoirs of his own Life*, pp. 136–37.
[55] Melville's instructions are in his *Memoirs*, pp. 112–15, and in Labanoff, *Recueil*, I, 231–34. The variations between the two versions make it clear that Melville cannot always be trusted. He wrote his memoirs at an advanced age, and his memory evidently played him tricks.
[56] *C.S.P., Scot.*, II, 79–80. For Melville's mission, see his *Memoirs*, pp. 115–29.
[57] The instructions of Bedford and Randolph are dated October 7, 1564. *C.S.P., Scot.*, II, 80–82.

Leicester, said the English envoys, Bedford and Randolph; if and when she did so, Elizabeth would look into the matter of the succession. Moray and Maitland, the Scottish representatives, were very angry. Such a position was totally unacceptable, as the English well knew.[58] Small wonder that Moray and Maitland told the understandably abashed Englishmen that they found Elizabeth's proceedings "marvelous strange," and that the only conclusion they could draw was that Elizabeth was procrastinating once more.[59]

The two irritated statesmen, on their return home, found, much to their surprise, that Mary was not as angry as they had feared.[60] Naturally not, for Mary was preparing against just such a contingency. She could not break with Elizabeth at once, however: Darnley was still in England, and Elizabeth had not yet said an irreversible and official "No" on the succession question. So she instructed the two to continue the negotiations with Cecil, and to include in their letters some distinct, and entirely fabulous, hints that unless the English made some concessions, Mary would certainly marry an unspecified Continental Catholic prince, for which marriage the negotiations were simultaneously going on. There can be no doubt that on this point Moray and Maitland were acting under Mary's instructions, for the Queen, in a letter of January 28, 1565, informed the Archbishop of Glasgow, her ambassador in France, of her plan, and instructed him to take the necessary steps to carry out his end of the bluff.[61]

Now we find Moray and Maitland writing a pair of joint letters to Cecil. This was one of the few occasions in their ten years of close political association on which they did so. There was a good reason for this. The pair had been badly worried by the fiasco at Berwick. They now took advantage of Mary's authorization to continue negotiations to make promises to Cecil far beyond anything Mary would have approved. In their first letter, dated December 3, they expounded the difficulties of their position. It was dangerous, they said, to meddle in the matrimonial affairs of

[58] October 31–November 3, 1564, Randolph to Cecil, *ibid.*, pp. 89–92.
[59] November 23, 1564, Bedford and Randolph to Cecil, *ibid.*, pp. 94–95.
[60] December 2, 1564, Randolph to Cecil, *ibid.*, p. 95.
[61] Labanoff, *Recueil*, I, 250–51.

princes. Cecil well knew that they wanted Mary to make a marriage which would suit their English friends. But the latter must make concessions too, and that right early, or Mary would close with a foreign suitor. If Elizabeth made a satisfactory offer on the succession question, on the other hand, they virtually promised that Mary would accept Leicester.[62]

It was this last statement which contained the dynamite. Moray and Maitland had absolutely no assurance that Mary would have Leicester at any price. If Mary ever discovered what a promise they had made in her name, they would be ruined. They awaited Cecil's answer on tenterhooks. Finally it came, dated December 16. It was thoroughly unsatisfactory.[63] Moray and Maitland were very angry. In their reply, dated December 24, they tore Cecil's arguments apart, declared that Mary would never marry an Englishman without some satisfaction on the succession question, and wound up by caustically inquiring why Cecil had not seen fit to sign his letter.[64] On the following day Randolph reported that Moray and Maitland were "in great perplexity" because they had exceeded their instructions; some two weeks later, that they were "in great agonies and passions." [65] Cecil wrote them twice in January 1565; the first letter was not well received; the second was. Maitland, on receipt of this second, friendly missive, addressed an elevated plea to Cecil on February 1, saying that if they could reach a satisfactory arrangement on this question, their glory would equal that of Edward I and Robert the Bruce in their respective countries.[66] Cecil was not moved.

All this correspondence had little apparent effect on Cecil and his mistress, but in reality it gave them much food for thought. A great foreign match for Mary must be stopped at all costs. The offer of Leicester had been made to prevent such a match; but now it was clear that Leicester was unacceptable, even to the Protestant, Anglophile faction in Scotland, except on conditions which Elizabeth was absolutely unwilling to grant. And now the foreign threat was growing again. Elizabeth's envoy in France was much alarmed by the frequent comings and goings of mes-

[62] *C.S.P., Scot.*, II, 95–97.   [63] *Ibid.*, pp. 102–5.   [64] *Ibid.*, pp. 105–9.
[65] *Ibid.*, pp. 111–12, 113.   [66] *Ibid.*, pp. 117–18.

sengers from Scotland.[67] The "foreign threat" was a deception, as we know; but Elizabeth and Cecil did not know. They were completely taken in.

Under the circumstances there was only one card left for Elizabeth and Cecil to play—Darnley. They had no intention of allowing Mary to marry Darnley under any conditions, which had not been the case with Leicester. So they did not make a formal offer of Darnley's hand to Mary. They simply gave him permission to go to Scotland. Cecil well knew that Darnley and his father would strain every nerve to persuade Mary to wed the young lord.[68] Cecil hoped they would succeed, and thus scotch Mary's foreign suitors. Then, Cecil planned to recall Darnley and his father to England. Both of them had gone to Scotland with passports containing a time limit. Darnley was an English subject, a member of the royal house, and could not marry without Elizabeth's consent. The possibility that Darnley might refuse to return was discounted: his mother was retained as a hostage, and, more important, the valuable English estates of Lennox, who was a greedy man, could be confiscated if father and son did not dance to Elizabeth's piping. In all this line of reasoning the English seriously miscalculated, simply because Mary's foreign negotiations were, doubtless much to her regret, almost entirely fictitious.[69] Elizabeth was playing into her rival's hand.[70]

Darnley arrived in Scotland in mid-February 1565, and on the 17th made his future wife's acquaintance. He made a fair first impression on people, Randolph reported, although there were those who disliked his coming. Glencairn had fears for Protestantism, Morton, for his pocketbook.[71] On the twenty-seventh Randolph

[67] January 7, 1565, Smith to Cecil, *C.S.P., For., Eliz.*, VII, 280–81.
[68] See Andrew Lang, *A History of Scotland from the Roman Occupation*, II, 136–37, on this point. Lang unfortunately draws the wrong conclusion from the evidence, viz., that Darnley was sent to divert Mary's attention from Leicester, with whom Elizabeth could not bear to part.
[69] In the winter of 1564–65 there were foreign suitors, mostly French, for Mary's hand, but none of them were thought by Mary to be of sufficient importance to be seriously considered as husbands. Teulet, *Relations politiques*, II, 189–90. A. Chéruel, *Marie Stuart et Catherine de Médicis*, p. 37.
[70] This interpretation of English policy is essentially that of Henderson, *Mary Queen of Scots*, I, 300–6.
[71] February 19, 1565, Randolph to Cecil, *C.S.P., Scot.*, II, 126–27. Randolph him-

wrote that he and Darnley had dined with Moray and that Darnley had been to the sermon to hear Knox and had later danced with Mary, at the urging of her brother.[72] The combination of intrigues behind the arrival of the young man had not yet dawned on the Earl. As for Maitland, he wrote gaily to Cecil on the twenty-eighth that he was in love (with Mary Fleming, one of the Queen's Marys), and therefore in the best of spirits.[73]

Moray was still anxious for the Leicester match, but he was beginning to despair of its ever taking place, owing to English stubbornness. On February 27 he dined Randolph and Wishart of Pitarrow and unburdened himself to the ambassador. He still was not worried about Darnley; but in the Leicester affair,

I have the worst part . . . I am known to be a travailer to your effect, which I repent not, for before God I do think it the best. If it come well to pass, take the honor who will; it is enough for me to have discharged my duty to God and my country . . . if it go otherwise than well, the burden is wholly mine, for that I am the counsellor, the deviser, the persuader—and how well some already like of me, you know, and being ever had in suspicion for England, either I shall be forced to show myself their plain enemy, or every word that I do speak of them (be it never so true or just) shall be had in suspicion. If she marry any other, what mind will he bear me, that knoweth how much I do mislike therewith? If he be a Papist, either we must obey or fall into new combers, and I ever to be thought the ring-leader. But to speak these things, what doth it avail? . . . it is not the first time you have heard me say as much; I see nothing the better, but drift of time, delays from day to day, and to do all for nothing, and to get nothing for all![74]

Plainly the Earl was becoming discouraged.

Mary, who since Darnley's arrival was in a position to do so, began to apply pressure. She insisted that Elizabeth make some sort of statement on the succession question, and kept after Randolph day after day.[75] Finally Elizabeth, who evidently judged

self, as his letter of February 12, 1565, shows, was opposed to Darnley's coming: he feared it would ruin the chances of the Leicester match. *Ibid.*, pp. 124–25. Morton's worry was due to the possibility that Lennox might challenge his control of the Angus estates, to which the Countess of Lennox had a claim.
[72] *Ibid.*, p. 128.   [73] *Ibid.*, pp. 128–29.
[74] March 1–3, 1565, Randolph to Cecil, *ibid.*, pp. 129–34.
[75] March 15, 1565, Randolph to Cecil, *ibid.*, pp. 135–36.

that Darnley had done his work by now, made her answer, which was communicated to Mary on March 16: she would make no decision on the question of the succession until she had finally decided whether or not she herself would ever marry.[76]

This was the fatal blow. Mary was very angry, and Moray was "almost stark mad." [77] At last the truth began to dawn on him. Elizabeth was not going to make the necessary concessions, and the Leicester marriage would not take place. And now he realized the fatal significance of the negotiations in regard to Darnley, with whom Moray was already at odds. "How long the kindness will stand between my Lord of Moray and Lord of Lennox, your Honour may judge of by this, that my Lord of Lennox hath joined himself with those whom my Lord of Moray thinketh worst of in Scotland; what opinion the young Lord hath conceived of him that lately talking with Lord Robert (Stewart), who showed him in the Scottish map what lands my Lord of Moray had, and in what bounds, the Lord Darnley said that it was too much. This came to my Lord of Moray's ears, and so to the Queen, who advised my Lord Darnley to excuse himself to my Lord of Moray," wrote Randolph on March 20.[78] Mary, he felt sure, would almost certainly marry Darnley, with or without Elizabeth's consent, and Moray was sure that Elizabeth would not give that consent. Thus the Darnley marriage would spell his own ruin, and, unless Elizabeth acted quickly, that of Protestantism as well, for if Mary married Darnley in defiance of England, it could only be under Catholic auspices. "The devil cumber you," he burst out at Randolph on March 18, "our Queen doth nothing but weep and write. Amend this betimes, or all will go amiss." [79]

Mary was grievously disappointed at this blasting of her hopes. Nevertheless she wavered before taking the decisive step of allying herself to Darnley, since this would mean defying the English

[76] March 17, 1565, Randolph to Cecil, *ibid.*, pp. 136–37. See also J. Stevenson, ed., *Selections . . . Illustrating the Reign of Mary Queen of Scotland*, pp. 134–35.
[77] March 20, 1565, Randolph to Leicester, in Andrew Lang, "New Light on Mary Queen of Scots," *Blackwood's Magazine*, CLXXXII (July, 1907), 21.
[78] March 20, 1565, Randolph to Cecil, in R. Keith, *The History of the Affairs of Church and State in Scotland*, II, 268–75.
[79] Lang, "New Light on Mary Queen of Scots," p. 21.

and her own Protestant subjects as well. "What to do or wherein to resolve she is marvelously in doubt," wrote Randolph to Cecil on the twenty-seventh.[80] But the doubt did not last long. No official communication came from England; only the story, circulated by the Earl of Athol, a friend of Lennox and a promoter of the Darnley match, that one day, as Leicester and Norfolk were playing tennis in Elizabeth's presence, the former snatched the Queen's "napkin" from her hand without so much as a by-your-leave in order to mop his face. Norfolk thought to avenge the insult, and was much taken aback when Elizabeth rated him soundly for vilifying Leicester.[81]

Such behavior on the part of Leicester and Elizabeth, which Lang calls "indecent familiarity," [82] served to convince all parties in Scotland that Elizabeth had been insincere from the first in her offer of Leicester to Mary. The latter now scornfully turned her back on England. Darnley had his famous attack of measles in the first week of April. Mary nursed him through it, and became infatuated with him at the same time. From this point on, she was not to be gainsaid. She would have Darnley, in spite of Elizabeth and all the world, including her brother.

As for Moray, he was in despair. Ever since 1561 he had staked his political life on being able to make some arrangement between Mary and Elizabeth which would satisfy both, settle the succession question, and assure the supremacy of Protestantism. To accomplish this he had sought his sister's favor to the point of breaking with his old allies, the Protestant zealots, and had thus delivered himself into Elizabeth's hands. If she proved unreasonable, as she had, his influence with Mary would be gone, as it clearly now was. Riccio had the Queen's ear; so had Lennox, along with the latter's Catholic friends, Athol, Caithness, and Hume. He could not even be sure of Maitland, who, politically minded as he was, might decide that the advantages of the Darnley match outweighed its disadvantages. Moray's situation was perilous; he had gambled on Elizabeth and lost; one more error might mean his ruin, for he had

---

[80] C.S.P., Scot., II, 137–38.
[81] March 31, 1565, Randolph to Throckmorton, ibid., p. 140.
[82] Lang, "New Light on Mary Queen of Scots," p. 26.

many enemies, both political and religious. On April 3, ostensibly because Mary was planning to celebrate Easter in an "ungodly" fashion, he left the court and retired to St. Andrews to think out his next move. Randolph reported that he had departed under a cloud.[83] This was, if anything, an understatement.

[83] April 7, 1565, Randolph to Bedford, *C.S.P., Scot.*, II, 141–42.

CHAPTER VI

Moray's Revolt

MORAY was in deep perplexity when he left Mary's court in April, 1565. He had been hoodwinked by his English friends and overreached by his Queen, and for the only time in his career he was completely at sea. His policy during the next six months was confused and ineffective and brought about a fiasco which came perilously close to ruining him forever.

Moray's sojourn at St. Andrews, where he spent most of April, gave him a chance to take stock of the party situation in Scotland and to discover who his supporters were. He had already taken one precautionary measure: in the latter part of March he, Argyle, and Châtelherault had pledged support to each other in all legitimate enterprises.[1] Argyle was Moray's old companion in arms, and he had suffered from the restoration of Lennox, to whom he had to return some lands.[2] Moray's renewed alliance with Châtelherault, whose power he had been attempting to weaken for five years, was rather startling; their only common bond was a thorough fear and dislike of Lennox and Darnley. These two great lords formed the nucleus of Moray's party, but there were others, by and large the same men who had first taken arms against Mary of Guise in 1559, earnest Protestants who felt that if Mary wed Darnley, Protestantism would be in jeopardy.

Equally important was the closing of the breach between Moray and Knox. The Reformer had been as zealous as Moray in behalf of the Leicester match, and recent events convinced him

[1] This is noted in a chronology of events in Scotland, in Cecil's hand, printed in W. Murdin, ed., *The Burghley Papers (1571–1596)*, p. 758.
[2] October 31-November 3, 1564, Randolph to Cecil, *C.S.P., Scot.*, II, 89–92.

that the Earl had at last seen the error of his ways. Knox was badly worried by the Darnley match. "The godly cry out that they are undone," wrote Randolph.[3] Moray and Knox now drew together once more, and they remained in alliance, though not always in agreement, till Moray's death.

In appearance the alignment of parties resembled that of 1559, but in reality there was a vast difference. The position of Moray and Knox was far weaker at the present time, principally because they could not convince enough people that the religion was in danger. To a large number of Protestants it appeared that Moray was prosecuting a personal quarrel with his sister, or, worse still, was serving as a catspaw for Elizabeth—be it remembered that the English connection was by no means as popular in the country generally as it was with the leaders of the Anglophile party at court. The fact that Moray's principal allies, Argyle and Châtelherault, were obviously swayed by personal motives lent color to the general suspicion that the cry of "Religion in danger!" was a blind. The result was that the Protestant party was split, and a great many men who had been members of the Congregation, especially the greedy, now sided with the Queen for personal reasons.[4]

In addition to this Protestant support, Mary could also count on that of all the Catholic lords in Scotland. Furthermore, there was Lord Gordon, the eldest son of the ruined Huntly, and hence a bitter enemy of Moray; his resurrection might prove useful. Finally, there was Bothwell. The latter had, in fact, already put in an appearance; he had returned to Scotland early in March. Moray knew that the restoration of Bothwell could only mean trouble for him; he and Maitland urged Mary to put the adventurous Earl to the horn.[5] Mary agreed, and Bothwell was summoned to a "day of law," scheduled for May 2. On May 1 Moray and Argyle ap-

[3] April 18, 1565, Randolph to Cecil, *ibid.*, pp. 143-44.
[4] On this point see *Historical Manuscripts Commission, 3rd Report*, Appendix, p. 394; *The Register of the Privy Council of Scotland*, I, 344-46; December 21, 1563, Randolph to Cecil, *C.S.P., Scot.*, II, 29-30; John Knox, *History of the Reformation in Scotland*, II, 495. Randolph's letter of June 3, 1565, *C.S.P., Scot.*, II, 172-74, gives a substantially accurate list of the important partisans on both sides.
[5] March 10, 1565, Bedford to Cecil, *C.S.P., For., Eliz.*, VII, 312.

peared in Edinburgh at the head of more than 5,000 men, an argument so effective that their foe, getting wind of it, decided to wait for a more auspicious day. In fact, he had already embarked for France.[6]

The fact that Moray had left his sister's court was evidence of serious disagreement between the two, nothing more. It did not mean that a rebellion would break out at once. Everything hinged on the attitude of Elizabeth. It was barely possible that Elizabeth might not actively oppose the Darnley match, in which case, Moray thought, Protestantism and the amity with England might be safeguarded by negotiation. Mary felt that in this case Elizabeth would have to agree eventually to a favorable settlement of the succession question also, since the two strongest claims would be united by the marriage; if so, all of Mary's problems would be solved. The difference between Moray and his sister lay in the fact that Mary was planning to marry Darnley in any case; Moray wanted her to abandon the match if Elizabeth disapproved.

Both sides, therefore, waited in suspense for an indication of Elizabeth's attitude. The latter soon decided to send Sir Nicholas Throckmorton to Scotland to make it clear to Mary that England was unshakeably opposed to the Darnley match. Mary might have any English noble but Darnley, and Elizabeth would look into the succession question if she took Leicester. Mary was asked to send someone to England with full power to negotiate, since Maitland, who had been sent to England, was permitted by his instructions to talk only about Darnley.[7]

The fat was now fairly in the fire. Mary, who expected some such result, had ordered her recalcitrant brother to come to the court at Stirling. He was coldly received at first,[8] but the military power he displayed when he kept Bothwell's "day of law" evidently gave Mary a fright. When Moray returned to Stirling on May 4, she was all smiles. So were Lennox and Darnley. They all

---

[6] March 15, May 3, 1565, Randolph to Cecil, *C.S.P., Scot.,* II, 135-36, 152-55. March 31, 1565, Randolph to Throckmorton, *C.S.P., For., Eliz.,* VII, 325. April 28, 1565, Bedford to Cecil, *ibid.,* pp. 346-47.
[7] R. Keith, *The History of the Affairs of Church and State in Scotland,* III, 332. Throckmorton's instructions are in *C.S.P., Scot.,* II, 145-47, 150-52.
[8] April 29, 1565, Randolph to Cecil, *ibid.,* pp. 147-48.

did their best to cajole him into registering his approval of the marriage in writing. Moray refused. He was so suspicious of his sister, who, Randolph reported, had said that her brother had designs on the crown, that he and Argyle now never appeared simultaneously at court, for fear of a *coup de main*.[9] He told Mary that he could not approve the marriage now, because he feared that it would be harmful to Protestantism and that it would be a political blunder if England was opposed to it. He would reserve his decision till Maitland returned. Only if Mary agreed to turn Protestant and wipe out all vestiges of Catholicism would he consent at once.[10]

Mary, who by this time had fairly exact information as to what Elizabeth's answer would be, now decided to be forehanded with her "good sister." [11] She summoned the nobility to meet on May 14 (the meeting was actually held on the fifteenth) to give their consent to the marriage before the English attitude was officially communicated to her and became generally known. Maitland, who had started north after Throckmorton, was therefore ordered to return to present Elizabeth with a new letter from Mary, and also to delay Throckmorton as much as possible, so that he would not arrive before the nobility had met.[12]

Maitland felt that the basic policy of the Darnley match was sound but that Mary's tactics were deplorable, since they would probably lead Elizabeth not only to oppose the match but also to encourage a Protestant rebellion. As a result, he took the drastic step of refusing to obey Mary's orders. He hastened after Throckmorton, explained the situation to him, and urged him to hurry. Never, reported the envoy, had he known Maitland to be so perplexed or so angry.[13]

Throckmorton sped to Stirling, where he arrived on May 15,

[9] May 3, 1565, Randolph to Cecil, *ibid.*, pp. 152–55.
[10] May 8, 1565, Randolph to Cecil, *ibid.*, pp. 155–57. May 12, 1565. Throckmorton to Leicester and Cecil, *ibid.*, pp. 160–61.
[11] A servant of Lady Lennox arrived in Edinburgh about May 1, with a letter from Maitland. May 2, 1565, Bedford to Cecil, *C.S.P., For., Eliz.*, VII, 350. May 3, 1565, Randolph to Cecil, *C.S.P., Scot.*, II, 152–55.
[12] May 8, 1565, Randolph to Cecil, *ibid.*, pp. 155–57. May 11, 1565, Throckmorton to Leicester and Cecil, *ibid.*, pp. 158–60.
[13] May 11, 1565, Throckmorton to Leicester and Cecil, *ibid.*, pp. 158–60.

and noisily demanded an immediate audience. He found Mary surrounded by her leading nobles, Moray among them, and stated Elizabeth's opinion in no uncertain terms. Mary said she was much surprised, since her "good sister" had so often given her to understand that she might marry any English noble. However, she was willing to delay the marriage three months, and in the meantime she would send another ambassador to Elizabeth to try to straighten things out. After the interview with Throckmorton, Darnley was created Earl of Ross. His oath of allegiance to Mary was, in Elizabeth's eyes, treason to herself. Throckmorton departed from Scotland shortly thereafter; force alone, he now felt, would break up the marriage.[14]

The consequence of Throckmorton's embassy was a heightened tension between the factions in Scotland, but no definite break, because it seemed that even at this late date Elizabeth might back down in the face of Mary's determination. Moray, hesitating and uncertain, lingered on at court for some days. He attended the Privy Council meeting on May 19, when it was decided to hold a convention of the nobility on June 10 at Perth; this was later put off till the twenty-second because, Randolph said, too many Protestants planned to attend.[15] Moray had been making a serious effort to insure a Protestant majority, because one of the items on the agenda was to prepare business for a July Parliament, at which he was determined to push the religious question.[16] This Parliament was never held. The later date for the convention was evidently selected to conflict with the usual meeting of the General Assembly on June 25; this would keep many Protestants away.

Elizabeth, meanwhile, was still in a fume. On June 8 she instructed Randolph to promise her backing to those who were upholding Protestantism. Ten days later she ordered Lennox and Darnley home and talked menacingly of war to the French am-

<hr />

[14] May 21, 1565, Throckmorton to Elizabeth, *ibid.*, pp. 161–64.
[15] *Register of Privy Council*, I, 335–36. This was the last council meeting Moray attended before his rebellion. June 3, 1565, Randolph to Throckmorton, *C.S.P., Scot.*, II, 174. Throughout this period Randolph's letters have to be used with caution; his prejudice against Mary in the matter of the Darnley match led him into all sorts of misrepresentations.
[16] *Register of Privy Council*, I, 335–36. Knox, *History*, II, 483.

bassador.[17] Meanwhile Mary had sent John Hay, Commendator of Balmerinoch, a Protestant and a friend of Moray, to Elizabeth, in a last attempt to win her favor.[18] Hay got nowhere with Elizabeth, but his journey to London was not entirely fruitless. While there he saw De Silva, who notified him of Philip's approval of the Darnley match.[19] A few days later Charles IX informed Elizabeth that the marriage had the approval of France.[20]

Meanwhile, in the last days of June, curious things were going on in Scotland. Rumors of all kinds filled the air, and the intrigues of both sides became very involved indeed. Moray did not attend the Perth Convention; he went as far as Lochleven, and there he holed up. Knox's continuator says he was ill.[21] He may well have been, and he would have done well to plead illness; instead, he spread the story that the Lennox faction had plotted his assassination at Perth.[22] He was soon to be called to account for this.

We have no knowledge of what went on at the Perth Convention; it doubtless turned into a council of war of the Lennox party. Mary stayed on in the neighborhood of Perth for several days, amid growing rumors that Moray and his associates planned to kidnap Darnley and Lennox, who had refused to obey Elizabeth's orders of recall,[23] and turn them over to England. Mary suddenly became alarmed, and on July 1 made a rapid ride from Perth to Lord Livingston's house at Callendar. The journey was not so hasty but that Lord Erskine could not send a bantering message to Moray asking what he had done to frighten the Queen so. Moray, who was just out of bed, replied that he was sure he did not know.[24] This episode, as well as some statements in Randolph's letters of early July, have led many historians to accept the rumors as truth and to assert that Moray did plan to seize Darnley and his

---

[17] C.S.P., For., Eliz., VII, 390. C.S.P., Scot., II, 178. June 18, 1565, De Foix to Catherine de Medici, in A. Teulet, ed., Relations politiques de la France et de l'Espagne avec l'Ecosse au XVIe siècle, II, 207–9.
[18] Hay's instructions, dated June 14, 1565, are in A. Labanoff, ed., Recueil des lettres de Marie Stuart, I, 266–71.
[19] June 25, 1565, De Silva to Philip II, C.S.P., Span., I, 438–42.
[20] June 30, 1565, Charles IX to Elizabeth, C.S.P., For., Eliz., VII, 399.
[21] Knox, History, II, 484.
[22] July 2, 1565, Randolph to Cecil, in Keith, History, II, 296–309.
[23] July 2, 1565, Randolph to Cecil, ibid., pp. 296–309.
[24] July 4, 1565, Randolph to Cecil, ibid., pp. 309–21.

father, but the story has since been discredited, at least as far as this particular incident is concerned.[25] It is possible that Moray and his friends did have some such idea before July 1, but there is no proof one way or the other, so that any concrete assertion is impossible.[26]

Although they were not plotting the kidnapping of Lennox and Darnley, Moray and Argyle were up to something a good deal more serious. On July 1 they sent a note to Randolph telling him they had some important matters to discuss with him.[27] What they wanted, it developed, was a subsidy of £3,000 from Elizabeth, in the interests of religion and of the English alliance.[28] They were planning to take action, but as yet they had not definitely decided to revolt, since Hay was still in England and since there was an outside chance that Elizabeth might change her mind about the marriage. But Moray did not expect her to. What he was trying now was a cautious half-measure: he wanted to coerce his sister by a show of force into delaying or abandoning her marriage—he doubtless remembered the beneficial results of his display on Bothwell's "law day." He and Argyle decided to hold a meeting of their supporters at Glasgow on July 15; Moray then went to St. Andrews, and Argyle sped westward, where he sum-

[25] D. H. Fleming, *Mary Queen of Scots*, pp. 354–56, first showed that there was nothing in this story, which was known as the Raid of Baith. Andrew Lang, no favorer of Moray, accepted his conclusions. *A History of Scotland from the Roman Occupation*, II, 143–44.

[26] Mary herself, in a letter to De Foix on November 8, 1565, asserted that Moray had planned to seize Lennox and Darnley, not on the occasion of the ride from Perth to Callendar, but at the Perth Convention itself. Unfortunately for Moray's detractors, however, parts of the letter are demonstrably inaccurate. Mary said that Moray would agree to the Darnley marriage if Catholicism were definitely outlawed, for Mary as well as for others, and if he were vested with real control of all business. There is no corroborating evidence for the second part of this statement. Then Mary made a bad slip. Moray, she said, used the occasion of Bothwell's "law day"—May 2—to plot the seizure of Lennox and Darnley. But we know that the Perth Convention was not decided on till May 19. *Register of Privy Council*, I, 335–36. This would rather lead one to suspect that Mary was exaggerating her brother's villainy. The letter is in Labanoff, *Recueil*, I, 299–307. It is also worth noting that a message justifying her conduct sent by the Queen to France in September did not mention any kidnap attempt. September 29, 1565, De Foix to Catherine de Medici, in Teulet, *Relations politiques*, II, 229–37.

[27] J. Stevenson, ed., *Selections . . . Illustrating the Reign of Mary Queen of Scotland*, p. 118.

[28] July 4, 1565, Randolph to Cecil, in Keith, *History*, II, 309–21.

moned his levies and began to menace the lands of Athol.[29]

Mary, meanwhile, was not inactive. She was exerting herself to win to her side as many people as possible, as can be seen by the fact that since mid-March she had been using very freely the power given her by the Parliament of 1564 to confirm feu charters, in order to gain supporters.[30] By and large she was successful in splitting the Protestant party, as we have seen, mainly because the struggle appeared to be so largely a matter of personal and political rivalry; this in spite of the behavior of Darnley, who was beginning to show himself for the nonentity he was, and who was becoming more and more unpopular.[31] Hay returned on July 6 [32] and told Mary of his lack of success in England, a pill which was doubtless sweetened by the fact that he also brought the blessings of Philip. All hope of amity with Elizabeth gone, Mary now determined to take vigorous steps to overcome her disaffected subjects. Proclamations were issued to the effect that nothing would be done to alter the religious *status quo*. On July 15 a summons was issued for all men to prepare to turn out to fight for their Queen.[33] At the same time she sent to France to recall Bothwell.[34] The Earl's hour had struck.

Mary also forbade the adherents of Moray to meet at Glasgow; [35] they obeyed the order literally and came together at Stirling in mid-July. The situation had changed materially for them since the first of the month. It was clear now that the Darnley match would mean the collapse of the friendship with England. Elizabeth was irreconcilably hostile to it, and on July 10 had instructed Randolph to support Moray and to urge him and his partisans to collect sufficient military strength to defend themselves against all possible contingencies.[36] This letter, taken in conjunction with her previous letter, of June 8, amounted to a promise of aid. Furthermore, Moray had heard that Mary had

[29] July 6, 1565, Randolph to Cecil, *C.S.P., Scot.*, II, 179.
[30] *Registrum Magni Sigilli Regum Scotorum*, IV, 368 ff. See above, pp. 92–93.
[31] July 2, 1565, Randolph to Cecil, in Keith, *History*, II, 296–309.
[32] July 7, 1565, Randolph to Cecil, *C.S.P., Scot.*, II, 179–80.
[33] *Register of Privy Council*, I, 338–39.
[34] R. Gore-Browne, *Lord Bothwell and Mary Queen of Scots*, p. 193.
[35] *Treasurer's Accounts*, XI, 376.   [36] Keith, *History*, II, 321–23.

asked for and received Spanish support.[37] This could only mean that Mary was planning to restore Catholicism in the near future. Consequently, on July 18, Moray and his friends wrote to Elizabeth formally requesting assistance in their efforts to preserve Protestantism and the amity with England—in other words, asking her to repeat her actions of 1559–60.[38] They were about to launch a rebellion.

Just what Moray planned to do had his revolt succeeded is highly problematical. The best guess is that he would have insisted that Mary give up Darnley, turn Protestant, and ratify the Acts of the Parliament of 1560. If Mary refused, he would probably have elevated Châtelherault to the throne. The Duke was feeble, and his eldest son was insane; Moray could thus look forward to a long tenure of power for himself. Such a dynastic shift could be expected to have English support in the long run, in spite of Elizabeth's scruples as to the disrespectful treatment of crowned heads, for Châtelherault had no claim to the English throne, and the nagging problem of the succession would thus be eliminated as far as Scotland was concerned. The union of the crowns would be indefinitely postponed, it is true; but to Moray the safety of Protestantism was a more important consideration. All this is mere guesswork, however: Moray was never in a position to put any line of policy into effect.

In fact, Moray was completely outgeneraled at the very beginning. Mary resolved to force a showdown with her recalcitrant brother, and she chose a line of tactics which made it seem more obvious than ever that Moray was acting from selfish personal motives. On July 17 she and the council sent a message to Moray at Stirling, ordering him to state in writing all he knew about the alleged plot to murder him at Perth. Moray replied that he was willing to explain in person, if he were granted a safe-conduct. Mary granted it on the nineteenth and ordered him to appear three days after he received it.[39]

---

[37] Randolph implied as much to Cecil in a letter of July 19; he must have received his information from some member of Moray's party, with which he was in close touch throughout July. *Ibid.*, pp. 330–35.   [38] *Ibid.*, pp. 329–30.
[39] *Register of Privy Council*, I, 339–42.

Moray was caught. He could not prove his charge that Lennox and Darnley planned to murder him at Perth—indeed, no proof has ever been discovered. If he obeyed the Queen's summons, he would have to admit as much, and he and his cause would be hopelessly compromised. If he failed to appear, he would stand convicted in the eyes of many as a mere intriguer who was using Protestantism as a cloak to cover his ambitions. He took refuge in silence. Mary pressed her advantage. On July 28 she issued another safe-conduct for Moray and eighty of his followers, to make it clear that no treachery was intended against him.[40] On the twenty-ninth she and Darnley were married, in spite of the lack of a papal dispensation.[41] Darnley had been proclaimed King on the previous day.[42] On August 1 Moray was summoned once more, on pain of being declared a rebel if he disobeyed.[43] The council which issued the summons was a very large one, with a heavily Catholic membership. Moray, having refused to appear, was put to the horn on August 6. This sentence was to be communicated to his principal allies, Châtelherault and Argyle, who were not to aid him under pain of being horned themselves.[44] The die was cast.

ii

It became apparent to everyone in Scotland almost at once that Moray's was by far the weaker party. He had won no important adherents since April. Châtelherault and Argyle remained his principal supporters, and he had the backing of Knox and of a large number of Fife lairds, such as Kirkcaldy; but the Protestant strength was effectively split. Mary, on the other hand, was winning over the notable fence-sitters, such as Morton and Maitland, and was increasing her strength by such moves as the recall of Bothwell and the release of Lord Gordon.[45]

[40] Fleming, *Mary Queen of Scots*, p. 357. *Register of Privy Council*, I, 345.
[41] On the question of the papal dispensation, see J. H. Pollen, ed., *Papal Negotiations with Mary Queen of Scots*, pp. lxxix–xcviii. A dispensation was necessary because Mary and Darnley were cousins.
[42] *Register of Privy Council*, I, 345–46.   [43] *Ibid.*, pp. 346–47.
[44] *Ibid.*, pp. 349–50.
[45] In October Gordon was restored to the earldom of Huntly. T. Thomson, ed., *A Diurnal of Remarkable Occurrents that Have Passed within the Country of Scotland*, pp. 80, 84.

Under the circumstances Moray had only one chance of success: he must have English support. Elizabeth had promised help, and Randolph kept writing to his government on Moray's behalf.[46] But Elizabeth was to prove a broken reed; she and her advisers ultimately decided that they could not support Moray. The key factor in this decision was unquestionably the general European diplomatic situation. Spain was hostile, and, worse still, Spain and France had drawn closer together. The Conference of Bayonne had taken place in June 1565, and Protestant Europe seethed with rumors of a secret Catholic league which was planning to uproot heresy with fire and sword. Elizabeth was well aware that she could not defy the combined power of France and Spain, and she feared that any aid she might give Moray would produce just such an alliance, directed against England. So she threw Moray to the wolves.

Meanwhile Moray and his friends were in the west, which was the center of their strength. On August 15 they met in Ayr, and decided to collect their forces and take the field on the twenty-fourth.[47] Mary was moving equally fast, however. On the fourteenth the property of Moray, Rothes, Kirkcaldy, and the Provost of Dundee was seized.[48] On the twenty-second Mary issued a proclamation announcing her intention of marching against the rebels and ordering her southern lieges to meet her at specified dates, starting on the twenty-sixth.[49] Athol was given a commission of lieutenancy in the north, in order to hold Argyle in check.[50] Along with all this went further assurances that no religious change was intended.

Mary left Edinburgh for the west on August 26, swearing that she would rather lose her crown than her revenge on Moray. She was well aware of her brother's dealings with the English; she taxed Randolph with them, and confiscated the property of two

---

[46] E.g., July 23, 1565, Randolph to Elizabeth, C.S.P., Scot., II, 182–83. On July 25 Bedford wrote to Elizabeth and Cecil, asking them for permission to aid Moray by creating some diversions on the Border and urging them to take a definite stand one way or the other on the question of supporting Moray. C.S.P., For., Eliz., VII, 411–13.   [47] Knox, History, II, 496.
[48] Register of Privy Council, I, 353.   [49] Ibid., pp. 355–57.
[50] Ibid., pp. 357–60.

men who were detected delivering money to Moray from an English agent.[51] Mary's objective was Glasgow, which she planned to approach from the southeast. Moray resolved on a bold stroke. With a troop of 1,200 horse he and Châtelherault, accompanied by Glencairn, Rothes, and Boyd, slipped round north of the Queen's forces and rode into Edinburgh on August 31.[52]

They received a very cold reception. The Protestant citizens of the town would not join them. This disaster was due mainly to the long rift between Moray and Knox. Though the latter was once more on Moray's side, the bulk of the Protestants would not be convinced that Moray was engaged in anything more than a political wrangle with his sister, and defend him in such a cause they would not. Lord Erskine, now Earl of Mar, still captain of Edinburgh Castle, turned its guns on his nephew. Mary was returning posthaste. Without Argyle's forces Moray was far too weak to face his sister in the field, especially since he had no artillery; so he left the town early on the morning of September 2, after addressing a letter to Mary in which he protested that he and his friends were much maligned, that Mary was listening to wicked advice, and that he was quite willing to have his case tried by the council.[53] This letter was a feeler; Moray was trying to discover whether his sister was at all disposed to make an agreement. It was ignored.

Moray and his friends retreated rapidly. They were able to keep ahead of the Queen largely because their little force was a mounted one. They arrived at Dumfries, on the home ground of the Master of Maxwell, on September 5.[54] Mary, at the same moment, was at Glasgow, whither her pursuit of Moray had carried her. Here, however, she was in some danger. Her forces, feudal levies, of course, were slipping away, as they always did; and with Argyle north and Moray south of her, she might be taken at a disadvantage. She therefore decided not to try conclusions with

[51] August 20, August 27, 1565, Randolph to Cecil, C.S.P., Scot., II, 194-95, 196-98. Also, ibid., p. 199.   [52] September 1, 1565, Randolph to Cecil, ibid., pp. 199-200.
[53] Ibid., p. 200. September 2, 1565, Randolph to Cecil, ibid., p. 201.
[54] September 5, 1565, Scrope to Bedford, C.S.P., For., Eliz., VII, 452.

her brother until the northern levies could be collected; she ordered them on the fifth to meet her at Stirling on September 30.[55]
Leaving Lennox in charge in the west, Mary returned to the east
to await the meeting of the northern levies and to attend to the
seat of Moray's personal power, Fife.[56] Recalcitrant Protestant
lairds there were dealt with firmly, and money was raised by fines
and forced loans.[57] Mary also issued a proclamation which claimed
that Moray's true aims were revealed by his demand that the
Queen take advice from the nobility of the realm rather than from
base-born foreigners. This demonstrated, Mary argued, that what
her brother wanted was power, not security for Protestantism.[58]
On September 15 she issued another proclamation promising that
at the next Parliament there would be a definitive settlement of
the religious question.[59] The implication was that the settlement
would be a Protestant one, but there was chicane here, as we shall
see.

Meanwhile, Moray and his friends were in desperate straits. It
was perfectly clear to them after the fiasco at Edinburgh that the
only thing that would save them was English aid. They lacked
everything: money, artillery, ammunition; and throughout the
latter part of August and the month of September they kept appealing for help.[60] Elizabeth and Cecil were in a nasty dilemma.
They had promised to help Moray, and considerable pressure was

[55] *Register of Privy Council*, I, 362–63.
[56] *Ibid.*, pp. 364–67. Moray's allies were outlawed on September 27; Thomson,
Diurnal of Occurrents, p. 83.
[57] Knox, *History*, II, 503. *Register of Privy Council*, I, 367–69. September 19,
1565, Bedford to Cecil, *C.S.P., For., Eliz.*, VII, 463–65. Fleming, *Mary Queen of
Scots*, p. 116. Thomson, *Diurnal of Occurrents*, p. 84.
[58] *Register of Privy Council*, I, 369–71. This proclamation is dated September 3
but was inserted in the Council Register under date of September 12.
[59] *Ibid.*, pp. 372–73.
[60] See especially the correspondence to and from Bedford during September,
C.S.P., For., Eliz., VII, 446 ff., *C.S.P., Scot.*, II, 204 ff.; and Robert Melville's instructions of September 10, 1565, *ibid.*, p. 207. Melville while in London spread
Moray's version of the events of the past few months in Scotland: he had been
driven to take up arms because he wished Mary to wait till all powers concerned
approved the marriage before she went ahead with it. He had been the victim of
a plot. The religious question was played up to Elizabeth; to foreign envoys it
was scarcely mentioned. See De Foix's letter of September 29, 1565, to Catherine
de Medici, in Teulet, *Relations politiques*, II, 229–37.

being exerted on them to fulfill that pledge, but practical politics required a hands-off policy. At one point their good resolutions almost broke down: on September 12 Elizabeth notified Bedford that she was sending him £3,000. Moray was to be given £1,000 and 300 men, *sub rosa*, of course.[61] Bedford never got a chance to act on the latter part of these instructions, which was promptly countermanded, but he did send the £1,000, to which he added £500 from his own pocket.[62] As the month wore on, the rebel lords' appeals grew more pressing; finally, Elizabeth, on September 24, put the matter up to her council. The council decided, inevitably, although not unanimously, that it was impossible to help Moray.[63] This decision meant that Moray's cause was lost beyond hope. On September 30 Elizabeth instructed Randolph to resume negotiations with Mary and to work for a general pardon for the rebels.[64] The next day she wrote Moray to tell him that she could not help him but would give him asylum in England if necessary.[65]

While Moray's fate was being decided in England, there was little the Earl could do but wait patiently in Dumfries and hope against hope. He was so short of funds and equipment that he could not even begin to raise an adequate military force. He was cut off from his ally Argyle, who in any case was more interested in devastating the lands of his personal enemies Lennox and Athol than in the common cause.[66] About the only step Moray took during September, beyond appealing for English aid, was to issue, on September 19, a proclamation justifying his conduct. His purpose, he said, was to safeguard Protestantism, which was in danger, and to restore the chief posts in the state to the nobility, who traditionally filled them, instead of allowing them to remain in the hands of base-born foreigners—in other words, "Davie"—since from this arose most of the evils currently to be seen in the govern-

[61] *C.S.P., For., Eliz.*, VII, 458–59.
[62] September 28, 1565, Bedford to Cecil, *ibid.*, p. 473.
[63] October 1, 1565, De Silva to Philip II, *C.S.P., Span.*, I, 483–86. See also September 18, 1565, De Foix to Catherine de Medici, in Teulet, *Relations politiques*, II, 219–28.   [64] *C.S.P., Scot.*, II, 215–16.   [65] *Ibid.*, p. 216.
[66] On this point see M. Philippson, *Histoire du règne de Marie Stuart*, III, 17–18.

ment of Scotland. Moray further claimed, probably correctly, that the proclamation of Darnley as King without consent of Parliament was grossly illegal.[67]

It has already been pointed out that Moray's cry of "Religion in danger!" was not effective in winning him supporters. It would be well to pause here and consider whether or not he was justified in claiming that Mary was really planning the overthrow of Protestantism. The first piece of evidence that comes to hand is an incident in February 1565. A Catholic evensong was held in Edinburgh; Moray protested, and Mary promised that no such ceremonies would be permitted in the future, but she did not punish those involved.[68] In March Randolph reported that as many people now attended Mass in Edinburgh as the Protestant service, and that two "Papist" outrages had gone unpunished.[69] Also in March Mary had seen fit to appoint a Jesuit, William Chisholm, to the see of Dunblane—the first such appointment since her return.[70] Moray left the court early in April because Easter was to be celebrated in the Catholic manner. Later in the month a priest was caught celebrating Mass. His hearers were jailed, and he himself was pilloried and pelted with eggs. Mary was furious and ordered all concerned released; she then instructed the magistrates of Edinburgh to punish the Protestants who were responsible for this affair.[71]

All these were but confirmations of the suspicions roused in Moray by Mary's marriage diplomacy and by her choice of advisers. Riccio was her chief counselor; as the time of the marriage drew near, her council became increasingly Catholic in membership, Athol being the key man. Darnley himself went to Mass as well as to the sermon.[72] Moray knew that the Queen had French and Spanish backing. In fact, her promises to Spain and to the

[67] Moray's proclamation is given in D. Calderwood, *The History of the Kirk of Scotland*, II, 569–76. [68] Knox, *History*, II, 471–72.
[69] March 20, 1565, Randolph to Cecil, in Keith, *History*, II, 268–75. Be it noted that this letter was written before the period in which Randolph began obviously to misrepresent matters in his letters. [70] Philippson, *Histoire*, II, 331.
[71] April 22, 1565, Alexander Clerk to Randolph, *C.S.P., For., Eliz.*, VII, 340–41. April 24, 1565, Mary to the magistrates of Edinburgh, in Keith, *History*, III, 104–5. [72] July 19, 1565, Randolph to Cecil, *ibid.*, II, 330–35.

Pope were far more explicit than he knew. On July 24 Mary wrote
to Philip II, saying that she was now following a Catholic policy,
that she had always been loyal to Rome, and asking for aid.[73] The
newly elevated Bishop of Dunblane informed the Pope that Mary
was marrying Darnley in order to restore the Catholic religion in
Scotland; for this purpose she needed money, which was hard
to come by in Scotland, especially since she must not alarm her
Protestant subjects unduly until she was in a position to crush
them.[74]

After Moray's rebellion actually broke out, the signs of Mary's
Catholic leanings multiplied. Knox was forbidden to preach for
a time.[75] Payments from the thirds to the Protestant clergy were
ended, after the ouster of Wishart of Pitarrow, one of Moray's
supporters, from the comptrollership.[76] Late in August a Catholic
became Provost of Edinburgh.[77] For the Continental princes,
Mary cast herself in the role of the persecuted Catholic: her subjects had rebelled, she said, to enforce the outrageous demand of
the Kirk that she turn Protestant.[78] This was not entirely false;
the General Assembly had made such a demand in June.[79] On
September 10 she wrote another letter to Philip of Spain requesting aid and advice on how to go about the restoration of Catholicism. Philip gave both, but Mary's messenger was drowned on his
return voyage, and the money fell into the hands of the Earl of
Northumberland, who, though a Catholic, would not give it up.[80]
On October 1 Mary instructed the Archbishop of Glasgow to
ask for aid from France, but to do so secretly—presumably in
order to keep the request from the Spanish.[81]

It is perfectly evident from all this that Moray was quite right
in saying that the Darnley marriage was a serious menace to Prot-

[73] Labanoff, *Recueil*, VII, 339–41.   [74] Pollen, *Papal Negotiations*, pp. 207–9.
[75] Knox, *History*, II, 497–98. Keith, *History*, III, 117–18.
[76] Knox, *History*, II, 515. Randolph reported Wishart's removal on August 27,
1565. *C.S.P., Scot.*, II, 196–98.
[77] Keith, *History*, III, 235–37. August 28, 1565, Bedford to Cecil, *C.S.P., For., Eliz.*,
VII, 439.   [78] Pollen, *Papal Negotiations*, p. 228, note 1.
[79] Knox, *History*, II, 484–87.
[80] Labanoff, *Recueil*, I, 281–83. October 18, 1565, Philip II to Cardinal Pacheco,
in Pollen, *Papal Negotiations*, pp. 213–15. Fleming, *Mary Queen of Scots*, pp. 377–
78.   [81] Labanoff, *Recueil*, I, 288–90.

estantism. He did not, of course, know the details of Mary's negotiations with the Continental Catholics, but he suspected what
was going on. His misfortune was that not enough people would
believe him. He had denounced the bad faith of Mary's repeated
promises that Protestantism was not in danger, and he was borne
out by the events of the winter of 1565–66. The realization that
he had been right after all was partly responsible for the upheaval
that enabled him to return in the following year.

The rest of the disastrous story of Moray's rebellion, which is
known to history as the Chase-about Raid, is quickly told. Early
in October he learned the fatal news that Elizabeth would not
support him. Mary's levies were assembling. The Master of Maxwell, in whose territories he was, had been intriguing with both
sides for some time, and now was about to go over to Mary—
which he did after Moray's flight—in return for a pardon.[82] The
game was up. Moray notified Bedford that he proposed to take
advantage of Elizabeth's offer of asylum, and on October 6 he
crossed the border and entered Carlisle, accompanied by Châtelherault, Rothes, Glencairn, Boyd, and others.[83] Argyle, who was
perfectly safe in his mountain fastnesses, remained behind. Mary
had won.

Thus ended a fiasco to which Moray had laid himself open by
his policy of the last five years. His major error lay in assuming
that Elizabeth and Cecil, simply because they were Protestants,
would view the problems of Protestantism in the same light as he
did. He had believed that he and Maitland could bring about a
modus vivendi between Mary and Elizabeth. In working for this,
he alienated his former allies, the Protestant zealots, because they
disliked his "soft" policy toward the idolatrous Queen. Then his
whole system collapsed in his face. Elizabeth proved unmanage-
able. Mary turned to other advisers and another policy, both of
which were wormwood and gall to Moray, but which in the eyes
of most Protestants did not appear dangerous enough to Protestantism to justify drastic measures. Moray's opposition led him to

[82] Knox, *History*, II, 512.
[83] October 5, 1565, Bedford to Cecil, *C.S.P., For., Eliz.*, VII, 480–81. October 7,
1565, Bedford to Elizabeth, *ibid.*, p. 482.

a futile rebellion during which, first, large numbers of his one-
time supporters, then Elizabeth, despite her promises, abandoned
him. Deserted by his former comrades in arms, shamefully betrayed by Elizabeth, vengefully pursued by his sister, he fled to
the country of his betrayer because he could do nothing else.

CHAPTER VII

The Turn of the Tide

IT WAS WELL for Moray that he possessed a good deal of courage, for the fiasco of the Chase-about Raid and the almost hopeless situation that resulted from it were enough to drive a lesser man to despair. In adversity Moray was to display much the same sort of temper as did his French and Dutch coreligionists; he never gave up hope of finding a way to restore himself and the Protestant party to power in Scotland. This proved to be a difficult task, one which might well have been beyond his powers, had not events in Scotland presented him with a ready-made solution to his problem, which he eagerly adopted. What this solution was, we shall see in due course.

Moray felt, and with reason, that Elizabeth had treated him very badly by reneging on her promise of aid during the rebellion. After some days of deliberation he resolved to go to London and see the Queen personally.[1] He paved the way for this step by writing a wounded letter to Cecil and Leicester on October 14, in which he held the English government responsible for the pitiable position in which he now found himself.[2] This was basically true enough, although somewhat exaggerated in the telling. Elizabeth's first reaction, on hearing of Moray's approach, was to order him not to come at all. Her messenger caught Moray at Ware, some forty miles from London; the Earl replied that he would stay there and await a summons.[3] This came almost at once. Elizabeth had thought the matter over, and evidently decided that if she refused to see Moray, he might well broadcast her duplicity to the world.

[1] October 13, 1565, Bedford to Elizabeth, *C.S.P., For., Eliz.*, VII, 487–88.
[2] *C.S.P., Scot.*, II, 223–24.   [3] *C.S.P., For., Eliz.*, VII, 497. *C.S.P., Scot.*, II, 226–27.

On October 23 Moray and the Abbot of Kilwinning, one of the Hamiltons, modestly dressed in black, had their famous interview with Elizabeth, in the presence of the French ambassador. Elizabeth started out severely, telling Moray that she was surprised that he dared present himself before her. De Foix was there, she said, as an impartial witness, so that he could inform Mary that England had given her no cause for hostility, since she (Elizabeth) had heard that there was a lying rumor going around to the effect that she had encouraged Moray. She understood that Moray had rebelled because of the political and religious implications of the Darnley marriage. Was this so?

Moray evasively replied that these considerations had occurred to him, but that Mary had always been kind to him, and that his revolt had not been directed against her personally. Elizabeth's rejoinder was that Moray had sinned grievously in taking arms against Mary. Moray explained that he had been outlawed on account of the altercation that had arisen out of the Lennox plot against him at Perth in June. Moray had refused to reveal what he knew of the plot in order to protect the lives of his informants. He was thus more or less worried into rebellion. He closed by asking Elizabeth to intercede with Mary for him. The Queen replied that she did not see how she could, but that she would discuss it with her council. She then dismissed Moray with the reminder that he could be grateful that he had not been shown the inside of an English prison.

This interview has been described at length because most historians have come to conclusions of various kinds about it without taking the trouble to analyze exactly what was said. The above account is taken from a letter of De Silva, the Spanish ambassador, who got it from Elizabeth herself, and it is undoubtedly substantially accurate, since De Silva had his own sources of information, and had no interest in presenting the case of either Elizabeth or Moray in a favorable light.[4] De Silva added in his letter that he understood that Moray had been briefed the night

---

[4] The letter is dated November 5, 1565 (*C.S.P., Span.,* I, 499–502). This version is substantially the same as the official English account sent to the English ambassador in France; *C.S.P., Scot.,* II, 227–28.

before, and that therefore the interview was collusive. All the more reason for De Silva to report it accurately, just as he heard it from Elizabeth; if the whole affair was fraudulent, there would be nothing gained by a colored report.

The charge of collusion is borne out by the interview itself. Each side passed gracefully over a lie told by the other: Moray's statement of the reasons for the revolt, and Elizabeth's denial that she had aided the rebels. The general tone of the interview was friendly. Elizabeth did not indulge in name-calling, as Sir James Melville alleges.[5] If she had been unpleasant to Moray, she would certainly have so informed De Silva. The reasons for lies and friendliness alike are not far to seek. Elizabeth knew well enough that Moray's defeat was a serious matter for her, and that her own behavior during the rebellion had given Mary a perfect opportunity to summon her French and Spanish friends to war on England. Elizabeth, for her own sake, had to clear herself of the charge of complicity in the rebellion. She could not, therefore, afford to antagonize Moray. The primary object of Moray, on the other hand, was to get back to Scotland. A pardon might be obtained through Elizabeth's intercession. This could only be effective if Mary was convinced that Elizabeth had nothing to do with the revolt. Moray was doubtless aware that Mary knew far too much to be deceived by Elizabeth's protestations of innocence, but little could be lost by trying, and he could have Elizabeth's support on no other terms. And France and Spain, at least, might be fooled. So Moray played Elizabeth's game, in return for the latter's intervention on his behalf with his sister. Knox's continuator reports that after the French ambassador had departed, Moray rebuked Elizabeth in private for her behavior, but this is most unlikely, since Moray knew well that Elizabeth had to be handled with kid gloves.[6] Possibly the story was spread, by Moray himself or by others, as a face-saving maneuver.

This was very necessary, because Elizabeth's conduct had not sat well with the Scottish Protestants as a whole. Many of them, including several who had supported Moray during the rebellion,

[5] Sir James Melville, *Memoirs of his own Life*, pp. 135–36.
[6] John Knox, *History of the Reformation in Scotland*, II, 513.

were so angry that they decided to wash their hands of England completely: English friendship seemed to be as dangerous as English enmity, and far more humiliating. Argyle in particular felt this, and for the rest of his career was bitterly hostile to England. Châtelherault, a lukewarm Protestant at best, soon made his peace with Mary, on condition that he surrender his fortified places and live in exile for five years.[7] Moray was made of different stuff, however. He, who had the most reason to be angry with Elizabeth, never wavered from his conviction that Anglo-Scottish friendship was necessary and beneficial, for political and religious reasons alike. But the alienation from England of many of his coreligionists was to raise a host of difficulties for him in future.

After his interview Moray settled down rather miserably in Newcastle. He could do nothing for himself; he could but hope that Elizabeth's representations would have some effect. He wrote occasional letters to the Queen and Cecil, urging them to do something for him.[8] He was sinking into poverty: Elizabeth would give him no money, and of course he could get none from his estates in Scotland. By Christmas Randolph reported that he had less than 200 crowns to his name.[9] The new year, the Earl informed Leicester, would simply complete his ruin, unless something happened soon.[10] That something, fortunately for him, was to happen. To understand what it was we must consider what had been going on in Scotland.

Mary had every reason to congratulate herself in October 1565. She had outwitted Elizabeth, married the one man who would strengthen her claim to the English throne, and driven her rebels across the frontier in ignominious flight. This, she ultimately decided, was but the first step in the great Catholic design to which she had committed herself. The next move was to restore the old religion in Scotland; once this was accomplished she could come to grips with her "good sister" in London, with Spanish aid, and reign over a united, Catholic Britain. If Mary had succeeded in

[7] December 3, 1565, Châtelherault to Cecil, *C.S.P., Scot.*, II, 243. On December 4 Moray informed Cecil that he approved of the Duke's arrangements. *Ibid.*, p. 244.
[8] See *ibid.*, pp. 231 ff., for these letters.
[9] December 25, 1565, Randolph to Cecil, *ibid.*, pp. 247–48.
[10] December 25, 1565, Moray to Leicester, *ibid.*, p. 248.

this grandiose scheme, the death knell of Protestantism would have sounded all over Europe. It is not too much to say that the course of events in Scotland in the winter of 1565–66, which culminated in the ruin of Mary's plans, was one of the decisive factors in assuring the survival of British, and hence of European, Protestantism.

Mary did not adopt this Catholic plan without hesitation, however. She was well aware of the enormous risks involved. It was by no means certain that she could carry even her own coterie with her, since many of them were Protestants. Many influential people were not anxious to see extreme measures against the rebels carried into effect. Among them were the Master of Maxwell, who had played a double game during the rebellion, and Morton and Maitland. On November 12 Randolph reported that Maitland was trying to get Moray the right to live outside Scotland on his income from his Scottish estates.[11] Knox from his pulpit was urging the government to forgive the banished lords and, when Mary's courtiers murmured, found himself in the unusual position of having his language and intentions defended by Maitland.[12] Sir James Melville urged Mary to pardon her rebels, and thus end their dependence on England. If she were generous, he said, Moray and his friends would be everlastingly grateful and would turn their backs on England forever.[13]

Elizabeth was also putting pressure on Mary to the same end. On October 24, the day after her interview with Moray, she sent a message urging Mary to pardon Moray and ratify the Treaty of Edinburgh. Elizabeth, in return, would, among other things, look into the matter of the succession. But the main burden of the message was its insistence that Elizabeth had not aided Moray at all during the rebellion.[14] This overture met with some success: Mary could not as yet afford to come to blows with England, since her Catholic friends in Europe had given her nothing more substantial than encouraging words. On November 7 Randolph reported that Mary was willing to deal with England; at the same

11 *Ibid.*, pp. 237–38.   12 Knox, *History*, II, 514.
13 Melville, *Memoirs*, pp. 139–40.
14 *C.S.P., Scot.*, II, 229. October 29, 1565, Elizabeth to Randolph, *ibid.*, p. 230.

time the ambassador urged that Elizabeth intervene more decisively, or Moray would be lost.[15]

Mary showed no signs of relenting toward Moray, as the Earl himself knew well.[16] But in December she consented to a meeting of commissioners for Border questions.[17] Upon being notified of this, Elizabeth appointed Bedford and Forster to meet with Mary's nominees and informed Randolph that the purpose of the meeting, from her point of view, was the restoration of Moray.[18] By mid-January, then, it seemed that Mary might yield to this pressure and pardon her brother; she had been particularly impressed by the argument that this move would lead to the abandonment by the Protestants of their associations with England.[19] If Mary had pardoned Moray for these reasons, it would have meant no more than a change in tactics, not in overall purposes: she would try conclusions with Elizabeth before she attacked Protestantism, instead of afterwards. That she was seriously thinking of this alternative is shown by the fact that she postponed for a month the Parliament which was to have met in February to forfeit Moray and his friends.[20] On January 24 Randolph reported that Mary was perceptibly softening toward her brother.[21] Then, very suddenly, Mary abandoned all thought of pardoning Moray and decided to push her Catholicizing plans with vigor. Her change of heart was due to a letter from the Cardinal of Lorraine, which arrived on January 27, urging her to take measures against

[15] November 7, November 8, 1565, Randolph to Cecil, *C.S.P., For., Eliz.*, VII, 510; *C.S.P., Scot.*, II, 235–36.
[16] See his letters of December 31, 1565, to Cecil and Elizabeth, *ibid.*, p. 249. Mary throughout had refused to hear of any mercy for her brother. Her most outspoken declaration came in a letter to De Foix on November 8, 1565, in which she ridiculed Elizabeth's suggestion that she pardon Moray in return for the release by Elizabeth of Lady Lennox. A. Labanoff, ed., *Recueil des lettres de Marie Stuart*, I, 299–307.
[17] December 23, 1565, Randolph to Cecil, *C.S.P., Scot.*, II, 245–47.
[18] January 10, 1566, Elizabeth to Randolph, *ibid.*, p. 251. Moray was not pleased by the appointment of Bedford and Forster, against whom, he feared, Mary would be prejudiced. January 15, 1566, Moray to Cecil, in R. Keith, *The History of the Affairs of Church and State in Scotland*, III, 343–44.
[19] Melville, *Memoirs*, pp. 146–47.
[20] December 25, 1565, Moray to Leicester, *C.S.P., Scot.*, II, 248. Andrew Lang, *A History of Scotland from the Roman Occupation*, II, 155.
[21] Keith, *History*, III, 344–45.

her heretics now.[22] This familiar advice was almost certainly rein-
forced by some talk of a Catholic League. Father Pollen asserts
that no such league ever existed, and his reasoning is convincing.[23]
But all of Protestant Europe believed in it, and there was certainly
some discussion of it in Catholic circles. Mary had expressed to
Philip her desire to join such a league.[24] Probably Mary was induced to follow the Catholic policy, which she much preferred
in any case, by the representations of her French friends, who
either through ignorance or design informed her that the league
was in process of organization and that she must follow an un-
compromising policy in order to be accepted and helped by it.

Mary's letter of January 31 to Pius V, expressing the opinion
that now was the time to strike at Scottish Protestantism, was a
clear indication of how the wind was blowing.[25] There were other
signs, which could be read by all. Douglas of Lochleven, Moray's
half-brother, made a vain effort to bribe Riccio in behalf of the
exiled Earl.[26] On February 7 Randolph reported that Popery was
flourishing, that royal pressure was being used on various lords to
get them to go to Mass, and that Moray was certain to be ruined
unless Elizabeth gave ground on the succession question.[27] Next
day Bedford wrote that Moray's lands had been given to others.[28]
In mid-February Randolph himself was in difficulties. Mary accused him of having conveyed English gold to Moray during the
rebellion, and his recall was demanded.[29] Randolph left, but went
no further than Berwick, where he was able to keep in touch with
Scottish affairs. Mary was perfectly justified in ridding her court

---

[22] J. H. Pollen, ed., *Papal Negotiations with Mary Queen of Scots*, p. ci. Melville, *Memoirs*, pp. 147–48. February 7, 1566, Randolph to Cecil, *C.S.P., Scot.*, II,
254–55.　　　　　[23] Pollen, *Papal Negotiations*, pp. xxxviii–xliii.
[24] October 24, 1565, Philip II to De Silva, *C.S.P., Span.*, I, 497–99.
[25] Labanoff, *Recueil*, VII, 8–10.
[26] T. McCrie, *The Life of John Knox*, II, 144–45, note 2. The story that Moray
himself attempted to bribe Riccio, by means of a diamond, rests only on a passage
in Melville, *Memoirs*, pp. 146–47, and is most improbable. Moray knew well
enough what Riccio was up to, and must have known that such an attempt
would be futile. Douglas, as far as we know, acted without Moray's knowledge.
[27] *C.S.P., Scot.*, II, 254–55.　　　　　[28] Keith, *History*, III, 345.
[29] February 17, 1566, Mary to Robert Melville, in *Maitland Club, Miscellany*, III,
179–83. February 19, March 6, 1566, Randolph to Cecil, *C.S.P., Scot.*, II, 256–57,
261–64.

of a man who trafficked with rebels, but her timing of the move made it plain to everyone that she no longer cared for an agreement with Elizabeth.

By February, then, Mary had made up her mind to pursue the Catholic policy, and the crucial test would come at the March Parliament, when Moray was to be forfeited and Catholicism restored to at least an equal footing with Protestantism,[30] which would eventually mean, of course, the extinction of the latter. Only the extreme Mariolators have ever contended that Mary favored toleration as a long-run solution to the religious question; such a notion was foreign to sixteenth-century thought. It seemed, too, that nothing could stop Mary. Unfortunately for her, however, there were various weaknesses in her position, which she did not take seriously enough, and which were to ruin her.

The first of these lay in the personality and position of the two men who were closest to her, Darnley and Riccio. Even before Moray's rebellion, Riccio had become Mary's most trusted adviser; now he "ruled all," as Randolph never seemed to tire of saying. As has been pointed out, he was detested by the Protestants, not only by those who had rebelled but also by those who remained.[31] He was looked on as an arrogant upstart, a fact which Riccio himself seemed to recognize.[32] Under these circumstances it was absolute folly for Mary to favor Riccio as ostentatiously as she did. Her knowledge of Scottish history should have warned her of the fate of lowborn royal favorites. But Mary continued to ignore the storm signals in this direction.

Mary might have behaved more intelligently in regard to Riccio, but there was very little she could do about Darnley. It did not take her long to realize that she had married a man who was worse than useless to her politically, and who was becoming most objectionable personally. Even before Moray had been driven from Scotland there were domestic disputes in the royal household over the question of the appointment of a Lieutenant

[30] Mary indicated as much in a letter of April 2, 1566, to the Archbishop of Glasgow, in Labanoff, *Recueil*, I, 341–50.
[31] For the attitude of Morton and Maitland, see March 6, 1566, Randolph to Cecil, *C.S.P., Scot.*, II, 261–64; E. Russell, *Maitland of Lethington*, pp. 248–49.
[32] Melville, *Memoirs*, pp. 132–34.

of the Marches.[33] Darnley was further annoyed by the pardoning of the Hamiltons.[34] Mary soon discovered that her husband was quite unfitted for public business. A stamp bearing his signature was made and turned over to Riccio, Mary giving as her justification for this the entirely accurate reason that Darnley was generally absent from court, on pleasure bent.[35] By Christmas Randolph reported that husband and wife were quarreling frequently.[36]

The real root of the difficulty was that Darnley wanted the crown matrimonial, which Mary had evidently promised him in the first flush of her amorous enthusiasm.[37] Such a grant would have given him equal authority with Mary in public business and would further have meant that Darnley would be King in his own right if Mary predeceased him. If she died childless, the crown would pass to the Lennox family. Mary had no intention of granting her foolish husband such authority at this point, and Darnley by his displays of childish resentment simply confirmed her in her decision. The object of Darnley's wrath was Riccio, who, he felt, was urging Mary to deprive him of all authority. The King was getting into a dangerous frame of mind.

Darnley was not, as we have seen, the only person in Scotland who disliked Riccio. The large and powerful group of Protestant lords who still remained in Scotland was coming to view the development of Mary's policy with great alarm. Mary naturally pursued her negotiations with the Catholic powers with great secrecy, but the trend of her policy was unmistakeable.[38] Ever since Moray's flight the Protestant lords, led by Morton and Maitland, had been working hard on one point: Moray must be pardoned and recalled. If this were done, they felt, it would be an indication that Mary contemplated no attack on Protestantism, which it was vital to them to preserve. For a while it seemed that they might

[33] October 2, 1565, Cockburn to Cecil, *C.S.P., For., Eliz.,* VII, 477.
[34] D. H. Fleming, *Mary Queen of Scots,* p. 369.
[35] Knox, *History,* II, 520.
[36] December 25, 1565, Randolph to Cecil, *C.S.P., Scot.,* II, 247–48.
[37] On this point see January 16, 1566, Randolph to Cecil, in J. Stevenson, ed., *Selections . . . Illustrating the Reign of Mary Queen of Scotland,* pp. 146–48.
[38] See, for example, her demands on Morton and Douglas of Lochleven, *The Register of the Privy Council of Scotland,* I, 390–91, 396–97, 417; and her treatment of the Protestant ministers, Knox, *History,* II, 515.

succeed. Then Mary suddenly changed her mind, at the end of January 1566, steeled herself to push through her Catholic policy, and refused to hear any more of pardon for Moray. Maitland, on February 9, wrote to Cecil that now there was nothing for it but to "chop at the very root." [39] The lords, too, were getting into a dangerous frame of mind.

There was, thus, material enough for a first-class explosion against Mary's policy, and that explosion was almost certain to be directed against Riccio, who was regarded by all concerned as the man really responsible for that policy. Darnley was now becoming convinced of the truth of a rumor which had been current for some time: that Mary was Riccio's mistress.[40] As early as October 1565 Randolph reported this story, and used it to explain Mary's implacable hatred of Moray, who, said Randolph, had found out his sister's guilty secret.[41] Elizabeth herself repeated the tale to De Foix in this wise: Moray was being persecuted by Mary because he "wished to hang an Italian named David, whom she loved and favored, giving him more credit and authority than was consistent with her affairs and honor." [42] There was almost certainly no truth in this story, which doubtless grew from the undue amount of confidence placed by Mary in her Italian secretary; but Darnley believed it, unhappily for Riccio, for Mary, and for himself.

In such circumstances it was inevitable that a plot should develop against Riccio, and develop it did, in February 1566. It is of little importance whether the Protestant lords or Darnley was the prime mover—each party later threw the onus on the other [43]

[39] *C.S.P., Scot.,* II, 255.
[40] February 13, 1566, Randolph to Leicester, quoted in P. F. Tytler, *History of Scotland,* VII, 19. Fleming has collected these rumors (*Mary Queen of Scots,* pp. 380–81).   [41] October 13, 1565, Randolph to Cecil, *C.S.P., Scot.,* II, 222–23.
[42] October 16, 1565, De Foix to Charles IX, quoted in Fleming, *Mary Queen of Scots,* p. 381.
[43] Darnley's public declaration on this point is reported in T. Thomson, ed., *A Diurnal of Remarkable Occurrents that Have Passed within the Country of Scotland,* p. 96, and contained the palpable lie that he was entirely innocent in the affair. Ruthven's account is in Keith, *History,* III, 260–78. See also March 27, 1566, Morton and Ruthven to Cecil, *C.S.P., Scot.,* II, 270–71. Bedford and Randolph also put the blame on Darnley in a letter to the English Council of the same date, *Calendar of the Manuscripts of the Marquis of Salisbury,* I, 333–36.

—but by February 13 Randolph wrote that "if that take effect which is intended, David, with the consent of the King, shall have his throat cut within these ten days." [44] Darnley's motives were to eliminate a man who, as he thought, had dishonored him, and also to get the crown matrimonial. The purpose of the lords was to end the danger to Protestantism and to get Moray and his friends home, at the very least. It is quite possible that they also had designs against the Queen's person. Mary believed that they did, but the evidence that the lords had such a scheme is inconclusive. [45]

It was necessary to make haste, since the Parliament which was to forfeit Moray was approaching. On February 25 Randolph reported that Lennox had gone to see Argyle. If the latter and Moray would consent to the granting of the crown matrimonial, the rebels would be pardoned and all possible security given to Protestantism; Darnley had agreed to these conditions already. [46] It was necessary for Darnley to agree to safeguard Protestantism, which he did not care about, and to restore Moray, which he must have disliked intensely, [47] because it was on these conditions alone that the support of the lords—Morton, Maitland, Ruthven, and Lindsay were the most important—could be had. Furthermore, Darnley had to put his pledges in writing, for he was not trusted by his associates, most of whom were his relatives. [48] In return for all this, Darnley was to be freed of his rival and to have his crown matrimonial.

There now remained the business of revealing the plot to Moray and his friends. It was certain that Moray would consent to it, since it would at one stroke accomplish all he desired. He had pinned his hopes on Elizabeth, as we have seen, and especially on

[44] February 13, 1566, Randolph to Leicester, quoted in Tytler, *History of Scotland*, VII, 19.

[45] April 2, 1566, Mary to the Archbishop of Glasgow, in Labanoff, *Recueil*, I, 341–50. See also the account of Claude Nau, Mary's secretary during her confinement in England: Nau, *The History of Mary Stewart*, pp. 3–16.

[46] *C.S.P., Scot.*, II, 258.

[47] Randolph felt that Darnley had been opposed to Moray's pardon throughout. December 25, 1565, Randolph to Cecil, *ibid.*, pp. 247–48.

[48] See Ruthven's account of the conspiracy, in Keith, *History*, III, 260–78. Lang calls the plot a typical Douglas treason: *History of Scotland*, II, 158. See also Randolph's letter of February 25, 1566, *C.S.P., Scot.*, II, 258. The list of those in the plot is in *Register of Privy Council*, I, 436–37.

the proposed Anglo-Scottish conference; [49] but it soon became clear that Mary had no intention of permitting the conference to take place before the meeting of Parliament. Moray was becoming desperate. On receiving assurances that the Earl of Sutherland —a Gordon and a Catholic—would say a good word for him if released by Elizabeth, he asked Cecil to permit Sutherland to go home.[50] Moray's state of mind was clearly indicated by a mournful letter to his wife, written on February 17, in which he exhorted her to trust in God and to commend him to his friends, "that are friends indeed, the number whereof is grown marvelous scant." [51]

In late February or early March a messenger from Scotland, possibly Lennox himself,[52] repaired to Moray at Newcastle and informed him of the plot. Bands were drawn up. Darnley promised in writing that he would grant Moray and his fellow rebels a remission for all crimes they might have committed, would restore their lands to them, and would stand by them in all just quarrels. Parliament was to be dissolved, so that no forfeitures would take place. Finally, Darnley guaranteed that the Proclamation of August 1561 on religious matters would remain in effect.[53] Moray and his friends promised in return that they would be true to Darnley, would undertake to obtain the crown matrimonial for him at the first Parliament after their return, and would uphold the right of the Lennox Stewarts to the crown if Mary died childless. They would use their influence with Elizabeth in behalf of Darnley and his mother. They would support the settlement of August 1561 on religion.[54] It will be noted that there is no mention anywhere of any proposed action against Riccio. Moray knew well enough what was contemplated, of course, and, in fact, had made careful provision to avoid involving himself in a possible charge

[49] January 15, 1566, Moray to Cecil, in Keith, *History*, III, 343–44.
[50] January 27, 1566, Randolph to Cecil, January 29, 1566, Moray to Cecil, *C.S.P., For., Eliz.*, VIII, 12.   [51] C. Innes, ed., *Registrum Honoris de Morton*, I, 14–15.
[52] Tytler, *History of Scotland*, VII, 22, and M. Philippson, *Histoire du règne de Marie Stuart*, III, 140–41, say that Lennox was the go-between, but the evidence is inconclusive.
[53] This band was dated March 6, 1566. *Historical Manuscripts Commission, 6th Report*, Appendix, p. 641.
[54] This band was dated March 2, 1566, and was signed by Moray, Rothes, Glencairn, Argyle, Boyd, and Ochiltree. *Maitland Club, Miscellany*, III, 188–91.

of being an accessory before the fact. He inserted in the band which he signed two important modifying phrases: he would support Darnley in all "lawful and just" actions, and would help set forward Darnley's honor "according to the Word of God."[55] Moray also provided himself with a further alibi: he planned his entry into Edinburgh for the day following the coup, which was set for March 9.[56]

Randolph had known of the plot from its inception, but his first official communication of it to his government was evidently that of February 25.[57] By March 3 Elizabeth was aware of it, for her letter of that date to Mary was minatory. She was, she wrote, extremely irritated by Mary's treatment of Randolph and Moray.[58] She evidently judged that further conciliation of Mary was unnecessary. She also suddenly discovered that Moray, who was about to regain his influence in Scotland, had been living in poverty for some time, and sent him a thousand pounds.[59] On March 6 Randolph and Bedford wrote a full account of the conspiracy to Cecil, and included a list of the important people who knew of it.[60] This list points up one aspect of the affair which was significant for the future: the contemplated attack on Riccio had reunited the Protestant party in Scotland. Moderates such as Maitland joined with zealots such as Lindsay. Knox was not informed of the conspiracy beforehand, but he heartily approved of the result.[61] Mary's behavior during the winter had done what Moray had been unable to do: it had convinced the Scottish Protestants that their religion was in danger.

The plot also brought to the forefront of Scottish politics a man who was to loom large in the history of his country for the next fifteen years, James Douglas, Earl of Morton. Morton was a man whose personal character was unlovely and whose political intelligence was late in developing. But he was forceful, shrewd, and

[55] March 6, 1566, Randolph and Bedford to Cecil, *C.S.P., Scot.*, II, 259–61.
[56] March 8, 1566, Randolph and Bedford to Cecil and Leicester, *ibid.*, pp. 264–65.
[57] *Ibid.*, p. 258.   [58] *Ibid.*, p. 259.
[59] March 16, 1566, Bedford to Elizabeth, *C.S.P., For., Eliz.*, VIII, 33.
[60] *C.S.P., Scot.*, II, 259–61.
[61] Knox, *History*, I, 235. Fleming discusses the evidence as to Knox's foreknowledge of the plot, and dismisses it. *Mary Queen of Scots*, pp. 395–98.

powerful, and from this time on became Moray's close ally. His Protestantism was more a matter of convenience than conviction: he had profited from the spoils of the Catholic Church, and was to profit still more in the 1570s, when he became Regent. Moray was chiefly responsible for the victory of the twin policies of Protestantism and the English alliance, but to Morton must be given the credit for assuring the victory. When resistance broke out on Moray's death, Morton stamped it out and by nine years of iron rule made impossible for the future any really serious threat to those policies.

Many historians have pointed accusing fingers at Moray for his behavior in this affair. What are we to think of a man who, six short months ago, raised a rebellion because Darnley was to be made King of Scotland, and who now promised to get the crown matrimonial for this same Darnley? Thus his detractors. By and large those who take this position are confused by their belief that Moray's sole motives were personal. It is certainly true that Moray wished to return home. If it is remembered, however, that his major motives were his desire for friendship with England and for the security of Protestantism, all apparent inconsistencies vanish. He had not swerved from his policies; instead, Darnley had been brought round to the point of aiding and abetting him in pursuing them, in order to satisfy his—Darnley's—personal desires. Darnley was now the tool by means of which the Catholic threat was to be broken forever, just as he had once been the tool Mary had thought to use in her campaign for the English throne and the restoration of Catholicism. So thought Moray and the lords in Scotland. A pitiful tool, to be sure. They did not know as yet just how pitiful.

Meanwhile Mary, all unwittingly, was rushing toward disaster. On March 7 Parliament met, and was at once placed under severe pressure by Mary to draw up a bill against Moray, who had been summoned for March 12 to hear his forfeiture.[62] Then, on Saturday March 9, the conspirators struck.

To describe the murder of Riccio would be superfluous, since

---

[62] Knox, *History*, II, 520. The official summons to Moray was made on December 19, 1565. *Treasurer's Accounts*, XI, 452.

the details of that famous scene are familiar to everyone who has ever concerned himself with Mary's tragic story.[63] At first all went well for the lords. Mary was taken by surprise: Riccio was slain, and after the event the Queen was closely guarded. Darnley quieted a group of townspeople who had been aroused by the commotion, and ordered the Parliament dissolved.[64] That very evening, however, difficulties began to arise. Bothwell and Huntly, who had been in Holyrood at the time of the murder, contrived to escape. Mary herself, whose courage in this crisis was immense, began to consider what might be done. Obviously she must escape, and in order to do this she would need the help of someone in the plot. The logical choice was Darnley. That spineless young man was easily won over by the Queen, who pointed out to him how criminal and foolish his behavior had been. She probably even affected to be convinced by his protestations of innocence, in order to regain him.

Moray meanwhile had left Berwick on March 10, after writing a thank-you letter to Cecil for all his and Elizabeth's favors.[65] He was met by Hume with a large body of horsemen, which formed his escort to the capital.[66] News of the murder reached him en route, at Dunbar.[67] He went at once to Holyrood, saw Darnley, and then repaired to his house for supper. He was summoned thence by the Queen, who received him affectionately, according to Melville.[68] Moray was much moved by his sister's distress. There is no reason to believe that his compunction was not sincere; Moray was no sentimentalist—he knew that Riccio would die— but he was not cruel, and he may well have felt that the brutality of the murder had been unnecessary.[69]

---

[63] Fleming, *Mary Queen of Scots*, pp. 387–90, has listed the contemporary accounts. Of the later ones, that of J. A. Froude, *History of England (1529–1588)*, VIII, 250–57, deserves mention as a literary masterpiece.
[64] Thomson, *Diurnal of Occurrents*, p. 91.
[65] March 8, 1566, Moray to Cecil, *C.S.P., Scot.*, II, 265.
[66] March 11, 1566, Bedford to Cecil, *ibid.*, pp. 265–66.
[67] March 11, 1566, Randolph to Throckmorton, cited in T. F. Henderson, *Mary Queen of Scots*, II, 384.
[68] Melville, *Memoirs*, p. 150. See also Ruthven's account in Keith, *History*, III, 260–78.
[69] It is possible, as Morton and Ruthven later claimed, that the original plan was merely to seize Riccio and not to put him to death until he had been tried. Ac-

Monday, March 11, was the crucial day. By this time the Queen had won over Darnley completely. In the morning, in the presence of his fellow conspirators, the King asked Mary for pardons for all concerned. He and Moray had a long private conference with her, Mary evidently having decided that it was necessary to convince her brother that she honestly meant to pardon the plotters. Although Ruthven does not say so in his account of the events of that day, it is probable that Mary succeeded in disarming Moray's suspicions.[70] Ruthven and Morton were less easily convinced. They knew Darnley better than Moray did; nevertheless they were forced to trust him. In the afternoon the lords were ushered into Mary's presence to ask for pardon. Moray joined in the pleading, not as one who had anything to be forgiven him, but on behalf of those who did. According to Nau, he included in his speech a little lecture on the virtues of clemency.[71] Mary promised to sign written articles of pardon in the morning. Hearing this, the lords left Holyrood and took their guards with them, on Darnley's promise that nothing would go amiss during the night. This was a very serious blunder, for on Tuesday morning the lords awoke to discover that the birds had flown. Mary and Darnley were safe behind the walls of Dunbar.[72]

This was a frightful blow to the lords, who realized at once that a rebellion was out of the question, since Mary was certain to have public opinion behind her, owing to the very brutality of the murder. They spent the next few days in rather panicky inactivity. Moray, however, did retain sufficient presence of mind to ride to the Tolbooth of Edinburgh on March 12, the day for which he had been summoned, and to announce to the empty room wherein the now defunct Parliament was to have met that

cording to this theory, the feelings of the participants simply got out of hand, and Riccio was summarily dealt with. This is unlikely, however, for there was no ground on which Riccio could be tried except that of adultery, and it is not probable that Darnley planned to drag the man who had cuckolded him, as he thought, into court. Henderson discusses this point: *Mary Queen of Scots*, II, 378–79.

[70] The continuator of Knox seemed to think so. Knox, *History*, II, 523.

[71] Nau, *History of Mary Stewart*, pp. 12–15.

[72] Ruthven's account, in Keith, *History*, III, 260–78, is the basis of most of this paragraph. See also Melville, *Memoirs*, pp. 150–51, and Knox, *History*, II, 523.

he assumed that the charges against him had been dropped, since no accuser appeared.[73]

Mary was burning for revenge. Nevertheless, she realized that she could not cope with all the lords at once; so she resolved to pardon the rebels of 1565 and thus neutralize them, in order to pursue those who had actually committed the murder.[74] Immediately after her arrival in Dunbar she sent Hay of Balmerinoch to Moray to offer him a pardon.[75] Moray was not willing to desert the men who had risked so much for him, but it soon became clear that resistance to the Queen was impossible. Led by Bothwell and Huntly, fighting men were streaming into Dunbar. On March 17 the lords realized that the game was up and fled from Edinburgh in all directions. So did Knox, who retired to Ayrshire.[76] Moray went to Linlithgow, where he found Argyle; they were met by another messenger from Mary, Sir James Balfour. This time Moray, with Kirkcaldy and Pitarrow, came to terms: Morton had informed them that it would be foolish for them to refuse to do so; they could do more for Morton by remaining in Scotland and working for a pardon.[77] Morton, Ruthven, and the other perpetrators of the murder fled to England. On March 20 Moray and Argyle, having made their submission, were ordered to retire to Argyle's estates in the west.[78] Mary had sought to stipulate that Moray agree never to aid those who had committed the murder; he promised to serve her loyally, but his conscience, he said, would not permit him to oppose Morton and his friends.[79] With this Mary had to remain content.

Mary entered Edinburgh in triumph on March 18, with a force of eight thousand men.[80] To all outward appearance she had triumphed over a dangerous conspiracy and had emerged from the affair with her power unimpaired. Actually, how-

---

[73] *Ibid.*, p. 524.
[74] On this point see March 21, 1566, Randolph to Cecil, *C.S.P., Scot.*, II, 269–70.
[75] Melville, *Memoirs*, p. 151.
[76] Knox. *History*, II, 525–26. Thomson, *Diurnal of Occurrents*, p. 94.
[77] March 21, 1566, Randolph to Cecil, *C.S.P., Scot.*, II, 269–70.
[78] Thomson, *Diurnal of Occurrents*, p. 95. April 2, 1566, Mary to the Archbishop of Glasgow, in Labanoff, *Recueil*, I, 341–50.
[79] March 30, 1566, De Silva to Philip II, *C.S.P., Span.*, I, 537.
[80] Knox, *History*, II, 525.

ever, the murder of Riccio marks the turning point in Mary's career, both personally and politically. The character of her husband had been laid bare; henceforth she could feel for him nothing but contempt and loathing. Bothwell she could not but regard as the prop of her throne: coming events were casting their shadows. Far more important, the murder of Riccio demonstrated that the Catholic policy that Mary had been pursuing for the past year was utterly bankrupt. Even with many of the Protestant nobility in exile, those who remained had been sufficiently strong to invade her palace, carry off her trusted servant from her side, and cruelly murder him almost under her eyes. True, the murderers were now fugitives, but this had been accomplished only at the price of compounding with the rebels of 1565. The marriage on which she had based her hopes of Catholicizing both England and Scotland had turned out to be the means of ruining her hopes. Mary abandoned the Catholic policy, and never revived it while she was on the Scottish throne. In fact, in the remaining fifteen months of her reign, she followed no well thought-out foreign policy at all, and her conduct of domestic business hinged mainly on questions of personality. The murder of Riccio spelled the ruin of the old religion in Scotland, and that meant that England, too, was safe. It was a decisive event in British history.

As for Moray, he had cause to congratulate himself on the outcome of the whole affair. He had been saved from impending ruin —and, more important, so had his religion. True, he wielded no political power as yet, but he knew that in time he would regain his influence since he was the recognized leader of the most powerful political party in Scotland, that of the Calvinist nobility. Many of his confreres were now fugitives from justice, to be sure; but he knew he could save them from forfeiture, and he was reasonably certain that in time he could bring them back home. It was simply a matter of time, and he was in no hurry, since the Catholic threat had faded into the background. Short of an armed invasion by Spain or France, it could, he felt, be dismissed almost entirely. Furthermore, he had learned a valuable political lesson from his experiences in the past year. Never again, he resolved, would he permit the Protestant party to become disunited. His task was made easier for him by the fact that the other Protestants had also discovered the fatal consequences of disunion. Many powerful Protestants were to oppose Moray in the future, either, like Maitland, because they considered other things more important than Protestantism, or, like Argyle, because they could not stomach the English alliance, to which Moray steadily adhered. But by and large Moray was able to hold his party together, and because of this he was able to surmount successfully the crises of the next few years.

CHAPTER VIII

Mary, Bothwell, and Darnley

ON MARCH 19, 1566, the day after her return to Edinburgh, Mary summoned Morton and his fellow conspirators to appear before her in six days' time, or to suffer the consequences. Within two weeks they were put to the horn.[1] The list of those summoned is an interesting one: it consisted mostly of servants and relatives of Morton, Ruthven, and Lindsay. None of those who had rebelled with Moray in 1565 were included. No Protestant minister was summoned, nor was Maitland, although he was certainly guilty.[2] Although many were charged with the crime, only two men, minions of Ruthven, actually suffered death as a result.[3]

The craven Darnley publicly proclaimed on March 21 that he was entirely innocent of the murder, although he had, he confessed, consented to the return of Moray and his friends without Mary's knowledge.[4] Mary doubtless encouraged this as a necessary political maneuver: no doubt must be cast on the legitimacy of her unborn child by the scandalous rumors which had circulated concerning her relations with Riccio. It is quite possible, too, that Mary did not realize just how deeply her husband was involved. If this was the case, she was quickly undeceived. Darnley's fellow conspirators were enraged by his betrayal, and they re-

[1] *The Register of the Privy Council of Scotland*, I, 436–37. T. Thomson, ed., *A Diurnal of Remarkable Occurrents that Have Passed within the Country of Scotland*, pp. 97–98.
[2] D. H. Fleming (*Mary Queen of Scots*, pp. 395–98), discusses the evidence against Maitland. Besides the proofs he adduces, there is also a draft circular by Maitland justifying the murder in *C.S.P., Scot.*, II, 268–69.
[3] Fleming, *Mary Queen of Scots*, pp. 131, 404.
[4] Thomson, *Diurnal of Occurrents*, p. 96.

taliated by sending to Mary the bands her husband had signed.[5] Moray did likewise a few weeks later.[6] Mary's feelings, on seeing these edifying documents, can be imagined.

Thus Darnley, having systematically betrayed virtually every important person in Scotland, was cordially detested on all sides. Every man's hand was against him: that of his wife, and those of Morton and of the other conspirators against Riccio. As for Moray and his friends, who of all those involved had been least injured by Darnley's treacheries, Randolph wrote on May 13 that Moray and Argyle had "such misliking of their King as never was more of man." [7] To the rough and ready Scottish mind, there was only one way of satisfactorily repaying Darnley's unspeakable behavior. His doom was sealed. The only real questions that remained were those of the time, the place, and the perpetrator of the deed.

Mary, badly shaken by her unpleasant experiences and far gone with child, now had only one thought: to reconcile the leaders of the two factions, her own and that of the Protestants, and thus to create some semblance of peace while she suffered in childbed.[8] In April Kirkcaldy, Glencairn, Moray, and Argyle were summoned to court, and the latter three resumed their seats on the Privy Council. One of the conditions of their return was that they reconcile themselves with Bothwell and Huntly.[9] This they did, superficially, although mutual suspicion and intrigue continued to flourish.

One point of disagreement between Moray and Bothwell was over the return of Maitland. Moray wanted to restore the Secretary, who once more was an advocate of the Protestant, Anglophile policy to which he had taught Moray and his followers to adhere. Bothwell was bitterly opposed to this, partly, at least, because he had received the lands of the Abbey of Haddington,

[5] April 2, April 4, 1566, Randolph to Cecil, *C.S.P., Scot.*, II, 273, 274–75.
[6] April 27, 1566, Maitland to Randolph, quoted in M. Philippson, *Histoire du règne de Marie Stuart*, III, 187.   [7] *C.S.P., Scot.*, II, 278.
[8] *Ibid.*, p. 273.
[9] April 4, 1566, Bedford to Cecil, *C.S.P., For., Eliz.*, VIII, 45. April 20, 1566, Drury to Cecil, *ibid.*, p. 52. Thomson, *Diurnal of Occurrents*, p. 99. *Register of Privy Council*, I, 454. April 25, 1566, Randolph to Cecil, *C.S.P., Scot.*, II, 276.

which Mary took from Maitland after the murder of Riccio.[10]
Mary refused to countenance Bothwell's attempt to get Maitland's
commission as Secretary revoked, but she would not pardon the
Secretary as yet. At one point it was reported that Maitland would
go to Flanders, but he did not go; early in June he was ordered to
ward himself in Caithness.[11]

Moray also began to apply himself to the far more difficult task
of obtaining a pardon for Morton and his associates—vainly, as
it turned out, although he evidently had some success in respect
to their subordinates.[12] Moray's object, of course, was to rebuild
the Protestant party to its full strength, to the power and numbers
it possessed before the disaster of 1565. Bothwell liked this maneuver no better than the one in behalf of Maitland; he countered by
attempting to win a pardon for George Douglas, one of the principal conspirators, who in return was to accuse Moray of complicity
in Riccio's murder. Fortunately for Moray, Drury and Morton
got wind of this plot, and Douglas was arrested by the English
government before it could be put into execution.[13]

The question of Morton was the principal aspect of official relations with England in this period. Mary did not want to quarrel
with Elizabeth at this point, when her policy was to be friendly
to everyone not directly connected with the murder. Nevertheless she wrote to Elizabeth on April 4, requesting that Morton and
the others be seized and handed over to her.[14] Moray at the same
time was urging Elizabeth to shelter and befriend the exiles.[15]
Morton and Ruthven were doing their best to help themselves
by bombarding Cecil with accounts of the slaying which put all
the blame on Darnley.[16] Morton was formally ordered to leave

---

[10] E. Russell, *Maitland of Lethington*, pp. 259–60.
[11] Claude Nau, *The History of Mary Stewart*, pp. 20–21. April 25, June 7, 1566,
Randolph to Cecil, *C.S.P., Scot.*, II, 276, 283–84. The reason for Maitland's failure
to go to Flanders was that he understood that Bothwell was planning to capture
him at sea. June 24, 1566, Killigrew to Cecil, *ibid.*, pp. 288–89.
[12] May 2, June 7, 1566, Randolph to Cecil, *ibid.*, pp. 277, 283–84.
[13] June 20, 1566, Drury to Cecil, *C.S.P., For., Eliz.*, VIII, 91. July 11, 1566, Leicester to Cecil, *ibid.*, p. 104. July, 1566, Morton to Forster, *C.S.P., Scot.*, II, 296.
[14] *Ibid.*, p. 275.
[15] April 2, 1566, Randolph to Cecil, *ibid.*, p. 273. May 1, 1566, Maitland to Ruthven and Morton, in Philippson, *Histoire*, III, 193.
[16] See *C.S.P., Scot.*, II, 270–72, 273–74.

England, and was informally told to hide somewhere, or he really would have to leave.[17]

Elizabeth was forced to be circumspect in regard to Morton because Mary had a potent weapon against her, in the person of Shan O'Neill, who, for the moment, constituted the Irish Question. O'Neill was the friend and ally of Argyle. As long as Argyle was friendly to England, O'Neill was not particularly dangerous, but now Argyle was no longer friendly. Mary was straining every nerve to win Argyle completely to her devotion, and thus to persuade him to reinforce O'Neill.[18] On May 4 Randolph announced that O'Neill had entered into direct negotiations with Mary.[19]

This affair frightened Moray. He realized that if Argyle helped O'Neill, a severe blow would be dealt to his policy of Anglo-Scottish friendship, which would be made still worse by the fact that the man responsible would be Argyle, who had so long followed Moray in all his political maneuvers, and who had been a mainstay of the Protestant party. Moray appealed to his old friend's religious feelings and to his duty to Morton and Ruthven, who had risked all for him. This appeal was partially successful; on May 13 Randolph wrote that Argyle would refuse to help O'Neill if Elizabeth openly favored Morton and Ruthven and vigorously supported Protestantism.[20] Moray, aided by Kirkcaldy, was able to keep Argyle more or less in line, in spite of Elizabeth's tactless attempt to get something for nothing by asking Argyle to oppose O'Neill out of gratitude for past favors.[21] Moray assured Randolph that he would do all he could to prevent O'Neill from getting aid, but that he did not have enough influence openly to oppose Mary's policy.[22] In July, for reasons

[17] May 7, 1566, Elizabeth to Forster, in J. Stevenson, ed., *Selections . . . Illustrating the Reign of Mary Queen of Scotland*, pp. 159–60. May 16, 1566, Morton to Cecil, *C.S.P., Scot.*, II, 278. July 11, 1566, Leicester to Cecil, *C.S.P., For., Eliz.*, VIII, 104. Morton's letter announced the death of Ruthven, who had risen from a sickbed to murder Riccio.
[18] See March 31, 1566, Mary to Argyle, in A. MacDonald, ed., *Letters to the Argyle Family*, pp. 5–6.
[19] *C.S.P., For., Eliz.*, VIII, 60.   [20] *C.S.P., Scot.*, II, 278.
[21] May 23, 1566, Elizabeth to Randolph, *ibid.*, p. 279. June 14, 1566, Randolph to Cecil, *ibid.*, pp. 285–86.
[22] June 7, June 13, 1566, Randolph to Cecil, *ibid.*, pp. 283–84, 284–85.

which will be made clear below, the matter faded into the background. But before it did so, there were repercussions. Mary certainly came to know of her brother's behavior in this business.[23] She was, naturally enough, very angry with Moray, whose recent experiences had not chastened him, and who evidently would work with her only as long as she adopted his policies. On June 24 Killigrew, the new English resident in Edinburgh, wrote Cecil that Moray had told him that his influence now was virtually non-existent.[24]

Amidst all the fuss about O'Neill, Mary was preparing for the arrival of her child. It had been decided early in April that Edinburgh Castle should be its birthplace, since it was deemed the safest spot in Scotland.[25] As her hour approached, Mary did her best to provide that nothing should disturb her kingdom. She reconciled herself with Darnley, for the moment,[26] because it was absolutely necessary that he acknowledge the child as his own. Of the two Scottish factions, she trusted her own absolutely, and Moray's only conditionally; so she surrounded herself with members of her brother's party, in order to keep them faithful at this time. The key members of the party, Moray, Argyle, Athol, and Moray's uncle Mar were asked to occupy the castle with her.[27] Bothwell disliked the favor shown to his rivals. He, with Huntly and John Leslie, now Bishop of Ross, a shrewd, shifty, and sancti-

---

[23] On June 17 Randolph complained to Cecil that the contents of his recent letters—full of the O'Neill affair as they were—were getting out. There was a leak somewhere in England, and it was evidently Elizabeth herself, who had made derogatory remarks about Moray and Argyle because they did not follow her blindly in the question of O'Neill. Information was getting back to Scotland. S. Haynes, ed., *The Burghley Papers (1542–1570)*, pp. 447–48.

[24] *C.S.P., Scot.*, II, 290.   [25] *Register of Privy Council*, I, 445.

[26] June 7, 1566, Randolph to Cecil, *C.S.P., Scot.*, II, 283–84. See also J. Robertson, ed., *Inventaires de la Royne Descosse Douairière de France*. This volume is mainly devoted to an inventory of Mary's personal property, drawn up at this time in case she died in childbirth; the inventory contained many bequests to Darnley.

[27] June 7, 1566, Randolph to Cecil, *C.S.P., Scot.*, II, 283–84. June 24, 1566, Killigrew to Cecil, *ibid.*, pp. 288–89. The Catholic Athol, a friend of Maitland, was, for the moment, supporting Moray. Mar is a good example of a Protestant moderate who had learned his lesson from the events of 1565–66. He was not involved in the rebellion or the murder plot, but henceforth he threw his influence behind Moray, and was Regent for a time after his nephew's death.

monious prelate, whose loyalty to the Catholic faith and to Mary was marred by a penchant for chicanery and by physical cowardice, attempted to persuade Mary to ward her brother during her confinement, alleging that Moray planned to take advantage of the moment to bring Morton home. Mary refused to do this, and Bothwell retired to his Border estates to sulk.[28]

On Wednesday, June 19, Sir James Melville set out for England; he was the bearer of the glad tidings that Mary had been delivered of a son. On the twenty-third he arrived in London to notify Elizabeth, who put as good a countenance as she could on the matter, though she was far from pleased. An heir strengthened enormously Mary's claim to the English succession. And, indeed, in the fullness of time, this infant was to sit on the English throne, and thus to realize the ambitions of Moray and Maitland, though neither of them lived to see the day.

ii

On June 24, as we have seen, Moray told Killigrew that he had no influence with Mary at all. And yet, less than three weeks later, on July 11, he conveyed to Cecil the astonishing news that he had been restored to power and favor.[29] Nor was the Earl exaggerating; he really had recovered power. From now on, no one worried very much about O'Neill. The records of the Privy Council indicate that Moray's strong hand was at the helm again: on July 17 Lord Livingston and Lord Robert Stewart, the Queen's half-brother, were ordered to stop feuding.[30] On the twenty-first it was announced that Mary would go on a justice eyre on the Borders to restore law and order there, another cause dear to Moray's heart.[31] At the end of July Mary settled a property dispute between Moray and Huntly on terms favorable to Moray.[32] In August the feckless Darnley threatened his life; Mary informed him of this, and together they forced a public apology from the

[28] June 24, 1566, Killigrew to Cecil, *ibid.*, pp. 288–89. Sir James Melville, *Memoirs of his own Life*, pp. 154–55.   [29] *C.S.P., Scot.*, II, 294.
[30] The command was repeated on July 24. *Register of Privy Council*, I, 470, 473–74.   [31] *Ibid.*, p. 473.
[32] July 27, 1566, Bedford to Cecil, *C.S.P., For., Eliz.*, VIII, 110. The final settlement is printed in Malcolm Laing, *The History of Scotland*, II, 101–4.

hapless youth.[33] In the teeth of bitter opposition from Bothwell, with whom he openly quarreled, Moray finally obtained the pardon of Maitland, who was restored to favor early in September. Mary even patched up a reconciliation between Bothwell and Maitland, who got his abbey lands back again.[34] Lady Moray was put in charge of little Prince James.[35] Mary apparently also informed Moray of her recent dealings with the new papal legate to Scotland, Laureo, Bishop of Mondovi, whose efforts to secure the execution of the Scottish Protestant leaders in return for funds came to nothing.[36]

Favors began to be shown once more to the Kirk. On September 17 all pensions granted from the revenues of the thirds were annulled.[37] Once again the ministers began to receive their stipends. An even more important concession, one for which Knox and his followers had long been clamoring, was made on October 3. It was decreed on that day that the General Assembly could appoint to all benefices of less than 300 marks' annual rental. The Queen would continue to appoint to the greater benefices, but she would exact a pledge from her appointees that they would observe the provision made for small benefices.[38] This offered the Kirk for the first time a solid legal foundation for the elimination of pluralism and lay engrossment of small benefices. This desirable reform could not take place all at once, since the law provided that the benefices must be vacant before the Assembly could appoint to them. And, of course, ways were found of evading the purpose of the enactment. But it did represent a considerable step forward.

[33] August 15, 1566, "Advertisements out of Scotland," *C.S.P., For., Eliz.,* VIII, 118.
[34] August 14, 1566, R. Melville to Cecil, *C.S.P., Scot.,* II, 299. August 28, September 8, September 19, 1566, Forster to Cecil, *C.S.P., For., Eliz.,* VIII, 124, 128, 131–32. September 20, 1566, Maitland to Cecil, *C.S.P., Scot.,* II, 300. Russell, *Maitland,* p. 263.
[35] September 8, 1566, Forster to Cecil, *C.S.P., For., Eliz.,* VIII, 128.
[36] See J. H. Pollen, ed., *Papal Negotiations with Mary Queen of Scots,* pp. cvii–cxix for a complete account of Laureo's mission. See also Laureo's letters of August 21 and September 9, 1566, *ibid.,* pp. 274–78, 282–84. Bishop Leslie believed that Moray had prevented the arrival of Laureo in Scotland. Leslie, "Paralipomena ad historiam Scotiae," in W. Forbes-Leith, ed., *Narratives of Scottish Catholics under Mary Stuart and James VI,* p. 115.
[37] *Register of Privy Council,* I, 477–79.   [38] *Ibid.,* pp. 487–88.

The real question is, why did Mary restore her brother to power? We have seen that she must have known of, and been angered by, his dealings with Elizabeth in the business of O'Neill. She knew what Moray's policies were, and she did not like them, unless they led to the English crown; yet the succession question was not really revived until several months after Moray's return to power. Furthermore, informed Englishmen, such as Killigrew and Bedford, pointed out to their government that it was not Moray but Bothwell who was the Queen's favorite.[39] Scottish contemporaries also said as much.[40] Bothwell was absolutely loyal to Mary and could be counted on to govern as she wished. Why, then, did she restore her brother to power, and even side with him against Bothwell in such matters as the restoration of Maitland?

If there is an answer, it must be almost entirely psychological. Mary, like most women born to the purple, was egocentric. Her happy childhood, while it had taught her much, had never taught her to control her feelings. She was headstrong and highly emotional. A comparison with Elizabeth is revealing. Elizabeth had been schooled in adversity before she came to the throne, and sentiment almost never, if ever, got the upper hand with her. Her public displays of temper were far more numerous than Mary's, but, unlike Mary's, they were never genuine. They were the calculated rages of a supremely intelligent actress. Love never was able to captivate Elizabeth. She flirted with her Leicesters and her Raleighs and her Essexes; they were but mirrors to her vanity, and she never would have dreamed of marrying any of them, not even Leicester, of whom she was as fond as she could be of anyone other than herself. Not an attractive person, perhaps. But a far more intelligent one than the woman in Edinburgh with whom she traded feline amenities for so many years. Mary was by no means stupid, but she was emotional, and she was vain. And her vanity was both greater and smaller than Elizabeth's. She did not care unduly for the petty personal compliments by which Elizabeth set so much

---

[39] June 24, 1566, Killigrew to Cecil, *C.S.P., Scot.*, II, 288–89. July 27, 1566, Bedford to Cecil, *C.S.P., For., Eliz.*, VIII, 110.
[40] John Knox, *History of the Reformation in Scotland*, II, 532–33. Melville, *Memoirs*, p. 154.

store, but neither was she vain for her country, as Elizabeth was. Elizabeth identified herself with England; her glory was England's, and England's, hers. Englishmen at the time and since have forgotten her numberless meannesses and treacheries in their pride at the accomplishments of "Good Queen Bess."

Mary's vanity was of a rather different type. What she thirsted for was personal glory. She desired the crown of England, as she had once desired those of France and Spain, in order to raise herself in the eyes of the world, and consequently in her own. For six years and more she had relentlessly pursued her ambition, by one path and then another, and had sacrificed all her feelings, her womanliness, to her political ends. She had even convinced herself that she loved a feckless and foolish boy because her marriage to him would further her plans. Then, with shocking suddenness, her political designs were wrecked, the bubble of her ambition burst. The emotions which she had suppressed, the sexual passions which her marriage had stimulated but not satisfied, began, especially after the birth of her child, to work heavily within her. They found their object ready to hand—Bothwell.

Bothwell was a typical Border noble in most ways, but in certain respects he was unusual. He was well educated, had good literary taste, and was courtly enough when he chose to be, which was not often. Although lacking in political intelligence, he had the virtue of absolute political loyalty to the crown. He had been Mary's right hand through the later phases of the Chase-about Raid, and above all, in the Riccio crisis. He was also a lady-killer with a long string of discarded mistresses, vaultingly ambitious, and very bad-tempered. But he was a man, which Darnley was not. It is not surprising that Mary fell in love with him.

For fall in love she did, although she probably did not realize it herself at first. The feeling probably began in the days of her convalescence, after the birth of James, after she had heard of Moray's dealings in the O'Neill affair, and realized, with a shock, that her brother, despite his recent pardon, was loyal to some thing or things other than herself. She realized how alone she was, politically and personally. Darnley was impossible. Her one true friend was Bothwell. Yet, instinctively, she fought against her growing feeling for the Border Earl. Mary was not immoral, and the idea of taking Bothwell as a lover, if it had yet occurred to her, was thrust aside. Yet she showed great favor to him—so said Killigrew and Bedford. Dimly she struggled against her womanly nature, which, now that her political dreams had vanished, was so imperiously asserting itself. She cast about for a protector against herself, and found her brother. Thus it was that Moray was restored in July, and thus it was that he was able to carry the pardon of Maitland in the face of his foe. Mary was, subconsciously, mortifying her flesh.[41]

Yet in spite of this she continued to smile upon Bothwell. He was in charge of the arrangements for her journey to Alloa, a seat of the Earl of Mar's, at the end of July, and with him, and Moray and Mar, she went hunting in August. Throughout this period she and Darnley were becoming more and more estranged, owing chiefly to Darnley's erratic behavior, until, indeed, they were no longer civil to each other.[42] One consequence was a band which, according to Moray, consisted of a formal promise of friendship between himself and Bothwell and Huntly.[43] Moray had probably promised to sign such a band at the time of his restoration in April, but its timing indicates that Mary now felt that this important formality was necessary because of Darnley's foolish carryings-on.

In the midst of all this, preparations were going forward for

41 There can, of course, be no evidence of the usual type adduced to support this theory. It rests principally, as is clear, on an interpretation of Mary's character which is certainly open to debate. As for the question as to whether Mary was ever in love with Bothwell at all, the evidence for this is far clearer, and will be dealt with when the circumstances surrounding the murder of Darnley are discussed.

42 For the story of Darnley's actions in this period, see Fleming, *Mary Queen of Scots*, pp. 135–37, 410–12; Knox, *History*, II, 533–34; September 30, 1566, Mary to Lennox, *Historical Manuscripts Commission, 3rd Report*, Appendix, p. 395; October 8, 1566, the Scottish Council to Catherine de Medici, in A. Teulet, ed., *Relations politiques de la France et de l'Espagne avec l'Ecosse au XVIe siècle*, II, 282–89; October 15, 1566, Du Croc to the Archbishop of Glasgow, in R. Keith, *The History of the Affairs of Church and State in Scotland*, II, 448–53; October 17, 1566, Du Croc to Catherine de Medici, in Teulet, *Relations politiques*, II, 289–93; November 13, 1566, De Silva to Philip II, *C.S.P., Span.*, I, 597. Du Croc had been appointed permanent resident in Scotland by France earlier in 1566.

43 Moray's declaration of January 19, 1569, *C.S.P., Scot.*, II, 599–600. See also Andrew Lang, *The Mystery of Mary Stuart*, pp. 74–78.

the justice eyre in the Border districts. Mary left Edinburgh on October 7.[44] On that very day Bothwell, who in his capacity as a Border Warden had been sent ahead to round up lawbreakers, ran afoul of one of them and was severely wounded, so severely that the first rumor was that he was slain.[45] Mary heard the news almost at once but did not hasten to Bothwell's side; instead she remained in Jedburgh for a week, holding her justice court, which was evidently very thinly attended.[46] It was not until the fifteenth that she made the long ride to Hermitage, where the wounded man lay. Moray apparently accompanied her. She remained but a few hours, returning to Jedburgh the same day.[47]

Immediately after her return to Jedburgh Mary became seriously ill. For a time her life was despaired of, even by herself, for she called her nobles about her and made a deathbed speech, in which she pleaded with Moray not to persecute the Catholics of Scotland after she was gone.[48] However, by the end of the month she was well on the way to recovery, which was not retarded even by the sight of Darnley.[49] Various causes for this illness have been mooted; that which seems to come nearest the truth, and to which the Queen herself attributed her sickness, is an emotional one. This was no new thing for Mary. Her bad health in the winter of 1563, for instance, was ascribed to disappointment over the failure of the Spanish match.[50] Maitland, after a conversation with Mary, informed the Archbishop of Glasgow that Darnley's behavior was responsible for the Queen's illness. "She has done him so great honor . . . contrary to the advice of her subjects, and he . . . has recompensed her with such ingratitude . . . that it is a heartbreak for her to think that he should be her husband, and how to

[44] Thomson, *Diurnal of Occurrents*, p. 100.
[45] October 8, 1566, Scrope to Cecil, *C.S.P., For., Eliz.*, VIII, 136–37.
[46] *Register of Privy Council*, I, 489–90.
[47] October 15, 1566, Forster to Cecil, *C.S.P., For., Eliz.*, VIII, 138–39. October 17, 1566, Scrope to Cecil, *ibid.*, p. 139. Thomson, *Diurnal of Occurrents*, p. 101.
[48] Nau, *History of Mary Stewart*, Introduction by J. Stevenson, pp. cxxxvii–cxli. November 6, 1566, John Hay to Cardinal Borgia, in Pollen, *Papal Negotiations*, pp. 502–4. Nau's story (*History of Mary Stewart*, p. 32), that Moray at one point, believing his sister to be dead, began to gather up miscellaneous valuables such as plate and rings, is not very plausible.
[49] Fleming, *Mary Queen of Scots*, pp. 140, 418–19.   [50] *Ibid.*, p. 94.

be free of him she sees no outgait." [51] Maitland's deduction is borne out by Mary's talk during her illness, which was recorded by Bishop Leslie.[52]

But even vexation at Darnley does not account for the severity of the seizure. In the writer's opinion, this was caused by Mary's sudden realization of the fact that she was in love with Bothwell— a natural enough discovery after her visit to his sickbed. This inference is borne out by the profound melancholy that gripped Mary during the next few months. From Jedburgh she proceeded to Kelso, where she received letters from Darnley that caused her to exclaim that unless she could somehow be rid of her obnoxious husband she would slay herself.[53] In December Du Croc, writing to the Archbishop of Glasgow, stated that she was continually sorrowful and was still uttering suicidal threats.[54] There was, indeed, "no outgait"—or so it seemed.

On November 20, after a slow progress through the Border districts, Mary came to the Castle of Craigmillar.[55] Here some sort of conference was held, the participants being Mary, Bothwell, Huntly, Maitland, Argyle, and Moray, on the problem of Darnley. This much is certain. It is also certain that the possibility of a divorce for Mary was discussed and rejected on the ground that it might destroy the legitimacy of Prince James. Mary talked of retiring to France. Our evidence for all this comes from a document known as the "Protestation of Huntly and Argyle." [56] This was drawn up by Mary and her advisers in the last days of 1568, when the Queen was a prisoner in England, and was sent to Huntly and Argyle, then the leaders of Mary's party in Scotland, for them to alter as they saw fit, and then to sign and publish.[57] The paper evidently never reached them; Lord Hunsdon seized

[51] October 24, 1566, Maitland to the Archbishop of Glasgow, in Malcolm Laing, *History of Scotland*, II, 73–75.
[52] On the subject of Mary's illness see J. Small, "Queen Mary at Jedburgh in 1566," *Proceedings of the Society of Antiquaries of Scotland*, new series, III (1881), 210–23. [53] D. Calderwood, *The History of the Kirk of Scotland*, II, 326.
[54] Keith, *History*, I, xcvi–xcviii.
[55] Thomson, *Diurnal of Occurrents*, p. 102.
[56] This document is printed in J. Anderson, ed., *Collections Relating to the History of Mary Queen of Scots*, IV, Pt. II, 188–93.
[57] January 5, 1569, Mary to Huntly, *ibid.*, pp. 185–87.

the messenger on the border and sent the documents he was carrying to Cecil.[58] In the evidence thus far cited the "Protestation" is
noncontroversial. Where it becomes doubtful is in its report of
the speech of Maitland, who evidently took the lead in the conversation. After the divorce had been suggested and rejected,
Maitland said that something would be done, and "Albeit that
my Lord of Moray here present be little less scrupulous for a Protestant than your Grace is for a Papist, I am sure he will look
through his fingers thereto, and will behold our doings, saying
nothing to the same." This sounded sinister, and Mary protested
that she would consent to nothing her conscience would not approve. Maitland told her not to worry: "Let us guide the matter
amongst us, and your Grace shall see nothing but good, and *approved by Parliament*" (italics mine).

Two other pieces of evidence are germane here. Moray, when
he saw this document, drew up a reply, on January 19, 1569, in
which, while not denying the general accuracy of the "Protestation," he stated categorically that he had been party at Craigmillar
to nothing that tended to any illegal or dishonorable end, and that
he had signed no bands except that of October 1566 referred to
above.[59] This latter statement was necessary because early in 1568
one of Bothwell's henchmen, Hay of Talla, had made a public
confession on the scaffold, in which he said that a band for Darnley's murder had existed, signed by Huntly, Argyle, Maitland,
Bothwell, and Sir James Balfour.[60] It will be seen at once that a
great deal hinges on the phrase of Maitland italicized above. If
Moray's bitter enemies, at a time when he was charging Mary
with complicity in the murder of her husband, could not accuse
him of anything worse than consent to some unspecified action
which would have Parliamentary approval, it is perfectly evident
that he had no hand in the murder. Nor, indeed, was he ever accused of having participated in the actual slaying, or of having

[58] January 10, 1569, Hunsdon to Cecil, *Calendar of the Manuscripts of the Marquis of Salisbury*, I, 390.   [59] *C.S.P., Scot.*, II, 599–600. See above, p. 181.
[60] Thomson, *Diurnal of Occurrents*, pp. 127–28. Hay's further statement that
Morton had not signed the band lends verisimilitude to his confession. On the
problem of the two bands, see Lang, *Mystery of Mary Stuart*, pp. 74–78, 118–21,
and Randolph's letter of October 15, 1570, *C.S.P., For., Eliz.*, IX, 354–55.

signed any murder band. The most serious charge that has been leveled against him, that of passivity in the face of guilty fore-knowledge, will be dealt with below.

In fact, it is unlikely that the idea of murdering Darnley was broached at all at Craigmillar, either in or out of Moray's presence. If we accept the "Protestation" and Hay of Talla's confession as both being more or less accurate—both are open to doubt, of course—the question arises as to just what was proposed there. It is the writer's opinion that what was decided was to arrest Darnley for treason, and to kill him if he resisted or attempted to escape —a device which has had its uses in our own enlightened age. This was the later opinion of Lennox.[61] Rumors of this leaked out and were circulated by the town clerk of Glasgow, a Lennox man.[62] The story of Lord Robert Stewart's last-minute "warning" to Darnley sounds like a twisted version of the same thing.[63] This would explain Maitland's phrase: if Darnley were to be eliminated in such a way, Parliamentary approval would follow. But the solution was uncertain; Darnley might give them no chance to kill him, and, while he might be convicted of treason and thus eliminated, Mary's reputation would suffer. The whole thing was very harassing; quite enough to keep the Queen plunged in gloom.

Early in December Mary returned to Edinburgh, and from there moved on to Stirling for the baptism of Prince James. She was beginning to succumb to her love for Bothwell. On December 11 Forster informed Cecil that Bothwell had been made Lieutenant of all the Marches and had also been put in charge of the arrangements for the baptism.[64] This was extraordinary, since the little prince was to be baptized in the Catholic faith, and Bothwell was a Protestant. James's sponsors were Charles IX, the Duke of Savoy, and Elizabeth. The latter and Mary were on very friendly terms at this time, owing to the restoration of Moray to

[61] Andrew Lang, *A History of Scotland from the Roman Occupation*, II, 172. Lang made an intensive study of the Lennox MSS. and incorporated his findings in his *History* and in his full-length study of the problem of the Darnley murder, *The Mystery of Mary Stuart*. On this point see this work, pp. 85–89.
[62] January 20, 1567, Mary to the Archbishop of Glasgow, in Keith, *History*, I, xcix–ci. [63] Melville, *Memoirs*, pp. 173–74.
[64] *C.S.P., For., Eliz.*, VIII, 155.

power, and Elizabeth on this occasion so far forgot her parsimony as to send a massive gold font as a baptismal gift through her envoy, the Earl of Bedford.[65] Mary had decided to take advantage of the fact that her brother had been restored to reopen the question of the succession; Elizabeth might now be willing to do something about it.[66] Elizabeth was not unwilling to discuss matters: in her instructions to Bedford she promised that she would do nothing to oppose Mary's rights, and that she would look into the matter of Henry VIII's will, which allegedly constituted a barrier to Mary's succession. She was even willing to negotiate a revision of the Treaty of Edinburgh, still unratified.[67] Mary was delighted, and replied that she was prepared to appoint commissioners to discuss these points, and anything else, with Elizabeth's representatives.[68] Before any concrete results could be obtained from these promising beginnings, however, tragedy intervened.

It was at the time of the baptism, which took place on December 17,[69] that the murder of Darnley was decided upon. There is good evidence for this. Mary's attitude toward her husband underwent a change. She now railed at him publicly, according to Lennox: he would benefit, she said, by being "a little daggered, and by bleeding as much as my Lord Bothwell had lately done." [70] On December 20 the Privy Council decreed that the ministers should have £10,000 a year, plus victuals, from the thirds.[71] This move was made to soften in advance the volume of protest which Mary knew her next step would arouse: a few days later she restored Archbishop Hamilton to his consistorial jurisdiction. The Kirk was wild about this; the General Assembly protested violently in its December meeting, and Knox addressed an inflammatory letter to the Protestant nobility.[72] Moray was taken by surprise, and was annoyed; he protested to Mary and, according to Bed-

[65] Thomson, *Diurnal of Occurrents*, p. 103.
[66] See her letters of November 18, 1566, in Labanoff, *Recueil*, I, 380–81, 382–84.
[67] Keith, *History*, II, 477–83. J. A. Froude regards Elizabeth's attitude at this time as a virtual admission of Mary's right to the succession. *History of England (1529–1588)*, VIII, 335.
[68] Mary's letter is dated January 3, 1567. *Register of Privy Council*, Addenda, XIV, 262–65.   [69] Thomson, *Diurnal of Occurrents*, p. 104.
[70] Lang, *History of Scotland*, II, 172.   [71] *Register of Privy Council*, I, 494–95.
[72] Knox, *History*, II, 539–44.

ford, got the commission revoked.[73] Bedford seems to have exaggerated, for the Archbishop's court did sit once, later in 1567,
for one purpose: to grant a divorce to Bothwell.[74]

But the strongest evidence that the King's death was now decided was the fact that on December 24 Mary pardoned Morton
and almost all of his associates. We have seen that Moray had
long been working for this, in order to bring his party back to
its full strength. According to the "Protestation of Huntly and
Argyle," he proposed at Craigmillar to trade his help against
Darnley for this pardon. But so far none had resulted: Mary and
Bothwell had had no reason for wanting Morton back. Now,
however, they had. Morton and his companions mortally hated
Darnley, as everyone knew. If they were pardoned, Morton might
be persuaded to kill Darnley, and thus keep the hands of Bothwell and his mistress clean. The decisiveness of Bothwell's influence in this business did not escape Bedford. On December 30
he wrote that, although Moray and others had been pleading for
Morton's pardon, they would have failed if Bothwell's voice had
not been added to theirs.[75]

The scheme failed, because Morton was shrewd enough to
realize that the murder was politically extremely dangerous. In
mid-January 1567 Bothwell and Maitland visited him at Whittingham to persuade him to join them in the plot. Morton refused to
do so unless Mary authorized the deed in writing. Mary, of course,
was not so foolish as to do any such thing; consequently Morton
would have nothing to do with the affair.[76]

It was, therefore, necessary for Bothwell to undertake the job
himself. From this point on, history, as Lang puts it, "becomes a
mere criminal trial, wrangled over by prejudice and confused by
dubious evidence." [77] The evidence, *pace* Mr. Lang, is not, per-

[73] January 9, 1567, Bedford to Cecil, *C.S.P., Scot.*, II, 309–10.
[74] The continuator of Knox says merely that Moray prevented the Archbishop
from entering Edinburgh in force to resume his powers, not that he obtained a
revocation of the commission. Knox, *History*, II, 548–49.
[75] *C.S.P., Scot.*, II, 308.
[76] The Whittingham meeting was reported in Drury's letter to Cecil of January
23, 1567, *C.S.P., For., Eliz.*, VIII, 167–68. Morton revealed the subjects discussed
in his final confession before his execution, in 1581. It is printed in Malcolm Laing, *History of Scotland*, II, 354–61.   [77] Lang, *History of Scotland*, II, 169.

haps, so dubious as he believed. The great question, of course, is whether Mary was guilty of foreknowledge of her husband's murder. The controversy has centered around the famous Casket Letters, a series of missives allegedly written by Mary to Bothwell between January and April 1567. I do not propose to discuss these letters; those who are curious are referred to the works of Lang and Henderson.[78] If the letters are genuine, Mary was undoubtedly guilty; but even if they were forged, the circumstantial evidence against her is overwhelming. And at this point we are confronted with another striking piece of it.

On January 20 Mary wrote to the Archbishop of Glasgow in scathing terms about her husband.[79] Yet on that very day she set out for Glasgow to see Darnley, who was lying there ill with smallpox.[80] So ably did she play her part that by the end of the month she had brought him back to Edinburgh with her, where, for reasons of health, as it was said, he was lodged at Kirk of Field. Seemingly they were entirely reconciled. Mary visited him with great frequency, and even spent two nights in the half-ruined house.[81]

In these weeks we hear little of Moray. We know that he entertained Bedford at St. Andrews after the baptism[82] and that he protested against the restoration of Archbishop Hamilton's court. We also know that he left Edinburgh for St. Andrews on the day before the murder of Darnley, on hearing that his wife had miscarried.[83] To many writers this sudden departure has smelled of more than coincidence. It is perfectly possible that Moray was deliberately getting out of harm's way, but it by no means follows that he knew that Darnley was to be slain that night.

If we accept the theory that Moray was expecting Darnley to be arrested for treason, and perhaps killed in a scuffle, his conduct throughout becomes completely intelligible. The Queen's

---

[78] Lang, *Mystery of Mary Stuart*. T. F. Henderson, *The Casket Letters and Mary Queen of Scots*. See also the studies by M. Philippson and R. Chauviré which appeared in the *Revue historique* (see Bibliography for full citations.)
[79] Keith, *History*, I, xcix–ci.   [80] Thomson, *Diurnal of Occurrents*, p. 105.
[81] For Mary's conduct during this period, see the deposition of Nelson, a servant of Darnley's. Anderson, *Collections*, IV, Pt. II, 166.
[82] December 30, 1566, Bedford to Cecil, *C.S.P., Scot.*, II, 308.
[83] G. Buchanan, *The History of Scotland*, II, 492.

behavior to Darnley at the baptism and the recall of Morton were to be expected. This last was the price Moray had exacted for his acquiescence. But the revival of the Archbishop's court puzzled and alarmed him; there was no need for any such tool to eliminate Darnley, and he protested against it. He did not suspect Mary's purpose in reviving it, for he did not become aware until after the murder that Mary was in love with Bothwell. When Mary seemingly reconciled herself with Darnley and brought him to Edinburgh, Moray must have become terribly alarmed. He knew those concerned well enough to realize that the reconciliation was only a sham. It dawned on him that the whole business was a trap. Darnley was to be murdered—he knew not how nor when, but he did know by whom. This being the case, he wanted to have nothing whatever to do with it. Hated though Darnley was, he was still a king, and if he were murdered, there would be an irresistable demand, both at home and abroad, that the crime be punished. Mary, in order to save herself and her good name, would have to turn on those who had done the deed and sacrifice them. Moray, not knowing his sister's love for the future murderer, fully expected her to do just this, as his behavior after February 10 shows. Furthermore, he wanted her to take that course, for Moray disliked Bothwell and regarded him as dangerous to his political and religious purposes. But he did not want to be involved himself or have any of his Protestant co-adjutors involved. Had he known of it, he would have blessed Morton's wariness. As it was, he must have been greatly relieved when he crossed the Forth on that February morning.

Let us now consider the theory that Moray was actively involved in the plot to murder Darnley. There are three possibilities here. The first is that Moray encouraged Bothwell—who undoubtedly committed the crime—with the knowledge that Mary knew of the plot and was in love with the Earl. This quickly reveals itself as absurd, for in that case Moray would have been exchanging one master for another, and Bothwell was far more dangerous to him and his plans than was Darnley in the latter's present isolated and helpless condition. Bothwell, though a Protestant, disliked Moray and was hostile to England; furthermore, Moray had great power in administrative affairs at the moment, and both Protestanism and the English alliance were flourish-ing.[84] The second possibility is that Moray encouraged Both-well, knowing that Mary was aware of the plot and believing that she was merely using Bothwell to get rid of a husband she hated. In this case the same reasoning would apply as in the case of what, in the writer's opinion, actually occurred: Moray would have been foolish to the point of rashness to have anything to do with such a plan, which, he knew, would recoil on its authors—as it did—and from which he could not be expected to gain. The third possibility is that Moray encouraged Bothwell without knowing anything of Mary's sentiments at all. Here again the same reason-ing applies, if anything, more forcefully than ever, with the recent case of Mary's vengeance on the murderers of Riccio on the records. This theory is further vitiated by the consideration that Bothwell, who was bold but not entirely lacking in sense, could not be expected to murder the King without knowing Mary's views on the subject. Finally, it should be pointed out that there is no evidence whatever, except the allegations of Moray's polit-ical enemies, to connect him with the murder. It is unwise as well as unjust to assume, as so many writers have done, that Moray, because he obtained power in the long run from Darnley's death, must therefore have been in some way responsible for it.

At about two o'clock on the morning of February 10 the silence of Edinburgh was broken by a shattering explosion. Kirk of Field had been blown up, and the King was dead. The details of the events of that famous night, like those of March 9, 1566, have been recounted many times.[85] As Moray had anticipated, the deed was to recoil frighteningly upon its authors.

[84] Relations with England have already been discussed. As for Protestantism: on January 10, one month before the murder of Darnley, a large commission, in-cluding Moray, was appointed by the council to look into burgh revenues and to be sure that burgh taxation was sufficient to care for the local ministers. *Regis-ter of Privy Council*, I, 497–98. This commission functioned, too, in spite of the murder: on May 7, 1567, Glasgow was ordered to make better provision for its kirkmen. *Ibid.*, pp. 508–9.

[85] R. H. Mahon, *The Tragedy of Kirk o'Field*, is a detailed study of the circum-stances of the murder itself. The works of Lang and Philippson on the Casket Letters, cited in note 78, also contain material on the murder. It was, of course, mentioned in all contemporary accounts.

CHAPTER IX

The Downfall of Mary

ALMOST IMMEDIATELY after the murder the new-made widow wrote an account of the affair to the Archbishop of Glasgow. It was only by the grace of God, Mary said, that she had not been killed as well; it was only because she had suddenly remembered the wedding of one of her servants that she had escaped. She was resolved to avenge her husband's death, she added.[1]

If Mary had followed the course of action outlined in this letter, in all probability she would have ended her days on the Scottish throne, even though she would have been a puppet in the hands of Moray and the Protestant party. This was the result Moray had anticipated. But Moray reckoned without Mary's passion for the slayer of her husband. No one expected the Queen to show any grief for Darnley, nor did she; but no one expected her to do what she did do, which was to behave, so far as possible, as if nothing had happened. True, two days after the murder, the Privy Council proclaimed that £2,000 awaited anyone who could give information as to the murderers,[2] but beyond that the Queen seemed determined to ignore the whole affair. Edinburgh was soon placarded with bills accusing Bothwell of the crime, and the Queen of guilty foreknowledge of it.[3] Mary paid no heed to this or to the advice of Elizabeth, the French government, and the Archbishop of Glasgow, the burden of which was to avenge the

---

[1] R. Keith, The History of the Affairs of Church and State in Scotland, I, ci–cii.
[2] The Register of the Privy Council of Scotland, I, 498.
[3] February 28, 1567, Drury to Cecil, in P. F. Tytler, History of Scotland, VII, 370–72.

murder.[4] She even attempted to put off Lennox when he demanded that some action be taken against the slayers of his son.[5]

Throughout the latter part of February, while all this was
going on, Moray was lying very low. He was both puzzled and
alarmed by Mary's do-nothing policy; this was not what he had
expected. Although he would not join the Queen at Seton, alleging that his wife was ill, he went to Dunkeld toward the end of
the month to meet with Morton, Athol, and others.[6] We do not
know what happened there, but from the future behavior of the
participants it may be deduced that they decided, for the moment at least, that there was nothing to be done. An impossible
situation had developed. Very soon Mary would be forced either
to sacrifice Bothwell or to defend him. In either case nothing
could be gained by action now; it was better to wait and see what
Mary would do, and then act accordingly.

Early in March Moray returned to court. On the thirteenth
he wrote to Cecil—his first pronouncement since the murder.
Naturally, he announced his disapproval of the crime, which he
called "odious and detestable"; but his main concern was to convince Cecil that he had had no hand in it.[7] This was necessary, for
Bothwell had been busily spreading the rumor abroad that Moray
and his fellow Protestants had killed Darnley, and, needless to say,
there were many, especially in Catholic circles, who believed it.[8]
It is worth mentioning here, however, that Du Croc and Moretta,
the two Catholic observers on the spot at the time of the murder,
both believed, with varying degrees of conviction, that Mary
was guilty.[9]

[4] February 24, 1567, Elizabeth to Mary, *C.S.P., Scot.*, II, 316. March 29, 1567,
Drury to Cecil, *C.S.P., For., Eliz.*, VIII, 198. Keith, *History*, I, cii–cv.
[5] Mary's correspondence with Lennox on this matter is given in J. Anderson, ed.,
Collections Relating to the History of Mary Queen of Scots, I, 40–49.
[6] February 28, 1567, Drury to Cecil, in Tytler, *History of Scotland*, VII, 370–72.
[7] *C.S.P., Scot.*, II, 318.
[8] G. Buchanan, *The History of Scotland*, II, 494. March 12, 1567, Laureo to the
Cardinal of Alessandria, in J. H. Pollen, ed., *Papal Negotiations with Mary Queen
of Scots*, pp. 364–66. March 20, 1567, Correr to the Signory, *C.S.P., Ven.*, VII,
389–90.
[9] For Moretta's attitude see March 1, 1567, De Silva to Philip II, *C.S.P., Span.*, I,
621–23. June 17, 1567, Du Croc to Catherine de Medici, in A. Teulet, ed., *Relations politiques de la France et de l'Espagne avec l'Ecosse au XVIe siècle*, II, 310–
12.

At the end of his letter to Cecil Moray asked for a passport. He was preparing to go abroad if necessary. This would be a drastic step, which Moray was probably not at all anxious to take. But circumstances were getting out of his control. It was obvious that some official action on the murder could not be put off much longer, and it became more and more apparent that Mary was going to shield Bothwell. Moray began to realize that she could have but one motive in so doing. Mary's love for her husband's slayer upset all of Moray's nice calculations, for he had no understanding of, or sympathy with, emotion as a political force. This is perhaps why, to the end of his life, he continued to repose the utmost confidence in Elizabeth and Cecil. Elizabeth was thoroughly untrustworthy, but Moray always felt that, in the end, she would support him, because her policy, thanks mainly to Cecil, was always a calculated one. But he had no idea how far Mary would go in defense of her lover. He certainly did not dream that she would go as far as she did. But he well knew that any attempt by Mary to protect Bothwell would sooner or later provoke a rebellion, for he knew the force of Calvinist public opinion in matters of morality, and he knew that many of the Protestant lords hated and feared Bothwell. He did not want to be involved in such a rebellion. He was certain that it would succeed in eliminating Bothwell, but, he calculated, once that was done, there would be a near-balance of factions, with the Protestants having a preponderance. Then he could return with clean hands, and, as the acknowledged leader of the Protestant party, his resumption of political control would be certain. With Mary's reputation somewhat tarnished, she would never again be in a position to do without him. So he decided to go sightseeing abroad.

The events of March confirmed Moray in his decision. On March 19 Mar was forced to give up the captaincy of Edinburgh Castle, which he had held since 1554, to Cockburn of Skirling, a henchman of Bothwell's. Mar in exchange received the hereditary captaincy of Stirling and once more was put in charge of the little Prince.[10] As Moray had foreseen, Mary, prompted perhaps

[10] March 21, March 30, 1567, Drury to Cecil, *C.S.P., For., Eliz.*, VIII, 194, 198–99. *The Acts of the Parliament of Scotland*, II, 549. The care of royal children was

by the Dunkeld meeting—she had come to be suspicious of noble
gatherings—at last decided to make concessions to public opinion.
On March 24 she wrote Lennox, consenting to the trial of Bothwell for the murder of Darnley.[11] But this was to be an unusual
type of murder trial, as was made manifest by the fact that Bothwell was permitted to sit at the Privy Council meeting which made
the arrangements for it.[12] And, although murder was a plea of the
crown in Scotland, as everywhere else, in this case the crown did
not prosecute. Lennox was forced to act as plaintiff, as in an ordinary civil suit.

By this time rumors were flying around to the effect that Mary
planned to marry Bothwell, who was to get a divorce on the
ground of his own adultery. So Drury reported on March 29.[13]
Moray thought it high time to depart. Mary was not anxious to
have him go. "She wept at his departure," said Drury, "wishing
he were not so precise in religion." [14] Brother and sister parted
on friendly terms. Moray's will, dated April 3, entrusted to Mary
the responsibility for seeing that its provisions were carried out.[15]
Mary in turn made him a gift of all the temporalities of the monasteries of St. Andrews and Pittenweem, of both of which he was
commendator.[16] On April 10 Moray was in Berwick.[17]

Moray's departure was followed by a series of extraordinary
events which are so well known as to require no detailing here.
The first was Bothwell's farcical "trial," which resulted in the expected acquittal.[18] Then came a meeting of Parliament, in which
Mary's attempts to mollify her potential enemies led her to give a
backhanded legal recognition to Protestantism.[19] There followed
the astonishing business of "Ainslie's Band," the collusive "kid-

virtually a prerogative of the head of the House of Erskine in the sixteenth
century.   [11] Anderson, *Collections*, I, 48–49.
[12] *Register of Privy Council*, I, 504–5.   [13] C.S.P., *For.*, *Eliz.*, VIII, 198.
[14] April 15, 1567, Drury to Cecil, Tytler, *History of Scotland*, VII, 372–76.
[15] C. Innes, ed., *Registrum Honoris de Morton*, I, 17.
[16] April 9, 1567, Moray to Wynram, *Historical Manuscripts Commission, 6th
Report*, Appendix, pp. 642–43.
[17] April 10, 1567, Drury to Cecil, *C.S.P., For., Eliz.*, VIII, 203.
[18] T. F. Henderson's account of the trial is a good one: *Mary Queen of Scots*, II,
451–55.
[19] All statutes contrary to the new religion were repealed. For the acts of this
Parliament, see *Acts of Parliament*, II, 547–79.

napping" of the Queen by Bothwell,[20] the latter's divorce, and
finally, on May 15, the marriage of Mary and the bold Earl, by
Protestant rites. For her lover Mary sacrificed her religion and
her Catholic friends throughout Europe.[21] This marriage was
the most serious blunder Mary ever made; it cost her her throne
and thus, indirectly, her life.

By the date of the marriage a formidable coalition had formed,
which in the space of one short month was to ruin both Mary and
her new husband. As early as April 20 Kirkcaldy had written in
rage to Bedford of the Queen's infatuation for Bothwell—she
would "go with him to the world's end in a white petticoat ere
she leave him. Yea! she is so far past all shame. . . ." He went on
to inform Bedford that he and his friends would undertake to
avenge Darnley if Elizabeth would support them.[22] But it was
the shameless, collusive "rape" that finally galvanized the lords
into action; they now realized that Bothwell and his friends, and
not they, were going to profit from the death of the King. The fact
that Darnley, whom they all hated, had been murdered with the
Queen's connivance was not enough to provoke a rebellion. Even
the judicial whitewashing of Bothwell might not have produced
an immediate upheaval, although sooner or later it probably would
have come. There were bribes for many in the form of parliamentary confirmations of their possessions, and Morton, in
Moray's absence the key man among the Protestant lords, had
received back his stronghold of Tantallon through Bothwell's influence, so that he would look through his fingers at the trial.[23]
But the permanent triumph of Bothwell the lords could not
stomach. It was not the murder of Darnley but her marriage to the
murderer that toppled Mary from her throne.

[20] On the question of collusion see Sir James Melville, *Memoirs of his own Life*,
p. 177; D. Calderwood, *The History of the Kirk of Scotland*, II, 356; May 3, 1567,
De Silva to Philip II, *C.S.P., Span.*, I, 638–39; and, most decisive of all, Kirkcaldy's
prediction, in a letter to Bedford written just before the event, *C.S.P., Scot.*, II,
324.
[21] After hearing of Mary's marriage to Bothwell by the Protestant ceremony, the
Pope refused to have any further dealings with her. A year or so later he said
that he did not know whether she or Elizabeth was the worse. Pollen, *Papal
Negotiations*, pp. cxxxiii, 397. M. Philippson, *Histoire du règne de Marie Stuart*,
III, 496.   [22] *C.S.P., Scot.*, II, 322–23.
[23] April 4, April 15, 1567, Drury to Cecil, *C.S.P., For., Eliz.*, VIII, 199–200, 207.

At the end of April the lords met at Stirling, and on May 1 a band was drafted, pledging the signatories to free the Queen and defend her and Prince James from Bothwell.[24] Nor was this merely a Protestant coalition; on May 7 Robert Melville informed Cecil that even the Catholics, outraged by Mary's behavior, were prepared to join the Protestants in an attack on Bothwell, and he urged Cecil to support them. France had made them an offer, he said, and unless England acted quickly, they might have to close with the French.[25] On the following day Kirkcaldy repeated this to Bedford and gave further details of the coalition. The key figures at the Stirling meeting had been Morton, Argyle, Athol, and Mar. The first three had separated to raise support in various sections of the country; Mar had remained to protect Prince James. They expected to win over not only assured Protestants such as Glencairn, Ruthven, and Lindsay but also Catholics such as Eglinton, Montrose, and Hume. Finally, Kirkcaldy asked Bedford to notify Moray of what went on, and to tell him to prepare to come home.[26]

Mary was not entirely unaware of the dangers confronting her. She proclaimed, both at home and abroad, that she had not married Bothwell under duress, in spite of the "rape." [27] On May 23 she issued a proclamation intended to reassure the Protestants on the score of religion.[28] Robert Melville was sent to England to pacify Elizabeth; Mary did not know that he had joined her enemies.[29] She endeavored to break up the noble coalition and succeeded in detaching Argyle, but an exchange of letters with Morton profited

[24] *Register of Privy Council*, Addenda, XIV, 315.
[25] *C.S.P., Scot.*, II, 326–27.   [26] *Ibid.*, pp. 327–28.
[27] In this connection see especially her instructions to the Bishop of Dunblane, who was sent to the French court with her explanation of her precipitate marriage. Anderson, *Collections*, I, 89–102.
[28] *Register of Privy Council*, I, 513–14. As an indication of how little Mary understood the causes of the Reformation, the temper of her people, and, indeed, the consequences of her own behavior, she picked this time to write to Pius V, asking that the commendatorship of Kelso be given to Bothwell's nephew, Francis Stewart, aged five. *Ibid.*, Addenda, XIV, 272–73. Francis Stewart was one day to become Earl of Bothwell himself and to have almost as spectacular a career as his more celebrated uncle.
[29] His instructions are in Anderson, *Collections*, I, 103–7.

her nothing.[30] Worse still, on June 6 Maitland deserted her to join the lords.[31]

The end came quickly. On Sunday, June 15, the two rival armies met at Carberry Hill. Neither side was anxious to attack, since, owing to the terrain, the attacking army would be at a disadvantage. Attempts at compromise failed. As the day wore on, desertion began to take its toll of Mary's army. Toward dusk the lords had obtained a decided superiority and began to prepare an attack. On perceiving this, Mary offered to put herself in the lords' hands, if they would return to their allegiance. These conditions were accepted, and she surrendered.[32]

As for Bothwell, he was permitted to escape to Dunbar. At first glance it seems surprising that the lords should have allowed this, since their avowed object was to punish him for his crimes. But Bothwell would have been far too dangerous as a captive. Maitland and Balfour,[33] at least, he could have dragged down with him if he were convicted in court of Darnley's murder, and Morton himself was guilty of being, in modern parlance, an accessory before the fact. The lords dared not, for their own sakes, bring Bothwell into court. It was decided to deal with him later.

It was quickly made clear to Mary that the lords, now that she was in their power, had no intention of restoring her to her former estate at once. It was as a virtual captive that she was led into Edinburgh on the night of June 15, amid the execrations of its Calvinist populace. She was furious with rage, feeling that she had been tricked. The lords did not improve her disposition by informing her that she would not be restored to her throne unless

[30] J. Spottiswoode, *The History of the Church of Scotland*, p. 204. Philippson, *Histoire*, III, 367–69, 487–91.
[31] June 7, 1567, Drury to Cecil, *C.S.P., For., Eliz.*, VIII, 245.
[32] The best account of the events of June 15 is that of Du Croc, written to his government on June 17, 1567, in Teulet, *Relations politiques*, II, 312–22.
[33] Balfour, Captain of Edinburgh Castle since May, deserted to the Lords before Carberry on receiving a promise of immunity for whatever crimes he may have committed. Moray later had to redeem this pledge. T. Thomson, ed., *A Diurnal of Remarkable Occurrents that Have Passed within the Country of Scotland*, p. 111. T. Thomson, ed., *The Historie and Life of King James the Sext*, p. 11. Innes, *Registrum Honoris de Morton*, I, 18–19. *Historical Manuscripts Commission, 6th Report*, Appendix, p. 642. Melville, *Memoirs*, pp. 180–81.

she renounced Bothwell once for all. This she absolutely declined to do. Consequently, on June 17, she was committed to the fortress of Lochleven, whose custodian, Sir William Douglas, was a near relative of Morton's and the half-brother of Moray.[34]

If Mary's behavior before the murder of Darnley lends color to the belief that she was guilty of foreknowledge of the crime, her conduct afterwards, in the writer's opinion, absolutely confirms it. She made no serious attempt to punish the criminals. When the man whom all Scotland knew to be guilty was brought to trial, she so arranged matters that the trial became a farce, heaped honors on him, and finally married him. Each one of her actions, from the restoration of Archbishop Hamilton's court to the marriage with Bothwell, is susceptible of an explanation which is consistent with innocence, and Mary has not lacked apologists who have exercised their ingenuity to explain them away. But, taken all together, these explanations simply do not ring true. The evidence for guilt is too overwhelming, even without the Casket Letters. Even such an ardent defender of Mary as Lang admits that, on the assumption of innocence, "Mary's conduct after Darnley's death remains an insoluble enigma." [35] When to all this is added the fact that virtually all her contemporaries who knew the facts—not only partisans, such as Morton and Knox, but men who wished her well, such as Moretta and Du Croc—thought her guilty, it becomes next to impossible to believe in her innocence. Alas for the romantics—it must be concluded that Mary was by no means the helpless victim of circumstances.

ii

In spite of Mary's numerous errors and follies, the movement against her did not have the support of all factions in Scotland.

[34] The warrant confining Mary to Lochleven is dated June 16, 1567. Her loyalty to Bothwell was given as the reason for her imprisonment. *Maitland Club, Miscellany*, I, 249–52. Maitland told Du Croc that, in conversation with him in Edinburgh after Carberry, Mary refused to be parted from Bothwell. June 17, 1567, Du Croc to Catherine de Medici, in Teulet, *Relations politiques*, II, 310–12. This appears to be true, since Maitland later repeated it, when he had become a member of Mary's party. D. H. Fleming, *Mary Queen of Scots*, pp. 464–65. See also June 20, 1567, Drury to Cecil, *C.S.P., For., Eliz.*, VIII, 256.
[35] Andrew Lang, *A History of Scotland from the Roman Occupation*, II, 174.

The leaders of the confederate lords were Moray's old friends and allies, Morton, Mar, Glencairn, Ruthven, Lindsay, and the like. With them stood the preachers, who had long detested the Queen and who rejoiced in her ruin, which they had done much to bring about by keeping Protestant opinion inflamed against Mary's real and supposed misdeeds. The Queen's inability to understand the nature of Calvinist morality, which had become deeply ingrained in the minds of her subjects, particularly those of the towns, was one of her most costly failings.

Allied to this solid core of Protestant strength were several diverse elements. Although Lennox himself had been in England since April,[36] the Lennox interest, which had never joined the Protestants except briefly during the conspiracy against Riccio, now became firmly attached to the Protestant lords: after all, their proclaimed purpose was to avenge Darnley. A number of Catholics were also members of their party, for the moment at least, either out of dislike of Bothwell, or, like Athol, out of family interest—Athol was a Stewart and an ally of Lennox. These men could be relied on to stand by the confederates as long as they did not proceed to extremities against Mary. Finally, there was Maitland, whose exact plans no one could be sure of. These disparate elements had been united by a common hatred of Bothwell. Whether that union would last, now that the latter's power had been broken, was highly problematical.

There was as great a diversity of purpose among those who still stood by the Queen. Some were her personal followers; some, confederates of Bothwell; some, enemies of Moray or other Protestant leaders. Also in Mary's camp was Argyle, whose motives are less easy to fathom. Moray's old friend stood aloof in the month preceding Carberry; he had, at one point, joined the lords, and then deserted them, but he did not join the Queen's party until after the ruin of Bothwell, whom he regarded as an enemy. He hated Lennox and disliked Athol, but probably the decisive considerations with him were suspicion of Elizabeth and personal loyalty to Mary, this last a quality he had developed after Elizabeth's behavior in 1565–66 had disillusioned him in regard to Eng-

[36] Thomson, *Diurnal of Occurrents*, p. 109.

land. From that time forward Argyle's anti-English bias was pronounced. Finally, the Hamiltons, led by the Archbishop, supported the Queen. The wily Primate was not moved by religious
considerations; as always, he had the interests of his family in view.
If Mary were deposed and Prince James crowned, the Hamiltons
might be excluded from the succession, in favor of the Lennox
family. The Archbishop had but little interest in Mary's welfare
as such, as we shall shortly see. What he was probably aiming for
was a compromise that would elevate the feeble Châtelherault to
the regency once more; this, he thought, would restore him to
the power behind the scenes which he had exercised in the early
1550s.

It is plain from this analysis that the division of parties was not
along religious lines. Nevertheless it appeared to be, with the
Archbishop the leader of the Marians. Therefore Morton and
his Protestant confreres dared not alienate their own most ardent
supporters, the ministers, who had done so much to pull Mary
and Bothwell down, especially since public opinion was becoming
more favorable to Mary, largely for sentimental reasons, according to Buchanan.[37] The lesson of 1565 had been well learned. As a
result a great deal of power was thrown into the hands of the
General Assembly, which postponed its regular meeting, scheduled for June 25, for a month. The reasons for the postponement
were the general confusion and the desire to make a special effort
in order to get the Protestants among Mary's supporters to attend.[38] When the Assembly came together again in mid-July, the
deposition of Mary had been decided on, and the support of the
ministers was more vital than ever to Morton and his friends. Consequently the demands of the Assembly were agreed to without
qualification and inserted in the Privy Council Register.[39] The
main things the ministers wanted were the complete abolition of
Popery, immediate possession of the total revenue of the thirds,
control of education, a requirement that all future rulers take an

---

[37] G. Buchanan, *The History of Scotland*, II, 524.
[38] Calderwood, *History of the Kirk*, II, 368–70.
[39] *Register of Privy Council*, I, 534–37. See also Calderwood, *History of the Kirk*,
II, 377–84.

oath to support Protestantism, and a pledge by the lords that the next Parliament would give the Kirk complete control of all Church property. That the lords would agree to such demands, especially that on Church property, indicates that the position of the confederates was far from secure.

That this was so was owing only partly to opposition at home. Equally important was the hostile attitude of England. Elizabeth, who had moved cautiously before Carberry, was profoundly shocked by the imprisonment of Mary; attacks of this nature on crowned heads were dangerous and might lead to a similar attack on her some day. She therefore determined to strain every nerve to secure the restoration of Mary. On June 23 she wrote to Mary, promising help in protecting her honor and life, and at the same time reading her a moral lesson on the iniquity of the Bothwell marriage.[40] Her next move was to send Sir Nicholas Throckmorton to Scotland. He was to see Mary and hear her side of the story, and inform the lords that it was wicked to imprison their sovereign, who must be restored. At the same time, the safety of the confederates and of Protestantism must be provided for in the terms of the restoration settlement, and the murderers of Darnley must be punished. He was also to try to have Prince James sent to his grandmother in England, a request the lords had already once refused.[41]

On July 12 Throckmorton saw Maitland, the official spokesman of the lords. The latter was very cautious, Sir Nicholas reported, and would not commit himself to following English advice; in fact, he would not even discuss releasing Mary. One of the reasons for the independent attitude of the lords was revealed by the Secretary: they had an excellent offer from France, and consequently were not dependent on English aid. Furthermore, said Maitland, Elizabeth's behavior in 1565–66 had alienated many people.[42] Maitland was not bluffing in the matter of the French

[40] C.S.P., Scot., II, 336–37.
[41] Throckmorton's instructions are dated June 30, 1567. Ibid., pp. 339–41. On the question of Prince James, see May 17, 1567, Elizabeth to Bedford, C.S.P., For., Eliz., VIII, 232; June 15, 1567, Bedford to Leicester, ibid., p. 252.
[42] July 12, 1567, Throckmorton to Cecil, C.S.P., Scot., II, 348–49. July 14, 1567, Throckmorton to Elizabeth, ibid., pp. 349–52.

alliance. A special French agent, Villeroy, had been sent to Scotland in June with instructions to renew the "auld alliance," at Mary's expense if necessary.[43] Catherine de Medici, like Maitland, felt that there were things more important than religion.

The most important reason for the lords' refusal to submit to Elizabeth, however, was the famous Casket. This had come into the hands of Morton on June 20 and was forced open on the following day in the presence of some ten lords, including Maitland, Athol, and Hume. Inside were Mary's letters to Bothwell, forged or genuine.[44] The letters are not necessary to prove Mary's guilt, as we have attempted to show. Nevertheless it is worth noting here that no one who saw the letters believed they were forged—or at any rate no one said so. Not even the three lords mentioned above ever suggested the possibility of forgery, although all three, at one time or another, became bitter opponents of Morton, who, if forgery there was, must have been responsible for it. The lords regarded the letters as trump cards against Mary, and rightly so. So, in his turn, did Moray, who certainly never questioned their authenticity, and who was to make good use of them in the future.

Throckmorton, in spite of Maitland's discouraging answer, continued to press his mistress's views. He had an ally in Maitland, who had told him that he did not favor a harsh policy toward Mary. Maitland's advice to Sir Nicholas was to bribe heavily and be silent on the question of Prince James; this, he said, was his only hope of success.[45] But Throckmorton was in a hopeless position, not only on account of the Casket and the French bid for the lords' friendship, but also because of Mary herself. The English envoy was not allowed to see the Queen, but he did get a message through to her, stating that he was there to help her but that she must divorce Bothwell before he could do anything for her. But Mary would not consider this, claiming that she was carrying Bothwell's child, which would be bastardized by a divorce.[46] Since Mary held to this attitude, it was a foregone conclusion that the lords would

---

[43] Teulet, *Relations politiques*, II, 322–25.
[44] Morton made a sworn statement before the Westminster Conference in December, 1568, as to the events of June 20–21. *C.S.P., Scot.*, II, 730–31.
[45] July 19, 1567, Throckmorton to Elizabeth, in Keith, *History*, II, 684–94.
[46] July 18, 1567, Throckmorton to Elizabeth, *C.S.P., Scot.*, II, 355–56.

refuse to release her. They left their future policy toward her vague; they would do as the "necessity of the cause" required. Maitland further told Sir Nicholas, in private, that Elizabeth's present policy of demanding Mary's release was the surest possible way of driving the lords to take Mary's life.[47] Throckmorton did not need to be told this; he had disliked Elizabeth's policy from the beginning.[48] It was high time to change it, he wrote Leicester on the twenty-fourth, especially since Elizabeth might be able to secure the person of Prince James if she promised him the succession.[49] This last idea, however, seems to have been mere wishful thinking on the part of the envoy.

Throckmorton's representations were put to skillful use by Cecil and finally had some effect. The Secretary at last persuaded Elizabeth that her policy might well defeat its own purpose. Throckmorton was told to continue striving for Mary but to be conciliatory, to leave open the door for a possible agreement based on something other than Mary's restoration, so that the lords would not ally themselves with France or take drastic steps against Mary.[50] This marks the beginning of a shift in Elizabeth's attitude toward Mary; politics now began to creep in beside questions of royal prerogative, and a year later, when the problem was tossed into Elizabeth's own lap, she adopted the same solution to which she had objected so violently when it was that of Morton and his friends.

Throckmorton had also been instructed by Elizabeth to open negotiations with Mary's supporters, to determine their strength and their views, so that, if the confederates proved recalcitrant, Elizabeth would have a party to back in Mary's behalf.[51] The envoy soon discovered that many of the Marians could not be relied on consistently to oppose the lords and in fact were already bargaining with their opponents.[52] On July 18 Throckmorton reported that even the Hamiltons were not to be trusted.[53] He was

---

[47] July 21, 1567, Throckmorton to Elizabeth, *ibid.*, pp. 358–60.
[48] July 2, 1567, Throckmorton to Cecil, *ibid.*, pp. 344–45.   [49] *Ibid.*, pp. 361–62.
[50] August 11, 1567, Cecil to Throckmorton, *ibid.*, pp. 378–79.
[51] July 14, 1567, Elizabeth to Throckmorton, in J. Stevenson, ed., *Selections . . . Illustrating the Reign of Mary Queen of Scotland*, p. 202.
[52] July 8, 1567, Melville to Drury, *C.S.P., Scot.*, II, 347. July 9, 1567, Scrope to Cecil, *C.S.P., For., Eliz.*, VIII, 277.   [53] *C.S.P., Scot.*, II, 355–56.

to receive proof of this some two weeks later, after the coronation of Prince James. Murray of Tullibardine and Maitland both informed him that Archbishop Hamilton, Kilwinning, and Huntly had offered complete submission if the lords would execute Mary. Huntly, who was deeply involved in the murder, was probably trying to save his own skin by this charming suggestion.[54] As for the Hamiltons, Tullibardine pointed out to the horrified Throckmorton that their motive was plain. "She being taken away, they account but the little king betwixt them and home (the crown), who may die." [55] It was a pretty desperate cause which had such backers as these.

Curiously enough, Archbishop Hamilton in this matter found himself in the same camp as Knox, although for entirely different reasons. The preachers, Throckmorton reported, were very "austere" in regard to Mary, and with them they carried public opinion, in Edinburgh at least.[56] The confederate lords were divided in opinion, but few of them favored extreme measures. Maitland wanted Mary's restoration, with safeguards; Athol, banishment; while the majority favored imprisonment, as long as she refused to be divorced from Bothwell.[57] Had Mary agreed to the divorce and, further, promised to allow the government to remain in the hands of the lords, she would certainly have been restored; this would have solved all of the lords' problems. The fact that they did not broadcast the Casket Letters to the world as soon as they laid hands on them shows that they did not wish to go to extremes against Mary. Right up to the time when it was resolved to force her to abdicate the lords did not reveal the contents of the Casket and still spoke in their public proclamations as though Bothwell was solely responsible for everything.[58] But Mary's refusal to desert Bothwell forced the lords' hand.

On July 18 Throckmorton reported the rumor that Mary had

[54] The rumor was current at this time that Huntly was anxious for the death of Bothwell also, and for the same reason. July 31, 1567, Throckmorton to Elizabeth, *ibid.*, pp. 369–71.
[55] August 9, 1567, Throckmorton to Elizabeth, *ibid.*, pp. 373–76.
[56] July 18, 1567, Throckmorton to Elizabeth, *ibid.*, pp. 355–56.
[57] July 19, 1567, Throckmorton to Elizabeth, in Keith, *History*, II, 684–94.
[58] See the proclamation of July 21 against the Bishop of Moray, Bothwell's uncle, in *Register of Privy Council*, I, 530–31.

offered to abdicate and turn over the government to Moray or to a council comprised of members of both factions.[59] Whether or not Mary ever made this offer, the lords now decided to force an abdication from her. If Mary refused to abdicate, the lords would proceed to a judicial condemnation of her, citing evidence in her handwriting as proof of her guilt. Thus Throckmorton wrote on July 24, the day the deputation was sent to Lochleven to obtain her renunciation of the throne.[60] Mary, however, did not refuse, either because she feared for her life or because she felt that any paper she signed under duress would be of no validity.[61] On July 24 she signed three documents: her abdication in favor of Prince James, the appointment of Moray as Regent, and—to become valid in case Moray refused that honor—the appointment of a council of regency.[62] Moray was the only possible choice as Regent. He had the confidence, for the moment at least, of all factions in the party in power, from that of Maitland to that of Knox. Even Mary seemed to trust him to some extent, for she knew that he was no extremist and that with him in power her life would be safe. Above all, Moray had not been involved in any of the compromising events which had occurred in such a steady stream since April, from the "trial" of Bothwell to the enforced abdication of Mary; his hands were clean. Moray had thus calculated correctly when he set out on his travels in April, although a regency was a bit more than he had expected.

Since Mary had abdicated, the next logical step was to crown her son; this was done on July 29 at Stirling, with Knox in the pulpit.[63] After the coronation, Throckmorton reported, the lords adopted delaying tactics with him; they were obviously waiting for the return of Moray.[64] It is true that the lords did very little

---

[59] C.S.P., Scot., II, 355–56.
[60] C.S.P., For., Eliz., VIII, 297–98. This letter is dated July 25, but internal evidence indicates that it was written on July 24.
[61] Robert Melville, in his letter of July 29, 1567, said Mary signed out of fear. C.S.P., Scot., II, 367–68. His brother James held to the duress theory. Memoirs, pp. 189–90. Mary, of course, agreed with James. See her proclamation of May 5, 1568, in Fleming, Mary Queen of Scots, pp. 512–14.
[62] The documents are given in Register of Privy Council, I, 531–33, 539–41.
[63] John Knox, History of the Reformation in Scotland, II, 566.
[64] August 5, 1567, Throckmorton to Elizabeth, C.S.P., Scot., II, 372.

in the first days of the new reign, beyond authorizing Kirkcaldy
and Tullibardine to set out after Bothwell, who thus far had been
pursued with suspicious lack of zeal.[65] Mary's husband had taken
to piracy in the north, and the lords doubtless hoped that Kirkcaldy would catch and kill him. Many great men would breathe
easier with the rascally Earl dead.

Meanwhile all eyes turned to the Berwick road, along which
the Regent-designate would travel on his way home. There was
considerable uncertainty as to what policy Moray would adopt,
which was not surprising, since the Earl had changed his opinions
frequently of late. We have seen why he left Scotland in April.
He told De Silva, with whom he had an interview on his way
through London, that he could not remain in Scotland as long as
the murder went unpunished: it would have been dishonorable
to do so. He further mentioned the rumors current as to Bothwell's collusive divorce, but he doubted that his sister would marry
her favorite.[66] Moray was probably sincere in this opinion. He
knew by now that Mary loved Bothwell, but he did not believe that her passion would entirely destroy her political intelligence.

On May 1, about two weeks after his conversation with De
Silva, Moray had arrived in Dieppe.[67] He spent the next three
months in France, where his movements were the subject of much
hostile Catholic scrutiny. On May 15 Alava, the Spanish ambassador in France, reported that he was at Orléans, thick as thieves
with Coligny and Condé.[68] When Catherine de Medici heard of
the troubles in Scotland, she attempted to win over Moray, as part
of her general wooing of the lords, without much success: one
of Cecil's agents reported that the Queen Mother had a low opinion of the Earl, terming him England's for life.[69] Catherine was
not easily discouraged, however; as soon as she heard the news
of Carberry, she sent urgently for Moray, who was at Lyons at

---

[65] *Register of Privy Council*, I, 543–46. For previous steps against Bothwell, see
ibid., pp. 524–25, 527–31.
[66] April 21, 1567, De Silva to Philip II, *C.S.P., Span.*, I, 634–36.
[67] *C.S.P., For., Eliz.*, VIII, 220.   [68] Teulet, *Relations politiques*, V, 24.
[69] May 24, 1567, Norris to Elizabeth, *C.S.P., For., Eliz.*, VIII, 236. June 9, 1567,
Cockburn to Cecil, *ibid.*, p. 246.

the time, in order to make one more effort to win him to an alliance with France.[70]

Moray's reaction to the news of Carberry and of Mary's imprisonment was one of annoyance. What he had expected was a revolution which would ruin Bothwell but which would not involve Mary's deposition. He wanted Mary to remain as Queen, since she would now be completely under the thumb of the Protestants. Furthermore, he knew that Elizabeth would not like the way the lords had treated their sovereign, and that a civil war would probably result. At this time, of course, Moray did not know of Mary's stubborn refusal to part from Bothwell, nor did he know of the Casket. He could see nothing but trouble arising from Mary's imprisonment and no advantage to be derived from it. Consequently his first action was to send a messenger, Nicholas Elphinstone, to Mary with a letter assuring her of his loyalty, and of his desire to serve her. Elphinstone passed through London on July 8, and saw Elizabeth on that day; the latter instructed Cecil to convey to Mary the welcome news of Moray's friendliness.[71] Moray's messenger was in Edinburgh by the sixteenth; on that day Throckmorton wrote that the lords would not permit him to see Mary or to deliver her brother's letter to her.[72] It is uncertain whether Elphinstone ever did see Mary—Throckmorton's letter of July 19 indicates that he did [73]—but the burden of his message almost certainly got to her, which explains why, if rumor was correct, she was willing to turn over the government to him.

Moray realized that he must get home as quickly as possible, and that this might prove difficult. The French were very pressing; he must avoid committing himself to them and at the same time must not give them reason to hinder his departure. He temporized skillfully in his negotiations with them. He told them that he wanted to help Mary, but that he could not say what he would do on his return, since the dominant party contained both friends and enemies of his; he must wait and see.[74] He would do nothing

[70] June 30, 1567, Alava to Philip II, in Teulet, *Relations politiques*, V, 26–27. July 2, 1567, Norris to Cecil, *C.S.P., For., Eliz.*, VIII, 269.
[71] July 8, 1567, Heneage to Cecil, *C.S.P., Scot.*, II, 346.
[72] *C.S.P., Scot.*, II, 353–54.   [73] Keith, *History*, II, 684–94.
[74] July 3, 1567, Correr to the Signory, *C.S.P., Ven.*, VII, 398.

which could be construed as an attack on Mary's title, and he
would welcome French friendship, since France and Scotland
were allies of such long standing. He would not be deterred from
going through England on his way home; he must urge the English
government to help him free his sister. He would not accept a
pension from France, but he did take a gift of plate.[75] At the same
time Moray requested the English ambassador, Norris, to provide
him with a means of getting out of France, which Norris did.[76]
The French probably did not put any great amount of confidence
in Moray's assurances regarding the alliance, since they knew him
to be pro-English; but their only chance of regaining influence
in Scotland was to pretend to trust him and to hope that Elizabeth
would continue to play into their hands. Therefore they let him
go and sent with him a special envoy, De Lignerolles, to negotiate
on the spot for a new Franco-Scottish alliance.[77]

Moray arrived in London on July 25.[78] Either just before his
departure from France or just after his arrival in England—more
probably the latter—he received information which changed his
whole attitude to the problem at home. For now he learned about
Mary's obstinate clinging to Bothwell and about the Casket. He
understood now why the lords had imprisoned Mary and why
they found it necessary to force her to abdicate. He also saw, only
too plainly, why they had dared do it. The deposition of a sovereign prince was no small matter in the sixteenth century, but the
contents of the Casket gave the lords an almost ironclad excuse in
the eyes of the world for doing so. Moray now concluded that
Morton and his friends had chosen the only possible course. He
had an interview with Elizabeth, in which he did not conceal his
change of view; harsh words were spoken, which left Moray very
angry.[79] In talking with the Queen he evidently relied on Mary's
continuing passion for Bothwell as his justification for his change
of attitude, for shortly afterwards he had a conversation with De

[75] July 13, July 17, July 24, 1567, Alava to Philip II, in Teulet, *Relations politiques*,
V, 27–31.
[76] July 13, 1567, Jeyne to Cecil, *C.S.P., For., Eliz.*, VIII, 281–82.
[77] August 12, 1567, Throckmorton to Elizabeth, *C.S.P., Scot.*, II, 380–81.
[78] July 26, 1567, De Silva to Philip II, *C.S.P., Span.*, I, 662.
[79] August 10, 1567, Bedford to Cecil, *C.S.P., For., Eliz.*, VIII, 315.

Silva, in which he summarized for the ambassador the contents of the Casket, prefacing his remarks with the statement that he had not mentioned any of this to Elizabeth. Moray also expressed to De Silva his conviction that Mary was guilty of foreknowledge of Darnley's murder. The ambassador gathered that Moray was not going to try to effect his sister's release.[80]

Moray's feelings as he rode northward to his native land were mixed. Now that he had the chance to put his two principles, Protestantism and the English alliance, fully into effect by becoming head of the Scottish state, he hesitated. The regency, he knew, would be a thankless and probably a dangerous task, and he was not anxious to undertake it.[81] The trappings of power meant but little to him, provided he had the substance; he had always preferred to work in the background. Yet he knew that he was the only man who could possibly prevent a civil war. Furthermore, if he declined, he would be gravely jeopardizing his life's work, and he was not the man to pass up a supreme opportunity to ensure the triumph of his principles. It was a foregone conclusion, really, that he would accept the new dignity which had been offered to him.

Moray rode into Edinburgh on August 11, accompanied by De Lignerolles, and was received with cheers by the Protestant citizenry of the capital.[82] He knew that he must make a rapid decision on the question of accepting the regency. For the next few days he worked busily, finding out what people thought, weighing the strength of the factions, assessing the differences of opinion in his own party. Information on these subjects had, in fact, been reaching him on his way north.[83] He finally concluded that he must accept the regency, but before doing so he wished

[80] August 2, 1567, De Silva to Philip II, *C.S.P., Span.*, I, 664–67. Moray's description of the contents of a Casket Letter or Letters, as given by De Silva, contained things which do not tally with the Letters as they were later given to the world. Out of this fact the defenders of Mary have postulated a "Pre-letter," which was the first version of Letter II and was later discarded as being too crude. See R. Chauviré, "Etat présent de la controverse sur les Lettres de la Cassette," *Revue historique*, CLXXIV (1934), 447–54.
[81] August 4, 1567, Mildmay to Throckmorton, *C.S.P., For., Eliz.*, VIII, 308. August 10, 1567, Bedford to Cecil, *ibid.*, p. 315.
[82] August 12, 1567, Throckmorton to Elizabeth, *C.S.P., Scot.*, II, 380–81.
[83] Melville, *Memoirs*, pp. 192–93.

to see the Queen. The lords were hesitant about permitting him to do so, since they evidently feared that he might yet return to a "soft" policy toward her, but they really had no choice but to give their consent, and on August 15 Moray, accompanied by Morton, Athol, and Lindsay, rode to Lochleven.[84]

The ensuing interview between brother and sister was extraordinary. Mary at first was full of passionate complaint, then of eager questions, then of fearful ones. Moray remained gloomily silent, until finally, after Mary had implored him to speak, he did so, with shocking severity. Step by step he detailed the events of her life in the past two years like a prosecuting attorney—or, as Throckmorton put it, like a "ghostly father"; by the time he had finished, Mary was firmly convinced that her death had been decided upon. Her brother thereupon left her for the night, advising her to recommend herself to the mercy of God. Mary must have spent that night in an agony of fear. She sent for Moray early the next morning; the Earl, seeing the impression he had made, softened considerably. He would do all he could to save her life, but, of course, in this matter the decision did not rest with him alone. She must help herself, too, by not intriguing against the new government, by changing her attitude toward Bothwell, and by bearing no grudge against those who had opposed her at Carberry. All this had the desired effect: Mary now urged her brother to take the regency. This was what Moray had wanted: to obtain a voluntary verbal confirmation from the Queen of the document she had signed on July 24. He made some show of reluctance, which may well have been sincere, but at last he gave his consent.[85] This whole scene has a rather unreal atmosphere to it. Moray was forced into a disreputable piece of duplicity by circumstances; he managed it well, but, it is to be hoped, did not much relish his part in the business.

And so, one week afterwards, on August 22, Moray was pro-

[84] August 13, 1567, Throckmorton to Elizabeth, in Stevenson, *Selections*, pp. 272–74. August 20, Throckmorton to Elizabeth, in Keith, *History*, II, 734–41.
[85] Moray himself described this interview to Throckmorton, who relayed it to his government on August 20, 1567. *Ibid.*, pp. 734–41. The truthfulness of Moray's account is confirmed by the fact that Mary turned over many of her jewels to him at the same time; Moray sold some and gave others to his wife.

claimed Regent of Scotland in the Tolbooth of Edinburgh. The Queen's abdication and designation of him as Regent were read, and Moray, after making a speech in which he protested his unfitness for the office, accepted it and swore a solemn oath to do justice, preserve the rights of the Crown, and uphold Protestantism. At the same time he made a written pledge, in much the same terms, to the Privy Council, with some additional stipulations, the most important of which was that he would do nothing to alter Mary's present status without the consent of the council.[86] It seemed as if the principle of the revolution of 1559–60 had finally triumphed, and with it that of the English alliance, which had sealed the revolution's success. And, in fact, so they had, barring a foreign invasion in force. With the downfall of Mary the last serious internal threat to British Protestantism had vanished, and the eventual union of the island under Protestant auspices was virtually assured. The twenty-nine months of Moray's regency were filled with desperate political struggles, but regardless of the outcome, the victors, by necessity or choice, would have to adhere to the two principles for which Moray had fought. Moray had won. It now remained for him to consolidate his victory.

[86] August 23, 1567, Throckmorton to Elizabeth, *C.S.P., Scot.*, II, 386–88. Stevenson, *Selections*, pp. 283–87. *Register of Privy Council*, I, 548–50.

CHAPTER X

Moray, Mary, and Elizabeth

FROM ITS INCEPTION Moray's government faced two major problems, which were to be the most vital questions of his regency. These were the relations of the new regime with England, and the restoration of order at home, either by the crushing of the adherents of Mary or by an agreement of some kind with them. The first of these Moray was able to handle successfully; the second was more difficult, but the Regent was well on his way to solving it at the time of his death. The removal of Moray from the scene meant only a temporary setback for his policies, however; eventually Morton succeeded in solving both problems and in assuring the permanent triumph of Moray's principles.

Moray had to define his position vis-à-vis England even before his proclamation as Regent. Throckmorton was still in Scotland and was still demanding, in Elizabeth's name, that the lords release Mary and restore her, even if they did so only under severe restrictions. Sir Nicholas had already warned his government that the advent of Moray to power was not likely to change the Scottish attitude.[1] Nor did it. On August 21 Throckmorton had an interview with Maitland and Moray, in the course of which the Secretary repeated all the old reasons for the lords' rejection of Elizabeth's advice. Moray emphatically seconded Maitland's views.[2] Throckmorton left Scotland shortly after this. He unsuccessfully made one more attempt to see Mary and, in a final inter-

[1] August 12, 1567, Throckmorton to Cecil, *C.S.P., Scot.,* II, 379–80.
[2] August 22, 1567, Throckmorton to Elizabeth, in R. Keith, *The History of the Affairs of Church and State in Scotland,* II, 741–47.

view with the Regent, found him discouragingly vague as to his future attitude toward his sister. Nevertheless, Moray and the other lords expressed their good will toward England, and offered Throckmorton, on his departure, the usual present of plate, which the envoy refused since it was offered in the name of King James.[3] Sir Nicholas's departure from Scotland was preceded by a few days by that of De Lignerolles, who had been courteously treated, but whose attempt to renew the Franco-Scottish alliance had come to nothing.[4]

After Throckmorton's departure Moray continued to be friendly to England, in spite of numerous rebuffs. He was anxious to send an ambassador to England, but Elizabeth, much to Cecil's regret, would not hear of it.[5] Moray felt that English aloofness could not continue indefinitely, however, on account of the problem of the Borders. To keep any semblance of order there, it was necessary for the Wardens on each side to meet in order to take concerted action against lawbreakers. Elizabeth would not yet permit her officials to deal with Moray's appointees,[6] but Moray was not offended by this. He told Bedford that his Wardens would always be prepared to meet with their English colleagues in the interests of justice.[7] Slowly Elizabeth's attitude began to alter; in November she ordered her Border Wardens to do business with Moray's.[8] This change on the Queen's part was certainly due to some extent to unremitting pressure from Cecil, who was Moray's steadfast ally, and to the fact that lack of cooperation was creating an increasingly grave administrative problem for the English Wardens. It was also due to Elizabeth's realization of the fact that Moray was having great success in dealing with the dissident elements in Scotland, and thus in stabilizing his regime.

[3] September 1, 1567, Throckmorton to Cecil, *C.S.P., Scot.*, II, 391–93.
[4] De Lignerolles's instructions are in A. Teulet, ed., *Relations politiques de la France et de l'Espagne avec l'Ecosse au XVIe siècle*, II, 327–29. He left Edinburgh on August 27. T. Thomson, ed., *A Diurnal of Remarkable Occurrents that Have Passed within the Country of Scotland*, p. 120.
[5] August 14, 1567, Throckmorton to Elizabeth, in J. Stevenson, ed., *Selections . . . Illustrating the Reign of Mary Queen of Scotland*, pp. 274–78. August 20, 1567, Cecil to Throckmorton, *C.S.P., For., Eliz.*, VIII, 324–25.
[6] September 8, 1567, Elizabeth to Bedford, *ibid.*, pp. 336–37.
[7] September 20, 1567, Bedford to Cecil, *ibid.*, p. 343. See also October 14, 1567, Moray to Cecil, *C.S.P., Scot.*, II, 396.   [8] *C.S.P., For., Eliz.*, VIII, 364.

Moray's most serious problem was, of course, the Marians, and he tackled it promptly and firmly, as Throckmorton had predicted.[9] On hearing that his opponents were planning a meeting in Glasgow early in September, the Regent decided to overawe his opponents by a show of force. On September 1 he ordered the lieges to be prepared to march with him against the rebels.[10] This move was successful; many Borderers acknowledged the Regent's government, and the Glasgow meeting was far more thinly attended than had been expected.[11] In fact, the Marians were thoroughly discouraged. Their meeting dissolved, and their leaders began to negotiate with Moray. Argyle, Boyd, and Kilwinning came to Edinburgh to offer their submission, and the latter was dispatched to France to obtain that of Châtelherault, the nominal head of the Hamiltons. The Master of Maxwell, now Lord Herries, and even Huntly, sent messages to the effect that they would like to make an agreement with the Regent.[12]

Moray pressed his advantage by moving against the fortress of Dunbar, which was still held for Mary by a henchman of Bothwell's, Patrick Whitelaw. The lieges were summoned, and on September 26 Moray rode out of Edinburgh to supervise the siege in person. Whitelaw was quick to make terms, and the fortress was surrendered on October 1.[13] The surrender of Dunbar left the Marians only the fortress of Dumbarton, which was strong but

[9] August 20, 1567, Throckmorton to Cecil, *C.S.P., Scot.*, II, 385–86. Throckmorton added that he felt that Moray sought "to imitate rather some which have led the people of Israel, than any captains of our age."
[10] September 2, 1567, Scrope to Cecil, *C.S.P., For., Eliz.*, VIII, 334. *The Register of the Privy Council of Scotland*, I, 560–61.
[11] September 5, September 11, 1567, Bedford to Cecil, *C.S.P., For., Eliz.*, VIII, 335, 337.
[12] September 11, 1567, Bedford to Cecil, *ibid.*, p. 337. September 12, 1567, Scrope to Cecil, *ibid.*, pp. 337–38. c. September 12, 1567, "Occurrences out of Scotland," *C.S.P., Scot.*, II, 393. September 15, 1567, Moray to Cecil, *ibid.*, p. 394. September 15, 1567, Moray to Throckmorton, *ibid.*, pp. 394–95. September 21, 1567, Herries to Scrope, *C.S.P., For., Eliz.*, VIII, 345. Argyle submitted in spite of the fact that he now had a personal quarrel with the Regent. He was anxious to divorce his wife, a half-sister of Moray's, with whom he had been on bad terms for years; Moray would not allow it. August 22, 1567, Throckmorton to Elizabeth, in Keith, *History*, II, 741–47.
[13] *Register of Privy Council*, I, 572–73. Thomson, *Diurnal of Occurrents*, pp. 124–25. The unfortunate Whitelaw had to pay for the cost of the siege, and of transporting Moray's artillery back to Edinburgh. October 9, 1567, Cecil to Norris, in Keith, *History*, II, 757, note 1.

not especially dangerous, since it was in an area where the Lennox interest was powerful. The remaining supporters of the Queen were further depressed. On the day of the surrender Kirk-caldy informed Bedford that the fighting was over, since Huntly and Herries were about to come in.[14] On October 14 Moray wrote to Cecil that all was quiet in Scotland.[15]

Moray also attempted to settle the question of Bothwell. The latter had escaped to Norway, where he was imprisoned by the Danish authorities. Among his papers was a letter from Mary which lamented their respective fates—sufficient proof, if any further were needed, that the lords had not invented Mary's affection for Bothwell as a mere pretext for imprisoning her after Carberry.[16] The King of Denmark imprisoned Bothwell but politely refused Moray's requests to extradite him to Scotland or to turn him over to any of the agents Moray sent to Denmark to take custody of him. The Regent asked Elizabeth to write to the King on this matter; she did so, without success.[17] What Moray and his friends would have preferred was that Denmark try and execute Bothwell or, failing that, hand him over to a Scottish agent, who would have tried him by drumhead court-martial. For reasons already indicated they were not anxious for a public trial in Scotland. As it turned out, what actually happened was satisfactory enough. Bothwell ended his days in a Danish prison and gave no more trouble to Moray and his party.[18]

[14] *C.S.P., Scot.*, II, 396. October 18, 1567, J. Melville to Throckmorton, *C.S.P., For., Eliz.*, VIII, 358.
[15] *Ibid.*, p. 356. When they submitted, the Marian lords had to sign a band acknowledging the legality of Mary's abdication and promising loyalty to James VI. Most of the prominent Marians, including Argyle and Huntly, signed; Herries did not. The band is printed in J. Anderson, ed., *Collections Relating to the History of Mary Queen of Scots*, I, 231–40.
[16] See H. Cockburn and T. Maitland, eds., *Les Affaires du Conte de Boduel*, Appendix, p. xl.
[17] December 30, 1567, Frederick II to James VI, *C.S.P., For., Eliz.*, VIII, 386. Thomson, *Diurnal of Occurrents*, p. 125. March, 1568, Moray to Cecil, *C.S.P., Scot.*, II, 401. March 29, 1568, Elizabeth to Frederick II, *C.S.P., For., Eliz.*, VIII, 434. Further correspondence by Elizabeth on this matter is given in Cockburn and Maitland, *Les Affaires du Conte de Boduel*, Appendix, pp. lx–lxiii.
[18] Bothwell was not the only supporter of Mary whom Moray pursued outside the limits of Scotland. The Bishop of Dunblane, who was especially disliked by the Protestants on account of his connection with the Jesuits, was ordered home, and when he failed to appear, his revenues were impounded. In November he

Once Moray had settled, as far as possible, the problem of Mary's followers, he turned his attention to the Borders, where matters had been going badly of late owing to the political confusion. After the seizure of Dunbar he proclaimed that certain of the lieges were to meet him early in November to carry out an armed pacification of the middle and western Marches.[19] The situation in the east was less serious, owing to the friendship of Hume. Moray's resolve had immediate effects; on the day following his proclamation a number of western lairds deserted Huntly and Herries.[20] The Regent then availed himself of a device he had found useful before: some ten days before the announced date of his eyre he quietly raided Hawick at night and caught some forty malefactors; this was "the greatest ruffle that ever the thieves of Liddesdale suffered," says Pitscottie.[21] Shortly after this, as we have seen, Elizabeth authorized her Wardens to collaborate with Moray's, and the situation on the Borders returned more or less to normal, except in the west, where Herries continued to cause trouble despite his submission to the Regent.

A more serious and more complicated problem for Moray than that of the Borders was that of dealing with his own supporters. There were two major difficulties here. In the first place, there was a serious difference of opinion as to what should be done with Mary, and Moray, by siding with those who insisted on her continued imprisonment, naturally alienated those who felt that Mary should be restored, now that Bothwell's power had been broken. For the moment this problem was not too serious, since Mary's own conduct testified to the futility of restoring her at that time. Nevertheless the Regent's attitude, combined with his religious policy, led to the departure from his camp of those Catholics, such as Eglinton and Montrose, who had joined Morton and the Protestant lords in June for the purpose of punishing Bothwell.[22] This

---

was officially forfeited. *Register of Privy Council*, I, 563, 569–70. Claude Nau, *The History of Mary Stewart*, Appendix II, p. 146.
[19] *Register of Privy Council*, I, 580.   [20] *Ibid.*, pp. 580–81.
[21] R. Lindsay of Pitscottie, *The Chronicles of Scotland*, II, 200–201. See also November 3, November 9, 1567, Drury to Throckmorton, *C.S.P., For., Eliz.*, VIII, 366, 367.
[22] For instance, early in September Eglinton, Cassilis, and others held a meeting

group was in no position to cause difficulty as things stood then; however, if Mary ever changed her mind about Bothwell, there were several of Moray's supporters, headed by the redoubtable Maitland, who would join it in an endeavor to restore the Queen.

More troublesome even than this was the fact that among the Regent's followers were many men who, rightly or wrongly, were regarded as Bothwell's accomplices in the assassination of Darnley. The principal excuse given for the rebellion of June was the desire of the rebels to punish this crime. Public opinion had been inflamed against Mary because of her part in the murder. Yet the government was doing nothing to punish these great men; on the contrary, they were among Moray's most trusted advisers. This was an unpleasant dilemma for Moray, and on moral grounds his behavior is indefensible. It was certainly unjust to heap the entire odium of the crime on Mary and Bothwell, guilty though they were, and at the same time to permit men like Maitland and Balfour to go free. But it is also true that from the point of view of practical politics Moray could have done nothing else. If he had moved against any one of these men, the one accused would have implicated as many others as he could, which would have meant a coalition of all those involved to protect themselves; and so many powerful people could be accused—Argyle, Huntly, and Morton, to name but three—that the resulting rebellion would undoubtedly have overturned the Regent. Moray had to accept this unpleasant situation and get along as best he could.

The Regent was well aware of the manifold difficulties confronting him, and he exerted himself to overcome them. He could not prosecute the great men involved in the murder of Darnley, but he tried to cajole people into overlooking this unpleasant fact by vigorously hunting down Bothwell's henchmen. He succeeded in laying hands on a number of them; their statements as to the methods used in killing Darnley, and as to those involved in the murder, were recorded, and they themselves were executed.[23]

in the west and agreed to remain neutral between the two factions. September 10, 1567, J. Melville to Throckmorton, *ibid.*, p. 337.
[23] Thomson, *Diurnal of Occurrents*, pp. 127–28. The confessions are in Anderson, *Collections*, I, 165–88, 192–205.

Unfortunately, the good impression made by all this activity was largely dissipated by the fact that one of those executed had stated on the scaffold, in the presence of a large gathering, that Argyle, Huntly, Maitland, and Balfour were all guilty of the murder.[24] This but confirmed the rumor that a murder band signed by these four and by Bothwell had existed and had been burned by Maitland and Balfour in Edinburgh Castle immediately before Carberry.[25] Moray did his best to avoid odium by making as little use as possible of these men in his government, with the exception of Morton, who was indispensable. Even Maitland was pushed more and more into the background, although as yet there was no serious difference of opinion between him and the Regent.[26] Nevertheless Moray's popularity unquestionably suffered heavily on this account.[27]

The Regent attempted to strengthen his somewhat precarious position by the judicious use of patronage. Maitland, Morton, Hume, Athol all received rewards of various kinds. Even Huntly and Argyle, so recently his enemies, were courted by Moray, who hoped to entangle them by means of advantageous marriages for some of their near relatives.[28] The greatest gains, however, were made by the Kirk, on whose unswerving support Moray counted heavily. In December 1567 Parliament met and confirmed most of the promises made by the lords to the General Assembly in July. The Acts of the Reformation Parliament of 1560 were re-

[24] January 7, 1568, Drury to Cecil, *C.S.P., For., Eliz.*, VIII, 393.

[25] October 28, 1567, Drury to Cecil, *ibid.*, p. 363. See above, p. 184.

[26] On the relations of Moray and Maitland, see Throckmorton's letter of May 6, 1568, to Melville, in Teulet, *Relations politiques*, II, 355-56.

[27] See the contemporary handbills quoted in P. F. Tytler, *History of Scotland*, VII, 171, and in G. Chalmers, *The Life of Mary Queen of Scots*, II, 443-49. It must be said in Moray's behalf that he did not condemn people indiscriminately, as a less scrupulous man might have done. Three of Bothwell's friends and relations, Cockburn of Skirling, Hepburn of Riccarton, and the Bishop of Moray, were declared innocent of the murder on October 28, when the Regent might well have increased his popularity by executing them. November 9, 1567, Drury to Throckmorton, *C.S.P., For., Eliz.*, VIII, 367. The Bishop, in April 1568, gave tangible evidence of his gratitude by granting a huge feu to the Regent; *Registrum Magni Sigilli Regum Scotorum*, IV, 481-83.

[28] *Historical Manuscripts Commission, 12th Report*, Appendix VIII, pp. 99, 111. Lindsay of Pitscottie, *Chronicles*, II, 202. Tytler, *History of Scotland*, VII, 172. *Reg. Mag. Sig.*, IV, 456-58. January 4, 1568, Drury to Cecil, *C.S.P., For., Eliz.*, VIII, 392.

affirmed, and Catholicism was utterly abolished. Appointments to benefices and to all teaching posts were to receive the approval of the Kirk, and only Protestants were to hold public office. The thirds were to be paid directly to the ministers, but an accounting to the Exchequer was required, and some part, at least, of the income from them was still to go to the government. On some further questions, particularly that of the legal jurisdiction of the Kirk, committees were set up to deliberate and report to the next Parliament. The one thing the Kirk did not get, never did get, was possession of the entire patrimony of the Catholic Church, although Moray attempted to obtain this for it too; the lords simply would not vote to despoil themselves thus.[29] The Kirk was duly grateful to the Regent and steadfastly supported his government. Nevertheless Moray, by his extreme Protestant policy, which placed the machinery of the state behind the Kirk's disciplinary measures, alienated a number of his supporters.[30] Furthermore, all these concessions, particularly those to the Kirk, threw a financial strain on the government which it could ill afford; by April 1568 Moray was pawning plate to Morton and others as security for loans and had sent a messenger to England to sell some of his sister's jewels to Elizabeth.[31] That Moray would permit himself to get into financial difficulties in this way is a good indication of the fact that he felt very uncertain of his position. His financial weakness, in turn, increased his perils, since he was too poor to stamp out all traces of resistance to his government.

Back of all these problems, of course, lay the question of what

[29] The Acts of the Parliament of Scotland, III, 14–25. The thirds had been paid directly to the ministers since November 2, on Moray's order; J. Stuart, ed., Miscellany of the Spalding Club, IV, 60. For Moray's attitude on Church property at this Parliament, see his letter of June 30, 1569, in D. Calderwood, The History of the Kirk of Scotland, II, 498–502.
[30] January 4, 1568, Drury to Cecil, C.S.P., For., Eliz., VIII, 392.
[31] Historical Manuscripts Commission, 6th Report, Appendix, pp. 643–44. April 20, 1568, Moray to Cecil, C.S.P., For., Eliz., VIII, 445. May 2, May 15, 1568, De la Forest to Catherine de Medici, in Teulet, Relations politiques, II, 352, 364–65. As early as the previous September Drury had indicated that Moray was in financial difficulties. C.S.P., For., Eliz., VIII, 349–50. Yet, despite this poverty, Moray was making further financial concessions to the Kirk in July. Calderwood, History of the Kirk, II, 425–27.

to do about Mary, who was still languishing in Lochleven. Moray paid her a visit in October and found her, so Bedford said, in good spirits.[32] They must have been considerably damped, however, by the action of the December Parliament, which pronounced all actions taken against Mary since the murder of Darnley legitimate, since she was guilty of foreknowledge of the murder and of marrying the murderer.[33] The language of this declaration indicates that the Casket Letters were exhibited in Parliament. It was not exactly fair to judge Mary unheard, as the Regent well knew. He later frankly admitted to her that he and the other lords had acted as they did in order to protect themselves from the legal point of view.[34] The policy thus laid down was one of continued imprisonment for Mary. As time went on, she became the center of rumors of various kinds. On March 20 Drury wrote that Moray was weary of the regency, and was planning to wed his sister to his relative, Lord Methven, and restore her to her throne.[35] Early in April the story was that on Moray's last visit to Lochleven, made because of an unsuccessful attempt to escape on the part of the Queen, Mary had asked for the hand of George Douglas, younger brother of the Laird, and Moray's half-brother; Moray put her off and expelled George from the Castle.[36] Moray should have been warned by this episode; it was clear that Mary had friends within the walls of her prison. But for once in his life Moray was incautious, trusted his relatives too fully. He was shortly to regret it.

In April of 1568, then, conditions in Scotland were in a state of uneasy, tense quiescence. Moray had achieved one of the objectives he had set himself in August: he had avoided civil war, in spite of a difficult party situation and of Elizabeth, who had even sent money to the Hamiltons in an effort to persuade them to rise.[37] Furthermore, he had forced the majority of Mary's sup-

[32] October 23, 1567, Bedford to Cecil, *C.S.P., For., Eliz.,* VIII, 359.
[33] *Acts of Parliament,* III, 5–14, 27–28.
[34] April 3, 1568, Drury to Cecil, in Keith, *History,* II, 789–93.
[35] *C.S.P., For., Eliz.,* VIII, 431.
[36] April 2, 1568, Drury to Cecil, *ibid.,* pp. 437–38. April 3, 1568, Drury to Cecil, in Keith, *History,* II, 789–93.
[37] September 10, 1567, J. Melville to Throckmorton, *C.S.P., For., Eliz.,* VIII, 337.

porters to acknowledge the new regime and had even induced a number of them to collaborate with him in the government, as the records of the Privy Council show.[38] He had also definitely established Protestantism as the state religion. Nevertheless there were weaknesses in his position. Mary's supporters were quiet for the nonce, but very little would be required to persuade them to revolt. If they did so, many of the Catholic nobility would almost certainly join them out of dislike of the religious settlement of the December Parliament. Even in Moray's own party there was a wing which could not be entirely depended on, the group headed by Maitland, whose principal backers were Athol and Hume. If Mary showed herself willing to abandon Bothwell and to agree to a compromise insuring the personal positions of the lords who had led the attack on her, this group would almost certainly join in the demand for her restoration. Furthermore, Moray's government was not popular in many circles, partly because of his inability to prosecute all those involved in Darnley's murder, partly because his determined effort to administer justice in other matters irritated all those who were unaccustomed to observing such laws as did not appeal to them, especially those which distinguished between *meum* and *tuum*.

Moray did have a group of dependable supporters, however: the great Protestant lords, the Protestant gentry of Fife and the Lothians, the Lennox interest, the Kirk, and the Calvinist towns. Furthermore, Moray's restrained and friendly attitude toward England was beginning to bear fruit. Elizabeth still refused to recognize his government, but she began to negotiate with him unofficially. In January the Queen wrote him a civil letter, for the first time since he had become Regent.[39] Thus encouraged, Moray began to negotiate with the English on a number of matters. As we have seen, he asked for, and received, English support in his efforts to obtain Bothwell's extradition from Denmark. He sold some of Mary's jewels to Elizabeth. He attempted to exert pressure on England by ostentatiously making friendly gestures to

---

[38] On this point see *Register of Privy Council*, Addenda, XIV, 23.
[39] January 31, 1568, Elizabeth to Moray, *C.S.P., Scot.*, II, 400.

France.[40] But Moray's most effective card in reestablishing relations with Elizabeth was the Border. The necessity for working together in the interests of justice in this area meant that a kind of de facto recognition of the Regent's government was extended every time the Wardens on opposite sides of the frontier consulted together, and the Regent made the fullest possible display of his pro-English sentiments by vigorously cooperating in the administration of justice.[41] This policy turned out well. A working entente with England was established; it would not be long, Moray calculated, before Elizabeth bowed to the facts and recognized his government.[42]

ii

On the morning of May 3 a messenger rode breathlessly to Moray at Glasgow. He had frightful news: on the previous night Mary had escaped from Lochleven, and even now was moving westward into Hamilton territory to rally her supporters around her.[43] Moray was "sore amazed" when he heard this, for he saw at once that at a single blow many of the gains of the past eight months had been wiped out.[44] Immediately, too, he was faced by a major strategic decision. He knew that all the men who had supported the Queen in 1567 would flock to her side; and a large part of the Marian strength was concentrated in western Scotland. Hence it seemed that the logical policy was to retreat. Moray,

[40] Teulet, Relations politiques, II, 349–50. April 1, 1568, De la Forest to Charles IX, ibid., pp. 344–45.

[41] For Moray's Border policy at this time, see his letters to Cecil and Drury: C.S.P., Scot., II, 401; C.S.P., For., Eliz., VIII, 424–25; Calendar of the Manuscripts of the Marquis of Salisbury, I, 356. See also March 6, March 13, 1568, Drury to Cecil, C.S.P., For., Eliz., VIII, 425, 428–29; April 23, 1568, Drury to Throckmorton, in Teulet, Relations politiques, II, 350–51; Register of Privy Council, I, 587–88; Thomson, Diurnal of Occurrents, p. 128.

[42] As early as February the Regent had informed Cecil of his suspicion that Elizabeth was more pleased with the state of affairs in Scotland than she admitted. S. Haynes, ed., The Burghley Papers (1542–1570), pp. 462–63. It is interesting to note that Moray, who refused to receive letters from Scots unless he was addressed as "Regent"—see Drury's letter of August 15, 1568, to Cecil, C.S.P., For., Eliz., VIII, 522–23—always signed himself "James Stewart" when writing to Elizabeth.

[43] A good contemporary account of the escape is contained in an anonymous letter from Scotland dated May 9, 1568, C.S.P., Scot., II, 404–5.

[44] Thomson, Diurnal of Occurrents, p. 129.

however, decided otherwise. He knew that he was safe enough in Glasgow for a few days at least, since the town and its immediate environs were loyal to him. If he retreated, he would give Huntly and the northern lords a chance to join forces with the western Marians. Furthermore, the psychological effects of a retreat on the waverers within his own party might well be disastrous. Consequently Moray decided to remain at Glasgow and to rally his forces there. On May 3 he summoned the lieges to Glasgow, and he followed this up with a second proclamation on the seventh.[45] His friends rallied round him.[46] In ten days Moray had an army of some four thousand men.

Meanwhile the Queen's supporters flocked to her headquarters at Hamilton. On May 8 they signed a band pledging themselves to restore her. It was signed by nine earls, nine bishops, twelve abbots and priors, eighteen lairds, and over ninety lesser men.[47] Mary's army swelled to six thousand men.[48] Nevertheless the Queen was not entirely satisfied with her present position, for she was in serious danger of becoming a mere puppet of the Hamiltons.[49] A military victory over the Regent would establish the Hamiltons' preponderance. So Mary attempted to make an agreement with her brother which would accomplish her restoration bloodlessly and thus, by preserving Moray's party intact, permit her to avoid domination by the Hamiltons. Moray, however, would not hear of any compromise.[50] In all likelihood it was the realization of the fact that a Marian victory would mean control of the government by the Hamiltons, as well as the Queen's silence

[45] *Register of Privy Council*, I, 622. *C.S.P., Scot.*, II, 402–3. See also Calderwood, *History of the Kirk*, II, 405–12.

[46] *Ibid.*, pp. 412–13. May 9, 1568, Drury to Throckmorton, in Teulet, *Relations politiques*, II, 359–60. Tytler, *History of Scotland*, VII, 177. May 9, 1568, "News from Scotland," *C.S.P., Scot.*, II, 404–5.   [47] *Ibid.*, pp. 403–4.

[48] May 9, 1568, "News from Scotland," *ibid.*, pp. 404–5. For a sample of Mary's proclamations at this time, see D. H. Fleming, *Mary Queen of Scots*, pp. 512–14. One extraordinarily venomous Marian proclamation exists in draft form. It was probably the work of Archbishop Hamilton, and in all likelihood was never issued. See *ibid.*, pp. 486–89.

[49] April 30, 1568, Forster to Cecil, *C.S.P., For., Eliz.*, VIII, 448.

[50] May 9, 1568, Drury to Throckmorton, in Teulet, *Relations politiques*, II, 359–60. May 17, 1568, Mary to Elizabeth, in A. Labanoff, ed., *Recueil des lettres de Marie Stuart*, II, 73–77.

regarding her intentions toward Bothwell, which kept Maitland and his friends from deserting the Regent, although, with the exception of Hume, they did but little to help him.

The one important fortress still in the hands of the Marians was Dumbarton, and it was resolved by the Queen's party to escort Mary there in force. Instead of trying to avoid the Regent's concentration at Glasgow, however, the Marians decided to march within striking distance of Moray's army, in order to provoke an engagement. Moray determined to accept the challenge: although he was outnumbered, he had a more experienced army, and, above all, he had far superior generalship on his side. On May 13 he intercepted Mary's army at the village of Langside, outside Glasgow, forced his rather disorganized foes to fight at a disadvantage, and won a decisive victory, thanks largely to the superb tactical skill displayed by Kirkcaldy. In about forty-five minutes all was over. Losses were almost nonexistent on the Regent's side, and were light on the other, mainly because Moray ordered the pursuit to bring in prisoners rather than corpses.[51]

Mary, seeing the disastrous result of the battle, lost her head and fled wildly in the direction of Dumfries.[52] For three days she remained in a state of panic, undecided as to what to do. She finally resolved, most unwisely, to throw herself on the mercy of Elizabeth, who had so often assured her "good sister" of her desire to help her regain her throne, and on May 16 she crossed into England, contrary to her friends' advice, and without a passport.[53] She was now fairly in the toils; from England she was never to depart, until death overtook her almost twenty years later.

The Regent determined to follow up his success by a thorough pacification of the Border, and his handling of this pacification is

[51] Sir James Melville, *Memoirs of his own Life*, pp. 200–202. Thomson, *Diurnal of Occurrents*, pp. 130–31. May 16, 1568, an anonymous report from Scotland, *C.S.P., Scot.*, II, 406–7. Tytler's account of the battle is a good one: *History of Scotland*, VII, 178–81. Morton evidently financed the Regent's army during the campaign. May 26, 1568, Drury to Cecil, *C.S.P., For., Eliz.*, VIII, 468.
[52] Melville, *Memoirs*, p. 202.
[53] May 17, 1568, Mary to Elizabeth, in Labanoff, *Recueil*, II, 73–77. Lord Herries, *Historical Memoirs of the Reign of Mary Queen of Scots and a Portion of the Reign of King James VI*, p. 103. May 17, 1568, Lowther to Cecil, *C.S.P., Scot.*, II, 408.

indicative of a change in his policy. His army, some seven thousand strong, set out on June 11.[54] In the area covered—principally the west and southwest—Moray's policy was one of ruthless destructiveness. There were no executions, but the castles of Mary's supporters were devastated, with few exceptions, and exceptions were made only for practical political reasons.[55] The policy seemed to work, too, for many of Mary's erstwhile supporters in the area flocked in to make amends for their recent behavior.[56] The importance of this expedition lies in the fact that it showed that, for the moment at least, Moray had abandoned the policy of conciliation toward most of his enemies that he had adopted on his assumption of the regency. The events of May had convinced him that that policy had been a mistake, since the Queen's supporters had repaid his concessions with a new rebellion the moment they thought the time was ripe. Moray's object now was to make it impossible for them ever to rebel again; he paid no heed to the reputed desire of Argyle and Huntly for reconciliation, and sent Sempill off to besiege Dumbarton, unsuccessfully.[57] This severity was not popular in Scotland, where any attempt at strong government was sure to meet with resistance, and hostility to the Regent was increased by the fact that Moray had perforce to refrain from prosecuting some of Darnley's murderers, in particular the treacherous Balfour, who was evidently thoroughly disliked.[58]

A far greater obstacle to the success of the policy of toughness than its unpopularity was the difficult attitude being taken by Elizabeth. Mary's unexpected arrival in England made it necessary

[54] June 17, 1568, Drury to Cecil, C.S.P., For., Eliz., VIII, 482.
[55] The castle of Lord Fleming, for instance, was spared in the hope that Fleming, who was Captain of Dumbarton, could be persuaded to surrender that fortress.
[56] There is an anonymous contemporary account of this tour of Moray's in D. Laing, ed., Miscellany of the Bannatyne Club, I, 19–29. The pacification was not entirely successful: Willock informed Cecil on July 8, 1568, that the confusion in the west was such that people went to Church in armor. C.S.P., For., Eliz., VIII, 495. G. Buchanan, The History of Scotland, II, 539–40, has misdated the expedition, placing it in September, and has led many later historians into the error of assuming that there were two expeditions instead of one.
[57] May 26, May 30, 1568, Drury to Cecil, C.S.P., For., Eliz., VIII, 468–69. Register of Privy Council, I, 624–25.
[58] On these points see Melville, Memoirs, pp. 198–99; July 10, 1568, Drury to Cecil, C.S.P., For., Eliz., VIII, 496–97.

for the English Queen to reconsider the whole basis of her Scottish policy, and the result was a drastic shift in that policy. Cecil at long last was able to persuade his mistress that the least dangerous course was to support Moray's government. This meant the retention of Mary in England, a policy fraught with difficulties.[59] It was not possible simply to imprison the sovereign of a neighboring state who had fled to England for protection and help without justifying that action in the eyes of the world, especially when that sovereign had powerful, if lately somewhat lukewarm, friends abroad.[60] It was necessary, therefore, for Elizabeth to find some pretext for retaining Mary in England, and at once she bethought herself of the reasons the Scots had had for deposing her. Elizabeth knew very well that Moray and his friends had in their possession some evidence or other—she did not as yet know exactly what it was—which was, presumably, absolutely damning. By hook or by crook Moray must be made to reveal that evidence to the world; then Elizabeth could morally justify her treatment of Mary. On the other hand, Elizabeth could not afford to approach Moray collusively to arrange to have these proofs of Mary's iniquity revealed. The evidence might turn out to be inconclusive after all, and even if it were not, Moray, if approached in this manner, would be in a position to drive a bargain as the price of his acquiescence, and that price would inevitably have something to do with the unpleasant question of the succession. Consequently Moray had to be forced into revealing what he knew in self-defense, and Elizabeth could do this only by pretending to favor Mary up to the decisive moment. Furthermore, for foreign consumption, it was necessary to favor Mary—but not too warmly, so that the eventual reversal of form would not seem too inconsistent.[61] This was *Realpolitik* with a vengeance!

[59] See Cecil's memorandum of May, 1568, *C.S.P., Scot.*, II, 418–19.
[60] The French could do nothing at this time, however, and neither Philip II nor the Pope was disposed to help Mary. June 27, 1568, the Bishop of Rossano to the Bishop of Ceneda, August 13, 1568, the Cardinal of Alessandria to the Bishop of Rossano, both quoted in M. Philippson, *Histoire du règne de Marie Stuart*, III, 495–96.
[61] Elizabeth told De Silva that what she really wanted was Mary's restoration as titular Queen, with Moray retaining the actual power. July 3, 1568, De Silva to Philip II, in Teulet, *Relations politiques*, V, 38–41.

That this was Elizabeth's policy is proved by her behavior in the summer of 1568. If she had really wanted to help Mary, she could have acceded to Mary's request either to restore her or to permit her to go to France to seek help there.[62] Elizabeth paid no heed to this. Instead she wrote to Mary on June 8, informing her that she would protect her and see that she was restored, but that first of all, since Mary wished it, all these unpleasant stories about Mary's connection with the murder of Darnley would be cleared up. Furthermore, the bearer of the letter, Middlemore, had instructions to go to Scotland to order Moray to cease persecuting Mary's supporters there and to justify himself against the charge of rebellion which Mary had leveled at him.[63]

Elizabeth in this letter was putting words into Mary's mouth. The latter had said nothing at all about wanting to clear herself of suspicion of guilt in the Darnley affair. But Elizabeth blandly assumed that Mary had, for she had now decided on the tactical device whereby to blast Mary's reputation and thus justify her imprisonment. Mary was to be cajoled into permitting Elizabeth to sit in judgment between her and her rebellious subjects, who were to be summoned to answer for their treason, and thus, Elizabeth calculated, forced into producing their evidence against Mary as a countermeasure. To spare Mary's susceptibilities, there would be no formal "trial"; Mary could hardly agree that any court could judge her, an anointed Queen. A commission of arbitration would be enough.[64] Mary was made to understand that without some such procedure, Elizabeth would not help her; [65] but if she did consent to it, Elizabeth would restore her regardless of what might be revealed, although if it turned out that Moray and his friends were to some extent justified in their behavior, there would be

[62] May 28, 1568, Mary to Elizabeth, in Labanoff, *Recueil*, II, 79–84.
[63] *C.S.P., Scot.*, II, 424–26.
[64] Although everyone was careful to avoid calling the forthcoming meeting of commissioners a "trial"—since Elizabeth's legal jurisdiction over the parties to the dispute was not recognized and, in fact, was nonexistent unless one accepts the old English feudal claim to suzerainty over Scotland—the affair nevertheless became a trial, as the next chapter will show. For the sake of convenience and brevity, therefore, the meeting will be termed a "trial" throughout this chapter.
[65] This policy was laid down by the English Council on June 20, 1568, *ibid.*, pp. 438–39.

some conditions to the restoration, notably that the lords of Moray's party go unpunished. Whatever the result, Mary was to turn Anglican and make a permanent alliance with England. After almost two months of negotiation and delay, the latter caused primarily by her well-founded suspicion of Elizabeth's ultimate purpose, Mary finally consented, on July 28.[66]

Elizabeth's devious policy made it necessary for her to take an outwardly very stern attitude toward Moray, which disquieted the latter not a little. The first message he had received from England after Langside was an oral one from Cecil, urging him to reduce the country to obedience as quickly as possible.[67] Assuming that official English support would soon be accorded to him, Moray sent his secretary, John Wood, to England at the end of May, to ask for that support and to give the English his official version of the recent happenings in Scotland.[68] He must have been startled to receive Elizabeth's reply, which was delivered to him by Middlemore in mid-June, while he was on his expedition of pacification on the Borders. He was peremptorily ordered to cease prosecuting Mary's friends and to prepare to defend himself against a charge of rebellion.[69] This was not what the Regent had expected at all, though the blow was somewhat softened by a secret message from Cecil to the effect that he was not to abandon his assaults on Mary's friends if any risk to himself or his government was involved in so doing.[70] A few days later a clarifying letter arrived from Wood. Elizabeth wanted Moray to send a com-

[66] Most of the relevant correspondence on the negotiations between Mary and Elizabeth on these matters is in *C.S.P., Scot.*, II, 431–66. Mary's letter of July 28, 1568, consenting to the commission of arbitration is in Labanoff, *Recueil*, II, 139–42. See also Mary's letter of July 5, 1568, *ibid.*, pp. 130–34, and that of Herries to Mary on June 28, 1568, in Teulet, *Relations politiques*, II, 380–87. Herries was Mary's principal agent at the English court. Mary was not entirely taken in by Elizabeth's specious promises; see her letters to De Silva in June and July, in A. Teulet, ed., *Papiers d'état rélatifs à l'histoire de l'Ecosse au XVIe siècle*, III, 47–48, 54–57, and that of June 21, 1568, to the Cardinal of Lorraine, in Labanoff, *Recueil*, II, 115–19.

[67] May 21, 1568, Elphinstone to Cecil, *C.S.P., Scot.*, II, 411.

[68] Wood's statement of June 5, 1568, *ibid.*, p. 423. May 21, 1568, Maitland to Cecil, *ibid.*, p. 412.

[69] June 8, 1568, Elizabeth to Moray, *ibid.*, pp. 426–27. June 17, 1568, Knollys to Cecil, *ibid.*, pp. 437–38.

[70] On this point see M. Philippson, "Etudes sur l'histoire de Marie Stuart," Pt. v, *Revue historique*, XXXVIII (1888), 13–14.

mission to England, to justify himself and his friends.[71] Moray was not happy about this. He refused to put an end to his attacks on the Marians, in the interests of justice, so he told Elizabeth in a letter of June 22. This letter was delivered to the Queen by Middlemore, who had been instructed by the Regent to ask the English government some questions. He did not object to this trial the English wanted, Moray said, but he wanted to be sure that he would be fairly treated. Wood had copies of the Casket Letters. If the originals of these letters were shown, Moray wanted to know, and Mary's guilt thus conclusively demonstrated, would the English government cease supporting Mary and recognize James VI? [72] In view of Elizabeth's promises to Mary, this was a most pertinent, and most embarrassing, question.

Elizabeth sent an equivocal answer to this query,[73] and Moray, feeling himself in a rather precarious position, adopted an ambivalent policy toward his opponents. It was possible that, in spite of all, some sort of compromise with Mary would be forced on him; so he strove to repair his personal ties with her, and as a starter, sent three coffers of her clothes to her from Lochleven.[74] At the same time he determined to continue his attempt to subdue her supporters at home, a task made far more difficult by Elizabeth's friendliness to Mary; her followers, hoping for English aid, were not prepared to submit to the Regent.[75] On July 13 two crucial decisions were taken. Moray realized that his government could not survive active English hostility. England had shown no real enmity thus far, but, not having fathomed Elizabeth's devious plans, the Regent feared that she might support his sister in good earnest if he hesitated on the matter of the trial. Accordingly, on that day, he notified Elizabeth that he awaited her pleasure as to the time and place of the meeting.[76]

---

[71] *Maitland Club, Miscellany*, IV, 120.
[72] *C.S.P., Scot.*, II, 441–43. Previously, on June 17, Drury had informed Cecil that Moray was willing to come to England to settle matters once for all. *C.S.P., For., Eliz.*, VIII, 482.
[73] Cecil's notes which served as the basis for the English reply are dated June 30, 1568. Anderson, *Collections*, IV, Pt. 1, 107–8.
[74] July 7, 1568, Knollys to Cecil, *C.S.P., Scot.*, II, 453.
[75] June 13, 1568, Drury to Cecil, *C.S.P., For., Eliz.*, VIII, 480.
[76] *C.S.P., Scot.*, II, 455. Throughout these months English Border officials con-

On the same day, July 13, Parliament was summoned for mid-August.[77] This move brought the opposition to Moray to a head. It was at once apparent that the principal business of the meeting would be the forfeiture of Mary's supporters; the result was a meeting of all Moray's foes at Largs, on July 28. Argyle, who had maintained a desultory military opposition to the Regent through the summer,[78] was proclaimed Mary's Lieutenant in Scotland, and the lieges were ordered to meet him on August 10 to march against Moray. Elizabeth was requested to restore Mary. The Marians even wrote to Alva to ask for troops.[79]

Moray met this challenge, further complicated by a demand from Elizabeth that he hold no Parliament until after the trial,[80] with steadfast determination. He gave Elizabeth an evasive answer at first, and then, just before Parliament met, informed her that, since his opponents were threatening him, he could not prorogue the meeting without losing prestige.[81] He continued his policy of conciliating Mary herself, writing her a very friendly letter on August 7.[82] He had good reason to feel kindly toward his sister at this point, for she was playing into his hands. On July 28, when she agreed to the trial, Mary also consented to order her partisans in Scotland to cease fighting, if Moray would do the same.[83] Moray would have liked nothing better, provided he could have his Parliament. After it was over, he could proceed against his op-

---

tinued to cooperate with Moray's, much to Mary's annoyance. See Knollys's letters of June 12, 16, and 21, 1568, *ibid.*, pp. 429–31, 436, 440–41.

[77] J. Stuart, ed., *Miscellany of the Spalding Club*, II, 109.

[78] July 4, 1568, Drury to Cecil, *C.S.P., For., Eliz.*, VIII, 493.

[79] *C.S.P., Scot.*, II, 466–69. *C.S.P., For., Eliz.*, VIII, 507. See also July 31, 1568, Argyle to Crawford, in Calderwood, *History of the Kirk*, II, 419–20.

[80] July 22, 1568, Elizabeth to Moray, *C.S.P., Scot.*, II, 461.

[81] July 31, August 12, 1568, Moray to Elizabeth, *ibid.*, pp. 470, 476.

[82] *Ibid.*, p. 473. Moray's overtures were received with the utmost coldness by Mary, who now suspected that Elizabeth was plotting with him. June 21, 1568, Mary to the Cardinal of Lorraine, in Labanoff, *Recueil*, II, 115–19. Moray himself expected very little from this attempt at friendliness; in a letter of August 7, 1568, to Scrope, he expressed serious doubt that a reconciliation satisfactory to all concerned could ever be worked out or that Mary's leaning to Anglicanism, evidently caused by the terms of her bargain with Elizabeth, was sincere. *C.S.P., Scot.*, II, 472–73. The Regent's scepticism on this latter point was quickly justified: Knollys reported on September 21 that Mary had become frankly Papist again. *Ibid.*, pp. 509–10.

[83] July 28, 1568, Mary to Elizabeth, in Labanoff, *Recueil*, II, 139–42.

ponents under color of law. He was not to have his way, however. Neither side paid any attention to the demands of Mary and Elizabeth. Argyle and Huntly continued their rather ineffectual campaigning.[84] Drury, in describing the situation in his letter of August 21, commented that Moray was not unduly bothered by his domestic foes; his one real fear was the possibility of a French invasion, led by Châtelherault, and paid for out of Mary's French dowry. The Regent need not have worried. Elizabeth had steadfastly refused Mary's pleas to allow her to send a messenger to France to ask for aid, and Mary, in accepting the trial, had agreed to ask no further.[85] Also, the French had rejected Châtelherault's request that they assist Mary.[86] It is probable that the Regent knew of this and was expressing entirely imaginary fears in order to obtain English support.[87]

Parliament met on August 16, and, as expected, its only business was to consider punitive measures against the Marians. Moray soon found, however, that his party was divided on the scope of these measures. Maitland and his friends argued that a blanket forfeiture would simply increase Marian resistance. Rather than risk a schism in his own party on this score, and influenced to some extent by Elizabeth's attitude, Moray gave in to the moderates and agreed to forfeit only the Hamiltons, Lord Fleming, and the Bishop of Ross. Certain other nobles, including Herries, were termed traitors, but no official action was taken against them. Argyle and Huntly were not mentioned at all. Parliament was dissolved on August 19.[88]

---

[84] August 1, 1568, "News from Scotland," *C.S.P., Scot.*, II, 471–72. August 15, August 21, 1568, Drury to Cecil, *C.S.P., For., Eliz.*, VIII, 522–23, 526–27.

[85] June 30, 1568, Elizabeth to Mary, *C.S.P., Scot.*, II, 448–49. July 28, 1568, Mary to Elizabeth, in Labanoff, *Recueil*, II, 139–42.

[86] July 5, 1568, Norris to Cecil, *C.S.P., For., Eliz.*, VIII, 494.

[87] See, for instance, the letter of John Gordon to Moray on July 12, 1568, *C.S.P., Scot.*, II, 454–55.

[88] *Acts of Parliament*, III, 49–55. Buchanan, *History*, II, 539. Thomson, *Diurnal of Occurrents*, p. 136. On August 16 the Archbishop of Glasgow was horned, but he was not yet forfeited. *Register of Privy Council*, I, 638. Moray himself attributed his leniency at this Parliament to Elizabeth, and explained the punitive measures that were taken on the ground that his enemies were still in arms against him. August 25, 1568, Moray to Elizabeth, *C.S.P., Scot.*, II, 489. The Marians seemed to appreciate the Regent's logic; after the Parliament they more or less

Moray's forfeitures were greeted with howls of rage by his opponents, who bombarded Elizabeth with protests, claiming that they had laid down their arms owing to Elizabeth's request to Mary that they do so, pending the outcome of the trial, and that Moray had behaved treacherously in the matter.[89] This charge has been echoed by numerous historians, including some not especially favorable to Mary. It is, however, palpably untrue. Moray never promised anyone that he would not hold the Parliament, even if his opponents did lay down their arms. And, as we have seen, the Marians had done no such thing, a fact which Mary herself admitted to Knollys on the very day that Parliament opened.[90] It is Mary's party, not Moray's, which deserves the label of hypocrite in this business.

The all-important question now was the preparation for the trial, which was due to begin very soon. Moray's efficient handling of the August crisis, coupled with his continued willingness to do Elizabeth's bidding in the matter of the trial,[91] was producing a shift in the English attitude which was artfully exploited by the adroit Wood. Once again the possibility of French armed intervention was being bruited about, since it was known that the French had granted permission to Châtelherault to return home.[92] Such a rumor was bound to increase English good will to the Regent, especially since Herries was using the report as a club in an attempt to bludgeon England into a pro-Marian attitude.[93]

---

obeyed Mary's order to remain passive. See September 1, 1568, Herries to Moray, *ibid.*, p. 495.

[89] August 23, 1568, Mary to Elizabeth, *ibid.*, p. 485. August 24, 1568, the Marian lords to Elizabeth, in Anderson, *Collections*, IV, Pt. I, 125–26. This letter was signed by Argyle, Huntly, Crawford, Eglinton, Cassilis, Fleming, Archbishop Hamilton, and a number of others.

[90] August 16, 1568, Knollys to Cecil, *C.S.P., Scot.*, II, 480–81. See also August 17, 1568, Herries to Scrope and Knollys, *ibid.*, pp. 481–82.

[91] See his letter of September 3, 1568, to Elizabeth, *ibid.*, p. 497.

[92] August 9, 1568, Elizabeth to Norris, *C.S.P., For., Eliz.*, VIII, 517. August 31, 1568, "Advices from Scotland," *C.S.P., Scot.*, II, 494–95. In fairness to Mary it should be stated that, according to this latter document, the Archbishop of Glasgow and the Bishop of Dunblane, not Mary herself, were responsible for the renewed attempt to get French help. See also September 7, 1568, Moray to Cecil, *ibid.*, p. 502; September 10, 1568, Knox to Wood, in T. McCrie, *The Life of John Knox*, II, 396–97.

[93] August 17, 1568, Herries to Scrope and Knollys, *C.S.P., Scot.*, II, 481–82. September 11, 1568, Scrope and Knollys to Herries, *ibid.*, pp. 503–4.

Elizabeth took these rumors seriously enough to take Mary to task for soliciting French assistance.[94] Wood, who had been in England most of the summer and was now on his way home, played his cards very cleverly at this juncture. He informed Cecil, with some accuracy, that Moray was worried about the forthcoming trial, so worried, in fact, that he wanted a safe-conduct, lest Elizabeth arrest him during his stay in England. The Regent also wanted a conference with Cecil before the trial began, if possible.[95] The impression left by Wood, taken together with Herries's behavior, Moray's queries of June 22, which had by no means been forgotten, and Elizabeth's promises to Mary, which the Marians were spreading far and wide,[96] was that the Regent was afraid that the English government was planning, regardless of the outcome of the trial, to force a restoration of Mary. Such an opinion was perfectly logical, and was strengthened by the fact that Elizabeth had refused Lennox's request to appear at the trial.[97] The story that Elizabeth would restore Mary in any circumstances was current in Scotland in September.[98] This being the case, it was perfectly apparent that Moray would not accuse his sister of a guilty connection with the murder of Darnley, in order to save himself from certain vengeance after her restoration. This would have defeated Elizabeth's whole purpose. Therefore, on September 20, the Queen wrote to Moray and promised him that, if Mary were guilty, she would not be restored.[99] On September 23 Cecil repeated this to the Earl of Sussex, one of the English commissioners for the trial.[100] This was what the Regent had been waiting for. If he could prove his case—and he was sure he could —England would be committed to support him, and Mary would be permanently erased from the political scene.

[94] August 31, 1568, Mary to Argyle, in A. Macdonald, ed., *Letters to the Argyle Family*, pp. 10–11.
[95] September 3, September 6, 1568, Wood to Cecil, *C.S.P., Scot.*, II, 497, 501. Moray himself asked for safe-conducts in a letter of September 7, 1568, to Cecil. *Ibid.*, p. 502. They were granted on September 16. *Ibid.*, pp. 507–8.
[96] On this point see August 7, 1568, Moray to Scrope, *ibid.*, pp. 472–73.
[97] August 18, 1568, Lennox to Cecil, *ibid.*, p. 482. August 25, 1568, De la Forest to Catherine de Medici, in Teulet, *Relations politiques*, II, 390–91.
[98] September 20, 1568, Hunsdon to Cecil, *C.S.P., For., Eliz.*, VIII, 551. Hunsdon, a relative of Elizabeth's, had been made Warden of the East March in August. *C.S.P., Scot.*, II, 486–87.   [99] *Ibid.*, p. 509.   [100] *Ibid.*, p. 510.

As a matter of fact, Moray did not receive Elizabeth's letter until after his arrival in England.[101] He had had some difficulty in forming his commission. His principal supporters were not anxious to go, since Mary might be restored after all, and all those who were on the commission could be assured of her undying animosity.[102] Finally he resolved to go himself, and with him as commissioners went Morton, Lindsay, the Bishop of Orkney, and the Commendator of Dunfermline. To these were added some assistants: McGill, Balnaves, Buchanan—and Maitland.[103] Maitland's inclusion, according to Buchanan, was due not to his diplomatic skill but to Moray's fear that he would cause trouble at home if he were left behind.[104] It is rather a pity that the Regent did not take Knox with him too; the conference would probably have been far livelier as a result.

Before setting out for England, on September 16, Moray took formal possession of the Casket.[105] On the twenty-seventh he and his fellow commissioners arrived in Berwick,[106] and a week or so later they entered York, which had been designated as the site of the meeting. The stage was set for the extraordinary drama which was to seal the Regent's triumph over his sister and to mark the end of Mary's career as an independent political agent. To a consideration of the events of this drama we must now turn.

[101] His acknowledgement is dated September 28, 1568, the day after his arrival in Berwick. *Ibid.*, p. 513.   [102] Buchanan, *History*, II, 540–41.
[103] Moray's commission is dated September 18, 1568. Anderson, *Collections*, IV, Pt. II, 35–37. Robert Pitcairn, Commendator of Dunfermline, was a comparative newcomer to high politics at this time. Moray made increasing use of him in various negotiations with England, and he served as Secretary of State during Morton's regency.
[104] Buchanan, *History*, II, 540–41. Mary had earlier expressed hope of winning Maitland over. July 27, 1568, Knollys to Cecil, *C.S.P., Scot.*, II, 461–62.
[105] *Register of Privy Council*, I, 641.
[106] September 27, 1568, Hunsdon to Cecil, *C.S.P., For., Eliz.*, VIII, 555.

CHAPTER XI

The York-Westminster Conference

THE MEETINGS between the English commissioners and those of the two Scottish factions during the winter of 1568–69, collectively known to history as the York–Westminster Conference, present a maddening problem to the historian. The difficulty is that the formal sessions of the conference, especially those at York, were almost meaningless. The really significant events of those weeks took place behind closed doors, and it is almost impossible to deduce with any certainty just what did occur. Though the upshot of all the devious machinations at the sessions at Westminster is plain enough, the course of events there had been largely predetermined by the clandestine intrigues at York. A good deal of the following account, therefore, is unproven and unprovable surmise, but it offers, in the writer's opinion, the most reasonable hypothesis which can be constructed from the conflicting and biased evidence available to us.

Elizabeth nominated a three-man commission to represent her at York. Two of its members, Sir Ralph Sadler and the Earl of Sussex, were loyal followers of the Queen and of Cecil. But the influence of these two was negligible; real control of the English commission lay in the hands of its principal member, the Duke of Norfolk—and Norfolk, who, though a Protestant himself, was hand in glove with the English Catholics, was by no means ill-disposed toward Mary. If we may believe Bishop Leslie, Mary felt confident of his friendship in mid-September, well before the conference opened.[1] Norfolk, however, was a man of no particu-

[1] November 6, 1571, examination of Leslie in the Tower, in W. Murdin, ed., *The Burghley Papers (1571–1596)*, pp. 52–54.

lar intelligence or courage. Had he been left to himself, he probably would not have dared to give rein to his pro-Marian proclivities. But he succumbed to an intelligence stronger than his own, and thus set his foot on the path that was to lead him to the block in less than five years.

Mary appointed a numerous commission, but for all practical purposes she had but two representatives at the conference, Lord Herries and Bishop Leslie. In her instructions, dated September 29, she insisted above all that the meeting was in no sense to be regarded as anything more than a conference; it was to have no judicial character. Furthermore, it was to be understood that the only purpose of the meeting was to arrange for her restoration. Her abdication was invalid, since it was signed under duress, and any evidence in her handwriting which Moray and his friends might produce which incriminated her in any way was discounted in advance as forged; it was very easy, she explained, to counterfeit her handwriting.[2] Mary's concept of the purpose of the conference squared with the promises Elizabeth had made to her, but had no relation to Elizabeth's real intentions. The instructions for the English commissioners contained an elaborate reconciliation scheme, it is true, but this plan would have been unacceptable to both sides, since it involved virtual English suzerainty over Scotland. It seems to have been included mainly to frighten Moray, since the instructions also authorized the English commissioners to renew Elizabeth's promise of September 20 to the Regent if he showed signs of wavering.[3] Worse still from Mary's point of view, her principal commissioners, while undoubtedly the ablest men she could find to represent her, did not really believe in her innocence. Herries had already indicated as much. In June 1568, when the possibility of a conference was being discussed, he had asked Elizabeth what her attitude would be if it were shown that Mary was not an injured innocent, and he had actually informed Mary that he had asked this question.[4] Bishop Leslie also had his doubts,

---

[2] A. Labanoff, ed., *Recueil des lettres de Marie Stuart*, II, 193–210.
[3] J. Anderson, ed., *Collections Relating to the History of Mary Queen of Scots*, IV, Pt. II, 8–25.
[4] June 28, 1568, Herries to Mary, in A. Teulet, ed., *Relations politiques de la France et de l'Espagne avec l'Ecosse au XVIe siècle*, II, 380–87. See also October

as his behavior during the conference, and in later years, was to make clear.[5] Mary's contemporary supporters were far less convinced of the justice of her cause than her champions of later days.

Moray was looking forward to the coming meeting with no great amount of joy. He was faced by a choice of evils. If Elizabeth really wanted reconciliation between the factions, he would have to acquiesce or face the consequences, which would doubtless be war. If, on the other hand, she wanted him to accuse Mary of murder and produce the Casket Letters, he would, of course, comply, but at the cost of permanently alienating all of Mary's well-wishers and perhaps provoking foreign intervention. The second course was less dangerous, and was preferred by Moray and by most of his fellow commissioners, who for one reason or another stoutly opposed any reconciliation, but there were grave perils in either policy.

The one man among the Regent's commissioners who took a different view was Maitland, and, curiously enough, it was Maitland who was the key figure in the early weeks of the conference. Maitland wanted a reconciliation and the restoration of Mary, for two principal reasons. In the first place, he feared that the open accusation and besmirching of the Queen by Moray would give Elizabeth a plausible pretext for barring Mary and her heirs from the English succession, which the Secretary still ardently desired for the Stewart line. Secondly, he was worried about his own safety. If Mary were accused of the murder, she might well reply by naming the others involved, including himself.[6] Spurred on by these considerations, the subtle Secretary set to work.

Maitland's carefully worked-out plans began to develop soon after the conference opened. The various parties to the meetings arrived at York early in October, and the first session of the conference was held on October 7. Mary's commissioners delivered

6, 1568, the English commissioners to Elizabeth, in Anderson, *Collections*, IV, Pt. II, 25–32, for Herries's behavior on the wording of the oath to be taken at the conference.
[5] For Leslie's character, and his curious confession after the uncovering of the Ridolfi Plot, see November 8, 1571, Wilson to Cecil, in Murdin, *Burghley Papers*, p. 57.
[6] On this point see June 12, 1568, Wood to Maitland, in *Maitland Club, Miscellany*, IV, 120–21.

their opening accusation of Moray and his friends, who were charged with treason and rebellion. Moray demanded time to study the charges and frame his answers; he also made a series of requests to the English commissioners which indicate the influence of Maitland. The Regent asked them to repeat Elizabeth's guarantee of September 20 that Mary, if found guilty, would not be restored, and Norfolk complied. This was all very well, said Moray, but Mary's followers were claiming that she had a written promise from Elizabeth that she would be restored in any case. Norfolk expressed his doubts, but Moray was not satisfied, and presented the Duke with four questions, to which he wanted precise answers: 1. Did the English commission have the authority to pronounce a verdict on Mary's connection with the murder? 2. If so, would they do so without delay, once the evidence was presented? 3. If Mary were found guilty, would England turn her over to the Scots? 4. In the same circumstances, would England recognize the government of James VI? Norfolk, caught unprepared, could only give tentative answers, until he could consult his government.[7] Consequently the Regent decided that until he was answered, he would refrain from making any serious accusations against Mary.

Maitland's hand is clearly visible in all of this. He had shaken Moray's confidence in Elizabeth's guarantee of September 20, which was sufficiently vaguely worded to justify a certain amount of doubt, and had succeeded in persuading the Regent to withhold his accusation until he had received more explicit promises from Elizabeth. Moray, who had suffered in the past from putting undue confidence in Elizabeth's word, was not unwilling, and on October 11, in his official reply to the accusations of the Marians, he defended himself merely on the grounds of the Bothwell marriage and Mary's voluntary abdication.[8]

Maitland had gained little more than time by this maneuver, but time was of the essence. He had already established contact with Herries,[9] and he even succeeded in turning Moray's next move

---

[7] October 9, 1568, the English commissioners to Elizabeth, in Anderson, *Collections*, IV, Pt. II, 41–48, 55–56.   [8] *C.S.P., Scot.*, II, 525.
[9] October 9, 1568, Knollys to Cecil, *ibid.*, p. 523.

to some account. The Regent, in the hope of getting a speedy and favorable answer to his demands, decided to tip his hand, unofficially: on October 11 the Casket Letters were privately shown to the English commissioners. The latter were properly horrified and wrote a fairly detailed account of them to Elizabeth.[10] Ultimately this maneuver won the game for Moray, because it confirmed Elizabeth in her decision never to rest until the Regent had been compelled to reveal the Letters officially. It was a damaging blow to Maitland's schemes, but he contrived to make the best of it by informing Leslie, and through him Mary, of what had occurred, so that the Scottish Queen would be more amenable to compromise.[11]

Norfolk was shocked; his letter of October 11 indicated that he was cured of whatever pro-Marian leanings he may have had.[12] Maitland, who desperately needed a friend in the enemy's camp, nevertheless realized that the Duke was the only possibility, and on October 16, he contrived to have a long private interview with Norfolk. The miracle was accomplished: Norfolk now became extremely favorable to Mary, and revealed to Maitland that the object of Elizabeth's policy was to force an accusation out of Moray. Maitland quickly passed this information on to Mary, though he concealed it from the Regent.[13] What had caused Norfolk's change of heart? Mary's defenders have maintained that Maitland must have proved to Norfolk that the Letters were forgeries. Possibly Maitland did attempt to shake the Duke's confidence in the genuineness of the Letters, but there is no real evidence for this, and there is nothing in Norfolk's record to indicate that he was such a disinterested lover of justice that the proof of Mary's innocence would cause him to place himself in dangerous opposition to his government, especially given the normal Tudor reaction to the disloyalty of noble subjects. One thing, and one

[10] October 11, 1568, the English commissioners to Elizabeth, in Anderson, *Collections*, IV, Pt. II, 58–63.
[11] October 14, 1568, Knollys to Norfolk, *C.S.P., Scot.*, II, 529–30. In June Moray had offered to show the Letters to the English, but there is no evidence to show that he actually did so at that time. See above, p. 229.
[12] *C.S.P., Scot.*, II, 528–29.
[13] C. October 18, 1568, Leslie to Mary, *ibid.*, pp. 533–34.

thing alone, could have caused Norfolk's *volte-face:* Maitland had held out hopes to him of an eventual marriage with Mary. Such a prize, with the prospect of the English succession, would be well worth the risk. Mary understood Maitland's game; on October 21, for the first time, she indicated that she was willing to be divorced from Bothwell.[14]

Norfolk now sought out Moray, and in an interview with him proceeded completely to misrepresent Elizabeth's policy. The Queen, he confidently predicted, would never hand down a favorable decision, which explained why she had refused to promise explicitly in writing that she would do so. Furthermore, if Moray produced his accusations against his sister, he would be jeopardizing the Scottish chances for the succession. Norfolk in his eagerness tipped his hand slightly and spoke of the advantages that would accrue to Scotland and to Moray personally if Mary had more children: with each child the Hamiltons' chances of obtaining the Scottish throne would become more and more remote. Moray was doubtless aware of what lay behind this rather transparent suggestion, but he was sufficiently impressed by Norfolk's arguments to agree to a compromise proposed by the Duke, which was that Mary should ratify her abdication and agree to reside in England, in return for which she would receive a pension from Scotland and Moray would remain silent on the matter of the murder.[15] This solution would preserve Moray's regency for him and assure the continued dominance of Protestantism; it would prevent civil war in Scotland; and it would be impossible for Elizabeth to object, since her avowed object was a reconciliation. The Letters could always be kept in reserve, to assure Mary's continued good behavior.

So the Regent sent Robert Melville to Bolton to propose this plan to Mary, and the latter, probably more frightened than she cared to admit by Moray's evident willingness to use the Letters if need be, assented. Success was within Maitland's grasp. On October 25 Melville set out for London to present Elizabeth with the

---

[14] Labanoff, *Recueil*, II, 219–22.
[15] Sir James Melville, *Memoirs of his own Life*, pp. 208–9. October, 1569, Moray to Cecil, in W. Robertson, *The History of Scotland*, III, 368–74.

fait accompli. There he was met by Herries, who, much to Melville's surprise, knew all about the negotiations, and who countermanded his instructions in Mary's name: the Queen had changed her mind. Maitland's laboriously built edifice came crashing to the ground. He had overreached himself in one particular, and that was enough to ruin him. Norfolk, who had been enticed into the scheme by the bait of a marriage with Mary, had become so bemused by the idea that he had decided that there was no profit in marrying an abdicated dowager when he could have a queen regnant who might, one day, elevate him to the English throne. He had urged Mary to refuse to ratify her abdication, and the latter, knowing that her main hope of success lay in retaining Norfolk on her side, and probably overestimating the influence of the Duke on the English government, had assented.[16]

Elizabeth, meanwhile, was becoming increasingly annoyed by the snaillike and friendly goings-on at York. This was not what she had had in mind at all. The glaring difference between Moray's private and public statements caused her to decide to expedite matters by removing the conference to Westminster, where she and Cecil could keep an eye on the proceedings; this was done on November 3.[17] She also began to put pressure on Moray by threatening to support Châtelherault's claim to the regency. Moray drew up a long statement to prove that, on constitutional grounds, his claim was superior to Châtelherault's; this matter was evidently argued out at York on October 20, at which time all parties were anxious to avoid discussing the real issues of the conference.[18]

There were difficulties involved in the transfer and continuation of the conference, as the English well knew. In order to persuade Moray to present his case against Mary, it would be necessary to make some sort of answer to the questions he had raised. On October 30 the English Council resolved to answer the Regent favor-

[16] This paragraph is based mainly on the confession of Robert Melville, made in 1573, when he was captured by Morton; Melville at that time had gone over to Mary's party. It is cited in Andrew Lang, *The Mystery of Mary Stuart,* pp. 206–7, 215–16. The date of Melville's departure for London is established by Knollys's letter of October 25, 1568, *C.S.P., Scot.,* II, 541.
[17] S. Haynes, ed., *The Burghley Papers (1542–1570),* p. 488.
[18] *C.S.P., Scot.,* II, 536–38. Haynes, *Burghley Papers,* pp. 484–86.

ably. It also decided that after Moray had produced his evidence, and the conference was over, he was to be permitted to resume his rule in Scotland. Mary was to be removed to a safer place of confinement, to obviate any possibility of her escape.[19] In other words, the threat of support for Châtelherault was simply a bogey to frighten Moray; and, more important, Mary's case had been virtually prejudged. Whatever one's opinion of Mary, it cannot be denied that Elizabeth's conduct of the conference was extremely unfair.

There was a further difficulty for the English in transferring the conference, which was that Mary would demand more forcefully than ever that she be allowed to appear and defend herself in person. Mary, in fact, did just that, on November 22, in her new instructions to her commissioners, and considerable weight was given to her demand by Elizabeth's blunder in receiving Moray in audience.[20] This problem had been anticipated by Sussex, who on October 22 warned Cecil against permitting Mary to appear. If she did, he said, it would prove very difficult to convict her.[21] Mary's defenders have taken this to mean that Sussex was not convinced of the authenticity of the Letters. This is possible, but it is at least equally likely that Sussex felt that if Mary were given an opportunity personally and publicly to repudiate the Letters, it would be extremely risky for Elizabeth to decide against her, especially in view of England's rapidly worsening relations with Spain, which reached the breaking point in December 1568. Mary's reputation must be blasted, and no opportunity for a real public defense was to be afforded, as the sequel was to show.

ii

Moray, as he awaited the reopening of the conference at Westminster, had reverted to his position of early October, with some modifications. The collapse of Maitland's reconciliation scheme ended any possibilities in that direction. So Moray prepared to

[19] *Ibid.*, pp. 487–88.
[20] Labanoff, *Recueil*, II, 232–37. Moray evidently arrived in London about November 13. November 7, 1568, Sussex to Cecil, *C.S.P., Scot.*, II, 546.
[21] This letter is given in J. Hosack, *Mary Queen of Scots and Her Accusers*, pp. 517–21.

accuse his sister of murder, provided Elizabeth gave him the necessary guarantees. But now he was willing to accept less definite promises from England. He was worried by the possibility of English support for Châtelherault. It also seems that Elizabeth had got wind of the Norfolk marriage plan, though not of Moray's connection with it. She warned Norfolk, but did nothing more.[22] At all events, Moray was now prepared to settle for something less than the formal guarantees he had demanded in October.

The conference reopened on November 25 at Westminster, with a much larger English commission this time, the most important addition being Cecil himself. On the following day the English answered Moray's questions in an entirely satisfactory manner.[23] Thus reassured, Moray produced his "eik," or addition to his previous statement, and accused his sister of murder. Melville, in recounting this scene, tells us that even after the English statement Moray was still hesitant, but that the Bishop of Orkney snatched the "eik" from the hand of Wood and threw it on the table, amid cries of "Well done, Bishop Turpy!" and that the Regent was greatly embarrassed.[24] If this is so, it is obvious that Moray had stage-managed the affair, so that he could claim, if necessary, that the accusation had been produced against his will.

The fat was now fairly in the fire. There could no longer be any reconciliation between Mary and her brother; furthermore, Moray and Maitland now stood at the parting of the ways. The two men drifted further and further apart, because the Secretary, obsessed by his desire to unite the kingdoms, felt that Moray had wrecked all possibility of this by destroying Mary's good name. Within a year there was an open break between them, and Maitland, after Moray's death, became, in Mary's behalf, the soul of the armed opposition to Moray's party. He had come to believe that Elizabeth could be made to grant the succession only by force, and he permitted this idea to dwarf all other considerations in his mind. Maitland adopted this extremely rigid view simply be-

---

[22] January 20, 1570, charges against Norfolk, in Haynes, *Burghley Papers*, pp. 573–75. Melville's story (*Memoirs*, p. 210), that Morton revealed the plan to the English is improbable. [23] *C.S.P., Scot.*, II, 554–55.
[24] Melville, *Memoirs*, pp. 210–12.

cause he was so politically minded. He failed to see that, in a religious age, religious considerations were bound to be decisive, even in political matters such as the succession. In this respect Moray was wiser than Maitland. He never mentioned the succession to Elizabeth again, trusting to time and community of interest, especially religious interest, to solve the problem. And solve it they did.[25]

Once Moray had made his accusations, the conference moved along at a rapid pace which was much more to Elizabeth's liking. Lennox was allowed to add his voice to those of Mary's other accusers.[26] Mary's commissioners indignantly denied Moray's charges and demanded that Mary be permitted to defend herself in person.[27] On December 3 Leslie informed Elizabeth that the admission of Moray's statement gave grounds for a dissolution of the conference, since the English Queen had promised to allow no mention of anything compromising to Mary.[28] The English Council met the next day to consider the matter. Before the meeting Leslie and Herries blundered badly, telling Cecil and Leicester that they still wanted a compromise and a reconciliation. Such a statement, after Moray had publicly accused Mary of murder, showed their lack of belief in the justice of their cause, and Elizabeth righteously informed them that the time for compromise was past. She meant, she said, to charge Moray with slander; pending his conviction or acquittal on this charge, it was impossible for her to see Mary.[29]

It was obvious now that Mary's commissioners were going to withdraw from the conference and declare it dissolved. Elizabeth and Cecil had no intention of ending matters until Moray had revealed his proofs, but it would look better, for foreign consumption, if Moray did this while the Marians were still officially participating in the conference. So, on December 6, Leslie's declara-

[25] This interpretation of Maitland's policy substantially follows that of E. Russell, *Maitland of Lethington*, pp. 403–5.
[26] Anderson, *Collections*, IV, Pt. II, 121–24. Lennox had been in York when the conference was in session there, but had not been permitted to appear before it. See his letter of October 9, 1568, to Cecil, *C.S.P., Scot.*, II, 523–24.
[27] Anderson, *Collections*, IV, Pt. II, 125–33.
[28] *Ibid.*, pp. 133–34, 158–61.   [29] *Ibid.*, pp. 134–40.

tion of dissolution was rejected on technical grounds, and pressure was put on Moray to justify himself. On that day the Regent handed in his *Book of Articles*, a chronological account of the case against Mary, which, if it is the one printed by Hosack, was largely the work of Buchanan and was highly inaccurate.[30] This by no means satisfied Cecil, and in the next few days, before the Marians presented a satisfactory proclamation of dissolution, he got what he wanted. Moray produced the Letters and a good deal of subsidiary material, including Morton's statement as to the discovery of the Casket and the depositions of Bothwell's henchmen, at least one of which was edited in order to protect some of Moray's allies, according to Lang.[31] This material was examined by the English Council on December 14 and 15, and they admitted, after studying Moray's proofs, that in the circumstances it would be dishonorable for Elizabeth to receive Mary.[32]

Elizabeth's objective had been attained, but the victory, she now realized, could not be turned fully to account. The situation in Europe was dangerous. England was on the verge of war with Spain, a war which neither Elizabeth nor Cecil wanted, but which might well come if Mary were too roughly handled at this juncture. Furthermore, there was some talk of a Franco-Spanish trade agreement directed against England.[33] Elizabeth therefore found it necessary to temporize. In spite of their "dissolution" of the conference, the Queen called in Herries and Leslie on December 16 and expressed her sorrow at Moray's unexpected revelations. She hoped that Mary would reply to them—not in person, of course; that was impossible—but by messenger. Otherwise it must be presumed that she was guilty.[34] Elizabeth nevertheless would not send copies of Moray's proofs to Mary until the latter promised to answer them.[35] Mary, however, refused to make any such

---

[30] *Ibid.*, pp. 144–49. Hosack, *Mary Queen of Scots*, pp. 522–48.

[31] Anderson, *Collections*, IV, Pt. II, 150–59. *C.S.P., Scot.*, II, 730–31. Andrew Lang, *A History of Scotland from the Roman Occupation*, II, 208, and *Mystery of Mary Stuart*, pp. 117–25. The Marian declaration of dissolution was accepted on December 9.   [32] Anderson, *Collections*, IV, Pt. II, 170–78.

[33] December 28, 1568, La Mothe-Fénélon to Catherine de Medici, in A. Teulet, ed., *Correspondance diplomatique de La Mothe-Fénélon*, I, 70–73.

[34] Anderson, *Collections*, IV, Pt. II, 179–82.

[35] December 20, 1568, Elizabeth to Knollys, *C.S.P., Scot.*, II, 586–88. Elizabeth's

promise—which would have been tantamount to acknowledging English jurisdiction over her—until she had seen the documents. A deadlock resulted. Elizabeth did not really want Mary to defend herself, however. Her real objective now was, curiously enough, very similar to Maitland's plan of October. On December 22 she instructed Knollys to suggest to Mary that she should ratify her abdication and recognize Moray's government. If Mary did this, the whole business would go no further—Elizabeth would pronounce no judgment.[36] Mary would have none of this, however. Now that she had been accused of the murder, her acquiescence in this plan would be a virtual admission of guilt.[37] Elizabeth was not to get out of her predicament so easily as that.

It was necessary, however, for the Queen to do something. Moray was clamoring for a decision; he had to go home, where conditions were most unsettled. On January 10, therefore, the Regent and his colleagues were summoned before the English commissioners, and Cecil pronounced his Queen's judgment: nothing had been said which in any way impaired their honor or allegiance. At the same time, they had said nothing which could induce Elizabeth to think badly of Mary.[38] In other words, both sides were innocent. As Tytler rightly observes, this "is perhaps the most absurd judicial opinion ever left upon record." [39] But Elizabeth, of course, was not concerned with justice. She had never had any intention of deciding in favor of Mary. But at this juncture it was politically impossible for her formally to pronounce in favor of Moray, on account of the danger of war with Spain.[40] Practically, of course, the decision was favorable to Moray. He was permitted to return home, and Mary was retained

---

decision on this point was supported by the English Council on January 13, 1569. *Ibid.,* pp. 600–601.

[36] Haynes, *Burghley Papers,* pp. 497–98. Whatever Mary's answer, however, the English had decided to support Moray's government. See Cecil's memorandum of December 22, 1568, *C.S.P., Scot.,* II, 589.

[37] January 9, 1569, Mary's Declaration, in Labanoff, *Recueil,* II, 274–77.

[38] D. Calderwood, *The History of the Kirk of Scotland,* II, 471–72.

[39] P. F. Tytler, *History of Scotland,* VII, 217.

[40] On January 3 the news of Alva's embargo on English property in the Netherlands reached London. Four days later England retaliated in kind, and on January 8, two days before Elizabeth's pronouncement, the Spanish ambassador was placed under house arrest. J. B. Black, *The Reign of Elizabeth,* p. 97.

in England as a prisoner. Small wonder that, as the French ambassador reported, Moray left for Scotland well pleased with the results of the conference.[41]

It is difficult to justify any of the parties to the conference on moral grounds. In spite of the accusations leveled against her, Mary emerges with more credit than anyone else, simply because her opponents, and Elizabeth in particular, were so manifestly dishonest and unfair. As Lang says, "It was the fate of Elizabeth and of Murray [sic] to make Mary's appear the better cause by the incredible dishonesty and hypocritical futility with which they handled her case." [42] For Elizabeth no defense is possible. Moray, at least, was not responsible for the fact that his accusations went unanswered. The principal charge against him is that he deliberately manipulated his evidence in order to protect those of his associates who were involved in the murder. We have seen why he found it necessary to do this. Aside from this, the Regent's role was not especially discreditable; he has suffered in the eyes of posterity more by association with Elizabeth's crookedness than for his own iniquities. The whole affair was a sorry business at best. It is not to be denied that the chief gainers were Moray and his party, for Mary's reputation was hopelessly besmirched, and her political prospects mortally damaged, and Elizabeth's triumph over her rival was to prove far more costly and dangerous to England than she had ever imagined it could be.

iii

Moray had been impatient for some time to get back to Scotland. As early as October 15 he had complained to Elizabeth that the conference was dragging and that, unless he could return home soon, Scotland would soon be in chaos.[43] Actually the situation in Scotland at this time was not particularly bad. There was a good deal of Border turmoil, as always, and an outbreak of the plague in Edinburgh, but until mid-December the Regent's parti-

[41] January 30, 1569, La Mothe-Fénélon to Catherine de Medici, in Teulet, *Correspondance diplomatique*, I, 160–62.   [42] Lang, *History of Scotland*, II, 209.
[43] *C.S.P., Scot.*, II, 530. See also his statement of October 21, 1568, *ibid.*, pp. 536–38.

sans, Mar, Kirkcaldy, and the rest, kept matters pretty well in hand.[44]

In December, however, the situation rapidly worsened. This was due to Moray's public accusation of Mary. No reconciliation between brother and sister was possible after this, and Mary began to do what she could to stir up trouble north of the Tweed. About December 10 she wrote to the Commendator of Arbroath, one of the Hamiltons, and to others, accusing Moray and Elizabeth of plotting to do what Henry VIII had attempted in the 1540s. Little James and the leading fortresses of Scotland were to be handed over to England. Moray planned to declare himself the next heir and to recognize English suzerainty over Scotland.[45] All of this was designed to rouse the country against Moray, and in spite of the falsity of Mary's charges she was successful in putting an end to the uneasy truce which had existed in Scotland since August. Argyle, Huntly, and the Hamiltons were preparing to rise, Hunsdon warned on December 20.[46] By the thirty-first things had become bad enough for Kirkcaldy to write a rather alarmist letter to Moray, urging him to hurry home as soon as possible.[47] The Marians made some progress against the Regent's men.[48] Early in January Mary attempted to add fuel to the fire by means of the "Protestation of Huntly and Argyle," discussed above, and by announcing to her friends the imminent prospect of French and Spanish aid.[49] Shortly thereafter Huntly and Argyle had the effrontery to request the officials of Edinburgh to issue their proclamation summarizing Mary's letter of December 10.[50] Kirkcaldy, far from making a defiant reply, wrote a polite letter to

[44] R. Lindsay of Pitscottie, *The Chronicles of Scotland*, II, 213. On the Border situation at this time, see Hunsdon's letters of November 15 and December 6, 1568, *Calendar of the Manuscripts of the Marquis of Salisbury*, I, 372, 376.

[45] *C.S.P., Scot.*, II, 574–75.   [46] Haynes, *Burghley Papers*, pp. 496–97.

[47] *C.S.P., Scot.*, II, 594.

[48] T. Thomson, ed., *A Diurnal of Remarkable Occurrents that Have Passed within the Country of Scotland*, p. 139. January 8, 1569, Huntly to Mary, in C. Innes, ed., *Registrum Honoris de Morton*, I, 39–40.

[49] See above, pp. 183–84. January 18, 1569, Mary to Archbishop Hamilton, *C.S.P., Scot.*, II, 604.

[50] Innes, *Registrum Honoris de Morton*, I, 40–41. Argyle actually did issue this proclamation, which is given in A. I. Cameron and R. S. Rait, eds., *The Warrender Papers*, I, 57–60.

Huntly. He was sure, he said, that Moray was being maligned.[51] Moray, on hearing of this, felt it necessary to ask Elizabeth to proclaim publicly that these stories were lies, which the Queen accordingly did, on January 22.[52]

Enough has been said to indicate that Moray's presence was urgently needed in Scotland. The conference had ended, and Mary's commissioners, when asked point-blank by the Regent if they wanted to accuse him of any connection with the murder of Darnley, had replied in the negative, after considerable shuffling.[53] The Border was rapidly being reduced to absolute chaos, and even Hume was having much ado to defend his position.[54] Yet still Moray delayed. One reason was his financial embarrassment; this was eased by a loan of £5,000 from Elizabeth.[55] But it was not primarily lack of money which kept the Regent in England. It was fear for his own safety.

Moray knew that Argyle and Huntly were preparing to resist his return by force.[56] But this did not worry him so much as his journey through northern England, which was heavily Catholic and very much aroused by his attack on Mary. He rightly discerned that the man chiefly responsible for this unhappy situation was Norfolk, who was embittered by the public accusation of Mary: it made his marriage to her far less feasible. Some writers have represented Moray's accusation of his sister as a "betrayal" of Norfolk, since he had agreed at York not to reveal the evidence against her. This is sheer nonsense. Moray made that pledge with specific reservations: he would honor it only if Elizabeth's policy turned out to be what Norfolk said it was, and if Mary consented

[51] January 14, 1569, Kirkcaldy to Huntly, *C.S.P., Scot.*, II, 607–8. Kirkcaldy had been Captain of Edinburgh Castle since September, 1567. Thomson, *Diurnal of Occurrents*, p. 124.
[52] January 21, 1569, Moray to Cecil, *C.S.P., Scot.*, II, 607. Elizabeth's proclamation is given in Calderwood, *History of the Kirk*, II, 474–76.
[53] *Ibid.*, pp. 472–73. G. Buchanan, *The History of Scotland*, II, 547–48. Leslie's "Discourse," in Anderson, *Collections*, III, 33–34. Moray took this step because Mary, in a set of instructions to her representatives, dated December 19, 1568, denied the charge of murder and accused Moray's party of the crime. Labanoff, *Recueil*, II, 257–61.
[54] January 15, January 19, 1569, Hunsdon to Cecil, *Calendar of the Manuscripts of the Marquis of Salisbury*, I, 391–92.   [55] *C.S.P., Scot.*, II, 603.
[56] January 15, 1569, Hunsdon to Cecil, in Haynes, *Burghley Papers*, pp. 502–3.

to ratify her abdication. On neither count did the conditions hold good: Elizabeth had promised, fairly definitely, to condemn Mary if the facts warranted an adverse judgment, and Mary had not ratified her abdication—at Norfolk's instigation. If anyone was guilty of betrayal in this business, Norfolk was.

Nevertheless the Duke was aggrieved, and the Regent, fearing that "my throat might be cut before I came to Berwick," as he put it, decided to approach him.[57] Moray met the Duke at Hampton Court, and, by his own admission, brought up the subject of Norfolk's marriage to Mary. The Regent said that he had been forced to accuse Mary in order to save himself, but that he really had nothing but affection for his sister, and could wish her no better husband than Norfolk—provided Elizabeth consented.[58] Norfolk, more ambitious than intelligent, was taken in by this, and ordered his friends in the north to stay their hands.[59] Mary was not optimistic about the situation, but she knew that her marriage to the Duke was, for the present, the only possibility that offered any hope at all of regaining her former position. So on January 30 she wrote Archbishop Hamilton, telling him to have her partisans in Scotland adopt a waiting game on Moray's return; she had reason to believe, she said, that the Regent would not attempt to handle them severely.[60]

Moray's behavior in this affair was certainly something less than straightforward. By no conceivable stretch of the imagination could he have desired a marriage between Mary and Norfolk, except on condition that Mary ratify her abdication, but of this he made no mention. His motive in bringing the matter up was, as he explained to Cecil, simply to make sure that he would get back home with a whole skin. In his description of the affair Moray went on to say that he adopted this course because he also feared that, in spite of all, some sort of compromise with Mary might be

[57] October, 1569, Moray to Cecil, in Robertson, *History of Scotland*, III, 368–74.
[58] October, 1569, Moray to Cecil, *ibid.*, pp. 368–74.
[59] Norfolk's northern allies obeyed his instructions, although the Catholic Westmoreland collected a force and demonstrated for Moray's benefit, by way of persuading the Regent to continue to favor Norfolk. Melville, *Memoirs*, p. 215.
[60] Labanoff, *Recueil*, II, 294–95.

crammed down his throat by Elizabeth, and he had good grounds for this fear, since Elizabeth had refused to render a favorable decision at the conference. Nevertheless, as the sequel was to show, even if Elizabeth did want a compromise, this particular one was most distasteful to her. Moray doubtless guessed as much, and by making his approval dependent on that of Elizabeth, he left himself with an almost infallible means of wrecking the whole marriage scheme. It was fortunate for Moray that Norfolk, whose head was turned by his dreams of a crown, did not see the pitfalls that awaited him.

By the end of January Moray was on his way north. Elizabeth provided him with an escort through northern England, and ordered her Marcher Wardens to recognize Moray's government and to admit no Scot to England who did not carry the Regent's passport.[61] This was further than Elizabeth had ever gone before on the path to complete official recognition of James VI. Moray on January 31 thanked her and Cecil for the escort and for publicly denying the rumors which the Marians were spreading, and urged Cecil to be sure that Mary could not escape.[62] These letters were written from Berwick; on February 2 the Regent entered Edinburgh.[63]

Moray had every right to feel satisfied with the results of his four months' sojourn in England. He had picked his way through a maze of intrigue and had come out with virtually all he wanted. From the strictly judicial point of view, of course, the conference had settled nothing. No verdict of "guilty" had been handed down. But Moray, and everyone else, knew that, allowance being made for the exigencies of the foreign situation, English support could now be depended on, and with that support the dominance of Protestantism was assured.

This did not mean, however, that the Regent's troubles were over. There remained the problem of Mary's supporters in Scotland, a problem which had increased in seriousness owing to the conference. The patent dishonesty of the proceedings at West-

---

[61] Haynes, *Burghley Papers*, pp. 501-2.   [62] *Ibid.*, pp. 505-6.
[63] Thomson, *Diurnal of Occurrents*, p. 139.

minster, coupled with Mary's belated decision to renounce Both-well, had produced a split in the Regent's party. Maitland and his friends must be regarded as enemies from now on. Moray had gained more than he lost, for the support of Elizabeth was more valuable than that of Maitland. Nevertheless the difficulties were great. To these difficulties the Regent now addressed himself.

CHAPTER XII

The Last Year of the Regency

THE REGENT now had less than a year to live. During that year the problems which confronted him were much the same as before. Mary's supporters in Scotland were still dangerous, and, in spite of the favorable result of the conference just held, relations with Elizabeth continued to be difficult. The source of all Moray's difficulties, of course, was Mary herself. In 1569 the presence of Mary in England, added to the tense domestic situation there, led to the last great internal crisis of British Protestantism in the sixteenth century. Moray had a hand in bringing the crisis to a head, and lived to see it pass. Then, as he was preparing the *coup de grâce* for his opponents, he was struck down.

Moray's first move after his return was to summon the Privy Council and request its approval of his actions in England, which was readily given, on February 12.[1] Two days later the lieges of the Lowlands were summoned for March 10, to march against the Marians.[2] The Regent's strong hand soon made itself felt. On February 16 Hunsdon reported that Moray had raided Jedburgh with a large body of horse and had captured some sixty malefactors.[3] Moray's activity did not mean, however, that he had returned to his post-Langside policy of attempting to crush his opponents by force. It was necessary to collect an army in order to demonstrate to those opponents that he could destroy them if he so wished, but what he really wanted now was to come to

---

[1] *The Register of the Privy Council of Scotland*, I, 644.
[2] *Ibid.*, pp. 644-45. [3] *C.S.P., For., Eliz.*, IX, 33.

terms with the Marians, on condition that they recognized his authority and that of James VI.

In reverting to a policy of conciliation the Regent was swayed by two considerations. In the first place, he felt that the result of the York-Westminster Conference would make the Marians amenable to compromise if he showed himself ready to go part way. The Marians had counted on English help in restoring the Queen, and Elizabeth's change of sides could not but dishearten them. In February Moray asked Cecil to send a token military force to join his levy against the Marians as an indication of English support. By March 10, however, the English had not yet agreed to do this.[4]

Moray's second motive for adopting a conciliatory attitude was his fear that a return to the policy of repression would lead to an open break with Maitland and his followers. He no longer trusted the Secretary, but he did not wish to add to the number of his enemies if he could avoid it. Once the Marian leaders had submitted, Maitland would be isolated and politically helpless, and then Moray could drop the mask in the matter of the Norfolk marriage. The Regent's seeming friendliness toward Norfolk served a dual purpose at this time: it kept Maitland from openly joining his foes, and it tended to make the Marians more willing to compromise, since they felt that Moray's support was necessary to get Elizabeth to agree to the marriage, which now was their best hope for Mary's restoration. Moray's real attitude toward the marriage had not changed, however; he was biding his time until he could smash the project beyond repair.

The rapidity with which Moray gathered his strength disconcerted and alarmed his opponents. Châtelherault, who arrived in Scotland late in February, wrote to the General Assembly on February 27, asking that body to prevent Moray from assailing him. The Assembly promised to present the Duke's request to the Regent; at the same time it showed what it thought of the Marians by denouncing them as Papists.[5] Moray, however, set out deter-

---

[4] February 17, 1569, Moray to Cecil, *C.S.P., Scot.*, II, 621. February 25, 1569, Moray to Elizabeth, *ibid.*, p. 625.
[5] D. Calderwood, *The History of the Kirk of Scotland*, II, 479–85.

minedly after Châtelherault, after issuing a proclamation which—
stretching the truth—declared that the English Council had admitted Mary's guilt.[6] The feeble Duke sent to dissuade Moray
from attacking him. To his surprise he found the Regent perfectly willing to treat. On March 13 an agreement was made between the parties. The Marians were to acknowledge the authority of James VI and the Regent. In return, some of them would be
admitted to the council, and their forfeitures would be revoked,
except in the case of those who had been involved in the murder
of Darnley. As for Mary, on April 10 there was to be a meeting
at Edinburgh between the Regent and four members of each
party—Châtelherault, Huntly, Argyle, and Herries on the one
hand, and Morton, Mar, Athol, and Glencairn on the other—and
the problem of Mary was to be discussed. In the meantime neither
side was to act against the other. Pledges were given by the
Marians that they would observe these terms.[7]

This agreement indicates clearly the direction of Moray's policy. He was willing to make concessions to Mary's supporters, on
condition that they submitted to his government.[8] At one stroke
he had neutralized half the opposition—or so it seemed. But Moray
well knew that Châtelherault was irresolute and undependable,
and he resolved to keep his army together until April 10, to guard
against all eventualities. On March 11 he had written to Elizabeth,
asking once again for support; this time his request was granted.
Two hundred foot, about forty horse, and some ammunition were
sent from Berwick on March 25.[9] The Regent found uses for
them. Since it was not necessary to turn his levies against the
Hamiltons, Moray decided to use them against the fractious Borderers. In spite of the presence of a number of the great Border
chiefs in Moray's army, the trip was not very successful, owing
largely to bad weather. It was not political differences, but the

[6] C.S.P., Scot., II, 631–32.
[7] T. Thomson, ed., A Diurnal of Remarkable Occurrents that Have Passed within
the Country of Scotland, pp. 140–42.
[8] Moray himself described his policy in these terms in a letter to Forster, of
March 15, 1569, C.S.P., For., Eliz., IX, 46–47.
[9] C.S.P., Scot., II, 630. April 8, 1569, Captain Reed to Cecil, Calendar of the Manuscripts of the Marquis of Salisbury, I, 405–6.

Borderers' dislike of Moray's evident determination to put an end
to their traditional occupation, that led them to oppose the Regent, Hunsdon opined.[10]

Early in April Moray returned to Edinburgh to await the forthcoming meeting with Châtelherault. As an earnest of good faith
he had ordered the release of a number of the prisoners taken at
Langside.[11] He evidently expected that the meeting would be
little more than a formality. He was to be surprised. As the first
order of business, Moray presented Châtelherault with a paper
acknowledging the authority of James VI. The Duke quite un-
expectedly refused to sign it. This was owing to his having just
received letters from Mary pleading with him to remain loyal to
her.[12] Moray was incensed at this violation of the March agreement and decided to make use of his superior force to execute a
coup de main. The Duke and Herries were promptly clapped
into Edinburgh Castle. The Earl of Cassilis, who agreed to recognize Moray's authority in spite of Mary's pleas, was permitted to
go free.[13]

The Regent did not neglect his other opponents, who were disconcerted by his evident strength and determination. In April
the revenues of the benefices of the Archbishop of Glasgow,
Mary's faithful ambassador in France, were confiscated and given
to Glencairn and the Laird of Minto.[14] The Regent issued proclamations against Huntly, his most powerful opponent, and prepared to march against him.[15] Huntly was loyal to Mary, to whom
he owed everything, and hung back as long as he could. He sent

[10] March 30, 1569, Hunsdon to Cecil, *ibid.*, p. 403. April 8, 1569, Captain Reed to
Cecil, *ibid.*, pp. 405–6. March 15, 1569, Moray to Forster, *C.S.P., For., Eliz.*, IX,
46–47. March 30, 1569, Forster to Cecil, *C.S.P., Scot.*, II, 636.
[11] Thomson, *Diurnal of Occurrents*, p. 143.
[12] April 23, May 6, 1569, La Mothe-Fénélon to Catherine de Medici, in A. Teulet,
ed., *Correspondance diplomatique de La Mothe-Fénélon*, I, 348–49, 369–70.
[13] Thomson, *Diurnal of Occurrents*, p. 144. T. Thomson, ed., *The Historie and
Life of King James the Sext*, p. 40. *Register of Privy Council*, Addenda, XIV, 27.
Mary's letter to Cassilis, dated April 7, 1569, is given in *Historical Manuscripts
Commission, 5th Report*, Appendix, p. 616.
[14] April 28, 1569, Thomas Archibald to the Archbishop of Glasgow, in A. Mac-
George, ed., *Miscellaneous Papers Principally Illustrative of Events in the Reigns
of Queen Mary and King James VI*, pp. 25–28.
[15] *Register of Privy Council*, I, 645–47, 656–57.

her a despairing letter in April, telling her that his military strength was rapidly waning, and that he needed some 1,500 to 2,000 French troops at once in order to maintain himself.[16] This was a vain hope, as Huntly well knew. By the beginning of May he found himself no longer able to control his own supporters. On May 6 one of his most important northern adherents, the Earl of Crawford, went to St. Andrews to make his submission to Moray and received his remission after promising to satisfy those who had complaints against him.[17] Four days later Argyle, who had been negotiating since February with the Regent, came in, and was granted a pardon also.[18]

Huntly now bowed to the inevitable and came to St. Andrews to treat with Moray. The latter was not disposed to be lenient. Huntly would be pardoned, and so would his followers, provided they all submitted quickly and personally to the Regent or his officials. Huntly had to give hostages for his future good behavior, and he had to promise further that he would deliver his cannon to Moray and would settle with all those who had financial claims against him for damages suffered at his hands during his rebellion. A three-man commission, none of whom had any love for Huntly, was appointed to pass on the claims. In this way Moray hoped to cripple Huntly's power and make it impossible for him to rebel again. The Earl had no choice but to accept these Draconian terms; on May 14 he submitted.[19]

According to Buchanan there was a long and heated debate in the Privy Council over the terms to be offered to Huntly, a number of members urging that he be accorded the same treatment as Argyle.[20] Moray decided otherwise, not so much because Huntly was an especially refractory foe as because his authority in the north was that of a petty king. It was high time, the Regent thought, that the strong hand of the central government made

[16] A. Teulet, ed., *Relations politiques de la France et de l'Espagne avec l'Ecosse au XVIe siècle*, II, 395–96.   [17] *Register of Privy Council*, I, 662–63.
[18] February 17, 1569, Hunsdon to Cecil, in S. Haynes, ed., *The Burghley Papers (1542–1570)*, p. 508. *Register of Privy Council*, Addenda, XIV, 27.
[19] *Register of Privy Council*, I, 663–65. J. Stuart, ed., *Miscellany of the Spalding Club*, III, 243–45. May 19, 1569, Hunsdon to the English Council, *C.S.P., For., Eliz.*, IX, 75–76.   [20] G. Buchanan, *The History of Scotland*, II, 557–60.

itself felt in the Highlands. He therefore decided, on May 16, to tour Huntly's domain in force.[21] His expedition set out from Brechin in early June; that month and almost all of July were spent by Moray in the north. He received the submissions of Huntly's followers, most of whom were heavily fined, a process which served the twofold purpose of weakening Huntly and of replenishing the Regent's treasury.[22]

Besides dealing with the former rebels, Moray also disposed of a good deal of ordinary judicial work in the Highlands, especially during his stay at Inverness in mid-June.[23] This fact indicates that he made this journey not only to insure the good behavior of Huntly but also to reassert the government's authority in the north, as he had attempted to do on the Border. The Highland problem was less pressing than that of the Border, because good relations with England did not depend on its settlement. But Moray had long realized that a powerful and orderly Scotland could be created only if the outlying districts were made to submit to the authority of the crown. His efforts in the Highlands were spasmodic because of his preoccupation with other affairs, and they ultimately proved unsuccessful. He had been prevented from fully exploiting the victory of Corrichie, and death intervened before he was able to take advantage of the situation created by his forcefulness in 1569.[24] His persistence on the Border bore fruit eventually, for his successors carried out his policy with the aid of England, and the job was completed by James VI after his accession to the English throne. The Highlands, however, remained a thorn in the side of the Scottish, and later of the British, government until the days of Bonnie Prince Charlie.

The Kirk made its presence felt during Moray's northern tour. The principal officers of the University of Aberdeen were ousted for Popery, and some witches were burned at St. Andrews and

---

[21] *Register of Privy Council*, I, 665–66.
[22] Thomson, *Diurnal of Occurrents*, pp. 144–45. Thomson, *Historie of James the Sext*, p. 42.   [23] *Register of Privy Council*, I, 670–73.
[24] A decision of the council on November 22, 1569, indicates that Moray probably planned to return to the Highlands in 1570. *Ibid.*, II, 56–58.

Dundee.[25] Not all of the favors went in one direction, however. The General Assembly, on July 5, in response to a request from Moray, voted to grant him part of the Kirk's income from the thirds to finance his expedition against Huntly.[26] During July, however, Moray's thoughts were not really centered on the Kirk, or even on Huntly. A most alarming situation had developed in England, which threatened once more to wreck all his carefully laid plans and which had to be handled with the utmost care if ruin were not, after all, to overtake him.

ii

Elizabeth and her advisers, as they surveyed the domestic and foreign scene in early 1569, found but little to cheer them. War with Spain was more than possible, and to this unpleasant prospect was added the equally unpalatable one of a war with France.[27] Because of the Spanish situation Elizabeth had been deprived of some of the advantages she had anticipated from the York-Westminster Conference, and a captive but uncondemned Mary was proving a serious embarrassment. The English government was bombarded with protests from the imprisoned Queen and her supporters, coupled with insistent requests that she be restored.[28] Elizabeth therefore decided to make one more effort to eliminate Mary as a possible source of danger by promoting a reconciliation between her and Moray. On May 1 Cecil drew up a memorandum embodying the English conditions. Three alternatives were to be laid before Moray. Mary might be persuaded to ratify her abdication and live in England; or she and her son might rule jointly; or she might be restored, under stringent guarantees for Protestantism and the security of Moray and his friends.[29] Cecil did not care for this policy. He felt that Mary's restoration would

[25] *Ibid.*, I, 675–76. Thomson, *Diurnal of Occurrents*, p. 145. R. Lindsay of Pitscottie, *The Chronicles of Scotland*, II, 218, 448.
[26] Moray's letter to the General Assembly is dated June 30, 1569. Calderwood, *History of the Kirk*, II, 498–502.
[27] For an account of England's relations with France and Spain in 1569, see J. B. Black, *The Reign of Elizabeth*, pp. 95–103.
[28] See, for instance, Mary's letter of April 25, 1569, to Elizabeth, in A. Labanoff, ed., *Recueil des lettres de Marie Stuart*, II, 329–30.
[29] *C.S.P., Scot.*, II, 642. Haynes, *Burghley Papers*, pp. 516–17.

be a positive evil more dangerous than the hypothetical perils it was designed to avert.[30] But for the moment his advice was disregarded.

Elizabeth's terms were dispatched to the Regent on May 16.[31] Before that date Leslie had made it abundantly clear that only the third possibility would be acceptable to Mary.[32] In spite of this, the alternatives were sent to Moray. It is difficult to avoid the conclusion that Elizabeth really expected and desired Mary's restoration; her anger when Moray rebuffed her seems genuine enough. Fear of war evidently caused the English Queen to lose sight of political realities for the moment. She should have known that Moray, after the revelations at Westminster, could countenance no scheme which would bring Mary back to Scotland except as a helpless captive.

At almost the same time Mary sent a message to her brother through the intermediary of Lord Boyd. He was to assure Moray that Mary, if she were restored, would abide by the guarantees included in Elizabeth's proposals. Mary also wanted a divorce from Bothwell, obviously to pave the way for her marriage with Norfolk.[33] A large number of English nobles were beginning to look favorably on the scheme for one reason or another—so many, in fact, that even Cecil had to pretend to have no objections to it.[34] The ultimate purpose of Norfolk and his friends was, of course, Mary's restoration in Scotland and her recognition as Elizabeth's heir. Hence they ardently supported Elizabeth's plan of coercing Moray into acquiescence in his sister's restoration, but they kept the rest of their designs carefully concealed from the Queen. They were attempting to use Elizabeth to force Moray's hand; they also hoped to use Moray to get Elizabeth to agree to the marriage of Mary and Norfolk. They dared not mention the subject to Elizabeth themselves, but they hoped that

[30] See his letter to Elizabeth of October 6, 1569, *C.S.P., Scot.*, II, 683–84.
[31] *Ibid.*, p. 647.
[32] On May 8, 1569. *Ibid.*, pp. 644–45.
[33] For Boyd's instructions see *ibid.*, p. 650. See also J. Maidment, ed., *Miscellany of the Abbotsford Club*, I, 23–27.
[34] Black, *Reign of Elizabeth*, pp. 98–99, 102. Andrew Lang, *A History of Scotland from the Roman Occupation*, II, 217–18.

Moray, when confronted with Elizabeth's demand for Mary's restoration, would propose the marriage to Elizabeth as the only means of safeguarding Protestantism and the Anglo-Scottish alliance in the event of Mary's restoration. Thus Norfolk and his friends hoped to maneuver the rulers of England and Scotland into compelling each other to accept a policy which they both disliked, and which had as its ultimate object the overturning of the policies of both.[35] It was a plan worthy of a Maitland.

Moray understood something of what was afoot in Norfolk's camp, but he was, unfortunately, in a false position owing to his involvement in the early stages of the marriage scheme. Since his return to Scotland he had continued friendly to Norfolk, probably in order to keep Maitland and his friends quiet while Huntly, Argyle, and the rest were being subdued. Even after the submission of Huntly he failed to indicate his real attitude to the marriage, in the hope that Elizabeth and Cecil would wreck it without his being involved; this would, he thought, prevent an open break with Maitland. Even Elizabeth's message on Mary's restoration did not worry him unduly, although he was surprised by it. Up to this time Elizabeth had been most friendly.[36] On June 5 Moray wrote to Elizabeth, expressing his surprise at her *volte-face*, and explaining that he could not give her a reply at once, since he was in the north and would have to consult with his supporters first.[37] Meanwhile, he sent Wood to check up on Maitland. Wood found the Secretary ill and noncommittal, but pleased with Elizabeth's message.[38] Even after this Moray remained on friendly terms with Norfolk, who as late as July 1 wrote the Regent a fulsome letter.[39] Moray evidently did not yet see in what direction affairs were tending.

The appearance of Boyd, however, made everything painfully clear. Be it remembered that the Regent did not realize that Eliza-

---

[35] On this point see July 20, 1569, Throckmorton to Maitland, in W. Robertson, *The History of Scotland*, III, 366–68. The plan had Catholic backing in England, of course, but for expediency's sake Mary was to turn Anglican. See Leslie's memorial of June 3, 1569, *C.S.P., Scot.*, II, 651–52.

[36] See, for instance, the arrangement made in March to supply Moray with food, ammunition, and specie, *ibid.*, p. 636.   [37] *Ibid.*, p. 652.

[38] June 10, 1569, Wood to Cecil, *ibid.*, p. 653.

[39] Haynes, *Burghley Papers*, pp. 520–21.

beth was no party to the marriage scheme. Since he knew that her favorite Leicester had known of the business almost from its inception, he naturally assumed that Elizabeth had heard about it.[40] He was aware of the threatening foreign situation, and assumed that Elizabeth had been frightened into adopting a policy which was not in her best interests and which was certainly not in the best interests of Scotland or Protestantism. Elizabeth might be frightened by this situation. Moray, however, was not.

In the first place, Moray had succeeded, for the first time since Mary's escape from Lochleven, in reducing all of Scotland to his will. He was, for the moment, safe from attack at home. Even if Maitland and his friends did rise, Mary's original supporters were in no condition to help them, and Maitland's party was too weak to challenge the Regent alone. Secondly, Moray felt that on this occasion he could defy Elizabeth with impunity. He knew that the foreign situation was responsible for Elizabeth's renewed friendliness to Mary. Consequently, the Regent thought, it was inconceivable that Elizabeth would use force in Mary's behalf. Therefore Moray decided unhesitatingly to reject both Elizabeth's and Mary's proposals. He had to walk warily, however, in order to avoid, if possible, any inconvenient revelations about his own share in the marriage scheme. To this end he decided to call a Convention of the Estates, which would actually do the rejecting; this would have the further advantage of demonstrating to Elizabeth and the world at large that Scottish opinion was solidly behind him on this question. On July 7 he informed Elizabeth that both her proposals and those of Mary would be submitted to a Convention, to be held at Perth toward the end of the month.[41] Elizabeth's impatience for an answer, and the threats of Norfolk's friends, failed to sway him or hurry him.[42]

[40] On this point see Moray's letter to Cecil in October, in Robertson, *History of Scotland*, III, 368–74. Maitland later opined that Moray's policy was based on the supposition that Elizabeth did not know of the marriage plan and would have opposed it had she known of it. Maitland here seems to be attributing to the Regent knowledge which was confined to the Norfolk camp, however. September 20, 1569, Maitland to Mary, *C.S.P., Scot.*, II, 676–77.   [41] *Ibid.*, p. 658.
[42] July 17, 1569, Elizabeth to Moray, *ibid.*, pp. 660–61. July 20, 1569, Throckmorton to Moray, *ibid.*, p. 661. July 24, 1569, Moray to Elizabeth, *ibid.*, p. 662. See also J. Spottiswoode, *The History of the Church of Scotland*, p. 230.

At the same time, he gave an indication of what his answer was likely to be by confiscating the revenues of Leslie's bishopric, in the face of Elizabeth's express prohibition.[43] Such a move would scarcely have been politic had he expected Mary's return to power.

The Perth Convention assembled on July 28. The first order of business was a discussion of the English proposals. The two alternatives suggested by Elizabeth which would have meant Mary's restoration were rejected out of hand. The third alternative, which involved Mary's recognition of James VI, and which therefore meant a strengthening of Moray's government, was, naturally, acceptable, and Moray was authorized to negotiate with Elizabeth on that suggestion only. After a day devoted to the affairs of the Kirk, the Convention on July 30 began its consideration of Mary's message. The key question, of course, was the divorce, and over this an acrimonious dispute broke out, Maitland and McGill being the principals. Moray remained studiously neutral throughout the debate, but everyone knew what his position was. Maitland had a difficult time. His followers were in a small minority, and Mary's tactlessness in referring to herself as Queen and to Archbishop Hamilton as head of the Scottish Church inflamed Protestant opinion. The question was put to a vote, and Mary's proposals were rejected by a count of 40 to 9. Included in the nine were Maitland, Huntly, Balfour, and Athol. Argyle, Herries, and Châtelherault were not present. With these exceptions, all the important men in Scotland supported the Regent. Maitland had to content himself with congratulating the victors on their solicitude for Mary's domestic happiness; for the moment, at least, he could do no more.[44]

Moray's decision spelled ruin for the elaborate plans of Norfolk and was indirectly responsible for precipitating the Northern Rebellion in England at the end of the year. Now Mary could be restored only by force, and Elizabeth could not be expected to

[43] June 1, 1569, Elizabeth to Moray, *C.S.P., Scot.*, II, 650–51. July 16, 1569, "Memorial by the Bishop of Ross," *ibid.*, p. 660.
[44] *Register of Privy Council*, II, 1–6, 8–9. August 3, 1569, Hunsdon to Cecil, *C.S.P., For., Eliz.*, IX, 106–7. August 3, 1569, Moray to Elizabeth, *C.S.P., Scot.*, II, 664.

go as far as this. Furthermore, Elizabeth could not now be coerced by the unanimous opinion of every important public figure in both kingdoms into consenting to the marriage of Mary and Nor-folk. The Duke's friends began to desert him. It was now only a matter of time before one of them would reveal the marriage pro-ject to Elizabeth.

But Elizabeth, for the moment at least, was very unhappy about Moray's rejection of her proposals. The foreign situation was still dangerous. In August she wrote the Regent two very angry letters, threatening him with reprisals if he continued intransigent, giving him orders on domestic policy, and dismissing his attempted explanation of the Perth decisions with contempt.[45] Moray re-fused to modify his position and ignored her advice on domestic affairs. But he was, as always, anxious to conciliate her. Early in September he sent the Commendator of Dunfermline to England, with a long and careful explanation of the political and religious dangers which would result if Mary were restored.[46] Before Dunfermline could deliver his message, however, the situation in England had radically changed, as we shall see.

Moray knew full well that his refusal to consider Mary's re-storation would raise up new enemies for him at home. Maitland and his friends, who thus far had acquiesced in the Regent's pol-icy, were now permanently alienated. Moray therefore decided that it would be well to stamp out the last vestiges of opposition on the part of Mary's other friends before Maitland could or-ganize his forces and rise against him. On August 1 Huntly was ordered to settle with all those who had complaints against him before the twentieth. At the same time Glencairn and Sempill were told off to conduct the siege of Dumbarton, the last impor-tant Marian stronghold.[47] On August 28 Moray announced plans for a forthcoming Border expedition.[48] Political fences also needed mending, especially in respect to the Kirk, whose support

---

[45] *Ibid.*, pp. 668, 670–71. At the same time Norfolk wrote Moray, in much the same vein. *Ibid.*, p. 669.
[46] Dunfermline's instructions are given in R. Wodrow, *Collections upon the Lives of the Reformers and Most Eminent Ministers of the Church of Scotland*, I, 325–37.   [47] *Register of Privy Council*, II, 9–12, 20–24, 25–26, 65–66.
[48] *Ibid.*, p. 19.

was now more than ever necessary owing to the defection of Maitland. In June and July the Regent promised to try to get all the manses and glebes required for the support of the ministers, even if an Act of Parliament were required; recognized the Kirk's jurisdiction over all cases involving witchcraft and divorce; and also acceded to a number of less important requests.[49] In return, the Kirk supported the Regent's policy loyally and continued to grant Moray part of their share of the funds raised from the thirds for the expenses of his government and for his private household.[50]

All these moves were but palliatives, however. The real trouble was Maitland. Moray therefore decided to strike at the root. After the Perth Convention Maitland had holed up with Athol; at the end of August the two were summoned to Stirling by the Regent, ostensibly to discuss what message Dunfermline was to carry to Elizabeth. Maitland was suspicious, but he decided to go, in the hope of persuading the Regent to alter the decision made at Perth. Moray greeted him in friendly fashion. On September 3, however, there was admitted to the council chamber Thomas Crawford, a retainer of Lennox, who, ostensibly on Lennox's behalf, accused Maitland of guilty foreknowledge of the murder of Darnley. This charge was based on the confession of French Paris, a servant of Bothwell's, who had been apprehended toward the end of 1568 and recently executed for his part in the murder. The council immediately voted that Maitland should be imprisoned until his trial, which was set for late November. At the same time Moray sent a force to Fife to arrest Balfour on the same charge; the latter was now a supporter of Maitland's.[51]

The Secretary was removed from Stirling to Edinburgh, where he was lodged in the house of a supporter of Moray's named Forrester. Thence he was carried off to the Castle by Kirkcaldy, on September 9, but not because Moray had so ordered.[52] Kirkcaldy,

[49] Ibid., pp. 6–7. Calderwood, History of the Kirk, II, 490–504.
[50] Ibid., pp. 535–36.
[51] August 30, 1569, Hunsdon to Cecil, C.S.P., For., Eliz., IX, 119. September 16, 1569, Maitland to Norfolk, in A. I. Cameron and R. S. Rait, eds., The Warrender Papers, I, 63–70. October 23, 1569, Maitland to Cecil, C.S.P., Scot., II, 691. Thomson, Historie of James the Sext, pp. 42–43. Paris's confession is dated August 10, 1569. J. Anderson, ed., Collections Relating to the History of Mary Queen of Scots, II, 192–205.   [52] Thomson, Diurnal of Occurrents, p. 149.

in fact, seems to have gone to the extent of forging the Regent's signature in order to get Forrester to surrender his prisoner.[53] Why Kirkcaldy did this is not entirely clear, for he certainly was absolutely loyal to Moray personally. Probably he was motivated by an outraged sense of justice. He had always advocated the prosecution of all the murders of Darnley, which, for political reasons, Moray could not undertake. Kirkcaldy had acquiesced in the punishment of Mary and Bothwell only, because he felt that theirs was the greatest guilt. But Maitland was no more guilty than half a dozen others, whom Moray was making no attempt to punish, and the political motive behind the accusation of Maitland was obvious.

Contemporary opinion tended to attribute the accusation of Maitland not to Moray but to a clique headed by Morton, with whom Maitland was bitterly at feud.[54] This attitude Moray affected to encourage, once Kirkcaldy had made his move. How far Maitland believed this is hard to say, but Kirkcaldy certainly did, and his personal loyalty to the Regent remained unshaken, despite his dislike of the latter's policy.[55] It is, nevertheless, very hard to believe that Moray was not involved in the accusation. Morton would hardly have made such a move on his own responsibility, and the whole affair was extremely convenient politically for the Regent. Furthermore, the stage-managing of the accusation was typical of Moray's methods of procedure, which involved a cautious avoidance of responsibility whenever it might prove politically advantageous to do so—witness his method of handling the "eik" at Westminster, as related by Melville.[56] In this case caution paid: Kirkcaldy remained loyal.

[53] So say Buchanan (*History*, II, 567), and Knox's secretary, Richard Bannatyne (*Memoriales of Transactions in Scotland* [*1569-1573*], p. 1).
[54] Thomson, *Diurnal of Occurrents*, pp. 148–49. In August rumors circulated of a plot being hatched against Morton by Maitland, Athol, Crawford, and Ruthven. *Ibid.*, p. 147. Sir James Melville (*Memoirs of his own Life*, p. 218), asserts that Kirkcaldy seized Maitland to prevent his being convoyed to Morton's stronghold of Tantallon. Melville is an unreliable authority for this period, however. He tended to support Maitland's general policy, and consequently much of what he says about Moray's motives and behavior must be discounted. On this point see T. McCrie, *The Life of John Knox*, II, 338–41.
[55] September 16, 1569, Maitland to Norfolk, in Cameron and Rait, *Warrender Papers*, I, 63–70. Buchanan, *History*, II, 568. October 23, 1569, Kirkcaldy to Bedford, *C.S.P., Scot.*, II, 691–92.   [56] See above, p. 243.

Moray sent an account of Maitland's arrest to England with Dunfermline.[57] By the time the latter arrived in London, however, his instructions on this matter and on the decisions at Perth had become obsolete. For early in September Elizabeth heard of the Norfolk marriage scheme. She was enraged at Norfolk and Mary, and all thought of restoring the latter vanished from her mind. Norfolk, who was contemplating rebellion with the aid of the Catholics of northern England, threw in his hand after a futile attempt to hide from Elizabeth's wrath by burying himself in the country. This broke the back of the conspiracy, but did not prevent his allies in the marriage plan, Northumberland and Westmoreland, from rising in November in behalf of the old religion, in what is known in English history as the Northern Rebellion.[58]

The revelation of Norfolk's plotting brought about an abrupt change in Elizabeth's attitude toward Moray. She was now more than willing to support him—but first she wanted to know all about his connection with the marriage plan. On September 17 Hunsdon met Moray at Coldstream on Border business. When queried, the Regent said that he had not objected to the marriage, provided Elizabeth consented to it.[59] Elizabeth, who evidently was anxious to pin a charge of treason on Norfolk if possible, was not satisfied with this; she wanted further information.[60] On October 29 Moray replied, giving a substantially accurate account of the development of the affair and of his attitude toward it, but omitting from his narrative his own part in the reopening of the question in January 1569.[61] In a letter to Cecil, written about the same time, however, Moray did admit to having opened the matter to Norfolk at Westminster.[62] The Regent tried to get Maitland to reveal his part in the business; the latter refused, probably in order to conceal his own treachery to Moray at York rather than out of fondness for Norfolk. The Regent thereupon sent a copy of Paris's confession, which implicated Maitland in

[57] C.S.P., Scot., II, 673.
[58] For an account of the Northern Rebellion, see Black, *Reign of Elizabeth*, pp. 103–12.   [59] Haynes, *Burghley Papers*, pp. 523–24.
[60] October 6, 1569, Cecil to Elizabeth, C.S.P., Scot., II, 683–84. October 13, 1569, Elizabeth to Moray, *ibid.*, p. 687.   [61] *Ibid.*, pp. 693–94.
[62] Robertson, *History of Scotland*, III, 368–74.

the Darnley affair, to Cecil.[63] By the time Moray's various explanations reached England, however, the Northern Rebellion had broken out, and we hear no more about the Norfolk marriage in Moray's lifetime.

Moray's critics have seized upon this affair as another example of his fathomless wickedness. Norfolk, they say, was "betrayed" by Moray, who was basely currying favor with Elizabeth. This is, to say the least, exaggerated. Moray did not reveal the marriage scheme to Elizabeth; and as soon as the Queen discovered it, she became favorable to Moray once more. On September 21 Henry Carew was sent to Scotland by Elizabeth to ask about the Norfolk business, and to try to work out with the Regent some plan whereby Mary could be returned to Scotland as a captive, with suitable guarantees that her life would be safe.[64] On October 7, long before Moray's official explanation reached London, Elizabeth ordered Scrope to cooperate as closely as possible with the Regent on the Border.[65] Moray did not need to purchase Elizabeth's friendship by revealing his dealings with Norfolk. Furthermore, Moray had expressly informed the Duke that his consent to the plan depended on that of Elizabeth. He had made no promise to approach Elizabeth on the matter or to keep it from her should she inquire about it. It is true that his letter to Elizabeth did not tell the whole truth; it was a politician's letter. But that to Cecil did. To argue that Moray should have denied all, as Maitland did, is to say that he should have jeopardized the English alliance, the work of a decade, on behalf of a man to whom he had committed himself only under certain conditions which had not been fulfilled, and of a policy which was thoroughly distasteful to him. Moray's detractors would have a case only if they could show that Moray himself revealed the marriage plan to Elizabeth. But this they cannot do.

While all this was going on, Moray was dealing with the old, familiar problem of the Border. From mid-September to mid-

---

[63] C.S.P., Scot., II, 698.
[64] Haynes, Burghley Papers, pp. 524–25. This was the solution Cecil desired: see his memorandum of October 17, 1569, C.S.P., Scot., II, 688.
[65] C.S.P., For., Eliz., IX, 129.

October he was at Kelso; the lieges assembled on October 18, and shortly thereafter Moray set out on a tour of pacification.[66] It was highly successful, so successful that, in the words of a contemporary, "there was such obedience made by the said thieves to the said Regent, as the like was never done to no king in no man's days . . . before." [67] Early in November Moray returned to Edinburgh, to prepare for Maitland's "day of law," which was scheduled for the twenty-second. Maitland, too, had been making preparations. On October 31 he sent out letters to all his friends, actual and potential, urging them to come to Edinburgh for the trial, in the good old Scottish fashion.[68] Come they did, in force, led by Hume. Moray was prepared for this, but he did not wish to precipitate a clash which, even if he won, would lead to a resumption of civil war. He therefore prorogued the trial, in a speech in which he reproached Maitland's followers, his former friends. They had, he said, elevated him to the regency without his encouragement, and had promised to help him administer justice. The cause of justice was not served by collecting an army to overawe the courts. He was not to be intimidated. Therefore the trial was postponed until such time as it could be held in a normal manner.[69]

In his letter to Cecil which recounted these events, Moray also informed the English minister that he had sent to the Marshal of Berwick to ask how he could help in suppressing the Northern Rebellion, news of which had just reached him. He did not wait on an official answer to act, however. Proclamations were issued strictly forbidding anyone in Scotland to aid any of the English rebels.[70] Then, at England's request, Moray began to collect an army to assist in the suppression of the revolt.[71] The domestic

---

[66] Thomson, *Diurnal of Occurrents*, p. 150. *Register of Privy Council*, II, 34 ff.
[67] Thomson, *Diurnal of Occurrents*, p. 151. See also *Register of Privy Council*, II, 41–51; October 22, 1569, Drury to Cecil, *C.S.P., For., Eliz.*, IX, 134; October 25, 1569, Scrope to Cecil, *ibid.*, pp. 135–36; October 31, Wood to Cecil, *C.S.P., Scot.*, II, 697; November 5, 1569, Drury to Cecil, *ibid.*, p. 699.
[68] *Ibid.*, pp. 697–98. [69] November 22, 1569, Moray to Cecil, *ibid.*, III, 7–8.
[70] *Register of Privy Council*, II, 66–67.
[71] December 5, 1569, Cecil to Sadler, *The State Papers and Letters of Sir Ralph Sadler*, II, 52–53. *Register of Privy Council*, II, 67, 72–73. December 8, 1569, Moray to the Council of the North, *C.S.P., For., Eliz.*, IX, 148.

situation was well in hand. The Scottish Catholics did not move, and, except for Hume, the Marians were quiescent.[72] Even Maitland was cowed; in fact, he was apparently trying to curry favor with the Regent by promoting a general band of the Scottish nobility against both English and Scottish Papists. Argyle was supporting this, and so was the Secretary's old enemy Knox.[73] Just what Maitland was up to is uncertain. Possibly he was frightened by the report that Balfour, who had been released on surety by Moray, was going to testify against him at his trial.[74] In all events Moray's hold on the country had never seemed more secure than at this moment.

By December 20, when the Regent's army assembled at Peebles, the back of the rebellion in England was broken. In fact, on that very day its leaders, Northumberland and Westmoreland, had entered Scotland, Sussex wrote to Moray, and would the Regent be good enough to capture them? [75] The Regent was willing, and on December 24 he laid hands on Northumberland, thanks to the greed of a Border thief, Hector of Harlaw, but Westmoreland he was unable to secure.[76]

The capture of Northumberland was greeted in Scotland, by the Borderers in particular, with rage. It was an age-old tradition that political offenders in either country, as opposed to common criminals, were to be protected if they fled across the border. Moray was blamed for refusing to Northumberland what Elizabeth had granted to him but four short years before. The Borderers still had no love for England, and the Regent was accused of base subservience to the "auld enemy." On December 30 Hunsdon wrote that "all sorts, both men and women, cry out for the liberty of their country, which is to succor banished men as they themselves have been received in England not long since." [77] On Janu-

---

[72] December 19, 1569, Drury to Cecil, *C.S.P., Scot.*, III, 26–27.
[73] December 5, December 20, 1569, Drury to Cecil, *ibid.*, pp. 18–19, 28–29.
[74] December 9, 1569, Drury to Cecil, *ibid.*, pp. 20–21. *Register of Privy Council*, II, 27.   [75] *C.S.P., Scot.*, III, 29.
[76] December 24, 1569, George Carey to Sussex, Hunsdon, and Sadler, *ibid.*, pp. 35–36. December 25, 1569, Sadler and Sussex to Elizabeth, *Calendar of State Papers, Domestic Series, Elizabeth, Addenda, 1566–79*, p. 167. January 14, 1570, Moray to Sussex and Sadler, *C.S.P., For., Eliz.*, IX, 171.   [77] *Ibid.*, pp. 157–58.

ary 11 Hunsdon informed Sussex that even Morton was staggered by Moray's move, and opposed the surrender of Northumberland to Elizabeth.[78] When one of Moray's captains was killed convoying Northumberland through Liddesdale, and when large numbers of men deserted when he attempted to move on Kerr of Ferniehirst, who was protecting Westmoreland, the Regent decided to tarry on the Borders no longer. He made for Edinburgh, and then for Lochleven, where his captive was lodged in the apartments formerly inhabited by Mary. At the same time he found it necessary publicly to declare that he had no intention of turning the Earl over to England.[79]

Moray was unprepared for the violence of the reaction to his seizure of Northumberland. He knew, of course, that there would be an outcry in some quarters, but he evidently felt that many would support him because Northumberland was a Catholic. He also overestimated the popularity of the English alliance. The animosities of three centuries cannot be eradicated in a decade. What is surprising is not that so many people disliked the English, but that so many did not dislike them.

Moray's main object in seizing the fugitive Earl was made clear by a memorial drawn up in December by the Regent and seven other lords. Mary, they declared, was really responsible for the Northern Rebellion. It was desirable that she be sent back to Scotland; hostages would be given to assure her personal safety.[80] Moray was evidently planning to exchange Northumberland for her. But the state of public opinion at home made him pause. It was rumored that Argyle and Huntly were preparing to rise. Worse still, Kirkcaldy, still Captain of Edinburgh Castle, was threatening to desert and to release Maitland, Châtelherault, and Herries if Moray made any further move in regard to either Northumberland or Westmoreland. Both Sadler and Hunsdon

[78] C.S.P., *Domestic Series, Eliz., Addenda*, pp. 191–92.
[79] December 26, 1569, Moray to Cecil, *C.S.P., Scot.*, III, 36. December 31, 1569, Forster to Sussex, *C.S.P., Domestic Series, Eliz., Addenda*, pp. 176–77. January 12, 1570, Constable to Sadler, *Sadler Papers*, II, 110–25. Lindsay of Pitscottie, *Chronicles*, II, 221.
[80] C.S.P., *Scot.*, III, 39. This document was signed by Mar, Glencairn, Marischal, Montrose, Lindsay, Ruthven, and Sempill, apparently the only lords who supported the seizure of Northumberland.

felt that Moray could not risk surrendering Northumberland, in view of the condition of public opinion.[81]

Nevertheless Moray had to do something. Elizabeth was of no help at all. In her own letters, and through her officials, she insistently demanded that Moray turn Northumberland over to her forthwith.[82] She showed absolutely no comprehension of the Regent's difficult political position. Moray decided that the only thing to do was to explain the situation fully to her and to demand that Elizabeth give him some tangible assistance if he surrendered his captive. To this end he sent Nicholas Elphinstone to London on January 2. Through Elphinstone Moray recounted the difficulties he had faced in the last three years. Scotland had been in constant turmoil and would remain so: all those who had anything to do with Darnley's murder, and the ambitious Hamiltons, aided by their relatives Argyle and Huntly, would never be content to submit to his government, whatever they might say from time to time. He had been forced to keep an army together almost continuously and had reached the end of his resources, and so had his friends, who were growing weary of the continual demands he had to make on them. If Elizabeth wanted Northumberland, she would have to do something substantial. The Regent needed £1,000 to pay his immediate debts, and an annual subsidy of £1,000 to maintain his army. Elizabeth must recognize James VI and guarantee his throne. Finally, she must do something about Mary—presumably, send her back to Scotland.[83] Moray's tale of

[81] January 3, 1570, Hunsdon to Cecil, C.S.P., For., Eliz., IX, 165. January 6, 1570, Allen King to Sir Henry Percy, C.S.P., Scot., III, 44–45. January 9, 1570, Sadler to Cecil, C.S.P., For., Eliz., IX, 168. January 12, 1570, Constable to Sadler, Sadler Papers, II, 110–25. January 21, 1570, Sussex and Sadler to Elizabeth, C.S.P., Domestic Series, Eliz., Addenda, pp. 202–3.

[82] See, for instance, her letters of January 2 and January 4, 1570, C.S.P., Scot., III, 39–40, 42, and Hunsdon's of January 9, 1570, in Haynes, Burghley Papers, p. 573.

[83] C.S.P., Scot., III, 53–55. Moray had already made one concrete suggestion to England. Both sides, he felt, should keep a standing force on the Borders at all times. He was prepared to do so if England would help finance it. December 22, 1569, Moray to Cecil, ibid., pp. 32–33. This was an eminently sensible plan; it was the only way thoroughly to stamp out Border lawlessness. The Regent's real purpose in all this seems to have been the creation of that standing army which the Stewart kings had never been able to afford and which the nobility had always so bitterly opposed. The reaction to the capture of Northumberland doubt-

woe was essentially accurate, and his demands not unreasonable, considering the services that he and his party rendered Elizabeth in the past decade. The English Queen was aware of this, and she ordered Hunsdon to give Moray assistance if he needed it.[84] Whether Elizabeth would have fully complied with Moray's requests will never be known. On January 24 she wrote, saying that she was willing to discuss the proposals, and was about to send Randolph to Scotland for this purpose.[85] Moray never saw this letter; at the time it was written, he was dead.

On his return from the Borders at the end of December, Moray heard that Dumbarton was on the verge of surrender. Anxious to hasten the process, he rushed Northumberland to Lochleven and hurried westward on January 2.[86] But, as it developed, the fortress was in better shape than had been anticipated; in fact, it had just been revictualed.[87] The Regent therefore returned to Stirling, where he transacted some unimportant business and told Gates and Drury, who had been sent by Elizabeth to get possession of Northumberland, that he would consult the nobility on this question as soon as he returned to Edinburgh.[88] Shortly thereafter he set out, and on January 22 he reached Linlithgow, where he proposed to spend the night.

Moray had been warned that his life was in danger and that he should avoid Linlithgow.[89] But such warnings came almost every day, and the Regent paid them but little heed. On the morning of January 23 he was told that an assassin awaited him that day. The informer offered to point out the very house in which he lurked. Moray apparently agreed to alter his route in leaving the town, in order to avoid passing in front of the killer's place of concealment, but the press of people in the street was so great that he changed his mind and followed his expected course.[90] Further-

less strengthened his conviction that such an army was necessary. This is mere speculation, however; the project, if project it was, died with him.

[84] January 22, 1570, Hunsdon to Cecil, *Calendar of the Manuscripts of the Marquis of Salisbury*, I, 462.   [85] *C.S.P., Scot.*, III, 58.

[86] Thomson, *Diurnal of Occurrents*, p. 155.

[87] January 14, 1570, Moray to Sussex and Sadler, *C.S.P., For., Eliz.*, IX, 171. Thomson, *Historie of James the Sext*, p. 44.

[88] January 20, 1570, Gates and Drury to Hunsdon, *C.S.P., Scot.*, III, 55-56.

[89] Bannatyne, *Memoriales*, pp. 289-90.   [90] Buchanan, *History*, II, 571.

more, he had to ride so slowly that he was an easy target. The murderer did not miss. We continue in the words of Buchanan: "The Regent leaped from his horse, saying, he was struck, and walked into his lodgings, as if he had not felt the wound. At first the surgeons pronounced it not mortal, but in a short time, severe pain arising, with great composure of mind, he began to think of death. When some, who were present, said repeatedly, that his own too great lenity had caused his ruin, as he had spared too many flagrant offenders, and, among these, his own assassin, who had been condemned for high treason, he replied mildly, as he was wont, 'Your importunity will never make me repent my clemency.' He then settled his family affairs, and having commended the king to those who were present, without having uttered one harsh expression, he departed before midnight, on the 23rd of January, A.D. 1570." [91]

The assassin was James Hamilton of Bothwellhaugh, who had been captured at Langside and pardoned by Moray and who, as Froude has demonstrated, was simply a professional murderer.[92] He had laid his plans with care. A mattress covered the floor of the second-story room in which he skulked, so that his footsteps would not be heard. The walls were draped in black, lest his shadow be seen from without. He had his horse waiting and had removed the keystone of the arch of the garden gate through which he must escape, so that he could ride through it.[93] The crime was planned by the Hamiltons, and carried out by one of their number, in order to remove the man whom they regarded as the greatest obstacle to their ambition to possess the Scottish throne. The brains of the family, the rascally Archbishop of St. Andrews, confessed on the scaffold three years later that he had instigated the murder.[94]

[91] *Ibid.*, p. 572. Buchanan, writing when the new year still began in March, gave the date as 1569. His translator made the correction in the date.
[92] J. A. Froude, *History of England (1529-1588)*, IX, 577-78. Calderwood, *History of the Kirk*, II, 416-17.
[93] Thomson, *Historie of James the Sext*, pp. 46-47.
[94] W. L. Mathieson, *Politics and Religion: a Study in Scottish History from the Reformation to the Revolution*, I, 169. The Archbishop also had personal reasons for the crime: on December 5 Moray had ordered the confiscation of his benefices. Lindsay of Pitscottie, *Chronicles*, II, 219-20.

The cold-blooded crime horrified Scotland. Even Maitland was shocked and proclaimed to the world his eagerness to see the murderers punished.[95] The Scottish factions, almost prepared to fly at each other's throats, were now almost ready to unite to exterminate the Hamiltons.[96] As for Elizabeth, she realized, too late, what a friend she had lost. "It is incredible," wrote La Mothe-Fénélon, "how deeply [she] felt Moray's death. . . . She exclaimed tearfully that she had lost the best and most useful friend she had in all the world . . . and carried on in such a way that the Earl of Leicester felt obliged to tell her that she was damaging her reputation by demonstrating that her safety, and that of her state, depended on one lone man." [97]

On February 14 Moray was laid to rest in St. Giles Church, in Edinburgh. Kirkcaldy of Grange bore the banner before his coffin, and eight lords were his pallbearers. His old companion in many struggles, John Knox, preached the sermon. His text was, "Blessed are the dead, that die in the Lord." [98]

[95] March, 1570, Maitland to Cecil or Leicester, in Cameron and Rait, *Warrender Papers*, I, 78–79.   [96] Lang, *History of Scotland*, II, 227.
[97] February 17, 1570, La Mothe-Fénélon to Catherine de Medici, in Teulet, *Correspondance diplomatique*, III, 54.
[98] February 22, 1570, Randolph to Cecil, *C.S.P., Scot.*, III, 83–84. Moray's epitaph was written by Buchanan and runs as follows: Jacobo Stewarto, Moraviae comiti, Scotiae proregi, viro aetatis suae longe optimo, ab inimicis, omnis memoriae deterrimis, ex insidiis extincto, ceu patri communi, patria moerens posuit. Calderwood, *History of the Kirk*, II, 526.

CHAPTER XIII

Conclusion

THE DEATH of Moray was a misfortune for Scotland, since it led to three years of bloody and unnecessary civil war. The arrest of Northumberland had alienated public opinion, and before the Regent had time to get the country in hand again, he was struck down. His importance to his party was quickly made manifest. There was no one who could take his place. Finally, after six months, in July 1570, a new Regent was chosen, under pressure from Elizabeth—Lennox.

The elevation of Lennox made civil war inevitable. He was at feud with the Hamiltons and was bent on avenging the murder of Darnley on Maitland. The natural result was a drawing-together of the Marians and the followers of Maitland. They were joined by many who looked on Moray's party as unduly subservient to England. The choice of Lennox as Regent, following on the seizure of Northumberland, made it appear that the King's Party, as Moray's friends came to be called, was little better than a tool of Elizabeth's. Moray alone could have prevented the conflict, for he was the only important man in his party who could command respect for character and ability alike.

The war dragged on from shortly after Moray's death until 1573, when the King's Party won out, with the active assistance of Elizabeth. In the meantime Scotland had undergone several changes of government. Lennox was killed in a scuffle at Stirling in September 1571, and was succeeded as Regent by Mar, a man of character but of no political ability. Mar was elderly at the time of his accession to power, and died after a year of ineffective rule, in October 1572. He was succeeded by Morton, who was a man of high political skill and no morals whatever. Morton did possess the virtue of the strong hand, and he quickly put an end to the civil war. He then hanged Kirkcaldy, and would have done likewise with Maitland, had not the Secretary opportunely succumbed to the disease which had been undermining his health for some time past.

Morton remained in power till 1581, and his regime marks a period of transition in Scottish history. The failure of the Marians meant that Mary and the Catholics could regain control of the country only by foreign invasion. Catholic intrigues and plots there were a-plenty—one of them resulted in the ruin and death of Morton himself—but in the last analysis they all depended, as their authors themselves realized, on Spanish or French armed support, and this was not forthcoming. Thus was the dominance of Protestantism assured, as was the English alliance. Morton was pro-English, and so was King James, when he began to rule personally. James swallowed the execution of his mother and stood by Elizabeth at the time of the Armada, and eventually he reaped the reward on which his heart was set—the English crown.

James's accession to the English throne marks the final triumph of Moray's policy. During the 1580s and 1590s the bases of that policy were not questioned; the great political battle of that period was waged between King and Kirk for control of the Scottish state, complicated, of course, by the continuing struggle for political hegemony between the Crown and the nobility, a struggle which was not finally resolved in the King's favor until after 1603, when James was able to bring the resources of England to bear on his recalcitrant feudality. The duel between King and Kirk had been foreshadowed during the early 1560s, in the intermittant conflict between Moray and Knox, which almost ruined both men. But the issue never came to a head during their lifetimes, because the danger to Protestantism was too great, and because after the crises of 1565–66, which marked the turning point of the struggle against the Catholic threat as represented by Mary, the two men realized that neither could get along without the other. Once the internal menace to Protestantism was removed, thanks mainly to the efforts of Moray and Knox, the stage was set for the struggle for control, which broke out after the domineering Morton had passed from the scene, the protagonists being King James himself on the one hand, and Andrew Melville and his cohorts on the other. Melville represented the policy of Knox, and James that of Maitland, which Morton had adopted, of political control over the Kirk. No Moray arose to keep the peace between them.

Few of Moray's Scottish political contemporaries outlived him by more than a decade. The ends of Archbishop Hamilton, Lennox, Mar, Maitland, and Kirkcaldy have already been noted. Knox died in 1572, prematurely aged by his unremitting struggles. In the next few years Argyle, Huntly, Glencairn, Châtelherault, and Athol all passed away, and in 1581 Morton was executed for his part in the murder of Darnley. Three years before, Bothwell, possibly insane at the end, succumbed in a Danish prison. In 1587 Mary went to the block; thus ended an imprisonment of almost twenty years. To the end she never ceased to hope and to plot for her restoration, and it was one of these plots which finally caused her reluctant "good sister" to sign her death warrant. Mary had behaved foolishly often, criminally occasionally; yet it is difficult not to feel a certain amount of sympathy for her. Be it remembered, however, that she rejoiced when she heard of her brother's murder, and even pensioned the murderer.[1]

ii

As might be expected, there are wide differences of opinion among historians as to Moray's character and accomplishments. To the more rabid of Mary's defenders no epithet is too strong to describe his villainy. To staunch believers in the "scarlet woman" interpretation of the Queen, such as Froude, her brother was "among the best and greatest men who have ever lived." [2] Among moderates on both sides of the fence Moray has excited a good deal of suspicion; while admitting his abilities, they question his motives.[3] In the opinion of the writer, virtually no one,

[1] August 28, 1571, Mary to the Archbishop of Glasgow, in A. Labanoff, ed., *Recueil des lettres de Marie Stuart*, III, 346–56.
[2] J. A. Froude, *History of England (1529–1588)*, IX, 581.
[3] See, for instance, the opinions of P. F. Tytler (*History of Scotland*, VI, 134–36,

with the exception of Hume Brown, has judged Moray correctly, because as a rule historians have not permitted themselves to consider him on his own merits. They have first made up their minds about Mary, and have judged Moray almost exclusively on the basis of his relations with her. This does somewhat less than justice to the Earl.

Hume Brown says that "of the two men (Moray and Knox) it was Moray who indubitably did the most to ensure the success of the Scottish Reformation." [4] This is, in the writer's opinion, an accurate judgment, and states succinctly one of the most important of Moray's achievements, and the least recognized. Knox has almost always received the lion's share, if not all, of the credit for the triumph of Protestantism in Scotland, because most people quite naturally assume that a religious revolution requires a religious leader to dominate it and to carry it through, Henry VIII being regarded as the awful exception. This is, of course, sometimes true, but there certainly would have been an upheaval in Scotland without Knox, as this account has demonstrated. When Knox appeared on the scene, in 1555, there were two questions to be answered: what form would the revolution take, and would it succeed? Knox definitively answered the first. Thanks to him, the Scottish Reformation became distinctively Calvinistic. He also helped to answer the second, by supplying the new movement with the type of leadership without which it could not succeed. This leadership was *not his own*, but that of the feudal nobles whom he converted, for in Scotland only the nobility could ensure the success of a movement of any sort.

Knox was fortunate in that he found the right man among his converts. The Protestant cause, in Scotland as elsewhere, attracted two sorts of men: those who joined out of religious zeal, and those who joined for worldly motives of one sort or another. The problem was to keep the two groups working together. This was Moray's great contribution to Scottish Protestantism. He was a man of great piety and of blameless personal life, who because of his austere morality could retain the loyalty and respect of the

VII, 254–55) and Sir Walter Scott (*The Monastery*, Everyman edition, p. 375).
[4] P. Hume Brown, *The History of Scotland*, II, 142.

Protestant zealots. At the same time he was a skillful soldier, politician, and administrator who could keep the materialistically inclined nobility in hand by moderation and concessions and extreme caution. In this respect Moray was unique, as the difficulties of the years 1570–73 show. There were some who were as pious as he, Glencairn and Lindsay, for instance; but they had no political ability. There were but a few with his political skill—Maitland, Morton, perhaps Archbishop Hamilton. None of these could command the respect of earnest Protestants, much less that of Knox. Moray was indispensable as a party leader; under his skillful guidance the Protestants, after overturning the old religion in 1559–60, weathered the fearful threat represented by Mary. He died a few years too soon, for he might have spared Scotland the civil war of the 1570s. Even so, by the time of his death his work was so well done that his party could continue to function with nonentities, and then a corrupt tyrant, at its head. It was Moray, then, who was chiefly responsible for the triumph of the Reformation in Scotland, for without him it is difficult to see how the new religion could have survived the challenge of Mary. In this way Moray has left his mark on the face of Scotland to this day.

Even more significant, perhaps, were Moray's more or less indirect contributions to Europe as a whole and to England in particular. As we have seen, the affairs of Scotland were of vital importance to the future of her southern neighbor, owing to one of those curious twists of fate which so often occur when governments are committed to dynasties. It was essential to England, for political and religious reasons alike, that Scotland be friendly. The Scottish Protestants quickly decided that it was equally important to them that England be friendly, since English aid was necessary in the establishment and defense of Protestantism against foes both foreign and domestic. And some day, many on both sides of the Tweed hoped, the island would be united under a single ruler. It was Maitland who first persuaded the Scottish Protestants to follow the policy of permanent friendship with England. Thus the Secretary brought about a revolution in Scottish foreign policy. Moray learned the lesson well, made this policy his own, and never wavered from it.

But from the very beginning there was a basic difference of purpose between Moray and Maitland. Both men agreed on the desirability of friendship with England, but for widely varying reasons. Maitland, always the politician, had the vision of union constantly before his eyes, and was willing to use any means to attain this end. He preferred to bring it about on a Protestant basis, through friendship with Elizabeth, but if this were not feasible, he would, and did, turn to other methods. Moray's purpose, on the other hand, was the safeguarding of Protestantism. Since England was Protestant, friendship was necessary and desirable. Union, too, was desirable, as a means of making the friendship permanent, provided it were carried through on a Protestant basis. This fundamental difference in aim eventually led Moray and Maitland to part company. In the end Moray's conception prevailed, for the island was united in the way in which he had always insisted it must be.

Moray's feat in retaining the good will of England, whose policy under Elizabeth was marked above all by vacillation and inconsistency, and at the same time keeping his party in Scotland together, was no mean accomplishment. A good deal of the credit must go to Cecil, who was always Moray's friend and who almost always sympathized with his policy. But Cecil did not have a free hand. Moray's unswerving loyalty to England despite Elizabeth's repeated bad faith is certainly one of the best examples of political consistency and devotion to principle in the face of overwhelming difficulties which is afforded by history.

The Protestant, Anglophile Scotland created by Moray and his friends was of cardinal importance to England. After Mary was eliminated, England was freed of her harassing dynastic problem, for there was but little doubt that James would succeed Elizabeth, barring a military catastrophe, and the future of Protestantism in the island was assured. Elizabeth and Cecil could pursue their devious foreign policy without having to worry about an attack from the north, and their successes, it is not too much to say, paved the way for England's future greatness. Certainly the whole history of England would have been different if Elizabeth had been confronted at every turn by a hostile Scotland ruled by a Catholic Queen who was her heir and who, in Catholic eyes, was already the rightful ruler of England.

The elimination of the possibility of a return to Catholicism in England, except through a foreign invasion, in its turn had profound effects on Europe as a whole. England was the only really powerful Protestant state in Europe, and was looked on by Protestants everywhere as their natural ally in their struggle against the aggressive Catholicism of the Counter-Reformation. Elizabeth supported the Protestants of France and of the Netherlands, not because they were Protestants, but because it was politically expedient to do so. She was aware that her chances for survival depended on her ability to prevent a Franco-Spanish combination against her. The easiest way to do this was to keep France and Spain occupied at home, by seeing to it that their rebellious Protestant subjects were not crushed. To what extent the French and Dutch Calvinists owed their ultimate successes to Elizabeth is debatable, but without her aid they might well have gone under, and if England had been Catholic, they certainly would have. It is most improbable that Elizabeth would have helped them, had she had a hostile, Catholic Scotland at her back. So it can be said with a good deal of justification that Moray contributed substantially to the survival of Protestantism in Europe by ensuring its triumph in Great Britain.

These are very considerable accomplishments, yet, strangely enough, they have gone virtually unrecognized. The reason is not far to seek, since they concern Moray's conduct toward Mary only in the most general way, and it is on this point that he has most frequently been judged. It would be well, therefore, to touch briefly on this subject.

Since Mary grew up in France, her brother did not know her at all at the beginning of his political career in the late 1550s. It is not improbable, though we have no proof of this, that he rather resented this sister—after all, but for an accident of birth, he might have been King. Personal feelings, however, Moray sternly refused to allow to affect his political judgments. After he became a Protestant, his determination that his religion should prevail was the underlying factor in his behavior, and in this respect he was entirely consistent. All his political moves were made in the belief that he was thereby benefiting Protestantism. From this point of view Mary was simply a piece in a highly complicated game. Because she was a Catholic, Moray could not be absolutely loyal to her; his religion came first. From this standpoint all of his so-called "betrayals" can be easily explained.

To say that Moray displayed unexampled ingratitude to his sister, since she showered him with favors, is sheer nonsense. When Mary returned to Scotland in 1561 Moray was one of the three or four most powerful men in the kingdom, and the earldom Mary gave him meant little besides an advance in rank. His political position was due to his own efforts, not to sisterly benevolence. To say that Moray overturned her because of his insatiable desire for power is equally foolish. Moray was certainly personally ambitious, but he did not permit his ambitions to interfere with what he considered to be sound policy, as his behavior in the affair of the Leicester marriage plainly shows. There is rather more substance to the charge that his political behavior was not always honest or moral. Certainly it cannot be considered honorable to connive at one murder, do nothing to prevent another, and to lend oneself to travesties of justice of the sort that took place at the York–Westminster Conference. All that can be said for Moray —and it is considerable—is that these actions were not undertaken merely for personal profit, and that almost every other contemporary statesman was tarred with the same brush. Let those defenders of Mary who point accusingly at the Riccio and Darnley affairs remember Mary's pension to Bothwellhaugh and the Babington Plot.

Moray's personality was one of cold and calculating reserve under a seemingly frank and open-handed exterior. His behavior was always Calvinistically correct and decorous; Buchanan tells us admiringly that his home resembled a "holy temple . . . free from impiety . . . [and] from improper conversation." [5] He was a shrewd and occasionally unscrupulous participant in the complicated trafficking in lands which characterized Scotland during this period, and at the same time he was evidently person-

[5] G. Buchanan, *The History of Scotland*, II, 573.

ally generous. While he could be rigorously just, he was not un-
merciful, and was never deliberately cruel. To the author of the
Diurnal of Occurrents he was the "defender of the widow and
fatherless." [6] Of his gifts as a statesman and administrator, no more
need be said. To the assertion of Sir James Melville, which has
been echoed by later writers, that he had no policy and ideas of
his own, but relied constantly on the advice of others, it is not
necessary to reply.[7] Enough has been said to indicate that, while
Moray certainly did make use of the ideas of other people, his
policy was distinctly his own. We can best close this work by
quoting once again from Hume Brown: "Like Admiral Coligny,
du Plessis-Mornay, and William of Orange, Moray is one of the
great public characters fashioned by the Calvinism of the sixteenth
century. In all of them there is discernible the same moderation
and breadth of view, the same practical statesmanship, penetrated
by profound religious feeling. . . . It was from a sure instinct of
his even justice, his consistent aims, and his capacity as a ruler,
that men spoke of Moray with affection and reverence as 'the
Good Regent.' " [8]

[6] T. Thomson, ed., *A Diurnal of Remarkable Occurrents that Have Passed within the Country of Scotland*, p. 156.
[7] Sir James Melville, *Memoirs of his own Life*, p. 222.
[8] P. Hume Brown, *John Knox*, II, 251.

Works Consulted

I. BIBLIOGRAPHIES

Read, Conyers. Bibliography of British History, Tudor Period (1485–1603). Oxford, 1933.

Tannenbaum, Samuel A., and Mary R. Tannenbaum. Marie Stuart, Queen of Scots. 3 vols. New York, 1944–46.

II. OFFICIAL PUBLICATIONS

Accounts of the Lord High Treasurer of Scotland. Vols. VI–XI (1531–66). Ed. by J. Balfour Paul. Edinburgh, 1905–16. [Abbreviated in the footnotes as *Treasurer's Accounts*.]

Acts of the Parliament of Scotland, The. Vols. II–III (1424–1592). Ed. by T. Thomson. London, 1814.

Calendar of State Papers, Domestic Series, Elizabeth. Addenda, 1566–79. Ed. by M. A. E. Green. London, 1871.

Calendar of State Papers, Foreign Series, Edward VI. Ed. by W. Turnbull. London, 1861.

Calendar of State Papers, Foreign Series, Mary. Ed. by W. Turnbull. London, 1861.

Calendar of State Papers, Foreign Series, Elizabeth. Vols. I–IX (1558–71). Ed. by J. Stevenson and A. J. Crosby. London, 1863–74. [Abbreviated in the footnotes as *C.S.P., For., Eliz.*]

Calendar of State Papers Relating to English Affairs (Rome). Vol. I (1558–71). Ed. by J. M. Rigg. London, 1916.

Calendar of State Papers Relating to Scotland and Mary Queen of Scots. Vols. I–III (1547–71). Ed. by J. Bain. Edinburgh, 1898–1903. [Abbreviated in the footnotes as *C.S.P., Scot.*]

Calendar of State Papers, Spanish (Elizabeth). Vols. I–II (1558–79). Ed. by M. A. S. Hume. London, 1892–94. [Abbreviated in the footnotes as *C.S.P., Span.*]

Calendar of State Papers, Venetian. Vol. VII (1558–80). Ed. by R. Brown and G. C. Bentinck. London, 1890. [Abbreviated in the footnotes as *C.S.P., Ven.*]

Calendar of the Manuscripts of the Marquis of Salisbury. Vol. I. London, 1883. Historical Manuscripts Commission.

Exchequer Rolls of Scotland, The. Vols. XVIII–XX (1543–79). Ed. by G. P. McNeill. Edinburgh, 1898–99.

Hamilton Papers, The. 2 vols. Ed. by J. Bain. Edinburgh, 1890–92.

Historical Manuscripts Commission Reports. London, 1874–.

Register of the Privy Council of Scotland, The. Vols. I–II (1545–78). Ed. by J. H. Burton. Edinburgh, 1877–78. Addenda to the above, ed. by D. Masson, in Vol. XIV. Edinburgh, 1898.

Registrum Magni Sigilli Regum Scotorum. Vols. III–IV (1513–80). Ed. by J. Balfour Paul and J. M. Thompson. Edinburgh, 1883–86.

Scots Peerage, The. 9 vols. Ed. by J. Balfour Paul. Edinburgh, 1904–14.

Treasurer's Accounts: see Accounts of the Lord High Treasurer of Scotland.

<h3 style="text-align:center">III. PRIMARY SOURCES</h3>

Anderson, J., ed. Collections Relating to the History of Mary Queen of Scots. 4 vols. Edinburgh 1727–28.

Anderson, J. M., ed. Early Records of the University of St. Andrews (1413–1579). Scottish History Society publication, 3d series, Vol. VIII. Edinburgh, 1926.

Bannatyne, R. Memoriales of Transactions in Scotland (1569–73). Ed. by R. Pitcairn. Edinburgh, 1836. Bannatyne Club publication.

Beaugué, Jean de. The History of the Campaigns 1548 and 1549. London, 1707.

Buchanan, G. The History of Scotland. Vol. II. Tr. and ed. by J. Aikman. Glasgow, 1827.

Calderwood, D. The History of the Kirk of Scotland. Vols. I–II. Ed. by T. Thomson. Edinburgh 1842–43. Wodrow Society publication.

Cameron, A. I., ed. The Scottish Correspondence of Mary of Lorraine. Scottish History Society publication, 3d series, Vol. X. Edinburgh, 1927.

———, and R. S. Rait, eds. The Warrender Papers. Vol. I. Scottish History Society publication, 3d series, Vol. XVIII. Edinburgh, 1931.

Cockburn, H., and T. Maitland, eds. Les Affaires du Conte de Boduel. Edinburgh, 1829. Bannatyne Club publication.

Dalyell, Sir John, ed. Fragments of Scottish History. Edinburgh, 1798.

———, ed. Scotish Poems of the Sixteenth Century. Vol. I. Edinburgh, 1801.

Dickinson, G., ed. Two Missions of Jacques de la Brosse. Scottish History Society publication, 3d series, Vol. XXXVI. Edinburgh, 1942.

Donaldson, G., ed. Accounts of the Collectors of Thirds of Benefices,

1561–1572. Scottish History Society publication, 3d series, Vol. XLII. Edinburgh, 1949.

Fleming, D. H., ed. Register of the Minister, Elders, and Deacons of the Christian Congregation of St. Andrews. Vol. I. Scottish History Society publication, 1st series, Vol. IV. Edinburgh, 1889.

Forbes-Leith, W., ed. Narratives of Scottish Catholics under Mary Stuart and James VI. Edinburgh, 1885.

Hannay, R. K., ed. Rentale Sancti Andree (1538–46). Scottish History Society publication, 2d series, Vol. IV. Edinburgh, 1913.

Haynes, S., ed. The Burghley Papers (1542–70). London, 1740.

Herries, Lord. Historical Memoirs of the Reign of Mary Queen of Scots and a Portion of the Reign of King James VI. Ed. by R. Pitcairn. Edinburgh, 1836. Abbotsford Club publication. [These memoirs have been attributed to Herries but may not have been written by him.]

Innes, C., ed. Registrum Honoris de Morton. 2 vols. Edinburgh, 1853.

Keith, R. The History of the Affairs of Church and State in Scotland. 3 vols. Ed. by J. P. Lawson. Edinburgh, 1844–50. Spottiswoode Society publication. [This work is not, strictly speaking, a primary source, but has been listed as such because its chief value lies in the documents included, which are given *in extenso*.]

Knox, John. Works. 6 vols. Ed. by D. Laing. Edinburgh, 1895. [The first two volumes comprise Knox's *History of the Reformation in Scotland*. The references to the *History* in this work are to the 1846 edition, edited by Laing, which was published by the Wodrow Society. Other references to Knox's *Works* are to the 1895 edition. There is a new edition of Knox's *History*, edited by W. C. Dickinson, 2 vols., New York 1950, which came into my hands too late to be consulted in the writing of this book. This is an excellent piece of scholarly work which does not supersede Laing's edition but should be used along with it.]

Labanoff, A., ed. Recueil des lettres de Marie Stuart. 7 vols. London, 1852.

Laing, D., ed. Miscellany of the Bannatyne Club. Vol. I. Edinburgh, 1827.

——— Miscellany of the Wodrow Society. Vol. I. Edinburgh, 1844.

Leslie, John. The Historie of Scotland. Ed. by T. Thomson. Edinburgh, 1830. Bannatyne Club publication.

——— The History of Scotland. 2 vols. Tr. by J. Dalyrimple and ed. by E. G. Cody and W. Murison. Edinburgh, 1888, 1895. Scottish Text Society publication.

Lindsay, R., of Pitscottie. The Chronicles of Scotland. 2 vols. Ed. by A. J. G. Mackay. Edinburgh, 1899. Scottish Text Society publication.

Macdonald, A., ed. Letters to the Argyle Family. Edinburgh, 1839. Maitland Club publication.

MacGeorge, A., ed. Miscellaneous Papers Principally Illustrative of Events in the Reigns of Queen Mary and King James VI. Glasgow, 1834. Maitland Club publication.

Maidment, J., ed. Miscellany of the Abbotsford Club. Vol. I. Edinburgh, 1837.

Maitland Club. Miscellany. 4 vols. Edinburgh, 1834–47.

Melville, Sir James, of Halhill. Memoirs of his own Life. Ed. by T. Thomson. Edinburgh, 1827. Bannatyne Club publication.

Murdin, W., ed. The Burghley Papers (1571–1596). London, 1759.

Nau, Claude. The History of Mary Stewart. Ed. by J. Stevenson. Edinburgh, 1883.

Patrick, D., ed. Statutes of the Scottish Church (1225–1559). Scottish History Society publication, 1st series, Vol. LIV. Edinburgh, 1907.

Pitcairn, R., ed. Ancient Criminal Trials in Scotland. Vols. I–II. Edinburgh, 1833. Bannatyne Club publication.

Pollen, J. H., ed. A Letter from Mary Queen of Scots to the Duke of Guise. Scottish History Society publication, 1st series, Vol. XLIII. Edinburgh, 1904.

———— Papal Negotiations with Mary Queen of Scots (1561–67). Scottish History Society publication, 1st series, Vol. XXXVII. Edinburgh, 1901.

Robertson, J., ed. Antiquities of the Shires of Aberdeen and Banff. 5 vols. Aberdeen, 1843–69. Spalding Club publication.

———— Inventaires de la Royne Descosse Douairière de France. Edinburgh, 1863. Bannatyne Club publication.

Scottish History Society. Miscellany. Vol. II. Edinburgh, 1904.

State Papers and Letters of Sir Ralph Sadler, The. Ed. by A. Clifford. 2 vols. Edinburgh, 1809. [Abbreviated in the footnotes as Sadler Papers.]

Stevenson, J., ed. Selections from Unpublished Manuscripts in the College of Arms and the British Museum Illustrating the Reign of Mary Queen of Scotland. Glasgow, 1837. Maitland Club publication.

Stuart, J., ed. Miscellany of the Spalding Club. 1st series, Vols. II–IV. Aberdeen, 1842–49.

———— Selections from the Records of the Kirk Session, Presbytery, and Synod of Aberdeen. Aberdeen, 1846. Spalding Club publication.

Teulet, A., ed. Correspondance diplomatique de La Mothe-Fénélon. Vols. I–III. Paris, 1838–40.

———— Papiers d'état relatifs à l'histoire de l'Ecosse au XVIe siècle. 3 vols. Edinburgh, 1851. Bannatyne Club publication.

———— Relations politiques de la France et de l'Espagne avec l'Ecosse au XVIe siècle. Vols. I, II, V. Paris, 1862.

Thomson, T., ed. The Booke of the Universall Kirk of Scotland. Vol. I. Edinburgh, 1839. Bannatyne Club publication.

———— A Diurnal of Remarkable Occurrents that Have Passed within the Country of Scotland. Edinburgh, 1833. Maitland Club publication.

———— The Historie and Life of King James the Sext. Edinburgh, 1825. Bannatyne Club publication.

Wodrow, R. Collections upon the Lives of the Reformers and Most Eminent Ministers of the Church of Scotland. Vol. I. Ed. by W. J. Duncan. Glasgow, 1834. Maitland Club publication.

Wood, M., ed. Foreign Correspondence with Marie de Lorraine, Queen of Scotland, from the Originals in the Balcarres Papers. 2 vols. Scottish History Society publication, 3d series, Vols. IV, VII. Edinburgh, 1923, 1925.

IV. SECONDARY WORKS

Allen, J. W. A History of Political Thought in the Sixteenth Century. 2d edition. London, 1941.

Bellesheim, A. History of the Catholic Church in Scotland. Vols. II–III. Tr. by D. O. Hunter Blair. Edinburgh, 1887–89.

Black, J. B. The Reign of Elizabeth. Oxford, 1936.

Brown, P. Hume. The History of Scotland. Vols. I–II. Cambridge, 1905.

———— John Knox. 2 vols. London, 1895.

———— Scotland in the Time of Queen Mary. London, 1904.

———— "The Scottish Nobility and their Part in the National History," Scottish Historical Review, III (1905–6), 157–70.

Bryce, W. M. "Mary Stuart's Voyage to France in 1548," English Historical Review, XXII (1907), 43–50.

Chalmers, G. The Life of Mary Queen of Scots. 2 vols. London, 1818.

Chauviré, R. "Etat présent de la controverse sur les Lettres de la Cassette," Revue historique, CLXXIV (1934), 429–66; CLXXV (1935), 41–82.

———— Le Secret de Marie Stuart. Paris, 1937.

Chéruel, A. Marie Stuart et Catherine de Médicis. Paris, 1858.

Dictionary of National Biography. New York, 1885-.

Dietz, F. C. English Government Finance 1485–1558. Urbana, Ill., 1920.

Donaldson, G. "The Scottish Episcopate at the Reformation," English Historical Review, LX (1945), 349–64.

Duncan, T. "Mary Stuart and the House of Huntly," *Scottish Historical Review*, IV (1906–7), 365–73.
———— "The Relations of the Earl of Murray with Mary Stuart," *Scottish Historical Review*, VI (1909), 49–57.
Elder, J. R. Spanish Influences in Scottish History. Glasgow, 1920.
Fleming, D. H. Mary Queen of Scots. London, 1897.
Froude, J. A. History of England (1529–88). Vols. VII–IX. London, 1862–70.
Gore-Browne, R. Lord Bothwell and Mary Queen of Scots. New York, 1937.
Grant, I. F. The Social and Economic Development of Scotland before 1603. Edinburgh, 1930.
Hannay, R. K. "The Earl of Arran and Queen Mary," *Scottish Historical Review*, XVIII (1920–21), 258–76.
———— "On the Church Lands at the Reformation," *Scottish Historical Review*, XVI (1918–19), 52–72.
———— "A Study of Reformation History," *Scottish Historical Review*, XXIII (1925–26), 18–33.
Henderson, T. F. The Casket Letters and Mary Queen of Scots. Edinburgh, 1890.
———— Mary Queen of Scots. 2 vols. New York, 1905.
Hosack, J. Mary Queen of Scots and Her Accusers. Edinburgh, 1869.
Hume, M. A. S. The Love Affairs of Mary Queen of Scots. London, 1903.
Laing, Malcolm. The History of Scotland. Vols. I–II. London, 1819.
Lang, Andrew. "Casket Letters," in Encyclopaedia Britannica, 11th ed., V, 449–52.
———— A History of Scotland from the Roman Occupation. Vols. I–II. Edinburgh, 1903.
———— John Knox and the Reformation. London, 1905.
———— "Knox as Historian," *Scottish Historical Review*, II (1905), 113–30.
———— The Mystery of Mary Stuart. London, 1904.
———— "New Light on Mary Queen of Scots," *Blackwood's Magazine*, CLXXXII (1907), 17–27.
MacKinnon, J. The Constitutional History of Scotland from Early Times to the Reformation. London, 1924.
Mahon, R. H. The Tragedy of Kirk o'Field. Cambridge, 1930.
Mathieson, W. L. Politics and Religion: a Study in Scottish History from the Reformation to the Revolution. Vol. I. Glasgow, 1902.
McCrie, T. The Life of John Knox. 2 vols. 5th ed. Edinburgh, 1831.
Mignet, F. A. The History of Mary Queen of Scots. Tr. by A. R. Scoble. London, 1861.
Muir, E. John Knox: Portrait of a Calvinist. London, 1929.

Murison, W. Sir David Lyndsay. Cambridge, 1938.

Neale, J. E. Queen Elizabeth. New York, 1934.

Pastor, L. von. History of the Popes. Vols. XVI and XVIII. London, 1928–29.

Percy, E. John Knox. London, 1937.

Philippson, M. "Etudes sur l'histoire de Marie Stuart," *Revue historique*, XXXIV (1887), 225–58; XXXV (1887), 21–58; XXXVI (1888), 28–61; XXXVII (1888), 1–48; XXXVIII (1888), 1–63; XXXIX (1889), 241–81.

—— Histoire du règne de Marie Stuart. 3 vols. Paris, 1891–92.

Pollard, A. F. "The Protector Somerset and Scotland," *English Historical Review*, XIII (1898), 464–72.

Rait, R. S. The Parliaments of Scotland. Glasgow, 1924.

——, The Scottish Parliament before the Union of the Crowns. London, 1901.

Ridpath, P. The Border History of England and Scotland. London, 1776.

Robertson, W. The History of Scotland. 3 vols. London, 1802.

Rose, D. M. "Mary Queen of Scots and Her Brother," *Scottish Historical Review*, II (1905), 150–62.

Russell, E. Maitland of Lethington. London, 1912.

Skelton, J. Maitland of Lethington and the Scotland of Mary Stuart. 2 vols. Edinburgh, 1894.

Small, J. "Queen Mary at Jedburgh in 1566," *Proceedings of the Society of Antiquaries of Scotland*, new series, III (1881), 210–23.

Spottiswoode, J. The History of the Church of Scotland. 3d edition. London, 1668.

Stevenson, R. L. "John Knox and His Relations to Women," in Stevenson's Works, ed. by C. C. Bigelow and T. Scott, X, 212–54. New York, 1908.

Tytler, P. F. History of Scotland. Vols. V–VII. Edinburgh, 1841–42.

Walker, W. John Calvin. New York, 1906.

Wilkinson, M. "The Mystery of Maitland," *Scottish Historical Review*, XXIV (1926–27), 19–29.

Zweig, S. Mary Queen of Scotland and the Isles. Tr. by E. and C. Paul. New York, 1935.

Index